GLOBALIZATION AND THE INTERNATIONAL FINANCIAL SYSTEM

Economic globalization has given rise to frequent and severe financial crises in emerging market economies. Many other countries have been unsuccessful in their efforts to generate economic growth and reduce poverty. This book provides perspectives on various aspects of the international financial system that contribute to financial crises and growth failures, and it discusses the remedies that economists have suggested for addressing the underlying problems. It also sheds light on a central feature of the international financial system that remains mysterious to many economists and most noneconomists: the activities of the International Monetary Fund and the factors that influence its effectiveness. Drawing on the views and proposals of leading scholars, Dr. Isard offers policy perspectives on what countries can do to reduce their vulnerabilities to financial crises and growth failures, as well as a number of general directions for systemic reform. The breadth of the agenda provides grounds for optimism that the international financial system can be strengthened considerably without revolutionary change.

Peter Isard is a Senior Advisor at the International Monetary Fund, where he has spent nearly twenty years in the Research Department and now teaches in, and helps manage, the IMF Institute. From 1972 through 1985, Dr. Isard held research and managerial positions in the International Finance Division of the Federal Reserve Board. He has published numerous articles on the behavior of exchange rates, strategies for monetary policy, and directions for reforming the international financial system. His book *Exchange Rate Economics* (Cambridge University Press, 1995) is widely acclaimed.

to my father, Walter Isard,

who inspired me to study economics

and strongly encouraged me to write this book

Globalization and the International Financial System

WHAT'S WRONG AND WHAT CAN BE DONE

Peter Isard

International Monetary Fund

CAMBRIDGE
UNIVERSITY PRESS

PUBLISHED BY THE PRESS SYNDICATE OF THE UNIVERSITY OF CAMBRIDGE
The Pitt Building, Trumpington Street, Cambridge, United Kingdom

CAMBRIDGE UNIVERSITY PRESS
The Edinburgh Building, Cambridge CB2 2RU, UK
40 West 20th Street, New York, NY 10011-4211, USA
477 Williamstown Road, Port Melbourne, VIC 3207, Australia
Ruiz de Alarcón 13, 28014 Madrid, Spain
Dock House, The Waterfront, Cape Town 8001, South Africa

http://www.cambridge.org

First published 2005

Printed in the United States of America

Typefaces Sabon 10/13.5 pt. and Melior   *System* LaTeX 2_ε [TB]

A catalog record for this book is available from the British Library.

Library of Congress Cataloging in Publication Data
Isard, Peter.
   Globalization and the international financial system : what's wrong and what
can be done / Peter Isard.
       p.   cm.
   Includes bibliographical references and index.
   ISBN 0-521-84389-8 – ISBN 0-521-60507-5 (pbk.)
   1. Financial crises – Developing countries.   2. Developing countries –
Economic conditions.   3. International Monetary Fund.   4. International finance.
I. Title.
HB3722.I83   2004
   332′.042 – dc22   2004049269

ISBN 0 521 84389 8 hardback
ISBN 0 521 60507 5 paperback

Contents

List of Figures, Tables, and Boxes

BOXES

List of Abbreviations

CCL	Contingent Credit Line
CFF	Compensatory Finance Facility
EC	European Community
ECB	European Central Bank
EFF	Extended Fund Facility
EMS	European Monetary System
EMU	European Economic and Monetary Union
ERM	Exchange Rate Mechanism
EU	European Union
FDI	foreign direct investment
FSA	financial sector assessment
FSAP	Financial Sector Assessment Program
FSF	Financial Stability Forum
G-5	Group of Five
G-7	Group of Seven
G-8	Group of Eight
G-10	Group of Ten
G-24	Group of Twenty-Four
GATT	General Agreement on Tariffs and Trade
GDDS	General Data Dissemination System
GDP	gross domestic product
HIPC	heavily indebted poor country
IMF	International Monetary Fund
IMFC	International Monetary and Financial Committee
ITO	International Trade Organization
LIBOR	London interbank offer rate
LOLR	lender of last resort
LTCM	Long-Term Capital Management
NAFTA	North American Free Trade Agreement
NDA	net domestic assets

NGO	nongovernmental organization
NIPA	national income and product accounts
ODA	official development assistance
OECD	Organization for Economic Cooperation and Development
OPEC	Organization of Petroleum Exporting Countries
PPP	purchasing power parity
PRSP	Poverty-Reduction Strategy Paper
ROSC	Report on the Observance of Standards and Codes
SAF	Structural Adjustment Facility
SBA	stand-by arrangement
SDDS	Special Data Dissemination Standard
SDR	special drawing right
SDRM	Sovereign Debt-Restructuring Mechanism
SRF	Supplemental Reserve Facility
UDROP	Universal Debt Rollover Option with a Penalty
WEO	*World Economic Outlook*
WTO	World Trade Organization

Acknowledgments and Disclaimer

This book was written during a leave of absence from the International Monetary Fund. I am grateful both to the IMF and to the Economics Department of the University of Maryland, which provided comfortable office facilities and an enjoyable and fruitful working environment.

Much of the book's material draws on contributions from other economists, who are extensively referenced throughout. Valuable comments and suggestions were provided by a number of colleagues at the IMF, including Andy Berg, Graham Hacche, Olivier Jeanne, Thomas Krueger, Jaewoo Lee, and Jeromin Zettelmeyer. I also gratefully acknowledge the questioning and feedback received from faculty and graduate students at the University of Maryland, the constructive suggestions provided by two anonymous referees, and the excellent assistance received from Ioannis Tokatlidis in putting together the figures and tables and from Nahid Mejid in preparing the manuscript. Special thanks go to my wife, Maggie, and children, Ben and Harsha, for bearing with me during prolonged periods of writer's distraction.

The analysis and opinions in this book are those of the author and, unless otherwise indicated, do not necessarily reflect the views of the IMF or others on its staff. The manuscript was submitted in October 2003; data have been updated through the end of 2003 or early 2004, but the book includes only a few references to material that has become available since October 2003. I have made considerable efforts to avoid factual errors and to provide balanced perspectives on the issues addressed, but the nature of the undertaking suggests that some sins of commission or omission will no doubt be discovered, for which I accept full responsibility.

PART ONE

Background

1

Introduction

This book is motivated by two major concerns about the globalization process and the international financial system: the prevailing global economic environment has given rise to frequent and severe financial crises in emerging market economies, and it has also left many countries unsuccessful in their efforts to generate economic growth and reduce poverty. In addressing these concerns, the book seeks to achieve three objectives. One aim is to provide perspectives on the various problems that contribute to financial crises and growth failures. A second is to describe the remedies that economists have proposed for mitigating these problems. The third is to shed light on a central feature of the international financial system that remains mysterious to many economists and most noneconomists: the activities of the International Monetary Fund and the factors that influence its effectiveness.

This chapter begins with some perspectives on the globalization process and then presents an overview of the book.

1.1 Globalization

Throughout the centuries, advances in transportation and communications technologies have brought people progressively closer together in space and time. By some measures, the process has accelerated since the mid-twentieth century.[1] Along with the advent and rapid growth of commercial air travel following the Second World War, the revolution in communication technologies during recent decades has profoundly affected the lives of people throughout the world. Thanks to a series of

---

[1] For example, Madison (2001) reports that, for the world as a whole, the ratio of merchandise exports to gross domestic product (GDP) rose from 5.5 percent in 1950 to 17.2 percent in 1995. See also Crafts (2000) and Masson (2001).

advances—including the laying of transatlantic and transpacific telephone cables beginning in the 1950s, the launching of communication satellites starting in 1960, the development of fiber-optic communications in the 1970s, the widespread adoption of personal computers during the 1980s, and the takeoff in use of the Internet and electronic mail during the 1990s—it is now possible to transmit information around the globe instantaneously and at negligible cost. As a result, countries and communities have become more closely connected in various ways, for better and for worse.

The process that has led to this increasing connectedness is often referred to as *globalization*, a term that crept into the common vernacular during the 1990s and is now widely used by business gurus, labor unions, antipoverty campaigners, environmentalists, politicians, and economists, among others. The increasing connectedness of people and countries—combined with the choices that policymakers have made in constraining or not constraining the behavior of individuals, businesses, and government agencies—has significantly affected the structure, growth, and vulnerabilities of national economies while also contributing to changes in cultural institutions, political regimes, and the environment.

Because groups with different economic, political, and social interests naturally focus on different issues, globalization has become a slippery term, with different connotations for different people. Certain aspects of the process have elicited harsh criticism. The media have been blamed for contributing to the breakdown of traditional family values and other cherished cultural institutions, but they have also been recognized for their role in energizing opposition to certain corrupt and inefficient bureaucratic practices and political regimes. The spread of large multinational conglomerates, with control over a significant share of the world's economic activity and substantial influence over national policy decisions, has triggered strong protest from advocates for the economic survival of smaller businesses and their employees and from groups concerned about the environment. The strength of these diverse concerns has led to an antiglobalist movement that national authorities and international policymaking institutions have appropriately been forced to take seriously.

This book focuses on issues associated with the process of international economic integration—or economic globalization—as evident in increasing flows of goods and services, financial resources, workers, and technologies across national borders. In doing so, it limits attention to the implications for economic welfare, ignoring implications for the environment, the stability of cultures and political systems, and other important noneconomic considerations.

Although international economic integration has increased substantially during recent decades, economic globalization is not a new process. The expansion of international trade and migration and the spread of economically useful knowledge and technology across national borders date back many centuries.[2] Advances in communication and transportation have provided a major driving force. Such advances do not occur spontaneously; they are themselves a reflection of the desire of people to take advantage of the perceived benefits of closer integration.[3] Public policies can have significant effects on the pace of economic globalization by providing stimulus or discouragement to innovations in communication and transportation technologies and by influencing the extent to which existing technologies give rise to cross-border flows of goods, money, people, and ideas.

Some of the consequences of economic globalization are quite visible, whereas others materialize slowly and are less widely appreciated. Proponents of economic globalization point to many significant benefits. Better communication mechanisms and lower transportation costs have provided consumers with access to lower-priced goods and a much broader range of products. International capital flows have financed production facilities in countries where labor is relatively abundant and ready to be profitably employed in more productive and remunerative activities. The spread of technological and marketing know-how and other ideas across national borders has also contributed to the more productive employment of local labor forces, enabling them to raise their standards of living. At the same time, opportunities for idle or low-wage labor to migrate to countries with relatively low unemployment rates have enabled workers to earn better incomes and acquire new skills while also easing labor shortages in the countries to which they have moved.

Nevertheless, globalization has also disrupted the economic circumstances of many people and bypassed the economies of many others. Accordingly, critics of economic globalization have strong reasons for

[2] For various historical perspectives, see Bordo, Eichengreen, and Irwin (1999); Crafts (2000); Williamson (2002); Baldwin and Winters, eds. (2004); and Bordo, Taylor, and Williamson, eds. (2003).
[3] See Mussa (2000).

concern. Some point to widening income gaps between rich and poor countries along with growing inequality and persistent poverty within countries. Many regard international capital flows as a force that has often destabilized economies and destroyed livelihoods.

Although they recognize that the benefits of economic globalization have come with some very high costs, most international economists regard it as a process that cannot be stopped or substantially reversed without very damaging consequences—results of the kind associated with the protectionist and other inward-looking beggar-thy-neighbor policies that contributed to the Great Depression of the 1930s.[4] It is also clear that economic integration within countries is much greater than economic integration across national borders,[5] suggesting that the process of economic globalization has the potential to extend considerably further. From these perspectives, the key challenge is not to resolve whether the pros outweigh the cons but rather to devise effective ways for national policymakers and international agencies to address the problems associated with globalization. The appropriate focus, in other words, is on how to strengthen both national institutions and policies and the international financial system to make the process of economic globalization work better.

1.2   Overview of the Book

The two major concerns about the economic aspects of the globalization process—financial crises and growth failures—have received considerable attention from policymakers and academic economists in recent years. This has led to a better understanding of the multiplicity of problems that contribute to the frequency and severity of international financial crises and that stand in the way of efforts to generate economic growth and reduce poverty.

As already noted, this book aims to provide perspectives on the various problems that underlie the bad side of the economic globalization process, to discuss the measures that have been proposed or initiated for addressing these problems, and to describe the activities of the International Monetary Fund (IMF) and the various factors that limit its effectiveness in preventing and mitigating financial crises and growth disappointments.

---

[4] See Bhagwati (2004) for a defense of globalization and James (1999) for a brief discussion of past episodes of turning back the clock on the globalization process.
[5] See Helliwell (1998).

The material is divided into three parts. Part One provides background on the evolution of the international monetary system and the functions and activities of its central institution, the IMF. Part Two discusses the factors that contribute to international financial crises, the effects of such crises, and the controversies over how policymakers should respond. It also provides various perspectives on the determinants of economic growth and the obstacles to poverty reduction. Part Three presents an agenda for reform, focusing both on a list of problems for countries to address individually and on a number of areas in which the international financial system can be strengthened.

The book is intended for a broad audience, including teachers, students, research economists, and policymakers. The level of exposition presumes familiarity with elementary macroeconomics, but beyond that most of the material is presented in a nontechnical manner, with boxes used to house more technical digressions. To cover the broad range of topics in a few hundred pages, the book provides relatively compact discussions of relevant historical and institutional material and the various proposals for strengthening national policymaking and the international financial system.[6] Readers who wish to pursue topics in greater depth will find an extensive list of references. Readers who already are well informed about some of the topics, or who have limited interest in them, will find summaries of the topics in the concluding perspectives of each chapter.

Chapter 2 presents background on the evolution of international monetary regimes since the late nineteenth century and on how the world economy performed under the successive regimes. It also describes the sea change that has taken place in international capital flows during the past several decades. The review of past international monetary regimes reveals that international financial crises have a long history, and that international monetary cooperation can have a very important influence on

---

[6] Other fairly extensive studies of how to make the economic globalization process work better include those by Bryant (2003), Eichengreen (1999b), Fischer (2001c, 2003), Goldstein (1998), Kenen (2001), and Tirole (2002), along with a number of reports surveyed by Goldstein (2003a) and the conference volumes edited by Feldstein (2002), Dooley and Frankel (2003), and Edwards and Frankel (2003). Most of these studies cover a somewhat narrower range of topics than this book but explore the topics they do cover in greater depth. Bryant (2003) devotes considerable attention to developing a basic understanding of the costs and benefits of domestic and international financial activity, and of how the needs for different types of international collective governance have changed and will continue to change as economic globalization proceeds.

the performance of the global economy. In addition, historical experience provides strong evidence that, unless countries can control international capital flows, they will not find it possible to stabilize the exchange rates between their currencies and simultaneously retain the autonomy to focus their monetary policies on achieving domestic economic growth and price stability. This fundamental impossibility theorem, when combined with political and financial market realities, helps explain why currency crises have become so intense under the prevailing international monetary system. It also sheds light on why the relatively high degrees of exchange rate stability that have been achieved under previous international monetary regimes—in particular, under both the international gold standard regime that prevailed prior to the First World War and the Bretton Woods regime that lasted from the mid-1940s until the early 1970s—are much less feasible today for exchange rates between the major currencies of the world. In many countries, the political empowerment of the working classes since the First World War has greatly reduced the scope for policy authorities to give exchange rate stability high priority over domestic macroeconomic stability, as was the practice during the gold standard era. And the rapid growth in the volume of internationally mobile private financial capital, together with its proven agility in evading official restrictions, has made it much less feasible for national authorities to control international capital flows effectively, as they were able to do until the latter part of the Bretton Woods era. By the same token, these political and financial market developments imply that the functioning of the global economy has become more dependent on effective international monetary cooperation.

Chapter 3 provides background on the functions of the IMF and how it operates. This includes descriptions of the purposes of the IMF; its decision-making structure; the nature of its surveillance over individual countries and the global economy; the broad guidelines that shape its policy advice; its lending policies and facilities; the process of designing and modifying the economic policy programs on which it conditions its loans; and the ways in which its activities and focus have changed over the past decade. In describing how the IMF operates, the chapter tries to convey a sense for various difficulties that hamper its effectiveness. It emphasizes that the IMF faces several types of constraints: namely, constraints imposed by its legal authority, by the views of its major shareholders, by the behavior of member countries, by its limited pool of financial resources, and by the state of economists' knowledge. The chapter lists a number of criticisms of the IMF, addressing several of them and leaving the rest for discussion in subsequent chapters.

Chapters 4 and 5 focus on international financial crises. Chapter 4 begins with some historical perspectives on crisis episodes and an overview of the conceptual literature on their underlying causes. It then provides brief case-by-case reviews of seven of the major currency crises experienced by emerging market countries since the mid-1990s—Mexico (1994–95), Thailand (1997), Indonesia (1997–98), Korea (1997–98), Malaysia (1997–98), Russia (1998), and Brazil (1998–99). The reviews concentrate on the contributing factors and the initial stages of the crises, with the objective of gaining insights relevant to crisis prevention. In general, these crises were not triggered by sharp and sudden changes in economic fundamentals, but all seven countries suffered from a buildup of large macroeconomic imbalances, major structural weaknesses, or both that gave market participants rational reasons for concern about their abilities to repay their debts and avoid currency depreciation. The reviews underscore several different types of macroeconomic imbalances and structural weaknesses that make countries vulnerable to financial crises. The chapter also tries to shed light on why the IMF has not been more effective in preventing crises. This issue is separated into two parts: one pertaining to the effectiveness of the IMF in detecting potential problems at an early stage and providing appropriate and timely policy advice, and the other relating to countries' willingness and political capacity to heed the IMF's advice.

Chapter 5 turns to the effects of financial crises and the issue of how policymakers should respond. The chapter focuses first on two common and troublesome patterns in international capital flows: *sudden stops*, in which large volumes of capital inflows are followed by sharp decelerations or reversals, and *contagion*, in which a financial crisis in one country triggers substantial financial market turbulence or crises in other countries. These phenomena are indicative of market imperfections and the need to address their underlying causes through reforms of the international financial system. The chapter next considers various controversies over how crisis-stricken countries and the international community should respond to financial crises, along with related criticisms of the IMF's policy advice. The topics covered include controversies about choices of exchange rate arrangements; about appropriate monetary and fiscal policy responses; about the extent to which the IMF should require countries to implement structural reforms as a condition for financial assistance; and about the moral hazard that may be generated by the practice of providing IMF bailout loans. The chapter also looks for lessons from the adjustment policies pursued by Korea, a country that engineered a relatively successful recovery from financial crisis.

In discussing ways to strengthen the architecture of the international financial system, the academic and policymaking communities have devoted considerable attention to the challenges of preventing and resolving financial crises. It is also important to focus on the longer-run objectives of raising living standards and reducing poverty. These longer-run objectives are the subject of Chapter 6. The chapter provides a condensed review of the literature on economic growth, focusing first on three proximate determinants—physical capital accumulation, human capital formation, and technological change or productivity growth—and then on a set of deeper determinants. It emphasizes the Schumpeterian view of economic growth as a process of creative destruction. This view highlights the importance of incentives for technological innovation along with the relevance of institutions and the openness of economies—factors that are highly influential in shaping the incentives of market participants and that can thereby play critical roles as deeper determinants of economic growth. The wide range of relevant institutions includes institutions for defining property rights and enforcing contracts; for regulating markets and correcting market failures; for stabilizing economies through monetary and fiscal policies and prudential supervision; and for legitimizing market systems through the provision of political voice and social safety nets. In addressing the issue of poverty, the chapter notes that economists generally regard economic growth as the most effective vehicle for reducing poverty. Hence, the quality of institutions has central importance not only for sustaining growth but also in determining outcomes for the poor. The chapter includes a discussion of the need for reforming the manner in which the international community provides debt relief and other forms of aid. It notes, on the one hand, that low-income countries face dim prospects of growing out of poverty traps as long as they are burdened with high levels of debt, and, on the other hand, that official development aid has not been very effective as a vehicle for promoting economic growth over the past half century.

For reasons discussed in Chapter 2, a complete rebuilding of the international financial system is not in the cards. However, there are numerous ways in which the current system can be improved, thus providing scope for making the economic globalization process work substantially better within the not-too-distant future. The last two chapters of the book describe an agenda for strengthening the system to mitigate its propensity to trigger and propagate financial crises and to enhance its capacity to promote economic growth and reduce poverty.

Chapter 7 considers a list of five broad challenges for countries individually. It reviews the pros and cons of capital controls, both in theory and in practice, as perspectives relevant to the challenge of devising a sensible strategy for liberalizing domestic financial markets and international capital flows. It describes the efforts that are underway to help countries address the challenge of strengthening institutions, information, and the financial and corporate sectors. It discusses the pros and cons of different types of exchange rate regimes and the challenge of adopting sustainable exchange rate arrangements. It provides perspectives on the challenge of maintaining sustainable levels of external and public debt, implementing sound fiscal and monetary policies, and responding expeditiously to events that threaten to erode market confidence. It also focuses on the challenge of opening the economy to trade and foreign direct investment in a manner that results in growth-enhancing activities.

Chapter 8 considers an agenda for systemic reform. One item on the agenda is to strengthen the quality and impact of IMF surveillance. Proposals here include the idea of prequalification requirements or ex ante conditionality—that is, linking countries' degree of prospective access to Fund credit, should they ever need it, to their track records in policy implementation and institution building prior to their requests for financing. Another piece of the agenda is to induce changes in the composition of international capital flows, with emphasis on discouraging debt-creating flows, particularly flows that involve short-term foreign-currency-denominated debts. A third idea is to create markets for contingent debt contracts or to establish other mechanisms that would allow emerging market countries to hedge themselves against macroeconomic risks; for example, a market could be created for debt instruments with payment streams that are contingent on outcomes for gross domestic product (GDP) or the prices of major commodity exports. A fourth direction for systemic reform would address informational imperfections and distorted incentives on the supply side of international capital flows. Some proposals here focus on providing market participants with more information about the IMF's assessments of individual countries; others address various practices, including the compensation systems of institutional investors, that contribute to herding behavior in international financial markets. A fifth avenue for reform involves revamping debt resolution procedures. Attention here has focused on collective action clauses, statutory mechanisms for sovereign debt restructuring, and the ideas of inserting standstill provisions and more explicit definitions of seniority rights into debt contracts. A sixth item on the agenda for systemic reform takes aim at strengthening the frameworks for development aid and official nonconcessional lending, giving consideration again to the idea of prequalification through demonstrated track records in policy implementation and institution building.

2

The Evolution of the International
Monetary System

At the core of the international financial system is a set of official institutions and arrangements that govern payments between nations and exchange rates among currencies—a core referred to as the *international monetary system*. By enabling monetary transactions to take place between the residents of different countries, the international monetary system provides "the glue that binds national economies together."[1] The nature of the system and the roles of its official institutions have evolved over time with developments in the world economy and associated changes in the economic interests and priorities of participating countries.

Many monetary transactions between countries involve exchanges of different currencies. Throughout time, accordingly, one of the central objectives of the international community has been to maintain an orderly system of exchange rates between national currencies—a system not characterized by excessive volatility. Underlying this objective is the general perception that orderly exchange rates are conducive to the expansion of international trade, which in turn is widely regarded as conducive to the more fundamental goal of promoting economic growth and the improvement of living standards.

To understand the performance of the world economy and the consequences of the economic globalization process, one must understand the international monetary system, the roles that countries expect it to play, and the factors that contribute to its effectiveness or ineffectiveness. Moreover, in analyzing the strengths and weaknesses of the prevailing system, one can gain valuable insights from reflecting on how the global economy performed under previous international monetary regimes, on

---

[1] See Eichengreen (1996: 3).

why the institutions that govern the present system were created, and on how the system and its institutions have evolved over time.

This chapter is divided into five main sections.[2] Section 2.1 presents perspectives on the rise and fall of international monetary regimes from the late nineteenth century through the mid-1940s, covering the classical gold standard regime that prevailed before World War I and the series of short-lived regimes that spanned the interwar period. Section 2.2 describes the Bretton Woods system that was put in place after World War II and survived until the early 1970s; it provides background both on the creation of the IMF and World Bank and on the functioning and collapse of the system. Section 2.3 discusses the international monetary regime that prevails today, describing the formal agreement regarding exchange rate arrangements, the move to a common currency in Europe, the wide variety of exchange arrangements that countries have adopted, and the nature of the agenda setting and international policy cooperation that has emerged. Section 2.4 turns to the liberalization of financial markets over the past several decades and the sea change that has taken place in international capital flows—key developments in the global environment that have had important ramifications for the functioning of national economies. The main points that the chapter develops are summarized in Section 2.5. (Readers without much interest in economic history may wish to skip much of the material in Sections 2.1–2.4.)

2.1 The Rise and Fall of International Monetary Regimes, 1870–1945

One of the fundamental theorems of international macroeconomics is that a country cannot simultaneously maintain a fixed exchange rate and the autonomy to direct its monetary policy at domestic economic stabilization objectives in the presence of large stocks of internationally mobile financial capital. This *impossibility theorem* was not developed formally until the early 1960s, when Fleming (1962) and Mundell (1960, 1961a, 1961b, 1962, 1963) published their pathbreaking analyses of the policy implications of perfect international capital mobility. However, the constraint on policy choice—also known as the *basic policy trilemma* of open economies—was already implicitly understood in the early 1940s by the

---

[2] Sections 2.1, 2.2, and 2.3 (specifically Subsection 2.3.2) draw heavily on Isard (1995).

architects of the IMF, who established a postwar international monetary system of fixed exchange rates, made no presumption that countries would cede autonomy over national monetary policies, and provided encouragement for countries to maintain restrictions on international capital flows.

The basic policy trilemma provides a useful framework for discussing the functioning and collapse of successive international monetary regimes.[3] In the context of that framework, this section develops several themes. One theme is that cooperation among major countries has, from time to time, been very important for mitigating international financial instability and prolonging the existence of international monetary regimes. The second theme is that international monetary cooperation has sometimes been extremely counterproductive. A third theme is that changes in the global environment have essentially precluded two of the three theoretically possible ways of resolving the basic policy trilemma. In particular, an attempt to return to an international monetary regime in which the key-currency countries gave exchange rate stability priority over domestic economic stability (such as the international gold standard) or a system that essentially relied on controlling international capital flows (such as the Bretton Woods regime) would have little chance of succeeding today.[4]

2.1.1 The international gold standard

The classical international gold standard regime took shape during the 1870s. At the end of the decade, it included the United States and most European countries.[5] Although the sustainability of the regime was rooted

---

[3] See Obstfeld and Taylor (2003) for an analysis of the evolution of international capital mobility within the framework of the basic policy trilemma, and Obstfeld, Shambaugh, and Taylor (2004) for statistical evidence in support of the trilemma.

[4] This is not to deny that strong political desires to strengthen economic integration among a group of countries, along with a willingness to undertake the process of achieving economic convergence, can allow the group to form a common currency area and establish mechanisms for limiting domestic economic instability within individual member countries to politically acceptable levels. Such a process has taken place within much of Europe. However, as elaborated later, a return to fixed exchange rates between the United States, Japan, and the Euro Area does not seem politically feasible in the foreseeable future.

[5] England had established a gold standard during the eighteenth century, which was abandoned in 1797 but revived in 1819. Germany adopted a gold standard in 1871 and was joined before the end of the decade by the Latin Monetary Union (France, Belgium, Switzerland, and Italy), Holland, the Scandinavian countries, and the United States. Austria–Hungary moved to a gold standard in 1892, followed by Russia and Japan in 1897. See Yeager (1976).

in commitments to convert national currencies into gold on request, by the 1870s, most of the countries operating under gold standards held large amounts of foreign exchange on deposit in London, Britain had accumulated substantial stocks of relatively liquid assets abroad, and international payments imbalances were generally settled by drawing down or accumulating stocks of (nongold) foreign exchange reserves. Moreover, beginning in the early 1870s, the Bank of England had started to manage money-market conditions more deliberately and, by 1890, had developed techniques for managing its policy interest rate in a manner designed to avoid large movements of gold by inducing short-term capital to flow in directions that accommodated imbalances in current account transactions and long-term capital flows.[6] The Bank "regarded the maintenance of the convertibility of sterling to gold as paramount and any sustained movement of gold always led to action sooner or later."[7]

Not even the hegemon country, however, could completely insulate its economy from external financial crises and the threats they posed to the international monetary system. The limited powers of the Bank of England were revealed on a number of occasions, including the 1890 Baring Crisis and the U.S. financial panic of 1907.[8] The former crisis was sparked by a revolution in Argentina that triggered a collapse in the market value of Argentine government bonds, a large quantity of which were held by the House of Baring. Because Baring had run up substantial debts to other financial institutions in Britain, its problems precipitated a general loss of confidence in the British banking system and resulted in deposit withdrawals by both foreigners and domestic residents, draining gold from the Bank of England. This raised doubts about the Bank's ability to defend its gold parity. Some foreign central banks withdrew gold from England, and it was anticipated that others would follow. Increases in the policy interest rate failed to stem the tide, and it seemed likely that the gold parity would have to be abandoned if the Bank tried to maintain the stability of the domestic banking system by fulfilling its role as lender of last resort. The Bank also experienced a strong drain of gold when financial panic broke out in the United States during the autumn of 1907. A downturn in the American economy had been followed by a rise in nonperforming loans, a wave of bank failures, a shift out of deposits, and a surge in the demand for currency and gold.

[6] See Scammell (1965).
[7] See Scammell (1965: 113).
[8] See Eichengreen (1992, 1996) for a more extensive discussion.

On each of these occasions, as on a number of others, the crisis was re-solved through international monetary cooperation. The 1890 crisis was defused after England obtained a loan of gold from the Bank of France and a loan of gold coin from Russia. By strengthening the Bank of England's capacity to provide support if necessary, the loans inspired renewed confidence, and a consortium of domestic banks then agreed to contribute the bulk of the financing required to reorganize Baring. The 1907 crisis was also resolved through the willingness of continental European central banks to part with gold, although in this case without any direct lending to the Bank of England. The Bank of France assisted indirectly by not follow-ing the rise in British interest rates, by reassuring market participants that it would release its gold, and by purchasing sterling bills to speed the flow. Of the gold shipped to the United States in the last two months of 1907, two-fifths was newly mined and most of the rest originated in France, Germany, Belgium, and Russia (largely transshipped through London).

As these episodes suggest, preservation of the international gold stan-dard regime required the core countries of the system not only to cooperate to help each other in times of crisis but also to accommodate over time the growing and somewhat volatile demand for gold in countries on the periphery of the system, including the United States. Partly because it had no central bank before the creation of the Federal Reserve System in 1913, the United States was not a party to the cooperative arrangements that were periodically required to support the gold standard. Moreover, in the absence of a central bank to react to shocks that influenced the demand for money, the United States was a leading source of disturbances to the center countries of the gold standard system; shifts in money demand in the United States were transmitted to shifts in the demand for gold with-out being mitigated by domestic monetary policy. Britain played a central role in accommodating the demand for gold at the periphery, but Britain's resources were stretched thin on a number of occasions, and in such times the core central banks had to defend the system collectively.

A second factor that contributed importantly to the credibility and longevity of the gold standard regime was a social and political environ-ment in which it was feasible for national monetary authorities to give the maintenance of currency convertibility precedence over other pos-sible goals of economic policy.[9] There was no widely accepted theory linking the state of the economy to monetary policy, and hence no general

[9] See Eichengreen (1996: 30–1).

perception that a tightening of monetary policy aggravated unemployment. Moreover, the working classes were not well positioned to protest effectively against monetary policies that defended the convertibility of currencies into gold at the expense of creating unemployment. In most countries, the right to vote was still limited to property holders (with women excluded virtually everywhere), and labor parties representing workers were still in their formative years. Furthermore, producers who competed with foreign products—notably French and German farmers— were placated with import tariffs. And in an age of limited government, limited social programs, and limited defense spending, there was limited pressure to run the monetary printing presses in support of the public sector.[10] All this made it politically feasible for countries to keep the world generally free of restrictions on international capital movements and opt for fixed exchange rates (gold parities) instead of autonomous monetary policies.

2.1.2   Wartime convertibility restrictions

During and between the two world wars, the international monetary system evolved through a sequence of short-lived regimes as stability proved elusive. By late July 1914, a month after the assassination of the heir to the throne of Austria–Hungary and just before the major European powers declared war, the strains on the international monetary system had intensified greatly. The impending war had heightened the perceived risks of holding various types of financial claims, which brought frantic attempts to adjust financial portfolios toward relatively safe assets. Investors hastened to sell securities, causing stock exchanges to close in the United States, England, and other European countries. With transatlantic gold shipments at risk from hostile cruisers on the seas, some Europeans who sought to convert the proceeds from sales of U.S. securities in New York had to pay as much as seven dollars in exchange for one British pound—well above the parity of $4.87 per pound implied by official gold prices.[11] Although the international gold standard did not completely dissolve, the era had effectively ended. Gradually over the next few years,

[10] See Eichengreen and Sussman (2000: 22).
[11] The disparity between market exchange rates and the official rate was reduced, however, after the Bank of England agreed on August 12 to accept gold deliveries in Canada. See Yeager (1976: 310) and Kindleberger (1984: 291–2).

countries imposed official or de facto restrictions on both the convertibility of paper money into gold and the free international movement of gold.

The introduction of convertibility restrictions helped to limit exchange rate fluctuations. At the end of 1915, the pound had depreciated by only about 3 percent from its prewar dollar parity, and the French franc by a little more than 10 percent.[12] In January 1916, the pound–dollar rate was pegged at \$4.76; and from April 1916, with foreign exchange resources replenished by advances from the U.S. Treasury, the exchange rate between the pound and the French franc was also stabilized through official support operations.[13] The support operations that maintained the wartime parities were terminated in early 1919, a few months after the armistice.

2.1.3 Free floating

Although the United States returned to a full gold standard in June 1919, the dollar was the only currency for which gold convertibility was restored. Thus, no effective constraints were imposed on the exchange rates between national currencies. The years that ensued were characterized by the virtual absence of official intervention to stabilize currencies—a regime of relatively freely floating exchange rates—until Britain returned to the gold standard in 1925.[14] Exchange rates between the key currencies fluctuated widely. By late 1920 the pound was more than 25 percent weaker than its wartime peg against the dollar, a trough from which it recovered considerably by mid-1922. The end of 1920 also marked a trough for the French franc, which bottomed out at a level nearly 70 percent below its value in early 1919.

In sharp contrast with the prewar gold standard era, the postwar period began with large divergences in the macroeconomic conditions of the key-currency countries, and with substantial differences in their economic policy priorities. Different policy priorities, as well as the lingering hostilities from the war, made international policy cooperation difficult. In general, countries sought to return to the gold standard eventually, but only the United States was prepared to do so immediately. Influential

[12] See the Board of Governors of the Federal Reserve System (1943: 670, 681).
[13] See Yeager (1976: 311).
[14] See Eichengreen (1989: 15–16).

British economists argued that the restoration of the gold standard was a necessary condition for financial stability, but they also stressed that balanced government budgets had to come first, along with actions to insulate central banks from pressures to provide credit to government agencies.[15]

The task of establishing macroeconomic stability proved difficult. Currency supplies and price levels had risen during the war years by comparable amounts in the United States and Britain, by about twice as much in France, and by significantly more in Germany.[16] Following the signing of the armistice in November 1918, the release of pent-up demands generated booming economic conditions in both Western Europe and the United States. Employment expanded rapidly. Prices and wages accelerated. Toward the end of 1919 and into the following year, central banks reacted by raising their discount rates,[17] which ended the boom. Wholesale prices peaked during the spring of 1920 and then fell sharply over the next year in Britain, France, and the United States. Economic activity also fell sharply, especially in Britain. Subsequently, prices stabilized in Britain and the United States, while inflation reignited in France. The German experience was far worse. By the end of 1921, wholesale prices were 35 times their prewar level; a year later, nearly 1,500 times.[18] One of the classic hyperinflations of history was underway, along with similar experiences in Austria, Hungary, Poland, and Russia.

The inflation that sprung up in Central and Eastern Europe was seeded in the physical devastation and financial strains that resulted from the war. The countries of continental Europe had seen their productive capacities sharply reduced, and they possessed limited financial resources. Moreover, in light of the credit risks, there was limited scope to borrow abroad and a large amount of debt to be paid. In addition, the terms of surrender included an agreement that the defeated powers were to pay reparations. The amounts were to be determined by a reparations commission, which announced its decisions in April 1921. Initially, the United States took a firm stance against debt forgiveness, insisting on prompt repayment of the war loans it had made to its European allies and also adopting a hard line on reparation settlements by Germany. Not surprisingly, the European

[15] See Eichengreen (1989: 127).
[16] See Yeager (1976: 312).
[17] See Tsiang (1959: 253).
[18] See Yeager (1976: 313).

countries turned to deficit spending to meet their excess demands for foodstuffs and raw materials and to finance the capital goods imports needed for reconstruction.

Although the prevailing macroeconomic conditions precluded an early return to an international gold standard, countries considered steps to promote international monetary stability and economic recovery in Europe. A series of international monetary conferences took place in the early 1920s, motivated in part by common interest in rebuilding the global economy. Beyond that common interest, however, the three leading countries had very different economic policy objectives.[19] At the time of the Genoa Conference of 1922, the Americans and the British agreed that recovery required a revitalization of foreign trade, whereas the French were strongly opposed to initiatives for easing protectionist barriers against imports. The British and French favored reducing reparations through renegotiations facilitated by concessions from the United States on the war debts of its Allies, but the Americans continued to resist such concessions. Although these conflicting national interests hampered significant cooperative actions to help rebuild the economies of the war-ravaged countries, a set of resolutions emerged with the aim of easing the transition back to gold.[20] In particular, the Genoa resolutions encouraged countries that had experienced sustained inflation to avoid the output costs associated with restoring prewar price levels by returning to gold at depreciated parities. They also urged governments to reduce the need for monetary gold by holding official reserves in the form of foreign currency balances rather than gold.[21]

Another significant step to ease the strains on the international monetary system was taken during 1924, when, after difficult negotiations, the major countries agreed to a package of policy measures known as the Dawes Plan.[22] The measures included an easing of German reparation payments along with the issuance of a new German currency, the reichsmark, which was pegged to gold. In addition, a successful international effort was launched to raise private sector funds for purposes of lending Germany the money to pay reparations.

---

[19] See Eichengreen (1989: 125–7).
[20] See Eichengreen (1989: 128–9).
[21] A further mechanism for economizing on gold was the substitution of bank notes and deposits for gold coins in circulation.
[22] See Kindleberger (1984: 302–4).

2.1.4 A gold-exchange standard

In April 1925, the British announced their return to the gold standard; by the end of the year, nearly three dozen currencies, in addition to the U.S. dollar, were either formally pegged once again or had been stabilized de facto for a full year.[23] For many of the countries, the adoption of new statutes, encouraged by the Genoa resolutions, permitted central banks to hold foreign exchange instead of gold in their legal reserves, thereby establishing a gold-exchange standard.[24] Notably, the official parities at which countries stabilized their currencies reflected national decisions and, in some cases, did not adequately allow for the different degrees of inflation that had occurred in different countries. The ramifications would be remembered in reforming the international monetary system after World War II.[25] Some countries had difficulty competing with foreign producers at the new exchange rates and, in light of pressures on their gold reserves, had to keep their monetary policies tighter than would have been appropriate for their domestic economies alone. Other countries experienced large current account surpluses under the new exchange rates and built up large official holdings of international reserves.

Britain found itself confronting the choice between tight monetary policies and substantial capital outflows. Churchill, then Chancellor of the Exchequer, had been swayed by advocates of returning to gold at the prewar parity, shunning the advice of some prominent economists, most notably Keynes, who had calculated that the pound would be significantly overvalued at that parity.[26] In the months immediately following the return to gold, the Bank of England maintained a tight monetary policy, and a considerable volume of bullion began to flow into its reserves. This obviated the need to rely on the safety net that had been put in place to defend the pound if downward pressures emerged.[27] However, Churchill had either misperceived or heavily discounted the consequences that

---

[23] See Brown (1940, Vol. I: 393–4).

[24] See Nurkse (1944: 28–30), who emphasized that the gold exchange system had been practiced in many cases before 1914 and was by no means invented in Genoa.

[25] See Yeager (1976: 330).

[26] See Keynes (1925: 11).

[27] During the year preceding the restoration of the gold standard, the British authorities had made efforts to bolster their ability to support the pound by negotiating lines of credit from the U.S. Federal Reserve and from a private syndicate headed by J. P. Morgan & Co. See Clarke (1967: 81–105).

defending the prewar parity would have for unemployment and industrial strife.

Given the weak state of the domestic economy, British monetary policy during the next several years was not kept sufficiently tight to prevent mounting claims on Britain's reserves. Substantial amounts of capital
flowed out of Britain and into Germany and France, particularly during
the period 1926–28. In Germany, where capital inflows were pulled to
a large extent by the rapid economic recovery, the Reichsbank became
concerned about the threat to monetary control. Until 1926, the Reichsbank had acquiesced in accumulating the sterling balances brought by the
capital inflow, but it then began to convert these balances into gold.

Similar developments were occurring in France. Successful fiscal stabilization measures taken in July 1926 by the newly formed Poincaré
government had induced a huge inflow of capital through mid-1927. The
French authorities, unable to agree on the exchange rate at which the
franc should be stabilized, let their currency appreciate moderately and
then pegged it de facto, in December 1926, at about the same level at
which it would subsequently be stabilized de jure in June 1928. During
the first half of 1927, the Bank of France, which had accumulated large
reserve holdings of sterling, began to convert these balances into both
dollars and gold while also converting dollar balances into gold. One of
its aims was to induce an increase in British interest rates, which it hoped
would discourage the capital flows into France.

With Britain in a vulnerable position, diplomacy came to the fore.[28]
The Bank of England emphasized Britain's domestic economic difficulties
to French officials, arguing that tightening its monetary policy would
aggravate those difficulties unacceptably. If pressed too far, Britain's only
alternative would be to abandon the gold standard. Apparently, the British
authorities also threatened to turn up the pressure on France to repay
its war debts. In the end, the impasse was broken partly by a degree of
accommodation on both sides and partly by the intervention of the United
States, which agreed to sell some of its own gold to France for sterling.

As these perspectives indicate, it would be wrong to conclude that international monetary cooperation broke down during the period of the interwar gold-exchange standard. However, because some countries had established gold parities without adequately allowing for the divergent amounts

[28] See Clarke (1967: 118–19).

of inflation that had occurred,[29] international cooperation aimed at preserving the interwar gold-exchange standard eventually became strongly counterproductive. In particular, monetary policy in the United States during the second half of 1927 was influenced by a desire to be cooperative in easing the strain on Britain's gold reserves, and the departure of U.S. monetary policy from the course most consistent with domestic needs in turn unintentionally fueled the boom and crash on Wall Street.[30] More generally, attempts to adhere to restored gold standards that had limited credibility under the prevailing economic conditions, exacerbated by inadequate and, in some cases, ill-conceived efforts at international cooperation, have been blamed for playing a major role in generating the Great Depression, which in turn catalyzed the political transformations that led to the Second World War.[31]

2.1.5 An uncoordinated hybrid system

Following the industrial downturn in the United States in mid-1929 and the stock market crash in October, the world economy plunged into depression. World industrial production dropped 32 percent between 1929 and 1932, "[w]idespread protectionism—in the form of tariffs, import quotas, foreign exchange restrictions, and the like—materialized overnight," and the volume of world trade fell 26 percent.[32] Although few economic historians blame the Great Depression on trade restrictions,[33] the resort to protectionism clearly signaled a breakdown in international cooperation.

At least seven countries left the gold standard between 1929 and August 1931. Britain followed in September 1931 after the collapse of several large banks in Austria and Germany had made financial asset holders wary and precipitated runs on a number of currencies, including the pound.[34] Britain's departure from gold was "unexpected."[35] Once unpegged, the

---

[29] Keynes (1925: 11) provides perspectives on Britain's choice of parity.

[30] See Yeager (1976: 336).

[31] See Eichengreen (1992) and Cooper (1992).

[32] See Irwin (1998: 337).

[33] In the United States, preparations for the 1929 Smoot–Hawley tariff increases began in late 1928, well before the industrial downturn; and much of the impetus for subsequent protectionist actions by other countries probably came from domestic economic stress rather than desires to retaliate. See Irwin (1998: 335–7).

[34] See Yeager (1976: 299).

[35] See Clarke (1967: 218).

pound depreciated substantially, falling 25 percent against the dollar in the first week of floating. In December, its average exchange value against the dollar was 30 percent below the pre-September parity.

The plunge of the pound may have induced various official and private asset holders to reduce their balances of financial assets and increase their holdings of gold. In any case, with market participants no longer able to obtain gold in London, bullion began to drain from the reserve holdings of the United States, which remained on a gold standard. This led the Federal Reserve to consider actions to push up interest rates. Some parties expressed strong opposition, given the depressed condition of the U.S. economy and the strength of the underlying U.S. balance of payments position.[36] However, concerns to stop the gold drain received priority over concerns about the domestic economy, and the Federal Reserve raised its discount rate sharply during October 1931. "With hindsight this is universally regarded as a serious mistake in monetary policy which deepened the depression in the United States and in the entire world outside the sterling bloc."[37]

With the world economy depressed, countries perceived advantages in cutting their ties to gold. Another sixteen countries left the gold standard in the last four months of 1931, and twelve more during 1932 and early 1933.[38] The United States abandoned gold unequivocally in April 1933, less than two months after the inauguration of President Franklin Roosevelt, whose views on economic policy were radically different than those of his predecessor.

Countries that had already unpegged their exchange rates sometimes found their competitiveness adversely affected when other countries decided to abandon gold. When the pound appreciated in the early months of 1932, the British government responded by establishing an Exchange Equalization Account to manage the exchange rate—in particular, to resist the appreciation. In the same spirit, the United States, after abandoning gold in April 1933, resisted international political pressures to limit the dollar's depreciation until, in January 1934, Roosevelt announced a return to a fixed gold parity at thirty-five dollars an ounce. At that price, the dollar, in terms of gold, was 40 percent cheaper than its pre-1933 parity. Notably, during the autumn of 1933, the United States

[36] See Despres (1973: xi–xii).
[37] See Kindleberger (1984: 380–1).
[38] See Yeager (1976: 299).

had probed whether the British were interested in stabilizing the dollar–pound exchange rate, only to find that the Bank of England was not ready to contemplate such an objective.[39]

2.1.6 Managed floating

By the mid-1930s, with the world economy suffering from the strongly adverse consequences of widespread resort to import restrictions and competitive devaluations, a renewed appreciation for the importance of international monetary cooperation had emerged. The unraveling of cooperation began to reverse in 1936. France, which had remained on a gold standard at the parity officially established in 1928, experienced downward pressure on its currency following the formation of a Popular Front Government in the spring of 1936. The French authorities contemplated devaluation. The Americans and the British were concerned that the franc might be devalued excessively. The French had reason to fear foreign retaliation. Negotiations led to the Tripartite Monetary Agreement of September 1936. As part of the agreement, the franc was devalued by roughly 25 percent.

The Tripartite Agreement established a process of coordination between the three major countries and a system of managed floating.[40] Although no formal coordination mechanism was specified in the agreement, arrangements for day-to-day collaboration among monetary authorities in managing exchange rates were soon worked out. The monetary authorities consulted daily to agree on appropriate levels for exchange rates and to decide on a common currency in which exchange market intervention would be conducted. When the parties agreed on both the exchange rate levels and the intervention currency, they further specified a price at which each central bank would exchange foreign currency for gold at the close of the business day.

Beyond efforts to coordinate day-to-day actions in exchange markets, the Tripartite Agreement did not constrain the three countries from pursuing independent policies aimed at domestic economic objectives. Formal coordination of monetary and fiscal policies was not taken explicitly into consideration.

---

[39] See Kindleberger (1984: 388).
[40] See Eichengreen (1989: 144–5).

2.1.7 Arrangements during World War II

The outbreak of World War II in 1939 ushered in a period of tight exchange controls. Exchange rates continued to be officially managed, with the pound rigidly pegged at $4.03. Given the scale and desperate nature of European needs for imported supplies, however, prevailing exchange rates would not have been sustainable without large-scale American assistance under the Lend Lease Act of 1941.

The total outflow of Lend Lease aid from the United States, net of eventual repayments, amounted to $37 billion at a price level considerably lower than today's. Thirty-eight countries were recipients of this aid, with about 65 percent of it channeled to the British Empire, 23 percent to the Soviet Union, and 7 percent to France and her possessions.[41]

2.2 The Bretton Woods System: 1946–1971

2.2.1 Creation of the IMF and World Bank

Plans for a new international monetary system began to take shape during the war. With recognition of the importance of international monetary cooperation, and in hopes of avoiding the international economic disorder that had followed World War I, the British and American authorities during the early 1940s assembled groups of governmental and academic experts to begin articulating ideas and negotiating rules and institutions for postwar monetary and financial relations.[42] The agreements that emerged were adopted by forty-four nations at a conference in Bretton Woods, New Hampshire during July 1944. The new international economic order was formally launched with the declaration of fixed exchange rate parities by thirty-two countries in December 1946.

Ideologically, the Bretton Woods agreement reflected a middle ground between the philosophies of laissez faire and interventionism. The negotiations sought to forge a coalition between those parts of the political

---

[41] See Yeager (1976: 378).

[42] See Ikenberry (1993) and Solomon (1982). Williams (1947) contrasts the strategy for economic reconstruction after World War II with the approach taken after World War I. Eichengreen and Kenen (1994) and Volcker and Gyohten (1992) credit the leadership role played by the United States during and after World War II, in contrast with U.S. isolationism after World War I, as a major factor in the design of relatively successful rules and institutions; they also suggest that success was facilitated by the fact that most of the negotiations involved only two countries.

establishments that lobbied strongly for free trade and those that sought arrangements to foster full employment and economic stabilization.[43] One of the objectives was to reach an agreement that countries with depressed economies would not resort, as they had in the 1930s, to beggar-thy-neighbor devices such as import restrictions or competitive devaluations. The outcome was a managed multilateral system that left individual countries with considerable autonomy to pursue domestic economic policy objectives but subjected their exchange rate practices and international trade and payments restrictions to international agreement.

Two new international organizations—the IMF and the International Bank for Reconstruction and Development (the World Bank)—were created at the Bretton Woods conference. The IMF was designed to promote international monetary cooperation and an orderly exchange rate system, and to provide short-term financial assistance to meet temporary balance of payment needs. The World Bank was established to finance economic reconstruction and development. The Bretton Woods conference also generated plans for an International Trade Organization (ITO) to establish rules, eliminate restrictions, and settle disputes relating to international trade. The ITO was never established, because the U.S. Congress did not approve its charter. In the late 1940s, however, the United States and many other countries adopted as treaty obligations the set of rules that had been developed for the ITO. The treaty was known as the General Agreement on Tariffs and Trade (GATT), and an informal secretariat for the GATT was created to provide a forum for addressing issues relating to international trade. During the 1980s and early 1990s it became increasingly evident that flaws in the institutional structure of the GATT impeded further progress in trade liberalization; and in December 1993, negotiations were completed to establish a new World Trade Organization (WTO), which came into existence on January 1, 1995.

The Articles of Agreement of the IMF defined a new international monetary system. Each member country was to fix, at a level approved by the IMF, a par value for its currency in terms of either gold or a currency fixed to gold. Each country was to keep its exchange rate within 1 percent of its par value, but it retained the right to adjust its central parity, upon securing the concurrence of the IMF, if ever a "fundamental

---

[43] See Ikenberry (1993: 157–8).

disequilibrium" developed in its balance of payments.[44] The IMF was to make credit available to members for the purpose of financing temporary and cyclical balance of payments deficits, subject to quantitative credit limits and to conditions linking the provision of credit to the implementation of policies aimed at correcting payment imbalances. Each country, after a transitional period, was to eliminate restrictions on currency convertibility for purposes of making payments for imports and other current account transactions. Countries were permitted, if not encouraged, to impose restrictions on undesired international capital flows.

In effect, the resulting system of exchange rates established an international gold-dollar standard. The United States was the only country to peg its currency to gold; most other currencies were pegged to the U.S. dollar. The U.S. par value was left at thirty-five dollars per ounce of gold, where it had been since 1934. The United States was also the only industrial country prepared at the outset to forego transitional arrangements and accept the obligation of avoiding restrictions on convertibility for current account payments.[45] Under a policy adopted in 1934, however, the United States sold gold only to foreign central banks and governments, and to licensed private users of gold for the industries and arts.[46]

2.2.2   Adjustment and collapse: the power of internationally mobile capital

The environment in which countries launched the new system of fixed exchange rates after World War II was fundamentally different from the environment that supported the fixed gold parities prior to World War I. As noted earlier, the spread of universal suffrage, and the more general breakdown of limits on the extent of democracy within countries—in part a reaction to the economic environment that the international gold standard regime had helped to shape—had considerably strengthened the political influence of the working classes and altered the incentives of

---

[44] Concurrence was automatic if the proposed adjustment, together with all previous adjustments, did not exceed 10 percent of the country's initial par value.

[45] El Salvador, Guatemala, Mexico, and Panama also accepted this obligation at the outset.

[46] The IMF's charter gave each country the option of converting its currency either into gold or into the currency of the country that was seeking conversion; see Yeager (1976: 352).

economic policymakers.[47] Before World War I, most countries attached high priority to maintaining their gold parities, which endowed the parities with strong credibility. In contrast, in the aftermath of World War II, elected officials who opted to incur high domestic economic costs for the sake of defending exchange rates faced dire political consequences.

As the incentives of economic policymakers changed, so did the behavior of international capital flows. As long as forward-looking market participants had no doubts about the commitment to maintaining fixed gold parities, internationally mobile capital had incentives to flow in directions that supported the parities rather than to speculate that parities would be adjusted. Thus, prior to World War I, international capital flows served to reinforce the commitment to fixed exchange rates, and governments had little or no incentive to impose controls on international capital movements. However, once it was no longer very credible that governments would incur high domestic costs, if need be, to defend their exchange rate pegs, capital controls were necessary to insulate national economies from speculative attacks on their currencies.

Through periodic adjustments of exchange rate pegs and a resort to capital controls, the Bretton Woods system survived for a quarter century. The demise came after internationally mobile private capital had grown substantially in both volume and agility, thereby becoming a major force that was difficult to control.

During the early years of the Bretton Woods period, par value changes occurred infrequently. In September 1949, the United Kingdom and most other European countries, with encouragement from the United States, devalued their currencies by about 30 percent against the U.S. dollar. In September 1950, after a 10 percent devaluation during the previous year, the par value of the Canadian dollar was suspended in favor of a floating exchange rate for a period that would last nearly a dozen years, albeit with very moderate fluctuations in the exchange rate between Canadian and U.S. dollars. And during 1957–58, the French franc was devalued in two steps by a total of 29 percent.

---

[47] Polyani (1944) was perhaps the first to develop the view that the rise in democratization and the associated politicization of economic relations was an endogenous response to the institutions of laissez faire that prevailed during the nineteenth and early twentieth centuries, with the gold standard prominent among them. See the discussion in Eichengreen (1996).

The postwar period through 1958 was characterized by a high degree of international economic cooperation. The industrial structures and financial positions of Europe and Japan had been devastated during World War II. In such circumstances, the war-torn countries looked to the United States for food, manufactures, and financial assistance. The United States offered the European Recovery Program, better known as the Marshall Plan. In addition to providing financial grants and loans, America encouraged the European countries to expand exports to the United States, and to liberalize trade among themselves, while maintaining restrictions on imports from outside Europe. The devaluations of 1949 were part of the effort to stimulate the expansion of European production by promoting exports and discouraging imports from outside Europe.

Along with reconstructing and expanding their production bases, the European countries sought to rebuild their depleted stocks of international reserves. Once the Bretton Woods system was in operation, most of the growth over time in official international reserve holdings took the form of dollar-denominated claims on the United States. By the end of the 1950s, U.S. liabilities to foreign monetary authorities had reached $10 billion, roughly equivalent in value to foreign official reserve holdings of British pounds, which had hardly changed during the decade.[48] In addition, U.S. gold sales to foreign countries amounted to $5.7 billion net during the period 1949–59.[49]

Although the architects of the Bretton Woods agreements regarded the recovery of international trade as important for the restoration of prosperity and economic growth, they allowed countries to maintain restrictions—for a transitional period—on the convertibility of their currencies to pay for imports and other current international transactions. By 1958, most European countries felt sufficiently secure with their expanded reserve holdings to remove the transitional restrictions on current account convertibility. Although only Germany took the further step of removing convertibility restrictions on capital account transactions,[50] the establishment of current account convertibility weakened the effectiveness of capital controls. Funds could now be readily shifted between currencies

---

[48] See Solomon (1982: 29).
[49] See Solomon (1982: 31).
[50] See Solomon (1982: 24). The Japanese yen was not made convertible for current transactions until 1964.

by leading or lagging payments for imports or exports, and invoices for merchandise trade could also be manipulated to move financial capital.

It would be more than another decade, however, before enormous flows of speculative funds brought down the system. In part this reflected the remarkably high degree of consistency, until the late 1960s, between the economic policy priorities of the industrial countries. The pursuit of export-led growth by Europe and Japan was not incompatible with domestic policy objectives in North America. Moreover, the maintenance of price stability in the United States provided a nominal anchor for other participants in the fixed exchange rate system, thereby permitting Europe and Japan to keep their policies oriented more toward promoting growth, and less toward resisting inflation, than might otherwise have been appropriate.

This is not to say that all was well in the world economy and the international monetary system. By the mid-1960s, many European countries had succeeded in reducing unemployment to relatively low levels, and wage and price pressures were intensifying. Moreover, by late 1964, growing concerns about the international monetary system were being openly discussed.[51]

The policy-oriented literature of the 1960s characterized the prevailing international monetary system as incapable of simultaneously resolving the problems of liquidity, adjustment, and confidence. With the production of new gold being inadequate to meet the increasing demand for official international reserves in a growing world economy, and with gold and reserve currencies comprising the principal reserve assets in the international monetary system, the liquidity problem could be solved, or so it was perceived, in only two ways: by continuing to increase the liabilities of the reserve-currency countries, especially those of the United States, or by raising the purchasing power of gold. This choice presented what was known as the *Triffin dilemma*.[52] The first solution would lead to a persistent balance of payments deficit for the United States on an official settlements basis,[53] which many economists viewed as an adjustment

---

[51] See Argy (1981) and Solomon (1982).

[52] See Triffin (1960).

[53] A country's official settlements balance amounts to its current account balance plus its balance of capital flows, excluding any changes in foreign official holdings of short-term claims on residents of the country. Thus, if a country in current account balance experienced a net increase in the short-term liabilities of its banks and other residents

problem.[54] The second solution, moreover, would create a confidence problem, undermining faith in the reserve system. In particular, an increase in the official dollar price of gold—or even the contemplation of an increase—could induce attempts by foreign governments to convert their dollar reserve holdings into gold and would also induce speculative investments in gold by private market participants. This would rapidly drain the gold reserves of the United States and destroy the ability of the U.S. authorities to defend any fixed gold parity for the dollar.[55]

The principal mechanism proposed to resolve this dilemma was for the IMF to create a new reserve asset. The formal creation of this asset—the *special drawing right* (SDR)—came with the approval in May 1968, and legal adoption the next year, of the First Amendment to the Articles of Agreement of the IMF. The initial allocation of SDRs took place in three stages during 1970–72; subsequent allocations were to be considered periodically as the global need for reserves expanded over time. In the event, however, the presumption that the expansion of dollar reserve holdings required an increase in the international indebtedness of the United States—or even in the short-term liabilities of U.S. residents to foreign monetary authorities—soon proved invalid. By the end of the 1960s, a large international market, known as the Eurodollar market, had developed outside the United States for the dollar-denominated liabilities of governments and reputable private borrowers. Official holdings of prime-grade dollar-denominated assets could thus be accumulated by borrowing from private financial intermediaries whose activities did not create balance of payments adjustment problems.

As it happened, the United States allowed a genuine adjustment problem to develop when it overheated its economy and fueled inflation by

to foreign monetary authorities, mirrored by outflows of other short-term or long-term capital, its official settlements balance would show a deficit.

[54] Notably, some economists correctly argued at the time that a persistent U.S. balance of payments deficit on an official settlements basis (in association with a continuing buildup of short-term liabilities of the United States to foreign monetary authorities) did not necessarily imply a continuing increase in the *net* international indebtedness of U.S. residents—as would be reflected in a continuing U.S. current account deficit—and thus did not really represent an adjustment problem; see Kindleberger (1965) and Despres, Kindleberger, and Salant (1966).

[55] During the 1960s, the United States and a number of other countries developed various policies to limit conversion of dollars into gold. These included the formation of the Gold Pool in 1961, the issuance of Roosa bonds, and the establishment of the Two-Tier Arrangement in 1968; see Solomon (1982) and Pauls (1990).

failing to push for a tax increase or expenditure cuts when the fiscal implications of the expansion of the Vietnam War were first anticipated in the mid-1960s.[56] Eventually, monetary and fiscal policies were tightened, which failed to stop the upward spiral of wages and prices but did generate a sharp slowdown and subsequent contraction of the U.S. economy. In those circumstances, short-term dollar interest rates declined considerably during 1970, while surging economic activity was pushing interest rates higher in Europe and Japan. The widening nominal interest rate differentials and continuing U.S. inflationary spiral eroded the attractiveness of dollar-denominated assets relative to both gold and assets denominated in other leading currencies. Private capital outflows from the United States rose sharply, mirrored by an increase in foreign official holdings of short-term claims on the United States. As a result, the foreign exchange value of the German mark (already raised by 9.3 percent in September–October 1969) came under strong upward pressure. In May 1971, the German authorities decided to abandon their official parity and let the mark float. A few other countries followed, but most European countries and Japan continued to maintain their fixed parities. Speculation against the dollar grew more intense. This led the U.S. authorities, on August 15, 1971, to suspend the convertibility of the dollar into gold for foreign monetary authorities.

The suspension of dollar convertibility marked the end of the Bretton Woods era.[57] Less than two weeks later, the Bank of Japan, after heavy official intervention to defend the yen–dollar parity, decided to let its currency float. By the end of August nearly all countries had relinquished their commitments to defend par values. Following the Smithsonian Agreement reached in December 1971, the Group of Ten countries,[58] in an attempt to restore the Bretton Woods system, established new par values and widened

---

[56] See Solomon (1982: 100–9).

[57] Notably, the collapse of the Bretton Woods system was not the result of reserve shortages. Had the United States imposed stronger self-discipline over its macroeconomic policies in the mid-1960s, the Bretton Woods regime might well have been prolonged without systemic reforms. From the obverse perspective, moreover, it is hard to conceive of systemic reforms that, on their own, could have generated significantly stronger macroeconomic policy discipline in the United States or other major countries at the time. It would thus be misleading to suggest that either the special drawing right (SDR) or international monetary reform came "too late."

[58] The Group of Ten was formed in 1962 by Belgium, Canada, France, Germany, Italy, Japan, the Netherlands, Sweden, the United Kingdom, and the United States. In 1964 it was expanded to include Switzerland.

the fluctuation margins to 2.25 percent on each side of the parities. As part of the agreement, the U.S. dollar was devalued by raising the price of gold from thirty-five to thirty-eight dollars per ounce, with the unwritten quid pro quo that the United States would not be pressed to restore the gold convertibility of the dollar at an early date.[59]

The new par values, however, proved difficult to defend. In June 1972, the United Kingdom decided to abandon the effort and floated its currency. Switzerland followed in January 1973, and Japan and Italy in February. In March, six members of the European Community (Belgium, Denmark, France, Germany, Luxembourg, and the Netherlands) announced that they would keep their currencies pegged against each other but let them jointly float in a so-called *snake* arrangement against other currencies. The international monetary system had evolved to a regime of *generalized floating* among the major currencies.

2.3   The Prevailing International Monetary System

2.3.1   *Amendment of the agreement governing exchange rate arrangements*

The central issue facing the IMF after the breakdown of the Bretton Woods regime was that of constructing a successor system of exchange rate arrangements. The move to generalized floating was widely regarded as a temporary solution. A Committee of Twenty—more formally, the Committee of the Board of Governors of the Fund on Reform of the International Monetary System and Related Issues—was established in 1972 with the mandate of developing a proposal.[60] This was planned as a two-year effort, with much of the work to be conducted by a group of six deputies. In June 1974, the Committee made public an Outline of Reform that called for a new exchange rate regime "based on stable but adjustable par values and with floating rates recognized as providing a useful technique in particular situations." The new regime was also to include a "symmetrical" process for balance of payments adjustment and "cooperation in dealing with disequilibrium capital flows."[61]

---

[59] See Solomon (1982: 205).
[60] See the discussions in Solomon (1982) and Pauls (1990).
[61] See the Committee of the Board of Governors of the fund on Reform (1974).

At the time the Outline was published, policymakers were focused on the difficulties created by the quadrupling of oil prices at the end of 1973 and by the onset of worldwide inflation. Many countries, including France, felt that a reformed system was possible only if it was based on par values. As of mid-1974, however, a return to par values still seemed far away. Moreover, some countries, in particular the United States, wanted a system that gave them the option of continuing to float their exchange rates. Following intensive negotiations between France and the United States, a compromise was reached in November 1975 at a meeting of the heads of government of six countries (France, Germany, Italy, Japan, the United Kingdom, and the United States) held outside Paris at the Chateau de Rambouillet. The Rambouillet Agreement led to the Second Amendment of the IMF's Articles, including substantial changes in Article IV, which deals with exchange rate arrangements. Although the amended Article IV provides scope for countries either to maintain par values or to implement other exchange arrangements of their choice, it begins with a statement of general obligations, emphasizing that each member must

collaborate with the Fund and other members to assure orderly exchange arrangements and promote a stable system of exchange rates. In particular, each member shall: (i) endeavor to direct its economic and financial policies toward the objective of fostering orderly economic growth with reasonable price stability . . . ; (ii) seek to promote stability by fostering orderly underlying economic and financial conditions . . . ; (iii) avoid manipulating exchange rates or the international monetary system in order to prevent effective balance of payments adjustment or to gain an unfair competitive advantage over other members.[62]

As Boughton (2001) and Kenen (2003) note, success in coming up with language—"promote a stable system of exchange rates"—that "equally supported two diametrically opposed visions is a remarkable tribute to the obfuscatory skills of the sherpas and their deputies."[63]

Indeed, no one has ever been able to give operational meaning to that phrase, but the agreement to put the word "stable" in an unnatural place played a key role in defusing the conflict between American and French views about the future of the monetary system.[64]

[62] See IMF (1993, Article IV).
[63] See Boughton (2001: 194).
[64] See Kenen (2003: 5). For a more extensive discussion, see De Vries (1985: 739–49).

2.3.2   European monetary integration

As pressures mounted on the Bretton Woods system toward the end of the 1960s, the opposition to greater flexibility of exchange rates was particularly strong among the European Community (EC) countries (France, Germany, Italy, Belgium, the Netherlands, and Luxembourg), which had moved considerably during the 1960s toward the unification of trade and tariff policies and the formulation of the Common Agricultural Policy. Indeed, the importance attached by the authorities of these countries to the preservation and strengthening of economic integration and cooperation, and the desirability of stable exchange rates from that perspective, led the EC to revive the idea of a monetary union "involving the reduction and eventual elimination of exchange rate fluctuations between the currencies of the EC countries and the complete liberalization of capital movements between them."[65] In pursuit of that idea, the EC decided in December 1969 to assemble a group of experts to come up with a detailed plan, which it endorsed in March 1971.

The plan, known as the Werner Report,[66] proposed a three-stage process for implementing monetary union. Stage I, from 1971 to 1974, would "create the machinery for coordinated policy making"; Stage II would "make exchange-rate changes depend on explicit member agreements"; and the final stage would create a "Community central bank shaped after the U.S. Federal Reserve System."[67]

As alluded to earlier, one of the first significant steps came in March 1972 when the six EC members, together with three soon-to-be members (the United Kingdom, Denmark, and Ireland),[68] established an independent currency arrangement (the snake) with narrower fluctuation margins than the IMF rules then allowed.[69] The international economic environment at the time, however, was unkind to the snake, in much the same manner as it contributed to a turbulent experience with managed floating within the broader international monetary system.[70] Britain, Ireland, and

---

[65] See De Vries (1985: 21).
[66] See the Council of the European Communities (1970).
[67] See Fratianni and von Hagen (1992: 13).
[68] These three countries joined the European Community (EC) on January 1, 1973.
[69] The Smithsonian Agreement in December 1971 had widened the IMF margins to 2.25 percent on either side of par values. The United Kingdom did not join the snake until May 1, 1972.
[70] See Goldstein (1980).

Denmark left the arrangement in June 1972, although Denmark rejoined in October; Italy left in February 1973; France left in January 1974, rejoined in July 1975, and left again in March 1976; and in the meantime, a number of small realignments took place.[71] To an important extent, the difficulties of holding the snake together reflected the fact that different countries—in the wake of the 1972–73 boom and the stagflationary oil price shock of 1973–74—chose different approaches to macroeconomic stabilization, giving rise, among other things, to different inflation rates. As a consequence, the process of monetary unification stagnated.

In October 1977 the British president of the European Commission launched a new drive for monetary union.[72] This led to the formation of the European Monetary System (EMS) in March 1979 and the creation of the European currency unit (ecu), a basket currency defined by fixed quantities of the currencies of participants in the EMS. At the beginning, all nine members of the EC except the United Kingdom participated in the fixed Exchange Rate Mechanism (ERM) of the EMS. One of the eight participants, Italy, was allowed to adopt wide fluctuation margins of 6 percent on each side of its par values; the others adopted margins of 2.25 percent. The United Kingdom remained outside the ERM until October 1990. Three more countries joined the EC during the 1980s—Greece in 1981, followed by Spain and Portugal in 1986—with Spain also entering the ERM as of June 1989 and Portugal as of April 1992.[73] Although the ecu was used as the common numeraire of the ERM and a means of payment among participating monetary authorities, the deutsche mark evolved, de facto, into the center currency, and monetary policies in countries other than Germany were effectively constrained to follow that of the Bundesbank.

Together, the fixed exchange rate system and the macroeconomic environment of the 1980s contributed to a dramatic convergence in inflation rates among countries participating in the ERM (Figure 2.1, top panel).

---

[71] See Solomon (1982), Kindleberger (1984), and De Vries (1985). Norway and Sweden joined in March 1973; Sweden withdrew in August 1977.

[72] See Jenkins (1978).

[73] On January 1, 1995, EC membership was expanded further to include Austria, Finland, and Sweden; Norway had been invited to join as well but rejected membership in a national referendum. Austria had, de facto, pegged its currency to the deutsche mark since 1981. Finland, Norway, and Sweden had shifted during 1990–91 from trade-weighted currency pegs to pegs against the European currency unit (ecu), but strong exchange market pressures had led all three countries to abandon their fixed exchange rate commitments by the end of 1992.

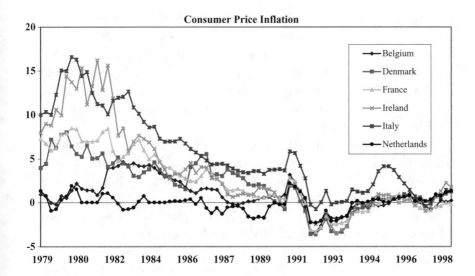

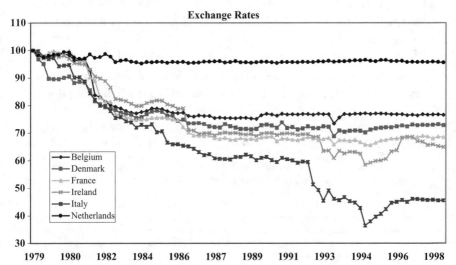

Figure 2.1. Inflation convergence and exchange rates in the ERM. Quarterly data. Consumer price inflation is excess over inflation in Germany in percentage points per year. The exchange rates show deutsche marks per national currency unit, March 1979 = 100. *Source*: IMF, *International Financial Statistics*.

The period also brought a steady decrease in the frequency of exchange rate adjustments; in particular, EMS central rates were realigned seven times between March 1979 and September 1983,[74] four times between October 1983 and March 1988,[75] and once between April 1988 and August 1992.[76] The infrequent realignments of central rates after the mid-1980s were reflected in the relative stability of market exchange rates (Figure 2.1, lower panel).[77]

These trends toward inflation convergence and exchange rate stability propelled the political process further. In June 1988, a decision was taken to require the lifting of all remaining capital controls by July 1990, and a committee was established to prepare a blueprint for European Economic and Monetary Union (EMU). The blueprint, known as the Delors Report,[78] was issued in April 1989 and adopted in June. Two and one-half years later, at the Maastricht Summit in December 1991, the member states of the EC adopted comprehensive amendments to their Charter, the 1957 Treaty of Rome, to allow, inter alia, for the transition to a single currency and the establishment of a central monetary policy institution for the Community.

The blueprint provided by the Delors Report and the Maastricht Agreement—including the holes left to be filled in the plan—elicited much controversy.[79] Moreover, for those who had disregarded the fault lines en

[74] During these seven realignments, bilateral central rates against the deutsche mark were changed six times for the Danish krone, five times each for the Belgian franc and Italian lira, four times each for the French franc and Irish pound, and twice for the Dutch guilder.

[75] On these four occasions, bilateral central rates against the deutsche mark were changed three times each for the Italian lira and the Irish pound and two times each for the Belgian franc, the Danish krone, and the French franc, with no change for the Dutch guilder.

[76] On the latter occasion, in January 1990, the central rate of the Italian lira was devalued by 3.7 percent against the deutsche mark as a "technical realignment" associated with a decision to narrow the fluctuation margins for the lira from 6 percent (on each side of the central rate) to 2.25 percent. The new central rate was fixed at approximately the prevailing market rate, and the lower intervention limit was not adjusted.

[77] The reduction in the variability of exchange rates, which was also evident for European countries that sought exchange rate stability but were not participants in the Exchange Rate Mechanism (ERM), did not come at the expense of increased interest rate volatility; see Artis and Taylor (1994).

[78] See the Commission for the Study of Economic and Monetary Union (1989). See Ungerer, Hauvonen, Lopez-Claros, and Mayer (1990) for a review of the European Monetary System (EMS) experience through October 1990.

[79] Kenen (1992) and Eichengreen (1993) provide overviews of the blueprint and the main issues it created, along with lists of other references. See also Giovannini (1990a, 1990b), Fratianni and von Hagen (1992), and Krugman (1992).

route to monetary union, a year-long period of turbulence in European exchange markets, beginning during the summer of 1992, forced a reexamination of the road map. By the end of January 1993, extremely strong market pressures had led to the withdrawal of the Italian lira and the pound sterling from the ERM; to the devaluations of the Spanish peseta, the Portuguese escudo, and the Irish pound within the ERM; and to the abandonment of the pegs of the Finnish markka, the Norwegian krone, and the Swedish krona against the ecu. By the beginning of August 1993, the peseta and escudo had been devalued further, the fluctuation bands of the ERM had been widened to 15 percent on each side of the central rates,[80] and the exchange market pressures had subsided.

The Maastricht Treaty prescribed that monetary union would be reached in three stages, as envisioned in the Delors Report. During the first two stages, which respectively began in 1990 and 1994, member governments strove to achieve convergence as measured by four criteria: inflation, interest rates, exchange rate stability, and fiscal positions consistent with specified upper bounds on general government deficits and public debt (as ratios to GDP). In May 1998, the fifteen members of the European Union (EU) agreed that eleven countries (Austria, Belgium, Finland, France, Germany, Ireland, Italy, Luxembourg, the Netherlands, Portugal, and Spain) would move to full monetary union—now known as the Euro Area—at the start of the next year.[81] The European Monetary Institute, established at the beginning of Stage II, was transformed into the European Central Bank (ECB) in July 1998. On January 1, 1999, the beginning of Stage III, the euro was created (superceding the ecu) and the ECB took over responsibility for the monetary policy of the Euro Area.[82] Greece became the twelfth member of the Euro Area at the beginning of 2002. Later that year, an agreement was reached that ten more countries (Poland, Hungary, the Czech and Slovak Republics, Slovenia, Estonia,

---

[80] Germany and the Netherlands agreed to maintain 2.25 percent fluctuation margins with respect to each other's currencies.

[81] The EC was essentially renamed the European Union (EU) on November 1, 1993, when the Maastricht Treaty entered into force. The EC continues to exist as a legal entity within the EU, but *European Union* has become the umbrella term. The four EU countries that did not join the Euro Area at its inception were Denmark, Greece, Sweden, and the United Kingdom.

[82] Bank notes and coins denominated in euro were not put into circulation until January 2002.

Latvia, Lithuania, Cyprus, and Malta) would join the EU on May 1, 2004, pending the fulfillment of several required economic and political conditions.[83]

2.3.3 Salient characteristics of the exchange rate system

Every country that has its own currency must decide what type of exchange rate arrangement to maintain. In academic discussions, the decision is often characterized as a choice between fixed and flexible exchange rates. In practice, however, countries have adopted a much wider variety of currency arrangements, rarely seeking to keep their exchange rates rigidly fixed (as distinct from pegged within narrow ranges) and rarely allowing them to float completely freely (i.e., without at least occasional official purchases or sales of currencies or interest rate adjustments aimed at influencing exchange rates).

The different types of exchange rate arrangements have been categorized in different ways. The IMF's *Annual Report on Exchange Arrangements and Exchange Restrictions*, published since 1950, has until recent years classified arrangements largely on the basis of what countries declare their exchange rate regimes to be. For much of the past two decades (1983–98), it divided exchange rate arrangements into four categories: pegged exchange rates, arrangements with limited flexibility, more flexible arrangements, and independently floating rates. Starting with the 1999 edition, this classification scheme was expanded to distinguish eight categories: exchange arrangements with no separate legal tender (i.e., in which the country uses a foreign currency as legal tender); currency-board arrangements (in which the exchange rate is fixed and changes in the domestic currency liabilities of the monetary authority must be fully backed by changes in its holdings of foreign exchange reserves); conventional pegged exchange rate arrangements with narrow fluctuation margins; fixed exchange rates with wider fluctuation bands; crawling pegs (i.e., narrow margin arrangements with central parities that are adjusted gradually over time in a preannounced manner); crawling bands; managed floating

[83] Accession was conditional on approval in national referendums of the prospective new members, or on ratification according to other procedures in the case of Cyprus. By October 2003, all ten countries had completed the national approval or ratification process, and in early November the EU's Executive Commission judged that all ten met the prerequisite economic and political conditions and would be ready to join on schedule.

with no preannounced path for the exchange rate; and independently floating arrangements.[84]

In reality, the observed behavior of exchange rates can be very different from the behavior suggested by the official classifications that countries give to their exchange rate regimes. Most industrial countries imposed restrictions, for significant parts of the postwar period, on the amounts of domestic currency that they would convert into foreign currency at their official exchange rates; in many developing countries, such restrictions remain in place today. These restrictions have often led to the development of active dual or parallel foreign exchange markets for currency trading at market-determined exchange rates that have frequently diverged significantly from official exchange rates.

This disparity led Reinhart and Rogoff (2004) to compile a new data set on market-determined exchange rates (by month since 1946) and to reclassify exchange arrangements on the basis of the actual observed behavior of these market-determined rates.[85] As it turns out, for the full sample of countries, the correlations between the Reinhart–Rogoff classifications (based on market-determined rates) and those of the IMF (based on official rates) are not very high. This finding calls into question much of

---

[84] The IMF classifies the exchange rate regime as an independent float if any official intervention purchases or sales are aimed primarily at moderating the rate of change and preventing undue fluctuations in the exchange rate. The regime is characterized as a managed float if the authorities intervene actively in exchange markets, or adjust monetary policy, to counter trends in the exchange rate that are judged to have undesirable implications for other objectives, such as the balance of payments or international reserve holdings.

[85] Previous attempts to reclassify exchange rate regimes have been based solely on official exchange rates; see, for example, Levy-Yeyati and Sturzenegger (2003a). Reinhart and Rogoff (2004) provide both a fine-grid classification scheme with fourteen separate categories and a coarse-grid classification with five separate categories, in each case distinguishing between freely falling rates (associated with high-inflation countries) and freely or managed floating rates. The fine-grid scheme includes hard pegs (i.e., currency-board arrangements and cases of no separate legal tender) and also distinguishes between fixed pegs, fixed bands, crawling pegs, crawling bands, moving pegs, and moving bands. To determine whether a rate should be classified as a de facto peg or band, Reinhart and Rogoff look at the time series of month-to-month percentage changes in the exchange rate and compute the probability, over a rolling five-year period, that the monthly absolute percentage change lies within a given threshold range (1 percent for a peg and, in most cases, 2 percent for a band). If the probability exceeds 80 percent, the exchange rate arrangement is classified as a de facto peg or band. The distinction between fixed, crawling, and moving pegs or bands depends on whether the time series of exchange rates has no drift over the five-year period, whether the center of the peg or band drifts in a single direction, or whether the central rate drifts both up and down over the five-year period.

the existing research on the macroeconomic consequences of alternative exchange rate regimes and the effects of exchange rate volatility, which has been based on either the IMF classification scheme or classifications that reflect the de facto behavior of official exchange rates.

In comparisons that are restricted to exchange rate arrangements among pairs of industrial-country currencies over the past three decades, the two classification schemes paint a broadly similar picture. Whereas many of the European industrial countries have chosen to permanently fix exchange rates within Europe by moving to a common currency, the non-European industrial countries have chosen to let their currencies float. The group of nonindustrial countries includes a substantial number with fixed or crawling pegs or bands—more so under the Reinhart–Rogoff classification than under the IMF classification—as well as a considerable number with floating rates.[86]

The pros and cons of different monetary policy and exchange rate regimes for different types of countries are discussed in Chapter 7. The remainder of this section focuses on the key currencies of the international monetary system—the U.S. dollar, the yen, and the euro (or the deutsche mark before 1999)—and addresses some issues raised by three aspects of the behavior of exchange rates among these currencies: short-run volatility, medium-run swings, and limited predictability.

Figure 2.2 shows the month-to-month variability of exchange rates among the key currencies since 1957, indicating that the breakdown of the Bretton Woods system in the early 1970s gave rise to a very sharp increase in short-term variability. As revealed in Table 2.1, in absolute value terms these key-currency exchange rates have moved more than 2 percent per month on average since the breakdown of the Bretton Woods regime. To put this number into perspective, note that these exchange rates have varied month to month five to six times as much over the past three decades as the prices of consumer goods and services in the United States and Japan, and eight times as much as consumer prices in Germany. At the same time, however, the key-currency exchange rates have exhibited somewhat less month-to-month variability than major stock market price indices, comparable variability to the prices of many primary commodities, but lower variability than the price of petroleum.

---

[86] See Rogoff, Husain, Mody, Brooks et al. (2004) for an analysis of the evolution and performance of different types of exchange rate regimes that distinguishes between advanced, emerging market, and developing countries and compares impressions from different regime classification systems.

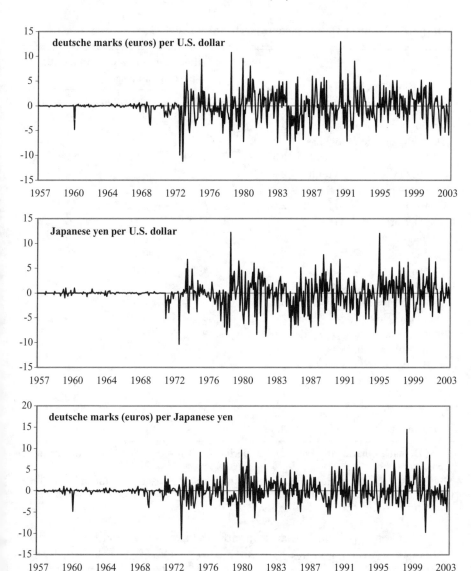

Figure 2.2. Month-to-month variability of key-currency exchange rates. Percent change from previous month. Deutsche marks are used for the period until the end of 1998; euros are used thereafter. *Source*: IMF, *International Financial Statistics*.

TABLE 2.1. Perspectives on exchange rate variability

	Average absolute values of month-to-month percent changes			
	1974–1983	1984–1993	1994–2003	1974–2003
Nominal exchange rates				
Deutsche marks (euros) per U.S. dollar	2.4	2.9	2.2	2.5
Japanese yen per U.S. dollar	2.3	2.5	2.4	2.4
Deutsche marks (euros) per Japanese yen	2.4	2.3	2.5	2.4
Consumer price indices				
United States	0.7	0.3	0.2	0.4
Germany	0.4	0.3	0.2	0.3
Japan	0.7	0.4	0.3	0.5
Stock market price indices				
United States (Dow Jones)	3.4	3.4	3.8	3.5
Germany (DAX)	3.0	4.5	5.6	4.4
Japan (Nikkei 225)	2.6	4.9	5.0	4.1
Commodity price indices				
Agricultural raw materials	2.5	2.2	2.2	2.3
Minerals and metals	2.6	3.1	2.6	2.8
Food	3.2	2.0	1.7	2.3
Gold	5.5	2.5	2.0	3.3
Petroleum	3.8	6.1	6.4	5.1

Note: Deutsche marks are used for the period until the end of 1998; euros are used thereafter.

Source: IMF, *International Financial Statistics*, for all series except for the Dow Jones (*Wall Street Journal*), the DAX (Deutsche Borse), and the Nikkei 225 (*Nihon Keizai Shinbun*).

Over intervals longer than a month, the successive month-to-month changes in exchange rates have often offset each other.[87] Nevertheless, some of the medium-term swings over the past three decades have been very large (Figure 2.3). One outstanding example was the dramatic appreciation of the dollar against the mark from the end of 1980 through early 1985, which nearly doubled the purchasing power of the dollar over the mark and greatly increased the propensity of U.S. residents to take

---

[87] From end of year to end of year during the 1974–2002 period, the percentage changes in these exchange rates were about four times as large in average absolute value as the month-to-month percentage changes.

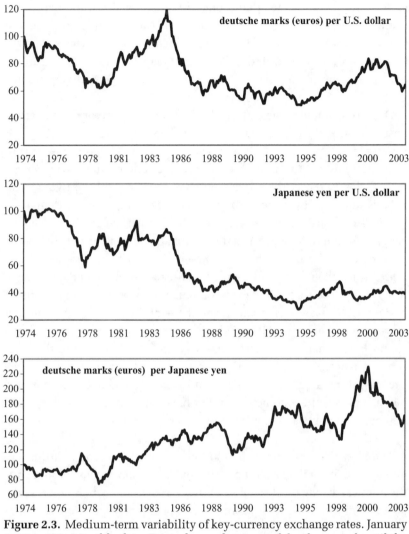

Figure 2.3. Medium-term variability of key-currency exchange rates. January 1974 = 100. Monthly data. Deutsche marks are used for the period until the end of 1998; euros are used thereafter. *Source*: IMF, *International Financial Statistics*.

European vacations and shopping trips. The rise of the dollar was followed by an even sharper fall through early 1987.

In addition to exhibiting short-term volatility and occasionally large medium-term swings, the key-currency exchange rates have been unpredictable. A series of pathbreaking econometric studies conducted in the early 1980s demonstrated that economists' state-of-the-art models of exchange rate behavior could barely outpredict a random walk model at horizons of up to twelve months, even when the models were given the benefit of ex post (realized) data on their explanatory variables[88]; numerous subsequent attempts to overturn that result have had very limited success.[89]

Over long horizons the empirical evidence is more favorable to economists' theories of exchange rate behavior. This is illustrated in Figure 2.4, which focuses on the purchasing power parity (PPP) hypothesis—that is, the hypothesis that the nominal exchange rate between any two currencies should closely reflect the relative purchasing powers of the two currencies, as indicated by national price levels.[90] The figure plots changes in nominal exchange rates between pairs of industrial-country currencies against differentials between national inflation rates for corresponding pairs of countries over different time intervals, with the 45-degree line representing the set of points that are consistent with the PPP hypothesis. It is readily seen that PPP becomes a much more respectable hypothesis as the time horizon is lengthened, and that—at least over the past quarter century—the long-run PPP hypothesis fits the data well for the industrial countries. Formal econometric analysis is not quite as kind to the long-run PPP hypothesis. Although they more rigorously establish that nominal exchange rates adjusted for inflation differentials tend to be mean reverting, a number of econometric studies have rejected the hypothesis that nominal exchange rates and inflation differentials have identical long-run trends.[91]

The view that currency values are not completely divorced from economic fundamentals is also supported by other frameworks for modeling the long-run behavior of exchange rates.[92] However, there is no generally accepted model that allows economists to place narrow confidence bands

---

[88] See Meese and Rogoff (1983a, 1983b, 1988). Hacche and Townend (1981) also concluded that existing empirical models were not useful for forecasting exchange rates.

[89] See Frankel and Rose (1995) and Rogoff (1999b).

[90] The term *purchasing power parity* (or PPP) was coined in the early twentieth century by Cassel (1918, 1922).

[91] See Breuer (1994) and Froot and Rogoff (1995).

[92] Such frameworks include the macroeconomic balance approach, which assumes that the real (inflation-adjusted) exchange rate adjusts over the long run to a level that equates the current account balance to an equilibrium saving-investment balance. See Isard, Faruqee, Kincaid, and Fetherston (2001) and references therein for descriptions of the macroeconomic balance approach and other frameworks. See Freund (2000) for evidence that lends support to the macroeconomic balance framework by establishing that large current account imbalances tend to lead to exchange rate adjustment.

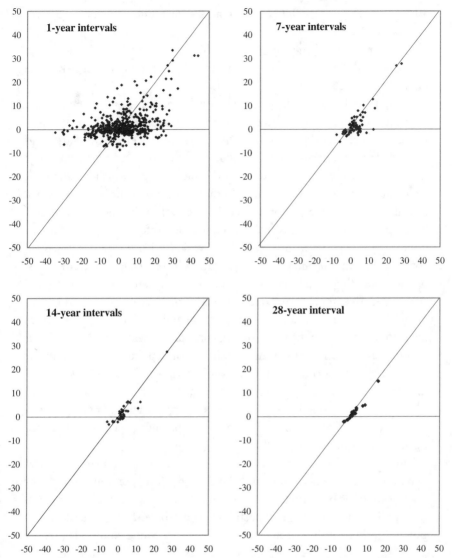

Figure 2.4. Exchange rate changes versus inflation differentials over different time intervals. Based on Flood and Taylor (1996). The plots are constructed from annual average data on the nominal exchange rates of twenty-one industrial-country currencies versus the U.S. dollar, along with corresponding consumer price indices, for the period 1974–2002. Changes in exchange rates are measured along the horizontal axes; changes in consumer price indices are measured along the verticle axes. The first panel plots 588 one-year changes (28 for each country); the second plots 84 nonoverlapping seven-year changes (at annual rates) corresponding to the periods 1974–81, 1981–88, 1988–95, 1995–2002, and so forth. *Source*: IMF, *World Economic Outlook*.

around estimates of the long-run equilibrium levels of exchange rates, or around predictions of how much exchange rates will change over the medium run.[93]

Does the behavior of key-currency exchange rates under the current international monetary regime have strong adverse effects on the performance of the world economy? One basis for concern is that large and unpredictable short-run fluctuations and medium-run swings in exchange rates can slow the growth of the world economy by distorting signals for trade and long-term investment.[94] In that vein, some who view exchange rate fluctuations as a major source of uncertainty in making contracts have emphasized that movements in exchange rates "can wipe out—or double—a 5 percent profit margin in a week."[95] Until recent years, such concerns have not found much support from formal econometric analysis. In particular, there is a long history of econometric studies that fail to find strong negative impacts of exchange rate variability on trade and investment,[96] as well as a number of studies concluding that transitions from fixed to floating exchange rate regimes sharply increase the variability of nominal and real exchange rates with no corresponding changes in the variability of most other macroeconomic variables.[97] In contrast, a new direction in the literature suggests that membership in a common currency area, other things being equal, has a very substantial positive effect on a country's trade with its currency-area partners, with an associated positive effect on its output.[98]

The pros and cons of common currency areas remain under active debate in both the academic and the policymaking communities.[99] The macroeconomic performance of the Euro Area in the years ahead will undoubtedly add important perspectives to the debate. The pros and cons of both adopting another country's currency and forming common currency

---

[93] See Isard (1995), Frankel and Rose (1996), Rogoff (1996), Obstfeld and Rogoff (2001), and Sarno and Taylor (2003) for a wide range of perspectives on what economists know about the behavior of exchange rates.

[94] See Tobin (1991).

[95] See Cooper (1990: 105).

[96] See Edison and Melvin (1990), Gagnon (1993), and Clark, Tamirisa, Wei, Sadakov et al. (2004).

[97] See Baxter and Stockman (1989) and Flood and Rose (1995).

[98] See McCallum (1995), Rose (2000), Frankel and Rose (2002), and Alesina, Barro, and Tenreyro (2003).

[99] For some important recent contributions to the academic debate, see the May 2002 issue of the *Quarterly Journal of Economics* and the summary volume by Alesina and Barro (2001).

areas among groups of developing countries are discussed in Chapter 7. Here the concern is with exchange rates among the key currencies of the international monetary system—the dollar, the euro, and the yen.

Several factors appear to argue strongly against an effort to stabilize key-currency exchange rates within narrow or even moderately wide target zones.[100] One set of considerations is that the United States, the Euro Area, and Japan are subject to different economic and political shocks, exhibit different responses to common shocks, and have well-developed policy institutions for stabilizing their own economies in reaction to shocks. A second consideration is that these are the economies on which the world relies most for growth and price stability. All three have established strong track records in maintaining price stability, and although Japan and the Euro Area have left much to be desired as locomotives for growth in recent years, their shortcomings in this regard have not stemmed from their giving exchange rate stability lower priority than domestic macroeconomic stability. A related consideration is that an effort to maintain greater stability of key-currency exchange rates would presumably require greater variability of key-currency interest rates, with adverse effects on domestic economic stability in the United States, the Euro Area, and Japan and without clear beneficial effects for the rest of the world.[101] A fourth consideration is that a policy of pursuing exchange rate stability at the expense of domestic economic objectives would find little political support within the United States, the Euro Area, or Japan.

Although these considerations seem to advise against target zones for the key currencies, they do not argue against periodic attempts to manage the key-currency exchange rates when markets seem disorderly or badly misaligned. Indeed, it can be contended that the sharp appreciation of the dollar between the end of 1980 and early 1985 resulted in part from the fact that the first Reagan administration pursued a hands-off or benign neglect policy toward exchange rates.[102] Since that time, substantial deviations of key-currency exchange rates from levels that appeared consistent with macroeconomic fundamentals have triggered occasional coordinated interventions by the authorities of two or three of the key-currency

---

[100] See Goldstein and Isard (1992) and Rogoff (2001).
[101] Reinhart and Reinhart (2003b) argue that neither theoretical nor empirical analysis supports the suggestion that limiting the variability of key-currency exchange rates would increase welfare for developing countries.
[102] See Isard (1995) and Bergsten (1999).

countries, as happened when the yen strengthened to 80 against the dollar in the spring of 1995 and when the euro was significantly depreciated in the fall of 2000.

2.3.4   Agenda setting and international policy coordination

The functioning of the global economy depends importantly on the effectiveness of the international monetary system and its central institution, the IMF. As the problems and needs of the global economy have evolved over time, so too have the focus and roles of the IMF. The key roles of the IMF are discussed in the next chapter. This section briefly describes how its member countries operate in identifying, analyzing, and setting an agenda for addressing issues relating to the functioning of the international monetary system. It also provides an overview of the extent to which the major countries of the system have acted to coordinate their policies.

As Chapter 3 describes in more detail, the day-to-day work of the IMF is carried out jointly by an internationally recruited staff, a management team, and a board of twenty-four Executive Directors that functions in continuous session. Ultimate oversight rests with a Board of Governors, which normally meets once a year at the annual meetings of the IMF and World Bank. Key issues relating to the international monetary system are usually considered twice a year by the International Monetary and Financial Committee (IMFC)—currently composed of twenty-four central bank governors, finance ministers, or others of comparable rank (reflecting the country composition of the IMF Executive Board, as described in Chapter 3).[103]

Most of the efforts made to coordinate national policies and, in effect, to set the agenda for the IMF have come from the major industrial countries. This reflects a number of related factors, including the importance of their policies for the world economy, the extent of their voting power in the IMF, and their position as large creditor countries in the

---

[103] The International Monetary and Financial Committee (IMFC) is a descendent of the Committee of Twenty (which operated from 1972 to 1974, when the IMF had twenty Executive Directors) and its successor, the Interim Committee (which met from 1974 to 1999). A joint committee of the Boards of Governors of the IMF and World Bank, named the Development Committee, advises and reports to the governors on issues of concern to developing countries.

international monetary system. Until 1986–87, the Group of Five (G-5)—established in the mid-1970s by France, Germany, Japan, the United Kingdom, and the United States—functioned as the main forum for discussions of policy coordination. Subsequently, this role has been played by the Group of Seven (G-7), comprising the G-5 plus Canada and Italy. Since 1975 these groups have held annual economic summits of heads of state or government, as well as periodic meetings of finance ministers and central bank governors or their deputies.[104] Numerous other groups have been formed to serve various functions in the international monetary system. Prominent among them are the Group of Ten (G-10) industrial countries that participated in establishing the General Arrangements to Borrow in 1962,[105] and the Group of Twenty-four (G-24), formed in 1971 to coordinate the positions of developing countries on international monetary and development finance issues and to ensure adequate representation of their interests in negotiations on international monetary matters.[106]

The process of policy coordination among the major industrial countries has consisted largely of information sharing and analytic discussions. These discussions pay serious and continuing attention to the outlook for the world economy, taking account of international economic interdependencies. Although it appears that countries have rarely been led to significantly modify their macroeconomic policies as a direct consequence of negotiations among the G-7 or G-5,[107] all countries take account of international economic interdependencies in setting national macroeconomic policies, and information sharing and analytic discussions among the G-7 have presumably contributed in an important way over time to the quality of national policy decisions. In the words of Larry Summers, former Secretary of the U.S. Treasury,

[104] Russia joined the annual economic summits on a permanent basis in 1998 (after participating in the 1994 and 1997 summits), which marked the establishment of the Group of Eight (G-8). However, the G-8 did not replace the G-7, which continues to function as a forum for discussion of economic and financial issues among the major industrial countries; see IMF (2003a).

[105] The G-10 actually includes eleven countries: the G-7 plus Belgium, the Netherlands, Sweden, and (since 1964) Switzerland. The General Arrangements to Borrow are described in Chapter 3.

[106] See IMF (2003a).

[107] The bargain struck between Germany, Japan, and the United States at the 1978 Bonn summit provides one of the few publicized examples of a coordinated adjustment in national policies.

[the] major accomplishment [of international forums such as the G-7] is not the specific decisions that are taken when they meet—sometimes there are none. Rather it is the gradual spread of common ways of thinking about and responding to economic developments. The value of the diffusion of best practice, or at least, better practice, is not to be discounted. Over time these forums provide important opportunities to use political pressure to nudge national policies in the right direction.[108]

Some economists and most policymakers look at policy coordination as a "regime-preserving" process designed to thwart various threats to international economic stability.[109] The regime-preserving perspective recognizes that wars among nations with weapons such as trade barriers are likely to be mutually destructive.[110] One example of regime-preserving coordination was the Plaza Agreement reached in late September 1985 by the G-5 finance ministers and central bank governors. In an effort to address what was generally perceived as a substantial misalignment of the strong U.S. dollar, and to ward off the protectionist pressures to which it was contributing, the G-5 issued a communiqué stating that "orderly appreciation of the main non-dollar currencies against the dollar is desirable," and that the G-5 countries "stand ready to cooperate more closely to encourage this when to do so would be helpful."[111] More recent examples, described in later chapters, have focused on various systemic reforms aimed at strengthening the effectiveness of the international financial system in promoting growth and preventing and resolving financial crises.

2.4   Liberalized Finance and the Sea Change in International Capital Flows

The past few decades have brought "a sea change in the global financial system, as the flow of private capital from industrial to developing countries has mushroomed."[112] Whether measured in gross or net terms, the expansion of cross-border capital flows has far outpaced the growth of

---

[108] See Summers (2000: 10).

[109] See Kenen (1988).

[110] See Tobin (1987: 68).

[111] See the Group of Five (1985). As Tobin (1987) notes, however, such agreements on exchange rate objectives have not been accompanied by understandings on how the countries participating in the agreements would use monetary or fiscal policies to achieve them.

[112] See Summers (2000: 2).

world GDP, and private capital flows to developing countries have expanded substantially faster than developing-country GDP. Like the rise of domestic financial activity, the expansion of international financial activity is potentially very conducive to economic growth over the long run, but the risks associated with ballooning financial obligations also make economies more vulnerable to major crises.[113]

To put the dramatic rise in cross-border capital flows into historical perspective, Figure 2.5 provides a rough description of the size of foreign capital stocks relative to GDP at eleven selected dates starting in 1870. The figure shows two different measures of foreign capital stocks, as constructed by Obstfeld and Taylor (2003), where a country's foreign capital stock is defined as the sum of its direct investments abroad plus the financial claims that its residents have on the residents of other countries. Long spans of historical data on foreign capital stocks are not available for many countries,[114] and the Obstfeld–Taylor measures are constructed from data for only seven major creditor countries before 1960, expanding to about thirty countries after 1980. One measure is the ratio of foreign capital stocks to GDP for the countries in the sample, with the sample of countries expanding over time. The other measure is the ratio of sample-country foreign capital stocks to world GDP, which corresponds to what the worldwide ratio would be if countries outside the sample had no foreign capital stocks. There is no attempt to separate foreign claims on developing countries from foreign claims on industrial countries. Both measures show substantial declines in foreign capital stocks between 1914 and 1930, relatively low levels between 1930 and 1960, and dramatic increases starting sometime after 1960.

---

[113] Chapter 6 addresses the relationship between financial development and economic growth. Bryant (2003) and Rajan and Zingales (2003) provide much more extensive and insightful discussions of the benefits and risks of financial activity within and between countries, and Obstfeld (1998) presents additional perspectives on the benefits and costs of increased international financial integration.

[114] Although long time series of balance of payments *flow* data are available for many countries, data on foreign capital *stocks* are difficult to construct for a variety of reasons—including capital gains and losses (such as those associated with exchange rate changes), retirements of principal and buybacks of equity, and defaults or reschedulings. An extensive data-construction effort by Lane and Milesi-Ferretti (2001) has generated estimates of foreign assets and liabilities, and the equity and debt subcomponents, for sixty-six industrial and developing countries for the period 1970–98. Lane and Milesi-Ferretti (2003) analyze and describe the availability of official estimates of external assets and liabilities for twenty-two industrial countries through 2001, as collected from IMF and national sources.

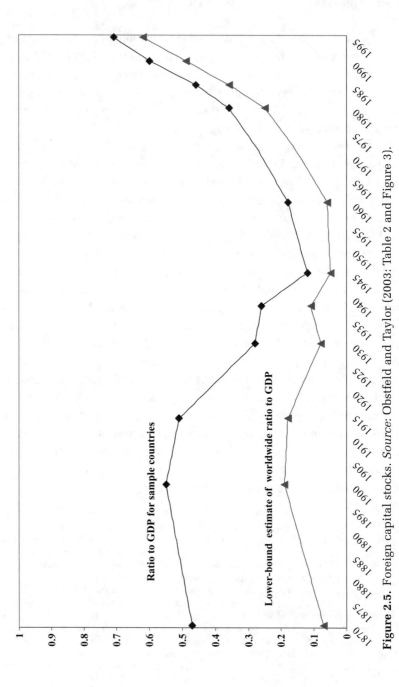

Figure 2.5. Foreign capital stocks. *Source:* Obstfeld and Taylor (2003: Table 2 and Figure 3).

Figure 2.5 also reveals that foreign capital stocks prior to World War I were comparable in magnitude (as a share of sample-country GDP) with the levels of the early 1990s. In addition, net capital outflows from the major creditor countries in the early 1900s, as well as the current account deficits of emerging market economies of the time (Australia, Canada, Argentina, Finland, Norway, and Sweden), were much larger relative to GDP than they are today. Nevertheless, in several relevant dimensions the degree of international financial integration prior to World War I was not as great as it is today. The bulk of foreign investments in the early 1900s consisted of long-term claims, with most of those composed of the securities of governments, railroads, and mining industries. Short-term flows were significantly smaller than long-term flows, in contrast to the situation today, and there was relatively little cross-border lending to banks and other financial institutions.[115]

The hiatus in international capital flows after 1914 reflected both the disruptions caused by the World Wars and Great Depression and the maintenance of comprehensive systems of capital controls in many countries during the 1950s and 1960s. The increase in foreign capital stocks between 1960 and 1980 received considerable stimulus from the quadrupling of oil prices at the end of 1973 and the subsequent recycling of oil revenues. Over the five-year period 1974–78, the Organization of Petroleum Exporting Countries (OPEC) generated an aggregate current account surplus of nearly $170 billion, while the non-oil-developing countries ran a cumulative deficit in excess of $140 billion.[116] These current account imbalances, of course, mirrored equal and opposite capital account flows (abstracting from errors and omissions), and hence they reflected both OPEC desires to accumulate assets abroad and the ability of non-oil-developing countries to finance their current account deficits.

Although the configuration of current account imbalances implied large net capital flows from the OPEC countries to the non-oil-developing countries, most of the capital took an indirect route. The members of OPEC, having nationalized foreign oil company subsidiaries, may have been sensitive to acquiring property abroad, and in any case they invested much of their surplus in the liquid assets or securities of industrial countries. In

---

[115] See Bordo et al. (1999).
[116] See Solomon (1982: 324).

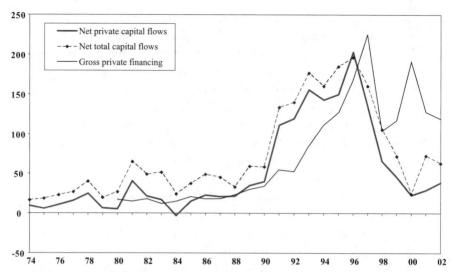

Figure 2.6. Capital flows to developing countries. Annual data in billions of U.S. dollars. *Sources*: IMF, *World Economic Outlook,* and Capital Data, *Bonds, Equities and Loans* database.

turn, the bulk of these investments were matched by capital flows from the industrial countries to the non-oil-developing countries. Much of the capital flowed in the form of syndicated loans from commercial banks, with many banks contributing shares of the loans, including smaller banks that had little previous experience in international lending. For the most part, these loans were denominated in dollars and carried floating interest rates linked to the six-month Eurodollar rate in London (the London interbank offer rate, or LIBOR). The bulk of these flows were channeled to Asian and Latin American countries.[117]

Figures 2.6 and 2.7 show developments since 1974 in three different measures of capital flows into developing countries—net total capital inflows, net private capital inflows, and gross private financing. Net total capital inflows are measured as net foreign direct investment plus net portfolio investments (bonds and equities) plus net bank loans and other investments. Net private capital inflows are net total capital inflows minus net official borrowing. Gross private financing excludes foreign direct investment flows and includes only primary issues in international markets

---

[117] At the end of 1978, nearly 70 percent of bank loans to the non-oil-developing countries was accounted for by eight recipient countries: Argentina, Brazil, Chile, Mexico, Peru, Philippines, South Korea, and Thailand. See Solomon (1982: 329).

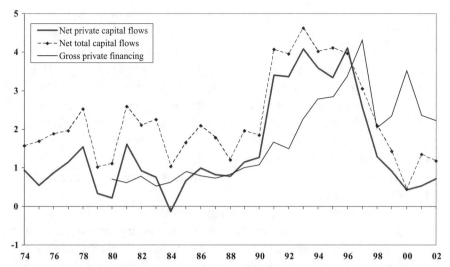

Figure 2.7. Capital flows to developing countries relative to developing-country GDP. Annual data as percentage of GDP. *Sources*: IMF, *World Economic Outlook*, and Capital Data, *Bonds, Equities and Loans* database.

of bonds, equities, and bank loans.[118] The figures show a substantial increase over time in capital flows into developing countries, with a particularly sharp increase at the beginning of the 1980s and another steep and much larger rise during the first half of the 1990s.

By the late 1970s, inflation rates in most industrial countries had risen significantly since the first oil-price shock, reaching double-digit levels in the United States; and following the appointment of Paul Volcker as Federal Reserve Chairman in August 1979, the stance of U.S. monetary policy was tightened sharply. Beginning in 1981, the fiscal deficits of the Reagan administration contributed further to high interest rates on dollar-denominated debts. As a result, the LIBOR rose from 9.2 percent in 1978 to 16.7 percent in 1981, and the interest costs of debtor countries soared. Furthermore, most industrial countries suffered recessions in 1982, which reduced their demands for developing-country exports. For Brazil, the

---

[118] The focus on these three measures follows Mussa, Swoboda, Zettelmeyer, and Jeanne (2000). Net total and private capital flows are constructed from balance of payments data, which are based on the aggregate of the information provided by individual developing countries. Gross private financing is based on information obtained from banks and other financial market institutions.

ratio of interest obligations to export earnings rose to nearly 50 percent in 1982, and for Mexico it reached nearly 40 percent.[119]

The rise in interest costs was a key factor in inducing developing countries as a group to add to their external debts during the early 1980s. However, with the emergence of a debt-servicing crisis in heavily indebted developing countries, the inflow of private capital dropped sharply after mid-1982 and remained fairly subdued throughout the 1980s. Then a second boom–bust cycle developed. This time a large part of the impetus came from a much less transitory factor than changes in the price of oil—namely, the liberalization of financial markets, which was not an entirely exogenous development.

Technological progress has been a prime mover of the liberalization of global financial markets and the sea change in international capital flows over the past three decades.[120] Rapid technological advances have dramatically increased information-processing capacities and drastically reduced computer costs while producing a revolution in electronic communications. This has made it much more feasible, and less costly, for financial institutions and other economic participants, including governments, to manage their financial affairs on a worldwide basis. It has also made it easy to vary the geographical location of many financial transactions, thereby undermining attempts by national authorities to maintain effective restrictions on financial activities, such as controls on interest rates, the allocation of credit, foreign exchange transactions, or the activities of different types of financial institutions. The development of the Eurodollar market, for example, can largely be attributed to the efforts of U.S. banks and securities houses to shift abroad those activities on which they faced domestic interest rate ceilings or other restrictions.

By the end of the 1970s, as a result in part of the increasing ability of financial market participants to evade regulations by shifting transactions to offshore centers, policy authorities in the industrial countries had come to question the usefulness of many of the official restrictions and controls that had long been features of their financial systems. Consequently, the 1980s and early 1990s gave rise to extensive liberalization of domestic financial systems, stock markets, and international capital transactions by

[119] See Solomon (1999: 37). It is also estimated that U.S. bank holdings of Latin American debt amounted to 97 percent of bank capital at the end of 1981, with higher exposures for some individual banks; see IMF (1997: 239).
[120] Harrington (1992) provides a lucid discussion of the global financial system in transition.

the industrial countries.[121] This can be seen in Figure 2.8, which is based on the data set described by Abiad and Mody (2003), who have compiled indices of six components of financial liberalization over the 1973–96 period for thirty-five countries disaggregated according to the World Bank's classification of income groups.[122] These indices, which range from 0 for full financial repression to 3 for full liberalization, distinguish between credit controls, interest rate controls, entry barriers, regulations and securities markets, privatization in the financial sector, and restrictions on international financial transactions.[123]

As can be seen in the figure, the gradual liberalization of financial markets in the high-income countries during the 1980s was followed by a less complete but much more rapid financial liberalization in the other groups of countries during the late 1980s and early 1990s.[124] In association with this liberalization, which the IMF and the major creditor countries generally welcomed (see Chapter 3), capital inflows to emerging markets accelerated during the early 1990s. Another factor coincident with the acceleration of financial investments in developing countries was the introduction of Brady bonds, beginning with the Mexican Brady exchange in 1989, which provided a new investment vehicle, gave rise to new information gathering and marketing activities, and may have had a general catalytic effect on investments in emerging market economies.[125]

Macroeconomic developments may have also contributed significantly, including the improving macroeconomic performances of a number of

---

[121] Bakker and Chapple (2002) describe, and draw some general lessons from, the experiences of the industrial countries with capital account liberalization.

[122] The sample includes thirteen high-income economies (Australia, Canada, France, Germany, Hong Kong, Israel, Italy, Japan, New Zealand, Singapore, Taiwan, the United Kingdom, and the United States), nine upper-middle-income countries (Argentina, Brazil, Chile, Korea, Malaysia, Mexico, South Africa, Turkey, and Venezuela), seven lower-middle-income countries (Colombia, Egypt, Morocco, Peru, the Philippines, Sri Lanka, and Thailand), and seven low-income countries (Bangladesh, Ghana, India, Indonesia, Nepal, Pakistan, and Zimbabwe). Figure 2.8 shows unweighted averages for each group of countries.

[123] Similar patterns are shown by Kaminsky and Schmukler (2003) and by Williamson and Mahar (1998), who provide details on liberalizations of restrictions on domestic financial transactions and international capital flows for similar lists of countries.

[124] Several of the upper-middle-income countries in Latin America had liberalized financial controls somewhat during the 1970s but tightened restrictions after the 1982 debt crisis.

[125] See Calvo and Mendoza (2000a). Named after former U.S. Treasury Secretary Nicholas Brady, Brady bonds were issued in exchange for syndicated commercial bank loans in transactions that allowed developing countries to restructure their debts and that were also attractive to industrial country banks, given the accounting practices under which they operated.

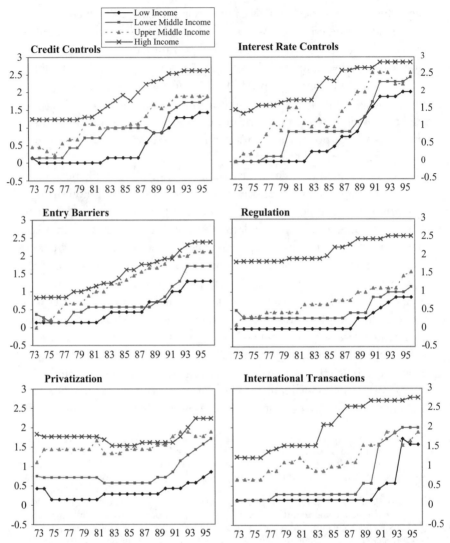

Figure 2.8. Financial liberalization by component and income group (0 = full repression and 3 = full liberalization; see text). *Source*: Abiad and Mody (2003).

developing countries, the strong performance and continuing buildup of financial wealth in the industrial countries, and, according to some research findings, the relatively low levels of industrial-country interest rates in the early 1990s.[126] Whatever the relative importance of these different factors, net private capital inflows jumped sharply at the beginning of the 1990s, and gross private financing rose from less than 1 percent of developing countries' GDP during most of the 1980s to a peak of more than 4 percent in 1996. Subsequently, the volume of capital inflows declined sharply in the wake of the financial crises that erupted from 1997 onward (recall Figure 2.7).

Figure 2.9 shows the composition of net private capital flows into developing countries, revealing the growing importance of portfolio investments (bonds and equities) during the first half of the 1990s. This development reflects the growing role of institutional portfolio investors in managing the savings of industrial-country households and businesses,[127] along with the financial liberalization and deregulation that opened up more channels for these institutions to invest abroad.[128] The figure also reveals that most of the decline in capital inflows after 1996—as well as most of the volatility of capital inflows during the 1990s—was attributable to the behavior of bank loans and net portfolio investments. Foreign direct investment flows into developing countries have risen gradually but fairly steadily over the past three decades.

The bank loans and portfolio capital that flow to developing countries are channeled predominantly through a set of less than 200 large financial firms (commercial banks and other institutional investors) based primarily in the G-10 countries and Spain.[129] By their nature, commercial banks

---

[126] See Calvo, Leiderman, and Reinhart (1993, 1996).

[127] Institutional portfolio investors include investment banks, wealth managers (e.g., mutual funds, pension plans, and hedge funds), and insurance companies. Investment banks bring to market nearly all public and private bonds, equity issues, and asset-backed securities; serve as pilots for privatizations, mergers, and takeovers; and trade securities for customers on secondary markets. Hedge funds are a class of portfolio investors that are organized in a manner that largely escapes regulation and enables the funds to take highly leveraged positions.

[128] Net portfolio flows rose from less than 6 percent of net private capital flows into developing countries during the five years preceding the 1982 debt crisis (1977–81) to roughly 40 percent during the five years preceding the 1997 Asian crises (1992–96). Correspondingly, bank loans declined from about 55 percent of the total to 15 percent while net foreign direct investment flows rose from under 40 percent to nearly 45 percent.

[129] See Dobson and Hufbauer (2001). Spanish banks are major creditors to Latin America.

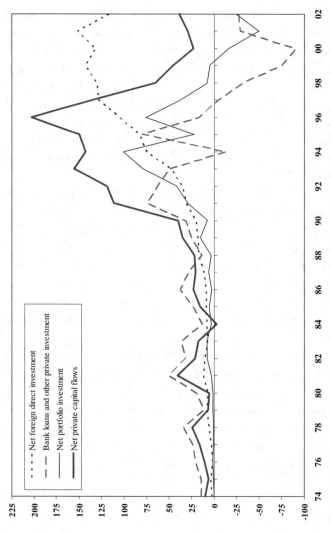

Figure 2.9. Composition of net private capital flows into developing countries. Annual data in billions of U.S. dollars. *Source:* IMF, *World Economic Outlook.*

are leveraged intermediaries that perform the valuable function of issuing liquid deposits and other short-term liabilities and acquiring longer-term assets. When liquidity crunches threaten, commercial banks have to cut credit lines and call loans. In contrast, with the exception of hedge funds, institutional portfolio investors are generally not highly leveraged. They face losses when markets turn, but they are not forced to sell bonds and equities in the same manner that commercial banks are sometimes forced to curtail credit and call loans.

Financial liberalization and deregulation in the industrial countries has resulted in both the elimination of restrictions that once prevented banking, insurance, and securities firms from entering each other's businesses and the rapid growth of derivative transactions (e.g., forward contracts, swaps, and options—see Chapter 7) that result in off-balance-sheet exposures rather than changes in recorded balance-sheet positions. These developments have greatly complicated the task of exercising prudential supervision over the major players in international capital markets.

2.5   Concluding Perspectives

This chapter has reviewed the performance and collapse of past international monetary regimes in the context of the fundamental impossibility theorem of open-economy macroeconomics—namely, that a country cannot simultaneously maintain a fixed exchange rate and autonomy to direct its monetary policy at domestic stabilization objectives in the presence of large stocks of internationally mobile capital. The longevity of the international gold standard from the 1870s through the outbreak of World War I, an era relatively free of restrictions on international capital movements, can be largely attributed to the absence of effective political resistance to the domestic economic instability associated with commitments to fixed exchange rates (gold parities). The success of the Bretton Woods system in surviving for a full quarter century, from the end of World War II through the early 1970s, can be associated with the fact that most countries maintained various restrictions and controls on domestic financial activities and international capital transactions, which did not begin to erode severely until the U.S. economy overheated at the end of the 1960s.

Neither an attempt to resurrect the Bretton Woods system nor a return to an international gold standard would have much chance of success today. The revolution in electronic communications and computer technologies has made it relatively easy for market participants to shift the geographical location of international financial transactions and to repackage financial products. Thus, efforts to reimpose restrictions on international capital flows would be highly ineffective in countries with sophisticated financial market participants. Moreover, with the spread of universal suffrage and democracy, the political empowerment of the working classes has increased considerably since the gold standard era, at least in the industrial countries. This would make it very difficult for policy authorities in the key-currency countries—the United States, Japan, and the Euro Area—to give priority to exchange rate stability over domestic macroeconomic stability.

Even if it were politically feasible for the key-currency countries to give priority to exchange rate stability over domestic macroeconomic stability, several considerations argue against that choice. First, the United States, Japan, and the Euro Area are subject to different economic and political shocks, exhibit different macroeconomic behavior in response to common shocks, and have well-developed policy institutions for stabilizing their own economies in reaction to shocks. Second, these are the economies on which the world relies most for growth and price stability; all three have established strong track records in maintaining price stability, and, although they have not all performed well as locomotives for growth in recent years, their shortcomings in this regard would not have been avoided by their giving priority to exchange rate stability over domestic macroeconomic stability. Third, an effort to achieve greater stability of key-currency exchange rates would presumably require larger and more frequent adjustments of key-currency interest rates, with adverse effects on domestic economic stability in the United States, Japan, and the Euro Area and without clear beneficial effects for the rest of the world.

Although these considerations would seem to question the wisdom of any attempt to stabilize the key-currency exchange rates within narrow or even moderately wide target zones, they do not argue against decisions to form common currency areas among groups of countries that seek to strengthen economic integration—provided that the countries involved have the wisdom and patience to take prior actions to achieve economic convergence and to establish mechanisms for limiting domestic economic instability within individual members of their groups. Nor does the case against efforts to tightly control the key-currency exchange rates argue for a policy of benign neglect toward those exchange rates. The prevailing international monetary system—under which exchange rates among the key currencies sometimes exhibit considerable short-run volatility and wide and unpredictable medium-term swings—has been well served by periodic actions to manage the key-currency exchange rates when markets seemed disorderly or badly misaligned.

The successes and failures of past international monetary regimes underscore the crucial role of international monetary cooperation. The history of the international gold standard reveals that even Britain, the hegemon of the system, suffered occasional financing and currency crises and had to be bailed out periodically by other countries; furthermore, this was during an era in which commitments to fixed gold parities had relatively high credibility. Obversely, the interwar experience with several short-lived international monetary regimes reveals the high costs that can result from either a lack of adequate cooperation (and sound analysis) in determining the levels at which to fix exchange rates or a complete breakdown of cooperation with widespread resort to import protection and competitive devaluations.

An important qualification is that international monetary cooperation can on some occasions be highly counterproductive. For example, the desire to be cooperative in easing the strain on Britain's gold reserves had an influence on monetary policy in the United States during the second half of 1927 that helped fuel the boom and subsequent crash on Wall Street.

This chapter has also provided perspectives on the sea change that has taken place in both the volume and the range of international capital flows since the early 1970s. Underlying this sea change has been the rapid advance in electronic communications and computer technologies, which has made it increasingly feasible for market participants to manage their financial affairs on a worldwide basis and to circumvent national restrictions on financial transactions, thereby helping to spur the widespread liberalization of domestic financial markets in the industrial countries and many emerging market economies. Although the magnitudes of foreign capital stocks and international capital flows today are comparable (when scaled by GDP) with those that prevailed prior to World War I, international financial markets are significantly more integrated now than they were during the gold standard era, when the bulk of foreign investments consisted of long-term securities and the only sectors with extensive access to international capital markets were governments, railroads, and mining industries.

The sea change in international capital flows has included a substantial rise in capital inflows into developing countries, with two boom–bust cycles superimposed. The first cycle began with the accumulation of financial wealth by oil-exporting countries during the 1970s, much of which was invested in industrial countries and recycled through banks into Latin American and Asian developing countries. The bust came in the early 1980s, following a sharp rise in world interest rates and the onset of recessions in most industrial countries. The second cycle, which featured a growing prominence of portfolio investments (bonds and equities) relative to bank loans, began in the early 1990s in association with rapid financial liberalization by many emerging market countries, as well as with the introduction of Brady bonds. Net private capital flows into developing countries more than quadrupled (relative to developing-country GDP) between the second half of the 1980s and 1996 and then turned sharply downward in the wake of a wave of international financial crises. Foreign direct investment flows into developing countries have exhibited a gradual but fairly steady uptrend since the early 1970s, which is in sharp contrast with the volatility of bank loans and portfolio flows.

3

The International Monetary Fund

Since its founding in the mid-1940s, the IMF has served as the world's principal forum for the promotion of international monetary cooperation. Its membership has expanded considerably over time, increasing from fewer than four dozen countries at the outset to 184 countries as of early 2004. With the return of China in 1980, Switzerland's entry in 1992, and the accession of many states of the former Soviet Union in the early 1990s, most of the world's economies are now members of the IMF and participants in the international monetary system.

3.1 Purposes and Activities

The architects of the IMF intended it to serve several purposes, which are spelled out in Article I of its statutes. These purposes include:

- providing an institution and forum for the promotion of international monetary cooperation;
- facilitating the expansion of world trade as a means of promoting high levels of employment and real income and the development of the productive resources of all members;
- maintaining an orderly system of exchange rates; and
- making financial resources temporarily available to members—under adequate safeguards—to lessen the impacts of balance of payments adjustment on national and international prosperity.

As noted in Chapter 2, the breakdown of the exchange rate system created at Bretton Woods led to the Second Amendment of the Articles of Agreement, which allowed countries greater freedom in their choice of exchange rate arrangements. The Second Amendment, effective in 1978, also specified that each member had certain general obligations, inter alia[1]:

- directing its policies toward the pursuit of orderly economic growth with reasonable price stability; and
- seeking to promote stability by fostering orderly underlying economic and financial conditions.

In addition, the amended Articles included a substantial redefinition of the Fund's responsibilities for overseeing the functioning of the international monetary system and the compliance of members with their general obligations.

The ways in which the Fund seeks to fulfill its multiple purposes are revealed by the activities in which it engages. Major categories of activity include:

- exercising surveillance over members' economic and financial policies, and over economic and financial developments in both individual countries and the world economy;
- providing financial assistance to members, conditional on agreements to implement policies designed to support macroeconomic adjustment and correct underlying problems;
- providing technical assistance and training to the governments and central banks of member countries in areas in which the IMF has expertise;
- conducting research and general policy analysis aimed at advancing economists' basic understanding of the functioning of national economies and the international monetary system, compiling statistics to support economic analysis, and in those ways contributing to both the quality of policy advice and the focus of deliberations on how to strengthen the international monetary system; and
- serving as a forum for ongoing dialog on issues relating to the performance of the world economy and the international monetary system.

3.2 Organizational and Decision-Making Structures

The day-to-day work of the IMF is carried out by a board of twenty-four Executive Directors, representing all of the IMF's 184 members, along

---

[1] See IMF (1993, Article IV, Section 1).

with an internationally recruited staff under the leadership of a managing director and three deputy managing directors. As noted in Chapter 2, ultimate oversight rests with a Board of Governors, which consists of one governor and one alternate appointed by each of the 184 member countries. The International Monetary and Financial Committee (IMFC), a subgroup of twenty-four governors or alternates (reflecting the composition of the Executive Board and representing all Fund members—see the paragraphs that follow) monitors the IMF's work program and exerts considerable influence over the issues that receive priority. The IMFC normally meets semiannually and reports to the Board of Governors.

Members of the Fund staff and management are international civil servants whose responsibility is to the IMF, not to national authorities. The organization has nearly 3,000 employees, spread over eighteen departments and a number of offices. The departments include five area departments as well as departments with various types of functional or administrative expertise. The area departments are primarily responsible for exercising surveillance over countries in different parts of the world, providing policy advice to the countries in their geographical domains, and helping national authorities design and implement economic adjustment programs when countries seek to borrow from the Fund. Among the functional departments, the Policy Development and Review Department keeps close watch over the Fund's country surveillance, economic program design, and lending activities in an attempt to maintain quality control and ensure consistency with guidance from the Executive Board; and as the needs of members evolve, it also plays a lead role in developing new policies and procedures for surveillance, program design, and lending. As a further mechanism for scrutinizing the Fund's work, an Independent Evaluation Office was established by the Executive Board in July 2001 to provide objective evaluations of issues relating to the IMF, operating independent of IMF management and at arm's length from the Executive Board.

In contrast to the Fund's staff and management, the Fund's twenty-four Executive Directors represent national authorities. The IMF's five largest shareholders—the United States, Japan, Germany, France, and the United Kingdom—have their own seats on the Executive Board, as do China, Russia, and Saudi Arabia. The rest of the Fund's 184 member countries are grouped into sixteen constituencies, each with one Executive Director who is elected for a two-year term. The Executive Board meets on a regular basis to discuss country matters, broader policy considerations, and administrative issues.

The IMF's financial resources come mainly from the quota (or capital) subscriptions that countries pay when they join the Fund, and from periodic increases in countries' quotas. In addition to defining required capital subscriptions, quotas determine the distributions of countries' rights within the Fund, including the voting power of Fund members, their access to the Fund's financial resources, and their shares in SDR allocations. The voting power of each Executive Director is proportional to the aggregate quotas of the countries in his or her constituency. General reviews of quotas are normally conducted at five-year intervals. To date, eight of the twelve general reviews that have taken place have led to quota increases, although the overall growth of quotas since the inception of the Fund, adjusted for changes in Fund membership, has been only about one third as large in percentage terms as the increase in the economic size (nominal GDP) of the Fund's largest share holders.[2]

From the earliest days of the Fund, the process of determining quotas has made reference to formulas that take account of each country's size (as generally measured by GDP), official reserve holdings, volume of trade, and variability of export receipts. These formulas have often been perceived as a way of taking account of both crude measures of financial strength and crude measures of potential needs for balance of payments financing. However, both the development and, over time, the modification and use of the quota formulas has been influenced largely by political negotiations, and efforts to rationalize the formulas from an economic perspective have never been very satisfactory. Fund publications tend to describe the relative magnitude of a country's quota as being determined "broadly on the basis of the economic size of the country, and taking into account quotas of similar countries."[3]

---

[2] The overall growth of quotas, adjusted for changes in Fund membership, can be calculated as the compounded value of the eight percentage increases in aggregate quotas that have resulted from the Fund's general quota reviews, each of which reflected the average percentage increase for the fixed group of countries that were members of the Fund at the time of the corresponding quota review. On that basis, adjusted aggregate quotas are 18.4 times as large today as the Fund's original quotas. By comparison, over the period 1952–2002 (starting seven years after the founding of the Fund, when data are readily available for each of the five largest industrial countries), nominal GDP expanded by factors of approximately thirty in the United States and Germany, sixty-five in France and the United Kingdom, and eighty in Japan.

[3] See IMF (2001a: 54).

Most of the decisions taken by the Fund's Executive Board require simple majorities of members' voting power, but decisions on major issues are made by the Fund's Board of Governors and require supermajorities of 70 or 85 percent. In particular, an 85 percent supermajority is required to amend the Articles of Agreement, to augment the pool of resources that the Fund has available to lend through an increase in Fund quotas, or to allocate SDRs or sell the Fund's gold. The United States, which currently holds the largest quota share of 17.5 percent—as much as the combined share of the three next largest countries[4]—has the power to block decisions on these matters.

3.3 Surveillance

The term *surveillance* refers to the many activities and mechanisms through which the IMF oversees the economic and financial policies and performances of its members in seeking to fulfill its purposes and thereby ensure the effective operation of the international monetary system. Surveillance is often viewed as having two broad components: *bilateral surveillance*, which is directed at developments and policies in individual member countries, and *multilateral surveillance*, which focuses on global and regional developments and issues.

The core activities of Fund surveillance have exhibited a high degree of continuity, yet there has also been considerable scope for the focus and breadth of surveillance to evolve over time to reflect changes in international financial markets and the global economy.[5] The semiannual meetings of the IMFC serve as an important forum for discussing and forging agreements on new directions for Fund surveillance. In addition, the practice and underlying principles of Fund surveillance are reviewed by the IMF Executive Board every two years, and separate reviews of Fund surveillance have recently been conducted by a group of external

---

[4] Other countries with relatively large quota shares are Japan (6.27 percent), Germany (6.12 percent), France (5.06 percent), the United Kingdom (5.06 percent), Italy (3.32 percent), Saudi Arabia (3.29 percent), Canada (3.00 percent), China (3.00 percent), and Russia (2.80 percent).

[5] Detailed treatises on the major activities of the Fund and how they have evolved over time are provided by Horsefield (1969), de Vries (1976), Boughton (2001), and James (1996). See also Bordo and James (2000).

evaluators and by the Fund's Independent Evaluation Office.[6] There is broad agreement on the general objective of making IMF surveillance as effective as possible in preventing macroeconomic crises and promoting a global economic environment conducive to sustainable growth.[7]

3.3.1 Country surveillance: core activities and policy advice

The mandate for country or bilateral surveillance comes from Article IV of the Fund's statutes. Article IV also provides underlying principles and broad guidance on the focus of surveillance, but it leaves the Fund's staff, management, and Executive Board to develop specific vehicles and practices to use in monitoring and analyzing economic and financial developments and policies in individual member countries. These vehicles and practices have evolved over time with the benefit of experience.

A general feature of bilateral surveillance is the conduct of regular (usually yearly) checkups or Article IV consultations with each member country. These consultations include a visit to the country by a team of IMF economists, who meet with government and central bank officials to discuss the country's economic policies in the context of recent and prospective developments.[8] Each IMF team includes economists who monitor and analyze economic and financial developments in their country throughout the year, and who are generally well prepared to discuss and provide advice on the country's economic policy strategy as part of a comprehensive analysis of its general economic situation. In compliance with guidance from the IMF Executive Board, the team's analysis is expected to include a review of the country's fiscal, monetary, and exchange rate policies; an assessment of the soundness of its financial system; and an examination of any industrial, social, labor, governance, environmental, or other policy issues that have a critical bearing on the country's macroeconomic policies and performance. Although the Fund's bilateral surveillance tends

---

[6] See Crow, Ariazu, Thygesen, and Portes (1999) and the Independent Evaluation Office (2003a, 2003b).

[7] As many economists have emphasized, however, there are elements of tension between preventing crises and promoting growth, and although the measures discussed in Chapters 7 and 8 can improve the trade-off considerably, a serious attempt to prevent crises completely would require draconian measures that would drastically suppress economic growth.

[8] The IMF teams also tend to meet with representatives of other groups during their country visits, such as trade unions, employer groups, academics, legislative bodies, financial market participants, and civil society organizations.

to give equal treatment to all members, there is significant scope to tailor the focus of Article IV consultations to relevant country-specific and global issues, recognizing that some members have a greater impact on the world economy than others, that some are more vulnerable to external developments, and that countries differ in their stages of development and their capacities to formulate and implement sound economic policies.

The country visits—commonly called *missions*—provide opportunities for extensive interactions between national authorities and the IMF and are typically regarded as the core of the Article IV consultations. Important scrutiny of the quality and cross-country consistency of bilateral surveillance is provided by procedures that take place before and after the country visits. Prior to the visits, the country teams prepare briefing papers that outline the main issues they intend to explore with the authorities, as well as the positions they plan to take in policy discussions. These briefing papers are reviewed by other members of the Fund's staff and must be approved by the Fund's management before the team begins its discussions with the national authorities; any significant differences of opinion about key issues or appropriate policy advice are generally resolved in meetings of the senior staff and management. Following the missions, the country teams prepare Staff Reports for review and discussion by the IMF's Executive Board, which officially represents the Fund and its general membership. The views of Executive Directors are recorded in a written Summing Up of the Article IV consultations, which is then transmitted to national authorities and serves as a focal point for the staff's ongoing surveillance. In an effort to make its economic analysis and policy advice more transparent, the Fund now publishes the Staff Reports for most Article IV consultations, along with Public Information Notices that combine the Summings Up of Executive Board discussions with summaries of the staff's analysis.[9]

Even at its best, the quality of the IMF's analysis and policy advice is limited by the accumulated knowledge and best judgments of the

---

[9] Under a policy of voluntary publication at the discretion of the countries on which surveillance material was prepared, the Fund published about 75 percent of the Staff Reports that were discussed by the Executive Board during the eighteen-month period through August 2003. After reviewing its transparency policy in June and September 2003, the Executive Board agreed to move from a policy of voluntary publication of Article IV Staff Reports to a policy of "presumed publication"; see IMF (2003a).

economics profession. As such, it is handicapped by the fact that economists have not yet discovered "the magic formula that assures rapid and steady economic growth, low inflation, financial stability, and social progress."[10] Accordingly, although bad policy advice usually has no good excuse, in some cases the Fund's policy advice is bound to be bad simply because economists' collective knowledge and judgments are limited. As many economists will recall,

"it used to be widely believed that industrial investment supported by subsidies or direct government involvement would launch the take-off into sustained development, that import substitution was a pro-growth strategy, and that there was an exploitable long-run trade-off between higher inflation and lower unemployment."[11]

Today, policy recommendations based on such consensus views of the past would be strongly challenged.

As is often noted, the effectiveness of the IMF's policy recommendations is in many respects analogous to the effectiveness of doctors' medical advice. In both cases, effectiveness is limited by existing knowledge and the best judgments that can be drawn from cumulative experience. In both cases, effectiveness in dealing with specific situations has tended to improve over time as experience has pointed to areas of deficient knowledge, as theorists and empirical researchers have succeeded in defining and analyzing the relevant questions, and as the interaction of research findings with additional experience has added to cumulated knowledge and improved best judgments. In both cases, new problems continue to emerge as time passes and the global environment evolves, creating situations in which past experience provides little or no helpful guidance. And in neither case can patients be turned away; the strategy of refusing to provide advice until the cure is known with certainty is generally not an acceptable option.

In early 1997, Michael Mussa, then Chief Economist of the Fund, described the broad principles that shape the IMF's policy advice as follows[12]:

[10] See Mussa (1997: 28).
[11] See Mussa (1997: 29).
[12] See Mussa (1997: 28–9). The wording follows Mussa verbatim; the sentences have been separated and the bullets added.

- Policies need to support an appropriate macroeconomic and microeconomic environment, but achieving high rates of sustainable economic growth depends primarily on private-sector activities.
- Market-oriented economic systems with high levels of competition are generally more efficient in allocating resources to meet consumer needs and to support worthwhile investment and growth.
- Openness to international trade and investment and to transfers of information and technology is vital for economic progress.
- Exchange rates should broadly reflect international competitiveness.
- Policies resulting in rapid inflation are generally injurious to economic performance.
- To maintain reasonable price stability and to counteract unwarranted fluctuations in output and employment, monetary policies typically need to respond to (and to anticipate) cyclical developments.
- The public sector has an essential role in fairly enforcing the rules of a competitive market system, in providing appropriate assistance to the vulnerable in society, in supporting investment in some key areas such as education and health and some components of infrastructure, and in countervailing identifiable and significant market failures.
- Public expenditure needs to be adequately financed by equitable and enforceable taxes with broad bases and with the lowest feasible tax rates.
- Fiscal deficits often have a desirable cyclical component reflecting the "automatic stabilizers"; but public-sector deficits and debt should be kept within reasonable limits lest they unduly mortgage future generations or contribute to economic and financial instability.

Although these broad principles still appear to have wide support within the economics profession, the continuing experience of disappointing growth in many countries has led to an expanded set of guidelines for sustainable growth.[13] In addition, the continuing experience with financial

---

[13] The October 1996 Communiqué of the Interim Committee contained a declaration on the Partnership for Sustainable Global Growth that outlined a wide range of principles extending beyond the guidelines relevant for maintaining macroeconomic stability. Among other things, the new principles attached importance to fiscal transparency, good governance, education, health care, poverty alleviation, and social safety nets. Subsequently, policy economists began to refer to *second-generation reforms*, with emphasis on various social goals and on the importance of well-functioning institutions in sustaining growth; see the papers prepared for the November 1999 IMF Conference on Second Generation Reforms, available at www.imf.org.

crises has raised several types of concerns about the effectiveness of Fund surveillance. One concern not listed in the aforementioned guidelines focuses on the need to strengthen national financial systems and to improve the Fund's ability to monitor economic and financial developments in a timely manner. A second concern relates to the specific types of policy actions that countries threatened or stricken by crises have been pushed to undertake as a condition for financial support from the Fund. A third is the concern that something is fundamentally wrong with the international monetary system—that regardless of their policies, countries face the threat of being overwhelmed by large inflows and subsequent reversals of internationally mobile capital. Measures taken in recent years to address the first of these concerns are described in the next section; the second and third concerns are addressed in subsequent chapters.

3.3.2   Country surveillance: new directions since the mid-1990s

The financial crisis that erupted in Mexico late in 1994, and the contagious effects it had on capital market conditions for other Latin American countries, provided a wake-up call for Fund surveillance.[14] The Fund had previously noted its concern with Mexico's large current account deficit in an Article IV Report discussed in early 1994. Moreover, the work of Guillermo Calvo and his collaborators[15] had created awareness within the Fund that, other things being equal, the upward trend in industrial-country interest rates would have adverse consequences for capital flows to developing countries.[16] Nevertheless, the crisis was a shock to the Fund's management and many others. As recalled by Stanley Fischer, then First Deputy Managing Director of the Fund,

Mexico's devaluation on December 20, 1994 (followed two days later by a forced decision to float) came as a surprise to many, in both the markets and the official sector, despite the famous warning by Rudi Dornbusch and Alejandro Werner ... that a "sad ending lies ahead unless the currency is devalued."[17]

[14] Chapter 4 provides a brief description of how the crisis evolved. Savastano, Roldos, and Santaella (1995) provide a more extensive review of Mexico's policy strategy and economic performance during 1988–94, underscoring the factors that contributed to the financial crisis.

[15] See, for example, Calvo et al. (1993).

[16] See Mussa (1997: 31).

[17] See Fischer (2001c: 8). The quote within the quote is from Dornbusch and Werner (1994: 287). A footnote to Fischer's statement clarifies the reference to Mexico's devaluation:

In the immediate aftermath of the Mexican crisis, it was reasonable to conclude that the responsibility for allowing events to reach a crisis stage was shared by the Mexican authorities, the Fund, and the official community more broadly.[18] The Mexican authorities had not reported key data to the Fund on a timely basis, thereby concealing the magnitude of their loss of foreign exchange reserves, and had also avoided politically difficult adjustments in monetary and exchange rate policies. The Fund's staff and management could be blamed for not being sufficiently aggressive, well before the crisis erupted, in insisting on having more complete and timely information and in pressuring the Mexican authorities to make appropriate policy adjustments. And the latter failures in turn could be partly attributed to the attitudes of the Fund's Executive Directors and the national authorities that own and control the institution, that wield considerable influence over the manner in which surveillance is practiced, and that are "not often enthusiastic to hear about potential crises that may beset their economies."[19]

By Spring 1995 the official community had focused on several directions for enhancing Fund surveillance—the first steps in an effort to strengthen the "architecture" of the international financial system.[20] Following its April meeting, the Interim Committee (precursor to the IMFC) issued a communiqué that, among other things, encouraged the Fund to be "frank and candid in its recommendations concerning the possible risks attached to policies followed by members"; stressed "the importance of regular and timely provision by all members of economic data to the Fund, thereby enabling the identification of emerging tensions at an early stage"; emphasized that "timely publication by members of comprehensive data would give greater transparency to their economic policies"; and requested the Fund "to work toward the establishment of standards to guide members in the provision of data to the public." In addition, the Interim Committee "invited the Fund to pay more attention to members' financing

---

"Mexico broadened its exchange rate band on December 20, and the exchange rate promptly moved to its upper limit, as capital outflows intensified."

[18] IMF (1995a: 45–6) summarizes the lessons that the Fund's Executive Board took away from the Mexican crisis.

[19] See Mussa (1997: 31).

[20] The reference to architecture was introduced three years later by Rubin (1998). Kenen (2001) provides an extensive discussion and evaluation of the architecture exercise through the summer of 2001. Eichengreen (1999b, Appendix A) summarizes the numerous architecture proposals that had surfaced by 1999, and Goldstein (2003a) assesses the leading proposals as of late 2001. See also the views of Summers (1999).

policies, and the soundness of their financial sectors, in its surveillance activities."[21]

Transparency. It would be generally inaccurate to suggest that the Fund's staff and management were not frank and candid in their confidential policy discussions with the authorities of member countries prior to the crises of the past decade.[22] However, by restricting frankness and candor to confidential interactions with national authorities, the Fund failed to adequately inform the public of the risks it perceived and left countries under relatively little pressure to take its policy advice seriously. Moreover, because the activities and policy advice of the Fund were not very transparent, the public could not evaluate and debate the quality of Fund surveillance in an informed manner.

The years since the Mexican crisis have marked a revolution in Fund transparency. Today, a majority of Fund members publish Staff Reports and Public Information Notices that describe their Article IV consultations, and the majority of countries that borrow from the Fund release descriptions of the policy programs they have agreed to undertake as conditions for the loans. In addition, the Fund staff now publishes almost all of its papers on general policy issues, sometimes also in preliminary form to solicit public comment. Public access to the Fund's publications has been greatly facilitated through the creation of an external website (www.imf.org); the release of news briefs or other statements following Executive Board discussions of important issues has become routine; and the Fund's senior staff and management now hold press briefings on a fairly regular basis.

The revolution in Fund transparency has not meant that nothing remains confidential. Many members of the Fund's Executive Board and senior staff remain concerned that full transparency would inhibit the frankness of the policy dialog between the Fund and its members. However,

[21] See the "Communiqué of the Interim Committee," as reprinted in IMF (1995a: 209–10). As noted by Fischer (2001c: 68), prior to the Mexican crisis, "the IMF did not make much effort to monitor market and financial developments in real time. It was only after the Mexican crisis that news and financial data screens were widely installed at the Fund." In addition, the Mexican crisis catalyzed the establishment of the Emergency Financing Mechanism within the Fund and the effort to expand the credit facilities available to the IMF under the New Arrangements to Borrow (see Subsection 3.4.1).

[22] See Fischer (2001c: 68). See also the external review of Fund surveillance by Crow et al. (1999: 6), who report that "in their own cases member country authorities did not generally regard the Fund's bilateral surveillance advice as insufficiently frank and direct."

the Fund has established policies and procedures that limit the extent to which information may be edited before Article IV reports and other studies prepared by the staff are made public.

Looking back over his tenure as the First Deputy Managing Director of the Fund, Fischer regarded "the transparency revolution as the most important change in the IMF during...[the seven years through 2001]. This is not simply a bureaucratic change; it is a culture change. It has some costs—but it is overwhelmingly a positive development."[23] Its benefits manifest themselves in many ways. Transparency

improves policy, because policymakers operating in the light of day cannot do some of the things they can do in the dark of secrecy. It also improves the quality of the Fund's work, for we are bound to be even more careful to get it right when we are subject to scrutiny.[24]

Standards, codes, and financial sector assessments. The financial crises of the 1990s gave rise to the development of internationally agreed standards and codes on various aspects of countries' financial systems, and to processes for assessing financial sector vulnerabilities and compliance with standards and codes. The first step, following the directives issued by the Interim Committee in April 1995, was the creation of a two-tier standard for the more complete and timely dissemination of economic and financial statistics by the Fund's member countries. A General Data Dissemination System (GDDS) was developed to provide guidance for all countries, and a Special Data Dissemination Standard (SDDS) was targeted at countries participating in international financial markets or aspiring to do so. The SDDS was established in March 1996, and, to implement it, an electronic bulletin board—the Dissemination Standards Bulletin Board—was made operational in September 1996 on the Fund's external website. The GDDS was established in December 1997. Each standard specifies a set of basic data to be provided, along with the periodicity of each data series and the lapse of time within which data are to be released. Among other things, the SDDS requires countries to report

---

[23] See Fischer (2001c: 71).

[24] Ibid. In contrast, on a related point, Tirole (2002: 119–20) takes a positive view of the Executive Board's practice of deciding most issues by consensus rather than making their votes transparent. By concealing their votes from the public, Executive Directors may have more scope to identify with the goals of the organization rather than catering to the wishes of their national electorates, who tend to have less time and incentive to acquire decision-relevant information.

foreign exchange reserves on a uniform basis, and with no more than a one-month lag; to reveal forward positions in foreign currencies; and to provide data on external debt.[25] The data standards also prescribe advanced dissemination of data-release calendars along with the provision of transparent descriptions of the procedures used to compile data and the policies for revising data. Subscription to the standards is voluntary, but countries wishing to establish and maintain their creditworthiness have incentives to subscribe.[26]

The push to strengthen surveillance over members' financial policies and financial sector soundness also resulted in more attention to financial matters in Article IV consultations, in the preparation of an IMF study outlining the broad principles and characteristics of stable and sound financial systems,[27] and in an expansion of the resources devoted to the Fund's ongoing multilateral surveillance of international financial markets. By late 1997, however, following the spread of financial crises from Thailand to other Asian countries, it had become clear that financial sector vulnerabilities were a major problem for many countries, and that the international community needed to make a much more extensive effort to help countries build sound financial sectors. This realization spurred a major effort to develop a set of standards and codes that could serve as benchmarks for good practice covering the government and the financial and corporate sectors.[28] It was hoped that providing internationally agreed benchmarks, and assessing countries against those benchmarks, would improve the quality of policymaking and the soundness of the financial and corporate sectors. Various public and private groups were

---

[25] Fischer (2001c: 66) emphasizes the importance of these innovations, many of which were triggered by the Asian financial crises and added through a strengthening of the Special Data Dissemination Standard (SDDS) in March 1999. Korea and Thailand had both subscribed to the SDDS prior to the 1997 financial crises, but the lack of timely and comprehensive reporting of data on their foreign exchange holdings and forward commitments kept market participants and the Fund largely in the dark about their reserve positions. Earlier and more complete awareness of their reserve positions by market participants and the Fund would have led to earlier and presumably less costly adjustment.

[26] See IMF (2003f, 2004). As of the end of 2003, fifty-three countries were subscribers to the SDDS and another sixty-three countries were participants in the GDDS.

[27] See Folkerts-Landau and Lindgren (1998). Meanwhile, the official community was undertaking a separate effort to prepare principles for banking supervision; see the Basel Committee on Banking Supervision (1997).

[28] Much of the inspiration for the standard-setting approach came from Goldstein's (1997) proposal for an international banking standard.

asked to develop standards or codes in their areas of expertise, and, at the initiative of the G-7 countries, a Financial Stability Forum (FSF) was established in early 1999 to promote information exchange and international cooperation among authorities responsible for maintaining financial stability.[29] For its part, the Fund during 1998–99 developed a Code of Good Practices on Fiscal Transparency and a Code of Good Practices on Transparency in Monetary and Financial Policies. In addition, a Data Quality Assessment Framework was officially approved in July 2001 as an enhancement to the data standards developed earlier by the Fund.

In May 1999, with a number of key standards and codes completed or under development, the IMF and World Bank took an important step toward strengthening surveillance of financial sectors by launching a joint Financial Sector Assessment Program (FSAP). Drawing on expert support from more than fifty cooperating institutions, including central banks and other supervisory agencies, FSAP teams provide comprehensive health checkups of countries' financial systems. These checkups focus on the whole range of financial institutions (including banks, mutual funds, and insurance companies) and financial markets (money markets, securities markets, and foreign exchange markets), as well as on the payments systems and the regulatory, supervisory, and legal frameworks that underlie the financial institutions and markets. The coverage includes assessments of the ability of the financial system to withstand various sources and degrees of stress; of various macroprudential indicators that have signaled crises in the past; of the extent to which relevant financial sector standards, codes, and good practices are being observed; and of the reform and development needs of the financial sector. Financial sector assessments (FSAs) are primarily intended to help member country authorities diagnose weaknesses in their financial systems, and participation is voluntary.

---

[29] As of April 2004, the Financial Stability Forum (FSF) included representatives of national authorities in eleven financial centers (the G-7 countries, Australia, Hong Kong, the Netherlands, and Singapore), four international financial institutions (the Bank for International Settlements, the IMF, the Organization for Economic Cooperation and Development, and the World Bank), four international regulatory and supervisory bodies (the Basel Committee on Banking Supervision, the International Accounting Standards Board, the International Organization of Securities Commissions, and the International Association of Insurance Supervisors), two committees of central bank experts (the Committee on the Global Financial System and the Committee on Payment and Settlement Systems), and the European Central Bank. The FSF tends to meet on a semiannual basis and maintains information about the various standards and codes on its website (www.fsforum.org).

Following the completion of an FSA, the IMF staff summarizes the main results in the form of a Financial System Stability Assessment, which serves as an input to the country's Article IV consultation and is discussed by the Executive Board. As of March 2004, FSAs had been completed for sixty-one countries, with work underway or waiting to be scheduled for another forty-six countries.[30]

As a separate but related initiative, a program to assess members' implementation and observance of standards in those areas of direct concern to the IMF, and for which the IMF has relevant technical expertise, was launched in early 1999. Later that year it was decided to expand the approach to include assessments by the World Bank of standards and codes in its areas of expertise, such as corporate governance, accounting, and auditing. If a country asks to be included in the program, documents known as Reports on the Observance of Standards and Codes (ROSCs) are prepared and published by the IMF or World Bank. This effort has focused on designated standards and codes in twelve areas: data dissemination, monetary and financial policy transparency, fiscal transparency, banking supervision, securities regulation, insurance supervision, payment and settlement, corporate governance, accounting, auditing, insolvency, and the combating of money laundering and terrorist financing.[31] ROSCs are conducted on a modular basis (separate modules for different standards and codes) and are intended to provide useful information for national authorities, as well as inputs for their policy discussions with the IMF and World Bank. The reports may also contribute to better risk assessments by the private sector and thereby provide stronger incentives for countries to comply with the internationally agreed standards.[32] By the end

[30] See IMF (2003g, 2004).

[31] See IMF (2003j). The effort focused initially on eleven areas but subsequently added a twelfth standard to include recommendations developed by the Financial Action Task Force to combat money laundering and the financing of terrorism.

[32] An econometric investigation by Christofides, Mulder, and Tiffin (2003), which uses existing indices of how well countries score on a variety of the characteristics addressed by the standards and codes, provides indirect evidence that compliance with standards has favorable effects on both the credit ratings of emerging market countries and the spreads that they incur on their foreign-currency-denominated sovereign debts. Accounting standards and property rights appear to be particularly relevant for spreads, whereas accounting standards and corruption appear especially important in explaining credit ratings. In Fischer's (2001c: 67) view, "Nothing would help improve standards more than if countries that met higher standards were rewarded with lower borrowing costs."

of 2003, ROSCs had been provided for 101 economies covering a total of 492 modules.[33] Although members are responsible for implementing standards, the IMF and other international bodies have been helping by providing technical assistance.

Poverty reduction. The new directions that IMF surveillance has taken in recent years have not been motivated solely by the challenge of living with potentially volatile international capital markets. A second motivation has been the desire to coordinate the Fund's surveillance with the international effort to reduce the stubbornly high incidence of extreme poverty in many parts of the world.[34] An important part of this effort, initiated in the late 1990s, has focused on easing the burdens of external debt for heavily indebted poor countries, with debt relief linked to the design of country-owned comprehensive policy strategies described in Poverty-Reduction Strategy Papers (PRSPs). A country's PRSP is formulated by its government, but it is expected to emerge from a broad-based participatory process involving domestic stakeholders and external donors. The objective is to outline an appropriate antipoverty strategy over a long-term horizon on the basis of an understanding of poverty and its causes within the specific circumstances of the country. Because PRSPs are intended to provide a framework for debt relief and concessional financial assistance, they are also expected to integrate poverty-reducing measures into a coherent, growth-oriented macroeconomic framework. Accordingly, although a key underlying principle is that national poverty-reduction strategies should be country driven, the design of PRSPs has in practice involved ongoing consultation with IMF and World Bank staff. As of May 2004, nearly forty low-income countries had completed PRSPs and another twenty or so had embarked on the process.[35] The debt relief and concessional financing associated with PRSPs is discussed later in this chapter; some general perspectives on poverty and poverty alleviation are provided in Chapter 6.

---

[33] See IMF (2004n).

[34] The International Development Goals adopted by United Nations conferences in the early 1990s, renamed the Millennium Development Goals following the UN Millennium Summit of Heads of State and Government in September 2000, aim to halve the incidence of extreme poverty by 2015 and achieve ambitious improvements in health, education, the environment, and gender equality.

[35] See IMF (2003k), as updated from www.imf.org.

3.3.3   Global and regional surveillance

The Fund is also extensively engaged in the surveillance of global and regional economic and financial developments and trends, often referred to as multilateral surveillance. One of the major products of its multilateral surveillance is the *World Economic Outlook* (*WEO*), normally published twice a year. The *WEO*, which is coordinated and largely prepared by the Fund's Research Department, results from an internal process of generating, aggregating, and analyzing short- and medium-term projections of key macroeconomic variables for each of the Fund's member countries under assumptions that ensure approximate global consistency. In addition to providing a comprehensive outlook for the world economy, individual countries, and regions, the *WEO* includes analytic discussions of topical issues. The *WEO* is read widely and given considerable attention in the press. The Fund also uses global macroeconometric models to analyze how the baseline *WEO* projections would change under different assumptions about key "exogenous" variables (such as the price of oil) or the course of policies in large countries.[36]

Along with producing the *WEO*, the Fund devotes considerable resources to monitoring and analyzing developments in international financial markets. Beginning in 2002, it has issued regular *Global Financial Stability Reports*, which seek to provide timely and comprehensive coverage of both mature and emerging financial markets.[37] As a separate initiative aimed at complementing and strengthening efforts for a faster and closer involvement of the private sector in crisis prevention and resolution, a Capital Markets Consultative Group was established in September 2000. This group, which brings IMF management and senior staff together with representatives of a range of financial institutions from all regions of the world, meets several times a year. The meetings are private and informal, held for the purpose of fostering a regular dialog between the IMF and the private financial sector.

---

[36] The main global model used in the *World Economic Outlook* (*WEO*) to date, MULTIMOD, is described by Laxton Isard, Faruqee, Prasad et al. (1998); see also Hunt, Isard, and Laxton (2002), as well as Isard (2000). Laxton and Pesenti (2003) and Pesenti (2004) describe a new Global Economic Model that the Fund began to develop during 2002.

[37] These reports, initially issued quarterly and now semiannually, replaced both the annual reports on *International Capital Markets* (issued from 1980 through 2001) and the quarterly reports on *Emerging Market Financing* (issued during 2000 and 2001).

The *WEO* and the reports on global capital markets are discussed by the IMF Executive Board and inform the semiannual discussions by the IMFC. When requested, related material is also put together by the IMF staff as inputs into meetings of other international fora, such as the Group of Seven major industrial countries (G-7). In addition, the Executive Board holds regular informal meetings, normally every six to eight weeks, to review world economic and market developments.

The Fund's tools for multilateral and bilateral surveillance have been further strengthened in recent years by the creation, testing, and ongoing application of early warning systems for analyzing the prospects of financial crises in individual countries,[38] and by the development and ongoing application of a multilaterally consistent methodology for assessing possible misalignments of exchange rates among the industrial-country currencies.[39]

IMF surveillance also extends to policies pursued under regional arrangements. This includes, for example, regular monitoring and Executive Board discussions of developments in the EU and Euro Area, the West African Economic and Monetary Union, the Central African Economic and Monetary Community, and the Eastern Caribbean Currency Union. In addition, Fund management and staff participate in surveillance discussions of various groups of countries, such as the G-7 and the Asia–Pacific Economic Cooperation Forum.

3.4   Lending and Economic Stabilization Programs

Along with its surveillance responsibilities, the IMF has the important purpose of providing financial assistance to member countries in order to lessen the impacts of balance of payments adjustment on national and international prosperity. The basic rationale for this role remains much the same as it was when the IMF was created—namely, that private international capital markets function imperfectly, and that many countries

---

[38] See Berg, Borensztein, Milesi-Ferretti, and Pattillo (2000) and Berg, Borensztein, and Pattillo (2004). Estimated models of how well a group of candidate variables predict currency crises, banking crises, or both can be a useful tool for helping to assess economic risks, but they display limited accuracy (erroneously predicting crises that never occur and failing to predict crises that do occur) both within the sample periods over which they are estimated and even more so in forecasting out of sample.

[39] See Isard and Faruqee, eds. (1998), and Isard et al. (2001).

have limited access to financial markets, especially when they have large balance of payments deficits that have to be corrected.

The imperfect functioning of private international capital markets can be attributed to various factors, including imperfect information about countries' policies and economic circumstances, coordination problems that lead to excessive lending or credit contraction, difficulties in enforcing loan contracts, and multiple equilibria.[40] Such market imperfections, together with the public goods aspects of balance of payments financing (e.g., the encouragement it provides to the expansion of international trade and the elimination of exchange restrictions), provide the justification for official financing, without which many countries could only correct large external payments imbalances through measures that had relatively adverse implications for national economic activity, and perhaps also for international prosperity. Moreover, by dealing directly with national authorities to secure commitments to policies designed to correct payments imbalances, the Fund can catalyze other sources of financing that would not be available in the absence of an economic stabilization program supported by the Fund.

The first part of this section provides background on several different lending facilities that are available to the Fund's member countries, and on the amounts of resources that members can access under these facilities. To understand the nature of the Fund's lending activities, it is essential to recall that under its legal charter, the Fund is only allowed to make its financial resources "temporarily available" to members, and "under adequate safeguards." These constraints require that the Fund condition its provision of credit to a member country on an economic stabilization plan that provides plausible assurance that the member will return to a sustainable external payments position within a reasonably short period of time (generally a few years, as elaborated later). The second part of this section provides perspectives on the manner in which economic stabilization programs are designed and implemented.

3.4.1 Lending policies and facilities

The policies and facilities through which the IMF lends to member countries have evolved over time. Until the 1960s, lending took place

---

[40] See Masson and Mussa (1995).

exclusively under the *credit tranche policies*, through which a country could draw up to a maximum of 100 percent of its IMF quota in tranches (or installments) of 25 percent of quota each. A drawing from the credit tranches, known as a Stand-By Arrangement (SBA), is intended to help a member deal with a short-term balance of payments problem. SBAs, which still account for the core of the Fund's lending activities today, typically disburse loans over a twelve- to eighteen-month period, with repayments expected within 2.5 to 4 years from the dates of disbursement. All SBAs in excess of 25 percent of quota are disbursed in phases and subject to conditionality, as described later.

Over time, the international community has established additional mechanisms for meeting the external financing needs of member countries, including mechanisms for addressing difficulties created by particular characteristics of the world economy (such as large fluctuations in commodity prices) and, more generally, for providing access to either longer-term, exceptional, or concessional financing.[41] Mechanisms for the use of IMF resources outside the credit tranches are generally referred to as *facilities*. Drawings on the credit tranches and IMF facilities are denominated in SDRs and carry interest rates equal to or at a premium above the SDR interest rate—a weighted average of market interest rates on three-month euro-denominated securities (the Eurobor rate) and three-month securities of the governments of the United States, Japan, and the United Kingdom.[42]

Apart from credit tranche drawings through SBAs, most Fund lending today takes place through the Extended Fund Facility (EFF) and the Poverty Reduction and Growth Facility. The EFF was established in 1974 as a vehicle for providing extended financing to members undertaking needed structural reforms. Loans under the EFF are typically disbursed over a three-year period with repayment expected within four and a half to seven years from the dates of disbursement. The Poverty Reduction and Growth Facility, which was established in 1999 to replace earlier concessional finance facilities, provides low-interest loans with long repayment periods to help low-income countries restructure their economies to

---

[41] See IMF (2001a) for an extensive discussion.
[42] The weights reflect the composition of the SDR, which is updated every five years and currently (since January 2001) comprises 29 percent euro, 45 percent U.S. dollar, 15 percent yen, and 11 percent pound sterling.

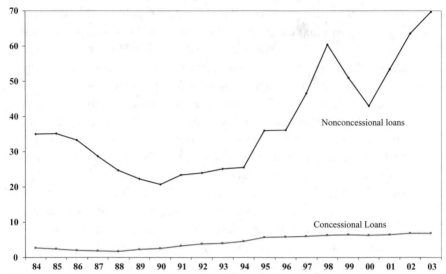

Figure 3.1. IMF credit outstanding. End-of-year data, except end of October data for 2003, in billions of SDRs. *Source*: IMF, IMF finances database.

promote growth and reduce poverty.[43] As can be seen in Figure 3.1, the volume of concessional credit outstanding has been expanding very gradually over the past two decades whereas nonconcessional credit outstanding has more than doubled since the mid-1990s. As of the end of April 2004, the Fund had nearly SDR 70 billion (equivalent to about $100 billion) in regular (i.e., nonconcessional) loans outstanding, SDR 20 billion (about $30 billion) of undrawn balances under SBAs and EFFs, and nearly SDR 7 billion (roughly $10 billion) in concessional loans outstanding.[44]

---

[43] The Fund began to provide concessional financing to low-income countries in 1976 through the establishment of the Trust Fund, which loaned the profits generated from the sale of part of the Fund's gold holdings during 1976–80. A Structural Adjustment Facility (SAF) was created in 1986 to recycle resources loaned under the Trust Fund, and a year later the Enhanced Structural Adjustment Facility was established to foster stronger adjustment and reform measures than those under the SAF and to augment the concessional resources available for that purpose. In October 1999, the Executive Board decided to change the name of the Enhanced Structural Adjustment Facility to the Poverty Reduction and Growth Facility.

[44] In addition to regular and concessional lending, the Fund's financial operations include the allocation of reserve assets through the creation of SDRs. However, the SDR mechanism, which was discussed briefly in Chapter 2, has been used to allocate reserves on only two occasions (the periods 1970–72 and 1978–81), with total allocations amounting to SDR 21.4 billion, equivalent to approximately US $33 billion at the end of 2003 exchange rate of $1.49 per SDR. For further discussion of the SDR mechanism and its history, see IMF (2001a, 2001c) and Mussa, Boughton, and Isard, eds. (1996).

Under the Fund's current policies, access to financing through SBAs or EFFs is normally constrained to an annual limit of 100 percent of a member's quota, and to a cumulative limit of 300 percent of quota. These limits can be waived in exceptional circumstances, as has been the case for a number of emerging market countries that have experienced severe financial crises since the mid-1990s. In that connection, at the end of 1997, as a reaction to needs created by the Asian crisis, the Fund established a Supplemental Reserve Facility (SRF) to provide exceptional financing to countries experiencing balance of payments crises associated with a "sudden and disruptive loss of market confidence."[45] SRF resources are provided in association with an SBA or EFF and governed by the same conditionality, with access under the SRF established on a case-by-case basis and not limited by any explicit ceiling. However, repayment of drawings under the SRF is expected within two to two and a half years—a shorter period than for SBAs or EFFs. Moreover, whereas SBAs and EFFs are provided at the SDR rate of interest with a surcharge of 100 basis points for drawings over 200 percent of quota and 200 basis points for drawings over 300 percent of quota, SRFs include an interest surcharge of 300 to 500 basis points.[46] As of the end of April 2004, five countries had outstanding drawings in excess of 300 percent of quota: Turkey (1,617 percent of quota), Brazil (597 percent), Uruguay (561 percent) Argentina (486 percent), and Indonesia (324 percent). Together these countries accounted for roughly five-sixths of the Fund's outstanding loans.

In addition to the aforementioned sources of Fund credit, member countries may currently qualify for financing through the Compensatory Finance Facility (CFF) and under some circumstances in the form of emergency assistance. The CFF, established in 1963, was intended to help countries suffering from temporary declines in export earnings—in particular, primary product producers confronted with declines in commodity

---

[45] Two years earlier, following the outbreak of the Mexican crisis and the provision of exceptional financing to Mexico, the Fund specified a set of streamlined procedures under an Emergency Financing Mechanism to facilitate rapid Executive Board decisions on IMF financial support in crisis situations.

[46] See IMF (2001a). Reviews of access policy by the Executive Board have established that exceptionally large access to Fund resources should be based on four criteria: exceptional balance of payments pressures; an assessment that the country's debt burden can be sustained; a judgment that the member has good prospects of regaining access to private capital markets within the period that Fund resources will remain outstanding; and agreement on a strong adjustment program together with indications that the government has the will and capacity to deliver on the agreed program. See IMF (2003h).

prices; access under the CFF is limited to 45 or 55 percent of quota. Emergency assistance, normally limited to 25 percent of quota, is available to countries experiencing natural disasters or struggling with postconflict situations.[47]

The IMF's regular lending operations are financed on a rotating basis from the fully paid-in capital subscriptions of member countries. To become a member of the Fund, a country is required to provide a capital subscription equal to its assigned Fund quota, with part of the subscription paid in the form of reserve assets (either foreign currencies acceptable to the IMF or SDRs) and the remainder in its own currency. In conducting its regular lending operations, the Fund disburses the reserve assets accumulated through quota subscriptions and also calls on countries that are regarded as financially strong to exchange the IMF's holdings of their currencies for additional reserve assets. As noted earlier, the quota resources available to support lending operations are reviewed every five years or so and have been increased from time to time when approved by members holding a supermajority (85 percent) of the Fund's voting power. As a backup, standing arrangements have been in place since 1962 to allow the Fund to borrow to supplement its quota resources when needed to "forestall or cope with an impairment of the international monetary system."[48]

Many people assume that Fund lending imposes a burden on creditor countries. This view has only a small element of truth. Countries

---

[47] The Fund has had a number of other facilities that no longer exist. The Buffer Stock Financing Facility, established in 1969 and eliminated in 2000, provided loans to help members finance their contributions to approved commodity price stabilization funds. A temporary Oil Facility was put in place from 1974 to 1976 to help recycle the surplus revenues of oil-exporting countries. A Systemic Transformation Facility, utilized from 1993 to 1995, provided loans to economies seeking to transform their economies from central planning to market-oriented systems. A Y2K Facility, created in September 1999 to deal with possible strains resulting from the Millennium, or Y2K, computer-dating problem, proved to be unnecessary and was allowed to lapse in early 2000. A facility of Contingent Credit Lines was created by the international community in 1999 as a mechanism for putting in place precautionary funds to help prevent the spread of financial crises and as an incentive for countries to make themselves less crisis prone; however, for reasons discussed in Chapter 8, the facility did not attract any applicants, and it was allowed to expire in November 2003.

[48] The quotas of IMF members currently total SDR 213 billion (equivalent to nearly $320 billion at the end of 2003 exchange rate). The standing agreements to borrow, known as the General Arrangements to Borrow (in place since 1962) and the New Arrangements to Borrow (in place since 1998) involve credit lines from twelve and twenty-five countries, respectively, totaling SDR 52.2 billion (about $78 billion) combined.

receive market-related interest rates on most of their reserve positions in the Fund[49]—that is, on the sum of the reserve-asset portions of their quota subscriptions, plus any of their own-currency subscriptions that are loaned out by the Fund, plus all of the reserve assets that they provide the Fund, when asked, in exchange for their own-currency subscriptions.[50] Moreover, as already noted, the Fund charges large-scale borrowers more than a risk-free market rate. Furthermore, as discussed at greater length in Chapter 5, borrowing countries to date have had a very good track record of repaying credit extended under the Fund's regular lending facilities, with full interest over the duration of the borrowing, although in some cases the repayment horizon has been effectively extended through the negotiation of successor arrangements.[51] Past experience, of course, does not imply that the very good track record will continue in the future; much depends on developments in Argentina, Brazil, and Turkey. However, among other crisis-stricken countries that have received large rescue packages from the Fund over the past decade, those that have adhered to their negotiated economic stabilization programs have not hesitated to repay the Fund, in some cases ahead of schedule. The last of Mexico's drawings under its 1995 and 1999 SBAs was paid off in August 2000; Korea completed repayments on its 1997 SBA ahead of schedule in

[49] To cover the administrative costs of operating the Fund, the rate of remuneration on members' reserve positions is reduced to as much as 20 percent below the SDR interest rate, but part of the burden of administering the Fund is also placed on debtor countries by setting the rate of interest on large drawings from the Fund's regular facilities at a premium above the SDR interest rate.

[50] Until April 1, 1978 (the date that the Second Amendment of the Articles of Agreement came into effect), members received no remuneration on their reserve tranche positions (i.e., the 25 percent of quota subscriptions paid in reserve assets); as members' quotas in the Fund have subsequently been increased, only the expanded portions of reserve tranche positions have been remunerated. Thus, every country that joined the Fund before April 1, 1978 has a non-interest-bearing (unremunerated) reserve tranche position amounting to 25 percent of its quota on that date. For a country that joined after April 1, 1978, the unremunerated reserve tranche is the same percentage of its initial quota as the average unremunerated reserve tranche was as a percentage of the quotas of all other members when the new member joined. At the end of 2003, the unremunerated portion of members' paid-in reserves averaged 3.8 percent of members' quotas. See IMF (2003c: 158).

[51] The Fund deals with overdue obligations through a series of actions that can lead to suspension of membership; see IMF (2001a). As of the end of April 2004, only four countries (Liberia, Somalia, Sudan, and Zimbabwe) had been in arrears for more than six months on drawings under the Fund's regular lending operations, whereas one other country (Iraq) had protracted arrears on interest owed for drawing down their SDR holdings. These were primarily countries facing domestic conflicts, international sanctions, or both.

August 2001; and Thailand finished paying off its 1997 SBA at the end of July 2003, also ahead of schedule.

The Fund's concessional lending is a different story. Although not envisioned by the Fund's original charter, the provision of concessional loans, grants, and debt forgiveness has come to be regarded as essential for the restoration of economic growth in many countries of the world. Because the Fund and the World Bank are jointly involved in exercising continuous surveillance over member countries and providing advice on macroeconomic and structural policies, the international community has found it attractive to provide official assistance to these countries through the Fund and the Bank and to condition this assistance on the implementation of negotiated adjustment programs. As mentioned earlier, debt relief is provided under a Heavily Indebted Poor Country (HIPC) initiative, launched in 1996, and is conditional on the design of comprehensive policy strategies described in PRSPs. The resources for financing the HIPC initiative and the Fund's concessional lending are separate from the general resources provided by quota subscriptions. Most of the resources reflect the contributions of a broad segment of the IMF's membership, with additional resources provided by the investment income on the proceeds from IMF gold sales made during 1999–2000.[52]

As of April 2004, twenty-seven countries (twenty-three in Africa) had become eligible for assistance under the HIPC initiative out of thirty-eight countries that potentially qualify, and HIPC relief was expected to reduce the external debts of the twenty-seven countries by two-thirds in net present value terms. Debt–service ratios for these countries were expected to decline from roughly 16 percent of exports before debt relief to about 8 percent of exports afterward.[53]

3.4.2 *Program design and conditionality*[54]

As a prerequisite for borrowing from the Fund, a country must negotiate a program of economic policies that provides adequate assurance that it will be in a position to repay the Fund within a well-defined time horizon. This practice derives from the IMF's legal charter, which specifies that the Fund's resources are to be made available to members on

---

[52] See IMF (2001a: 117–42).
[53] See IMF (2003i, 2004).
[54] This section draws extensively on Mussa and Savastano (2000).

a temporary basis and subject to appropriate safeguards. The negotiated programs often require countries to undertake certain policy adjustments as *prior conditions* for financial assistance from the Fund. In addition, when the IMF agrees to provide credit to a member country, it generally makes the funds available in several tranches over the period of the financial arrangement, conditioning the availability of each tranche on whether or not the country complies with the policies specified in its negotiated program. To enable the Fund to monitor compliance with policy objectives, the negotiated programs generally include quantitative targets or *performance criteria* for a small number of variables, and they may also list a set of *structural benchmarks*.[55] References to the economic policy programs negotiated with the Fund—often referred to as economic stabilization programs or economic adjustment programs—make extensive use of the term *conditionality*, sometimes in reference to the broad set of policies that a member is expected to follow in order to avail itself of credit from the Fund,[56] and sometimes as a narrower reference to the specific prior conditions, performance criteria, and benchmarks included in the program.

The nature of IMF conditionality has changed considerably over time.[57] During the 1950s and 1960s, most drawings on Fund resources were accounted for by the short-term needs of industrial countries. With private credit now readily available to these countries from international capital markets, however, no industrial country has chosen to borrow from the Fund since the mid-1980s. Moreover, in extending assistance to other countries, the international community has increasingly recognized that successful adjustment efforts require a medium-term outlook, with appropriate attention to the supply side of the economy and structural impediments to growth. The mandate for the Fund to broaden the scope and extend the time horizon of its conditionality, which first gained formal recognition with the creation of the EFF in 1974, received further

[55] Performance criteria can be defined in precise and objectively verifiable ways,—such as a quantitative ceiling on the fiscal deficit for a specific time period or a requirement that new provisioning requirements for commercial banks be put in place by a specific date. Structural benchmarks comprise either critical actions that cannot be specified in terms that can be monitored objectively or actions that are intended to serve as markers in assessing progress on critical structural reforms but for which nonimplementation would not, by itself, warrant an interruption of the scheduled disbursements of Fund financing. See IMF (2001b, 2002b).
[56] See Gold (1979).
[57] See Polak (1991).

impetus during the 1980s and early 1990s as the international community reflected on the policy needs of heavily indebted developing countries and of economies seeking to transform from centrally planned to market-oriented systems.

It is convenient to follow the common practice of referring to the economic stabilization plans that accompany IMF financial arrangements as IMF programs. It may be noted, however, that this terminology is somewhat misleading. Stabilization programs are developed jointly by the Fund and the national authorities, and the conditionality attached to the programs is generally the result of negotiations, with give and take by both parties. In that connection, moreover, the Fund's negotiating teams have learned from experience that stabilization programs tend to work best when the policy measures they include are extensively "owned" by the national authorities in charge of implementing them.[58] In addition, from a legal perspective, the economic stabilization program and associated policy conditionality, as described in a Letter of Intent and accompanying documents submitted to the Fund as a formal loan application, are regarded as the property of the national government. Furthermore, although reference to IMF programs accords well with the widespread impression that national authorities are at the mercy of the Fund in program negotiations, this impression is not accurate in all cases.[59]

The design and implementation of an IMF program is described in some detail by Mussa and Savastano (2000), who divide the process into six stages: inception, blueprint, negotiation, approval, monitoring, and completion. *Inception* occurs when the authorities of a member country request financial assistance. Typically such requests are communicated orally and informally from national authorities to IMF staff or

---

[58] See Mussa and Savastano (2000) and Goldstein (2001). As Drazen (2002) notes, however, the case for conditionality becomes more questionable when the IMF and the national authorities agree on what should be done—that is, when the national authorities have ownership of the program. In such circumstances, the case for conditionality appears to hinge on whether it can help national authorities either overcome political constraints or develop a clearer vision, through the process of discussing the economic rationale for various program conditions, of the policy measures they want the program to include.

[59] In particular, the authorities of countries of strategic interest to the United States or other major shareholders of the Fund have at times exerted strong pressure on the Fund's negotiating teams and management through the governments of the major shareholders. For example, press stories on January 20, 2003 reported that the G-7 countries had strong-armed the Fund into rolling over $6 billion of Argentina's debt. Paraphrasing Rudiger Dornbusch, Alan Beattie wrote in the *Financial Times* (January 21, 2003): "Argentina dialed 1–800-BAILOUT and the G7 made the IMF take the call."

management. Sometimes the requests follow Article IV consultations or other discussions in which the IMF staff encourages the national authorities to make policy adjustments necessary to address external and other macroeconomic imbalances. However, it is up to the national authorities to decide whether to follow such advice, and whether and when to request financial assistance in support of a stabilization program. Countries often delay policy adjustments and allow external and domestic macroeconomic imbalances to worsen significantly before requesting financial assistance from the IMF.[60] Consequently, countries applying for IMF programs often start from dire initial conditions.

Following inception, a *blueprint* of an economic stabilization program is prepared by, or in close consultation with, the IMF staff team that has been conducting regular surveillance and preprogram discussions with the national authorities. The blueprint takes account of important country-specific characteristics, including the country's exchange rate regime and monetary policy strategy; the size of the public sector; the volume and composition of its international trade; the state of its financial system; and its access to international capital markets. The blueprint for adjustment reflects both an analysis of the country's economic situation and preliminary assumptions about the amount and time profile of the financing that would be made available from the Fund and other sources. A briefing paper summarizing the blueprint and the staff's analysis of its quantitative implications is then circulated among the senior staff of the Fund for evaluation and comments, and a revised blueprint is subsequently prepared for inputs and clearance from the Fund's management, including inputs on any prior actions that the authorities should be asked to take.

After management clears the blueprint, the process enters the *negotiation* stage. This normally involves a series of meetings between the IMF staff and the national authorities to iron out disagreements over the goals of the program (i.e., over feasible objectives for key macroeconomic variables) and the policies necessary to attain those goals. In cases that prospectively involve large amounts of financing or are potentially controversial, the Executive Board is generally kept informed and given the opportunity to express its views informally. Sometimes the negotiations with national authorities proceed harmoniously and quickly; sometimes they

---

[60] See Santaella (1996) and Knight and Santaella (1997).

are contentious and prolonged. In addition to incorporating negotiated changes, the blueprint may have to be modified to take account of new information or evolving economic circumstances. Once agreement is reached on goals and appropriate policies, the negotiations focus on prior actions, quantitative performance criteria, and the plan for monitoring performance and phasing financial assistance. Mussa and Savastano (2000: 88–9) provide a general description:

After reaching agreement on numerical values for the main objectives of the program, normally for at least one year ahead, authorities and staff negotiate numerical values for the quarterly path of a small set of macroeconomic variables used to monitor the authorities' adjustment effort. Two such *intermediate variables* on which almost all IMF programs focus are the public sector deficit and creation of domestic credit by the central bank. Typically, the behavior of those variables during the first 6–12 months of the arrangement become formal performance criteria, while the numerical values for the outer dates are *indicative targets* subject to revision in the program's midterm reviews.

Once a program has been negotiated between the IMF staff and national authorities, it is summarized in a signed Letter of Intent from the national authorities, which is their formal request for IMF financing. The process then enters the stage of seeking clearance from IMF management and formal *approval* from the IMF's Executive Board. As an input to this part of the process, the IMF negotiating team prepares a Staff Report describing the discussions with the authorities and the policy understandings that were reached. The report generally includes a detailed description of the macroeconomic framework, a fairly extensive set of macroeconomic projections, the staff's appraisal of the main risks and uncertainties surrounding the proposed stabilization program, and a summary of the technical features of the proposed arrangement (i.e., the size, duration, and phasing of the IMF loan and the performance criteria that must be met prior to the release of each installment). The preparation process includes a review by a representative cross section of the Fund's senior staff, whose evaluations and comments are taken into account before the report is sent to management for clearance:

Management makes the final decision on the size and phasing of the IMF loan but generally makes no changes to the projections or other technical features of the arrangement or to the policy understandings agreed . . . [between the authorities and the IMF negotiating team]. Increasingly, especially in important cases, management's view and guidance are provided on a continuous basis throughout the negotiating process.[61]

Following clearance by management, the Staff Report and Letter of Intent are distributed to the IMF's Executive Directors and a Board meeting is scheduled to discuss the proposed arrangement. The Executive Board has the legal authority to reject the proposed arrangement, and "there often are expressions of concern or even occasional abstentions," but arrangements proposed to the Board by management "have invariably been accepted," largely because management and staff have been careful "to take to the Board only programs that they expect will command its support."[62] That being said, however, the Board discussions are used by Executive Directors to emphasize those aspects of the country-specific adjustment strategies that they regard as essential to their continuing support for each particular arrangement. "Through this process the Executive Board exerts, over time, considerable influence on IMF conditionality."[63]

The *monitoring* of IMF programs spans the period over which IMF loans are scheduled to be disbursed, which is normally one to three years. The monitoring process involves an ongoing assessment of developments in the borrowing country to determine whether performance is in compliance with the performance criteria and benchmarks of the program and, what is more important, to gauge whether developments are consistent with the general goals of the program. The process includes a sequence of formal reviews at the so-called *test dates* at which performance criteria are supposed to be met before the successive tranches of the loan can be disbursed.

More often than not, a country's progress under a Fund program fails to meet at least one of the initial performance criteria:

This is not surprising, when one considers the assumptions about the behavior of external and domestic variables and about the timeliness of policy implementation that need to be made when setting numerical values for the intermediate variables chosen as performance criteria and agreeing on the pace of structural reforms.[64]

Accordingly, in implementing conditionality, the IMF exhibits considerable flexibility to withstand departures from initial assumptions by

---

[61] See Mussa and Savastano (2000: 89).
[62] Ibid.
[63] Ibid.
[64] See Mussa and Savastano (2000: 94).

waiving or modifying various performance criteria and, more generally, by making midcourse revisions to the programs.

In deciding how to respond when a country fails to comply with one or more performance criteria, a key issue is whether noncompliance resulted primarily from slippages in the implementation of agreed policy measures or from factors beyond the authorities' control. Other key considerations, from a forward-looking perspective, are whether the goals of the program are seriously threatened by the breaching of performance criteria, and whether the national authorities can make a credible commitment to implement suitable policy adjustments. When the breaching of a performance criterion results from factors largely beyond the control of the authorities and does not seriously threaten the goals of the program, the IMF Executive Board is generally willing to modify or grant a "waiver" of the unmet criterion such that disbursements under the financial arrangement can proceed without interruption. In contrast, when the failure to meet performance criteria points to significant policy slippages or seriously threatens the goals of the program, disbursements under the arrangement are either interrupted (pending the negotiation of a revised program that receives the approval of the IMF Executive Board) or suspended.

An IMF program reaches *completion* when the borrowing country becomes eligible for the last tranche of the IMF loan. It may be noted that, out of the 615 Fund arrangements approved between 1973 and 1997, 428 (70 percent) reached completion on schedule, 73 (12 percent) were extended beyond their original durations, 70 (11 percent) were canceled early but followed promptly by successor arrangements, and 44 (7 percent) were effectively suspended.[65]

Many Fund programs involve demand-restraining measures that are consistent with the objective of restoring a sustainable current account position by bringing aggregate expenditure into line with estimates of prospective output and available external financing. As already mentioned, in seeking to ensure adequate demand restraint, macroeconomic performance criteria generally include upper bounds on both the size of fiscal deficits and the amount of domestic credit creation by the monetary authorities. In most cases the macroeconomic performance criteria also

---

[65] See Mussa and Savastano (2000, Table 3).

include lower bounds on international reserves, which have little bearing on the strength of aggregate demand but are often depleted at the outset of Fund programs and have to be rebuilt as part of the process of restoring confidence about the sustainability of the country's external position. Despite the common inclusion of these three types of macroeconomic performance criteria, however, Fund programs are fashioned to the particular circumstances of individual countries, which have different types of economies, face different types of balance of payments problems, display a variety of policy regimes, and differ in their capacities and willingness to implement policies to address their economic problems. Accordingly, the Fund's macroeconomic policy advice has a large country-specific component. In addition, for many program countries the restoration of confidence and external sustainability, as well as the country's longer-term macroeconomic goals, depends on measures to strengthen the institutional infrastructure of the economy; in such cases, IMF programs often include structural performance criteria or benchmarks along with macroeconomic performance criteria.

The policy advice embodied in Fund programs has elicited many different types of criticism (see Section 3.6). One strand of criticism contends that the financial programming framework used by the Fund to determine numerical values for macroeconomic performance criteria is based on an oversimplified representation of macroeconomic behavior and strong assumptions about the values of key parameters. This criticism is valid, but it is also narrowly focused. The financial programming framework combines a set of basic macroeconomic identities and balance sheet constraints with a small number of behavioral equations and arbitrage conditions, such as a demand for money equation, an import demand equation, and an interest rate arbitrage condition. Thus, the use of financial programming to derive numerical values for key performance criteria requires assumptions about (or estimates of) various behavioral parameters. Moreover, some of the behavioral relationships and parameters may be highly unstable—in particular, the demand for money relationship and the velocity of money parameter. This feature invites the criticism that it is not meaningful or desirable to impose performance criteria that are based on precise assumptions about the values of highly unstable parameters.

Such criticism loses some of its force when it is realized that reliance on any other macroeconomic framework for guidance would confront similar issues. The design of a stabilization program with quantitative performance criteria necessarily requires judgment or assumptions about which there is much uncertainty:

Macroeconomic outcomes are not certain: unforeseen or unpredictable future events (such as the prices of key exportable commodities or the weather), unpredictable or unanticipated (in terms of timing as well as of magnitude) responses of consumers and producers to altered relative prices, serious strikes, and changes in the government can all affect the speed of response.[66]

Furthermore, there is considerable flexibility to modify or waive unmet performance criteria, and it is standard practice to use such flexibility as long as national authorities pursue the objectives of their programs in good faith. As Mussa and Savastano (2000: 114–15) put it:

[T]he usefulness of financial programming depends not so much on the accuracy of its forecasts, as on the *flexibility* for revising the main numerical targets as new information becomes available. In fact, all performance criteria in Fund-supported programs are set *conditional* on assumptions about the behavior of a number of variables. The assumptions are rarely kept unchanged for the duration of the program. During the monitoring phase, assumptions are revisited using the latest information ... and, if necessary, numerical performance criteria are revised. The scope that this open-loop feature of the approach affords for exercising judgment when assessing the country's performance under the Fund arrangement is what explains why IMF financial programming has proved so resilient.

Nevertheless, the credibility and effectiveness of economic stabilization programs can be undermined by analytic deficiencies in the models of macroeconomic behavior that are used in designing the programs. In this connection, an ex post evaluation concluded that the Fund programs for the Asian crisis countries did not adequately capture the behavioral elements of modern financial crises, suffering, in particular, from insufficient appreciation of "the large currency depreciation which might occur in view of the possibility of multiple equilibria" and "the severe balance-sheet effects that might result."[67] Such analytic deficiencies call for ongoing efforts to adapt the Fund's analytic framework to relevant advances in models of macroeconomic behavior, and for more sensitivity analysis and attention to risks in designing economic programs (see Chapter 7, Section 7.4).

---

[66] See Krueger (2003a: 304).
[67] See Independent Evaluation Office (2003b: 16).

As one recent adaptation of its financial programming framework, the adoption of inflation targets in a number of emerging market countries with Fund programs has led in those cases to the replacement of the Fund's traditional monetary performance criteria with quantitative consultation bands for inflation. This change was initiated in the ongoing series of arrangements for Brazil. After floating its exchange rate in January 1999, Brazil stated its intention to move to formal inflation targeting, also indicating that this could not be done immediately and that, in the meantime, it would rely on a traditional framework with quantitative targets for the net domestic assets (NDA) of the central bank. Accordingly, the technical memorandums that accompanied its program reviews included performance criteria for NDA through 1999 and the first part of 2000 while the inflation-targeting framework was put in place and a mechanism was developed under which the Fund could monitor the performance of inflation relative to a set of consultation bands. Starting with the November 2000 technical memorandum of understanding, however, the performance criteria for NDA were dropped and replaced by quantitative consultation bands for inflation.[68]

3.5 Technical Assistance and Research

In addition to extending policy advice and making policy-based loans, the IMF provides technical assistance to member countries in a range of areas, aimed broadly at helping members strengthen government and financial sector institutions, policy formulation and management, and the statistical basis for policy analysis. These activities are carried out both by sharing the expertise of the Fund's regular staff and by securing the consulting services of outside experts.

The IMF began to provide technical assistance in the mid-1960s, when many newly independent countries sought help in setting up central banks and finance ministries.[69] The demand for technical assistance surged in the early 1990s, as many former centrally planned economies required

---

[68] See relevant documents for Brazil (available at www.imf.org), including the March 8, 1999 *Memorandum of Economic Policies* (paragraphs 14 and 15) and the November 3, 2000 *Technical Memorandum of Understanding*. Similar changes have since been made in the monetary performance criteria for several other inflation-targeting countries with Fund programs.

[69] See IMF (2001c).

help with the transformation to market-based systems; and a substantial further impetus has come with the effort to help countries comply with the broad range of standards and codes that the international community has developed since the mid-1990s. The IMF also offers training courses for government and central bank officials of member countries, both at its Washington headquarters and at regional training centers in Africa, Asia, Europe, the Middle East, and South America.

The range of IMF technical assistance and training can be broadly grouped into four categories:

- monetary and financial sector issues, including banking supervision and regulation, bank restructuring, foreign exchange management and operations, payments clearing and settlement systems, and the organization and operation of central banks;
- fiscal policy and management issues, including tax and customs administration, budget formulation, expenditure management, the design of social safety nets, and the management of internal and external debt;
- issues relating to the quality, collection, management, and dissemination of statistical data; and
- issues involved in drafting and reviewing economic and financial legislation.

Because its effectiveness obviously depends on the quality of its policy advice, the Fund maintains a Research Department that conducts conceptual and empirical analysis of important policy issues; stays informed about the research and thinking of the academic community and other policymaking institutions; interacts extensively with staff in other departments of the Fund; continuously analyzes and keeps management and the Executive Board informed of developments and prospects in the world economy; and prepares background papers for the board's deliberations on various policy matters. The head of the Research Department also serves as Economic Counselor to the Fund and provides regular inputs on analytic issues at meetings of senior staff and management.[70]

---

[70] The Fund's research activities are described in the quarterly *IMF Research Bulletin* and the files of IMF Working Papers and other publications, which can be found on the IMF website (www.imf.org).

3.6 Criticisms of the IMF

The IMF has been heavily criticized by academics, politicians, and public-interest groups. Much of the criticism is serious and well intended,[71] although it is not uncommon for national politicians to use the IMF as a convenient scapegoat to blame for austerity measures required to deal with economic problems that they themselves have allowed to develop.

In reflecting on the criticism, it is relevant to note that a number of the Fund's alleged sins have been denounced from both sides. As others have observed,[72] there are serious disagreements among the critics over whether the Fund has been too tough or too easy in pushing nonprogram countries to adjust policies, whether the Fund has advised countries to adjust policies in the wrong direction or in the right direction but not enough, whether the conditionality associated with Fund programs has been too austere or too lax, whether the scope of Fund conditionality has been too broad or too narrow, and whether the Fund has been too forthcoming and generous or too skimpy in providing financial assistance. Notably, on many substantive issues the lack of strong consensus among critics outside the Fund is also reflected in disagreements among the Fund staff, who provide the institution with perspectives drawn from a variety of academic backgrounds, different professional backgrounds, and national backgrounds that span the whole range of the Fund's membership.

Box 3.1 provides a list of eleven different criticisms of the Fund, along with a summary description of the assessment provided in this book and a parenthetical reference to the chapter and section in which the assessment can be found. The list is not exhaustive: for example, it does not include criticism of the distribution of members' voting power and quotas, or the charge that the Fund is undemocratic and heavily biased toward representing the interests of rich countries—two related issues that this book does not address. Among the items that are on the list, Criticism 9 has already been discussed, Criticism 11 has been partially addressed, and six of the remaining nine criticisms are considered in later chapters. Perspectives

---

[71] Indeed, the emerging market crises of the past decade have induced a number of groups to conduct studies aimed at providing constructive recommendations on the future role of the Fund. Many of the recommendations are discussed in later chapters. See Crow et al. (1999) and Independent Evaluation Office (2003a, 2003b) for reports commissioned by the overseers of the Fund; see Williamson (2001) and Goldstein (2003a) for summaries of other reports.

[72] See Frankel and Roubini (2003).

BOX 3.1. Criticisms of the IMF

1. The Fund should never have encouraged emerging market countries to liberalize domestic financial markets and international capital flows before they had strengthened financial institutions and supervisory frameworks.
   - It is widely agreed, in retrospect, that the Fund should have strongly discouraged premature liberalization. How much the Fund actively encouraged countries to liberalize inappropriately is arguable and has not yet been carefully assessed (Chapter 3, Section 3.6).
2. The Fund should have been able to prevent many of the financial crises of the past decade.
   - Yes, in principle, but crisis prevention requires actions by countries, and the Fund's effectiveness in warning countries of dangers and in persuading countries in danger to take preventive actions has been limited by various features of the environment in which it operates (Chapter 4, Section 4.3).
3. The Fund should not be so quick or generous in bailing countries out.
   - There is no consensus on this (Chapter 5, Section 5.4).
4. The Fund should attach less austere conditions to its loans, negotiating programs under which countries give higher priority to providing support for economic activity and perhaps lower priority to remaining current on payments to creditors.
   - Less austerity might be desirable in many cases, but countries borrow to finance an excess of spending over income and generally need to tighten their belts to reduce the gap between spending and income. Although loans from the Fund allow countries to tighten their belts more gradually, Fund lending is constrained by the size of the pool of resources it has available to lend and by its legal mandate (Chapter 3, Section 3.6).
5. The Fund should not have required the Asian crisis countries to tighten fiscal policies.
   - This is widely agreed, and the Fund reversed its initial advice fairly quickly (Chapter 5, Subsection 5.3.3).
6. The Fund should not have required crisis-stricken countries to raise interest rates at the outset of their economic stabilization programs.
   - There is no consensus on this (Chapter 5, Subsection 5.3.2).
7. Fund programs went overboard in requiring the Asian crisis countries to meet too many structural conditions.

- This is agreed, and the Fund has since streamlined its conditionality (Chapter 5, Subsection 5.3.4).
8. The Fund's approaches to restructuring the financial and corporate sectors in the Asian crisis cases contributed to the erosion of confidence and the depth of the crises.
   - Yes, in Indonesia; probably not in Thailand or Korea (Chapter 5, Subsection 5.3.4).
9. The quantitative performance criteria in Fund programs are based on simplified models and strong assumptions about parameter values, and so on.
   - True, but narrowly focused. Simplified models and strong assumptions are unavoidable, and Fund programs allow flexibility for midcourse adjustments (Chapter 3, Subsection 3.4.2).
10. Fund policy advice should pay more attention to growth, poverty reduction, and helping countries build institutions and climb ladders.
    - There is general agreement on goals, and growth and poverty reduction are now central objectives of programs for low-income countries. There is not much support for the view that the Fund's role in pursuing the latter objective should extend beyond seeking to understand the obstacles to poverty reduction and to ensure that its surveillance and programs are consistent with promoting economic growth and reducing poverty from a macroeconomic perspective (Chapter 3, Section 3.6).
11. The Fund should make its activities and policy advice more transparent and should try to understand legitimate alternative views on economic policy.
    - It is hard to disagree, and in recent years the Fund has been making a major effort to become more transparent and open to alternative views (Chapter 3, Subsection 3.3.2 and Section 3.6).

on the other three, along with additional comments on Criticism 11, are provided in the remainder of this section.

The first criticism blames the Fund for encouraging emerging market countries to liberalize restrictions on domestic financial markets and international capital flows prematurely, without recognizing what the consequences would be in the absence of prior measures to strengthen financial sectors.[73] This charge seems somewhat misleading insofar as it is not easy

[73] Such criticism has come from many prominent economists, including Bhagwati (1998), Rodrik (1998), Stiglitz (2002b, 2004), and Tobin and Ranis (1998).

to find clear evidence that the Fund actively encouraged countries to liberalize prematurely,[74] but, even so, the Fund can be strongly criticized for not adequately warning countries that they had not yet met the prerequisites for successful liberalization. Some economists regard the premature liberalization of financial markets and capital flows as "probably the single most important cause of the [Asian] crisis."[75] As noted in Chapter 2, the acceleration of capital flows into developing countries in the early 1990s, which raised their vulnerability to capital flow reversals, was closely associated with rapid financial liberalization by emerging market countries. Moreover, as emphasized in Chapter 4, the degree to which the Asian countries became vulnerable, and the virulence of the crisis episodes when they occurred, has been largely attributed to the weaknesses of financial institutions and prudential frameworks in the crisis-stricken countries.

The importance of strengthening financial institutions and prudential frameworks and addressing macroeconomic imbalances before liberalizing financial markets is now widely agreed. This principle has long been recognized within the Fund and World Bank by those economists with financial sector expertise.[76] As of the late 1980s, however, most Fund economists had little financial sector expertise, and the principle was not adequately reflected in the Fund's policy advice.

[74] Although the Interim Committee Communiqués and IMF Annual Reports for 1996–97 reflect a growing interest in amending the Fund's Articles of Agreement to include capital account liberalization as one of the purposes of the IMF, this development came several years after the period during which most of the financial liberalization took place. Moreover, although the Communiqués and Annual Reports issued between 1988 and 1995 contain a few passages that commend progress in liberalizing financial markets in many developing countries, they also contain passages that recognize the dangers of premature liberalization and they provide little evidence that the IMF was actively encouraging the process during that period. A somewhat similar impression comes from an internal IMF review by Quirk and Evans (1995: 6), who note that "[w]hile generally eschewing an activist policy of urging rapid liberalization, the institution has in some cases encouraged developing countries to open their economies to foreign capital inflows and to liberalize restrictions on capital account transactions." And in an econometric study of the factors that contribute to financial reforms, Abiad and Mody (2003) find that a country is more likely to undertake reforms if it is engaged in an IMF program, but that the effect of IMF programs is only marginally significant and appears to become insignificant when account is taken of the factors that lead countries to request IMF programs.

[75] See Stiglitz (2002b: 89).

[76] See for example, Mathieson and Rojas-Suarez (1993) and Caprio, Atiyas, and Hanson (1993).

Nevertheless, the Fund did not generate its policy advice in a vacuum. To the extent that it conveyed enthusiasm for financial sector liberalization without strongly warning emerging market countries of the dangers of liberalizing before they had adequately strengthened financial institutions and prudential frameworks, a significant part of the blame can be attributed to the attitudes of policy authorities in the United States, the United Kingdom, and other creditor countries with major financial market institutions that presumably had interests in expanding their opportunities to invest abroad. Moreover, although some voices within the academic community, the Fund, the World Bank, and the creditor-country policymaking communities were expressing strong concerns at the time, on the whole the economics profession did not sound loudly alarmed.[77] Indeed, most experts in open-economy macroeconomics seem to have been very surprised by the virulence of the crises that subsequently developed. In that connection, Willett (2000: 76) notes that the Fund's failure to pay sufficient attention to financial sector vulnerabilities "mirrors the traditional failures of most graduate classes in international money or open economy macro to give much attention to such issues." Willett also notes, however, that the Asian crises were not a new type of crisis, citing the experiences of countries in the Southern Cone of Latin America during the 1980s[78] and suggesting that the Fund was in a much better position to draw on those experiences than the typical international economist.[79]

[77] One of the main voices of concern within the Fund was the annual *International Capital Markets Report*. Within the U.S. policymaking community, according to Blustein (2001), the Council of Economic Advisors (Stiglitz and Blinder) expressed concerns, but on such matters the policy positions of the Clinton Administration were shaped predominantly by the views of the Treasury Department.

[78] In an important study of Chile's 1982 crisis, Diaz-Alejandro (1985) emphasized the dangers of financial liberalization without commensurate strengthening of regulation and supervision. See Mathieson and Rojas-Suarez (1993) for an IMF study that conveys a strong awareness of the dangers.

[79] In their external review of Fund surveillance, Crow et al. (1999) flagged the Fund's limited attention to financial sector weaknesses and capital account issues as a major shortcoming of Article IV consultations, also noting that financial sector weaknesses had played important roles in contributing to earlier crises in Finland, Norway, and Sweden, as well as in Argentina and Chile. In a separate review, the Independent Evaluation Office (2003b) noted that IMF surveillance did identify the banking sector vulnerabilities that would later become central to the crises in Indonesia and Korea, but it criticized the Fund for underestimating the severity of the financial sector problems and the macroeconomic risks they posed.

The fourth criticism on the list, which focuses on the conditionality attached to borrowing from the Fund, is motivated by the highly desirable objective of reducing the austerity encountered by countries with Fund programs. In assessing this criticism, it is important to recognize both the realities of macroeconomic adjustment and the constraints imposed by the international community on the financial resources that the Fund can provide to its members. Most of the countries that request the Fund's financial support have allowed large macroeconomic imbalances to develop, have consequently lost access to private capital markets, and do not have easy policy choices given the limited amounts of financing available from the Fund. Although it is true that additional financing, or longer-term financing, could reduce the need for fiscal and monetary tightening, thereby easing the austerity and supporting economic activity at a higher level, the financing that the management of the Fund is free to offer is constrained by the size of the pooled resources that the Fund has available to lend and by the access limits and repayment horizons that the international community—that is, the member countries of the Fund— have agreed to impose. In that connection, the international community took a major step toward relaxing these constraints when it created the SRF for countries facing exceptional balance of payments pressures (recall Subsection 3.4.1).

As an alternative way to ease financing constraints and the associated austerity, at least in the short run, countries can choose to suspend payments on their debts. Few countries have made this policy choice, however, and presumably for good reason. As discussed in Chapter 8, a country that defaults on debt obligations not only risks prolonging its loss of access to international capital markets but also can be confronted by litigation that ties up its overseas assets, adversely affects its international trade, or curtails its ability to participate in international payment clearing systems.

That being said, the quest for ways to more effectively prevent and resolve international financial crises has focused on a number of proposals that would ease the adjustment burden on crisis-stricken countries, including proposals for "bailing in the private sector" and for conditioning debt payment obligations on macroeconomic developments. These proposals are discussed in Chapter 8.

The tenth criticism on the list argues that the Fund should be more focused on the longer-run objectives of promoting growth and reducing poverty, and should help countries build institutions and climb ladders in pursuit of these objectives. This suggestion focuses on promoting two generally accepted goals of economic policy—economic growth and poverty reduction—and on an uncontroversial path toward these goals—building institutions and climbing ladders to higher productivity. In practice, the Fund has paid increasing attention to promoting growth since the 1980s, and growth and poverty reduction are now central objectives of Fund programs for low-income countries. Nevertheless, there remains the issue of whether the Fund plays a sufficiently large role in the effort to promote these objectives.

The issue of how large a role the Fund should play in promoting growth and reducing poverty elicits considerable controversy. Many economists have expressed the view that the Fund should stick to its traditional mandate of promoting macroeconomic stability and an orderly system of exchange rate arrangements. Consistently, many have emphasized that the Fund should not expand its mandate into the area of poverty reduction, where the World Bank is much more competent to carry the ball. As elaborated in subsequent chapters, however, it has become increasingly recognized that macroeconomic stability requires sound institutions, that efforts to promote sound institutions are conducive to economic growth, and that growth is the main road to poverty reduction.

The increasing realization that sound institutions are important for both macroeconomic stability and economic growth, resulting in part from the financial crises of the past decade, has significantly altered the focus of the Fund. As noted earlier in this chapter, the international community, in its efforts to strengthen the architecture of the international monetary system, has given the Fund and World Bank major roles in developing standards and codes for the types of institutions that fall under their competencies, in monitoring the progress of countries in achieving compliance with standards and codes, and in providing technical assistance where appropriate. In taking on such roles, the Fund is also playing a major indirect role in the effort to reduce poverty. The international community has also given the Fund an important role, along with the World Bank, in assisting low-income countries to develop country-owned poverty-reduction strategies and in evaluating whether HIPCs are eligible for debt relief under the HIPC initiative.

Although there is widespread agreement that growth and poverty reduction are important goals of economic policy, there is considerable disagreement on the types of policy programs that are conducive to achieving these goals. In particular, members of many advocacy groups and civil society organizations have difficulty understanding the sense in which the Fund's policy advice is conducive to growth, and some view the Fund as closely aligned with the financial community. Such perspectives provide the basis for the last criticism on the list—the suggestion that the Fund do more to explain its policy advice in a manner that can be clearly understood by those who view it as simply an agent of the rich and powerful.[80] As indicated earlier in this chapter, the Fund has made major efforts in recent years to make its policy advice transparent and to increase significantly its availability to the press and its interactions with civil society organizations. As discussed in Chapter 6, however, the perspectives and analytic frameworks that motivate the Fund's policy advice appear to differ in several dimensions from those that shape the views of its critics, many of whom command considerable respect.[81] And even though the different views may not be reconcilable, more effort to elucidate and understand the different analytical frameworks could be constructive.

3.7 Concluding Perspectives

This chapter has described some key features of the IMF, including its purposes; its decision-making structure; the nature of its surveillance over member countries and the global economy; the broad guidelines that shape its policy advice; its lending policies and facilities; the process of designing and modifying the economic stabilization programs on which it conditions its loans; and the ways in which its activities and focus have changed over the past decade. In doing so, it has tried to provide perspectives on the constraints under which the Fund operates—namely, constraints imposed by its legal authority, by the views of its major shareholders, by the behavior of member countries, by its financial resources, and by the state of economists' knowledge. The chapter has also listed a number of criticisms of the Fund, addressing several of them and leaving the rest to be taken up in subsequent chapters.

---

[80] From the somewhat different perspective of restoring public confidence in program countries, the Independent Evaluation Office (2003b) has recommended that the design of Fund programs should include strategies to communicate the logic of the programs and any subsequent program-related information to the public.

[81] See Kanbur (2001).

One of the Fund's major responsibilities is to exercise surveillance over the economic and financial policies of its member countries. In that respect, the Fund is often regarded as analogous to a medical doctor for national economies. The Fund provides each member country with regular checkups, and its effectiveness in preventing macroeconomic problems from developing is obviously limited by the quality of its diagnoses and policy advice. Its effectiveness is also limited by several other inherent difficulties. One difficulty is that preventive medicine can be hard to sell. Countries (people) are often unwilling to tighten their fiscal belts (diet), or to change their behavior in other ways, until their problems have reached a serious stage.[82] A related difficulty is that when countries (people) finally do become ready to address their problems, the prospect of a successful cure is often heavily dependent on fairly severe austerity measures. A third difficulty is that financial resources are limited, which reduces the scope for pursuing less austere cures. A fourth difficulty is that the prospect of cures is limited by the existing knowledge of the profession, and by the best judgments that can be drawn from cumulative experience. Although effectiveness in dealing with specific problems tends to improve over time, new problems continue to emerge with changes in the general environment, sometimes creating situations in which past experience provides little helpful guidance.

Some of these difficulties will be revisited later in the book. On the "what's right" side of the ledger, the international monetary system has at its center an institution that is well placed to serve as a forum for international monetary cooperation and to exercise surveillance over members' economic and financial policies. On the "what's wrong" side is the fact that, for various reasons, Fund surveillance has not been sufficiently effective to prevent a number of emerging market economies from suffering devastating financial crises over the past decade, or to pave the way for many of the low-income developing countries to substantially increase their growth rates.

Among other things, the list of what can be done includes the efforts that the international community has been taking to develop standards and codes covering government institutions and the financial and corporate sectors, and to implement processes to assess and help countries

---

[82] As reported by Fischer (2001c), for example, neither Thailand nor Korea took serious policy actions to try to avert their 1997 financial crises until they had exhausted virtually all of their foreign exchange reserves.

reach compliance with these benchmarks. As described in this chapter, the effort focuses particular attention on standards and codes in twelve areas: data dissemination, monetary and financial policy transparency, fiscal transparency, banking supervision, securities regulation, insurance supervision, payment and settlement, corporate governance, accounting, auditing, insolvency, and combating money laundering and terrorist financing. The standards and codes initiative is by no means all that should be done to reduce the frequency and severity of economic crises and to improve countries' prospects for take-off into sustained economic growth, but by seeking to strengthen a considerable range of institutions, it could well help countries become significantly less vulnerable to financial crises and low growth rates.

Starting several decades ago, initiatives have also been taken to adapt the Fund's lending facilities to address more effectively the financing difficulties created by the evolving characteristics of the world economy. In particular, the credit tranche policies established at Bretton Woods have been supplemented by mechanisms designed to address specific types of global shocks (e.g., large fluctuations in commodity prices); to provide access to longer-term credit for countries undergoing major structural reforms; to make exceptional amounts of financing available to countries experiencing balance of payments crises associated with sudden and disruptive losses of market confidence; and to facilitate the provision of concessional financing to low-income countries. For the most part, countries must pay market-related interest rates for the use of Fund credit, with penalty charges in the case of exceptionally large amounts of financing. Moreover, the repayment record on nonconcessional lending has been very good to date, challenging the notion that the interest rates attached to Fund lending have not adequately reflected the credit risks.

The Fund's concessional lending is a different story, but here it is relevant to recognize three points. First, the financial resources come from a separate pot than the resources for the Fund's other credit facilities and have largely been contributed by the Fund's creditor countries over and above the general resources that members provide through their quota subscriptions. Second, the international community has come to the recognition that concessional loans, grants, and debt forgiveness are essential for the restoration of economic growth in many countries of the world. Third, the rationale for channeling concessional resources through the Fund and the World Bank is that the two institutions, through their continuous surveillance over member countries, are well placed to help countries design growth-oriented economic programs and to negotiate the conditionality that the international community desires to attach to its provision of concessional financing.

The Fund's legal charter requires it to attach "adequate safeguards" to its loans. Moreover, the authority vested in the Executive Board to approve or reject loan requests gives the national authorities of member countries an ongoing role in shaping the general types of conditions that the Fund's staff and management negotiate in helping to design economic programs for countries that seek to borrow from the Fund.

This chapter has listed a number of criticisms of the Fund, addressing some of them and leaving others to be discussed in subsequent chapters. Among the many things for which the Fund has been criticized, perhaps the most serious is the fact that it failed to strongly warn emerging market countries of the dangers of liberalizing their restrictions on domestic financial activities and international capital flows without adequate prior actions to strengthen their financial institutions and establish appropriate prudential frameworks. Although the Fund was not the only guilty party, its negligence in this regard represents a major failure in carrying out its responsibilities for exercising surveillance and trying to prevent macroeconomic crises.

Other criticism faults the Fund for attaching austere conditions to its loans and for not paying more attention to growth and income distribution (poverty reduction). Although less austerity would certainly be highly desirable, such criticism often fails to recognize that the Fund's policy advice and conditionality are dictated in part by the amount of financial resources that the international community is willing to provide, and it is unrealistic to think that countries with large macroeconomic imbalances have easy policy choices when available financing is limited. This line of criticism also tends to overlook the roles that the Fund has recently been playing in the standards and codes initiative, which focuses on helping countries strengthen institutions in support of macroeconomic stability and growth, and in the HIPC initiative, which provides debt relief to low-income countries in support of country-owned poverty-reduction strategies.

Another charge that this chapter has addressed criticizes the Fund for relying on a highly simplified framework and strong assumptions when it calculates the quantitative performance criteria that countries must meet to remain automatically eligible for successive loan disbursements under a program with the Fund. Such criticism is valid, and, partly for that reason, a country's progress under a Fund program often fails to meet at least one of the initial performance criteria. However, the criticism is also narrowly focused, overlooking the flexibility that the Fund exercises in waiving or modifying performance criteria and, more generally, in making mid-course corrections to negotiated programs. When a performance criterion is breached, the Fund's response is governed by several factors: whether noncompliance with the performance criterion has been associated with slippages in the implementation of agreed policy measures; whether the goals of the program are threatened; and, if so, whether the national authorities can make a credible commitment to implement suitable policy adjustments. If the breach results from factors largely beyond the control of the authorities and does not seriously threaten the goals of the program, the IMF Executive Board is usually willing to grant a waiver of the unmet criterion such that disbursements under the program can proceed without interruption. The flexibility for exercising judgment when assessing a country's performance under a Fund program explains why the Fund's financial programming approach has proved so resilient.[83] As discussed in the next chapter, however, some critics include on the "what's wrong" side of the ledger the allegation that the Fund has gone too far in exercising its flexibility to waive performance criteria and in not being a sufficiently tough cop.

---

[83] Even so, the credibility and effectiveness of economic adjustment programs can be undermined by analytic deficiencies in the models of macroeconomic behavior that are used in designing the programs. This calls for ongoing efforts to adapt the Fund's analytic framework to relevant advances in models of macroeconomic behavior, and for more sensitivity analysis and attention to risks in designing economic programs (see Chapter 7, Section 7.4).

International
Financial Crises
and Obstacles
to Growth

4

Factors Contributing to International Financial Crises

The three chapters that form Part Two of this book provide perspectives on two major concerns about the economic aspects of the globalization process: the frequency and severity of international financial crises, and the difficulties of sustaining economic growth and reducing poverty. This chapter focuses on factors that contribute to international financial crises. It first presents some historical perspectives on crisis episodes and an over-view of the conceptual literature on their underlying causes (Section 4.1). Next it provides case-by-case reviews of seven of the major financial crises that emerging market economies have experienced since the mid-1990s, concentrating on the contributing factors and initial stages, with the objective of gaining insights relevant to crisis prevention (Section 4.2). These reviews are followed by a discussion of IMF influence during pre-crisis periods (Section 4.3) and some concluding perspectives (Section 4.4).

4.1 Historical and Conceptual Perspectives

Crises in financing international debts have been a prominent feature of the present era of high capital mobility. A defining characteristic of such events is a massive effort to shift financial capital out of claims on countries that come to be regarded as vulnerable to macroeconomic or political developments that would lead creditors to suffer capital losses—whether by reducing the real value of their claims (e.g., through inflation or confiscatory actions) or by making the countries unable or unwilling to comply with their debt payment obligations. Such capital outflows may start as a trickle but tend to feed on themselves in a vicious circle, as capital flight intensifies concerns about prospective capital losses, which in turn induces additional capital outflows. Sometimes the vicious circle can be broken through policy actions that effectively address the underlying source of concern to market participants. In other cases, the desired capital outflow can result in a substantial depreciation of the country's currency and can also substantially deplete the country's foreign exchange reserves, depending on whether and for how long the policy authorities try to resist currency depreciation. For countries that have built up large stocks of foreign-currency-denominated debt, currency depreciation raises the real burden of servicing and repaying that debt in terms of the domestic consumption that must be foregone, which heightens the prospect of debt payment difficulties and makes the vicious circle even more vicious. In such cases, financial crises have usually led to large declines in economic activity.

International financial crises are by no means a phenomenon new to modern times. On numerous occasions during the pre-1914 gold standard era, for example, countries either defaulted on international debt payments or encountered circumstances that strongly threatened their gold standard commitments.[1] Some historical comparisons suggest that currency crises during the gold standard era tended to be of longer duration than those during the past three decades, but the main difference identified by historical comparisons is that financial crises have been about twice as prevalent over the past three decades as they were during the gold standard period.[2] A second difference, found in analyses that distinguish between banking crises and currency crises, is that banking crises were less prone to undermine confidence in countries' currencies during the gold standard era.

As described in Box 4.1, a number of questions about currency crises and banking crises have been studied econometrically with data from the past three decades. Among other things, these studies suggest that although currency crises may have been more prevalent during the past three decades than during the gold standard era, the frequency of currency crises since the mid-1970s has been fairly steady.

Despite the regularity of international financial crises from the mid-1970s through the early 1990s, as well as the fact that many policymakers, financial market participants, and research-oriented international economists had lived and learned through the drama of the

---

[1] See Kindleberger (1978), Fishlow (1985), Bordo and Schwartz (1996), and Eichengreen and Bordo (2003).
[2] See Eichengreen and Bordo (2003).

BOX 4.1. Selected econometric studies of currency crises and banking crises

Different econometric studies have used different definitions of currency crises. A methodology advanced by Eichengreen, Rose, and Wyplosz (1995, 1996) and Kaminsky and Reinhart (1999, 2000) relies on a pressure index constructed as a weighted average of monthly percentage exchange rate depreciations and monthly percentage losses of foreign exchange reserves.[1] This approach defines a currency crisis as an event in which the pressure index exceeds some threshold. An alternative methodology adopted by Frankel and Rose (1996) defines a currency crisis as a monthly depreciation that exceeds a certain absolute threshold and also exceeds the country's average monthly depreciation over the previous twelve months by another threshold. The second criterion in the Frankel–Rose definition is intended to avoid the recording of a high rate of depreciation as a currency crisis when it simply reflects a trend associated with rapid inflation.

The study by Kaminsky and Reinhart (1999) has the feature of addressing both banking and currency crises, seeking to understand their causes and interactions.[2] It focuses on a group of twenty small open industrial and developing economies that had fixed exchange rates or crawling pegs or bands over the period 1970–95, identifying seventy-six currency crises and twenty-six banking crises during that period, along with nineteen "twin crisis" episodes in which the beginning of a banking crisis was followed by a currency crisis within 48 months.[3] The analysis reveals, among other results, that crises tended to be preceded by weak and deteriorating economic fundamentals, and that the conditional probability of a currency crisis given a banking crisis was significantly

---

[1] Some studies have extended the pressure index to take account of any interest rate changes that were implemented to resist exchange rate depreciation or reserve losses. Such an extension is not appealing, however, when the data set includes countries that had regulated financial markets with no market-determined interest rates during much of the sample period.

[2] Kaminsky and Reinhart define the timing of banking crises on the basis of records of bank runs, closures, mergers, and public sector takeovers. The weights in their currency pressure index are such that the two components have equal sample volatilities, and currency crises are defined as periods when the index was three standard deviations or more above its mean.

[3] In an earlier survey of the incidence of banking problems in Fund member countries between 1980 and Spring 1996, Lindgren, Garcia, and Saal (1996) documented 149 episodes of significant banking sector problems during the fifteen-year interval, distributed among 133 countries (nearly 75 percent of Fund members). They further classified 41 of these instances (affecting 36 countries) as banking crises, defined as involving "runs or other substantial portfolio shifts, collapses of financial firms, or massive government intervention." See also Caprio and Klingebiel (1996), who provide a database on episodes of major bank insolvencies (i.e., cases of negative net worth) since the late 1970s for 69 countries for which information was available.

higher than the unconditional probability of a currency crisis; however, banking crises were not necessarily the immediate causes of currency crises (there appear to be common roots).

Kaminsky and Reinhart (1999) also find that the incidence of banking crises was higher after countries liberalized financial markets than before, which is consistent with evidence reported by Demirguc-Kunt and Detragiache (1998) based on the experiences of fifty-three countries during 1980–95. Demirguc-Kunt and Detragiache conclude, however, that the effect of financial liberalization on the probability of a banking crisis is muted where the institutional environment is strong—in particular, where the rule of law is respected, corruption is relatively low, and contracts are enforced. They also find that financially repressed countries tend to have improved financial development after liberalization, even if they experience a banking crisis.

Mussa, Swoboda et al. (2000) study the incidence and severity of currency crises for a group of thirty-four emerging market economies—that is, developing countries with substantial links to international financial markets—over the period 1975–98. Using thresholds comparable with other studies, they identify sixty-six episodes as currency crises based on a pressure index and sixty-five episodes based on the Frankel–Rose criterion.[4] That amounts to roughly three currency crises per year on average among the group of thirty-four countries, and two currency crises per country on average over the twenty-three-year period. They also find that the incidence of currency crises was not much different during the 1990s than during the 1970s and 1980s.

[4] See Mussa, Swoboda et al. (2000, Table A9). The threshold for the pressure index is the mean plus three standard deviations, the same as that used by Kaminsky and Reinhart (1999). The thresholds for the Frankel–Rose criterion were chosen to generate about the same total number of crises as the pressure index.

developing-country debt crises of the 1980s, nobody was prepared for the succession of major financial crises that erupted during the decade beginning in Summer 1992.[3] First came the crisis among industrial-country participants in the European Exchange Rate Mechanism (1992–93). Then a series of crises broke out in emerging market countries, including Mexico (1994–95); a number of Asian countries, including Thailand, Indonesia, South Korea, and Malaysia (1997–98); Russia (1998); Brazil (1998–99); Turkey (2000–01); Argentina (2001); and others.

[3] Krugman (2000) speculates that economic historians may someday dub the 1990s the Age of Currency Crises.

Figures 4.1 and 4.2 focus on seven countries that have experienced currency crises since the mid-1990s. In most of these cases the crises were characterized by large reversals of net capital inflows, substantial declines in real GDP, steep nominal and real exchange rate depreciations, and recoveries of GDP growth after a year or two. Compared with international financial crises during the 1970s and 1980s, the currency crises of the 1990s were more virulent, involving much larger losses of output. By some estimates the number of crisis-stricken countries that experienced substantial losses in real GDP was three times higher during the 1990s than during the 1980s.[4] This contrast, moreover, is sharpened by the fact that the crises of the early 1980s followed a very steep and fairly prolonged increase in U.S. interest rates, whereas those of the 1990s were preceded by only mild tightening of monetary policies in the industrial countries. In addition, the crisis-stricken countries of the 1990s tended to account for larger shares of world output than those of the 1970s and 1980s.

As discussed in Chapter 5, the currency crises of the 1990s were also highly contagious: the Mexican crisis spilled over onto Argentina and other Latin American countries; the Thai crisis spread quickly to other Asian countries; and the Russian default affected the market conditions faced by emerging market countries around the world, triggered the near failure of a major U.S. hedge fund (Long-Term Capital Management), and generated extreme concerns about the risks to the financial systems of the United States and other industrial countries. This phenomenon is somewhat apparent in Figure 4.3, which shows sharp jumps in an index of interest rate spreads on emerging market bonds during the periods surrounding the Mexican and Russian crises.[5]

---

[4] See Mussa, Swoboda et al. (2000, Table 2), who define a "substantial loss" of output as a decline of more than 4 percent over a one-year period or a cumulative 12 percent over a three-year period. They also document (Table A8) that the incidence of large reversals in capital flows to developing countries, measured in terms of gross private financing, was significantly greater during the 1990s than during the 1980s.

[5] Contrasts have also been drawn between the amounts of official financing that the crises of the 1990s attracted relative to the crises of earlier decades. In making such comparisons, however, one should recognize that impressions of the size of Fund programs over the past decade can be somewhat misleading. In particular, press releases from the IMF and other official sources trumpeted the packages of the 1990s as large by characterizing them in terms of the sum of the IMF financing that was approved plus other bilateral financing that had been tentatively arranged but that in some cases did not actually become available. Fischer (2001c: 43) notes that "the amount the IMF lent in the seven years from 1994 to 2000, SDR 80 billion, was slightly smaller, relative to the global economy, than the SDR 50 billion it lent in the seven years starting 1981, i.e. during the Latin debt crisis."

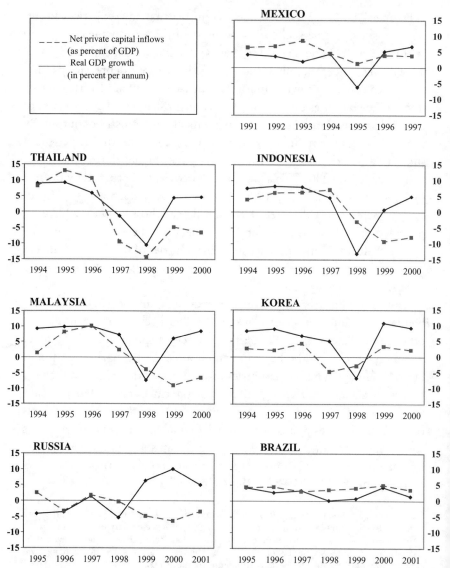

Figure 4.1. Sudden stops in net private capital inflows and real GDP growth. Annual data. *Source*: IMF, *World Economic Outlook.*

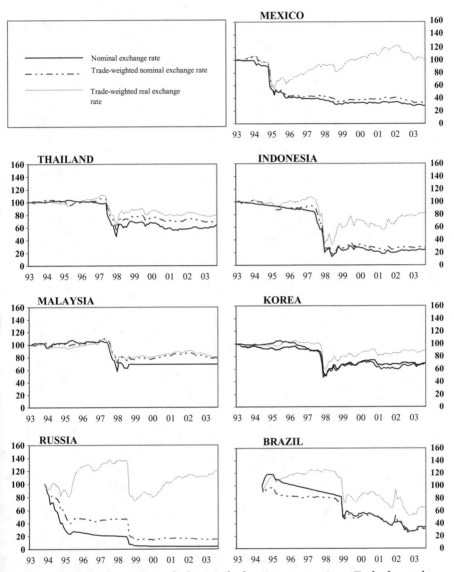

Figure 4.2. Exchange rates before and after currency crises. End-of-month data. January 1993 = 100 for all cases except Russia (November 1993 = 100) and Brazil (June 1994 = 100). *Source*: IMF, *International Financial Statistics*.

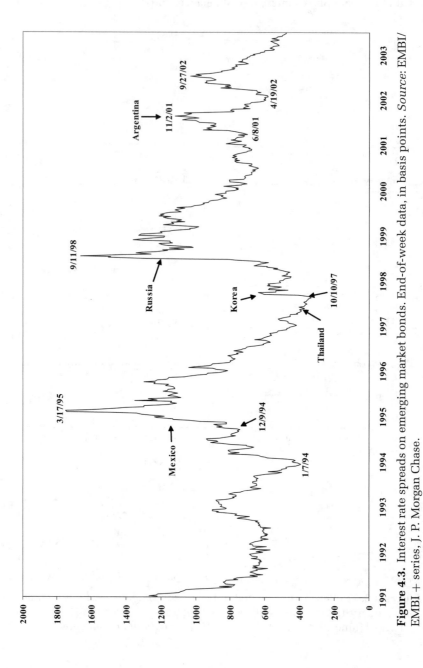

Figure 4.3. Interest rate spreads on emerging market bonds. End-of-week data, in basis points. *Source:* EMBI/ EMBI + series, J. P. Morgan Chase.

In addition to being more virulent than the financial crises of earlier decades, the crises of the 1990s did not fit neatly into the conceptual framework that economists had developed during the 1970s and 1980s.[6] The 1980s literature on speculative attacks, emanating from a pathbreaking paper by Krugman (1979),[7] emphasized that persistent balance of payments deficits would eventually exhaust the foreign exchange reserves of countries operating fixed exchange rate regimes and drew the celebrated insight that rational forward-looking market participants would inevitably attack a country's exchange rate peg before its official reserves were depleted. Another insight was that even when market participants projected an eventual depletion of a country's reserves under prevailing macroeconomic policies, they would not necessarily attack the exchange rate peg immediately. An exchange rate peg could thus remain "inconsistent with macroeconomic fundamentals" for some time before pressures on the exchange rate surfaced.

The Krugman model suggested that the leading indicators of speculative attacks were fiscal deficits, current account deficits, and dwindling international reserves. These indicators were broadly consistent with the events of the 1980s, when many of the countries that succumbed to currency crises had been running large deficits in their fiscal positions or current accounts. The relevance of the Krugman framework was called into question, however, by the European exchange market crisis of 1992–93. In the first place, the countries participating in the Exchange Rate Mechanism (ERM) of the European Monetary System had extensive access to borrowing facilities to replenish their reserves; second, some of the countries stricken by the crisis had not been running large budget or current account deficits; and third, the exchange market pressures were triggered by a national referendum (in Denmark) and public opinion polls (in France) indicating that voters had become reluctant to endure the high interest rates and depressed economies that the ERM countries had been experiencing in their efforts to meet the preconditions for joining the European common currency area.

[6] For perspectives on the conceptual literature, see Flood and Marion (1999), Jeanne (2000a), Dornbusch (2002a), or the discussion in Eichengreen (1999b, Appendix B).

[7] See also Flood and Garber (1984). The Krugman model was inspired by the literature on government price-fixing schemes in markets with exhaustible resources—in particular, the analysis of gold prices by Salant and Henderson (1978). See Botman and Jager (2002) for an extension of the Krugman–Flood–Garber framework that emphasizes the role of coordination among speculators in a multicurrency environment.

At the time of the ERM crisis, the analysis arrived at in policy circles gave considerable weight to the fact that the monetary policies needed to preserve exchange rate stability had become inconsistent with the needs of domestic economies.[8] Although budget and current account deficits were relatively large in several participating countries, policymakers and market participants tended to view weak economic activity as a more relevant threat to the sustainability of monetary policies. High unemployment rates cast doubt on the sustainability of prevailing interest rates and exchange rates, even in countries with balanced or surplus fiscal and current account positions (e.g., France).

These new perspectives soon gave rise to a second generation of speculative attack models that no longer relied on the assumption of an exhaustible supply of reserves, but rather analyzed the decision to realign a currency as the outcome of interactions between rational private market participants and a government pursuing well-defined policy objectives.[9] Such frameworks explicitly recognize that downward pressure on a currency arising from a shift in market expectations confronts the monetary authorities with a trade-off between stabilizing the currency (by raising the policy interest rate) or stabilizing domestic economic activity. A new feature of some of the second-generation models was the possibility of multiple equilibria and self-fulfilling or self-justifying speculative attacks. In particular, for a sufficiently large exogenous shift in market expectations, an exchange rate that the policy authorities would have chosen to sustain in the absence of the shift in sentiment would no longer be welfare maximizing once sentiment had shifted (given the implications for interest rates and economic activity), and the optimal policy response would involve an exchange rate adjustment that fulfilled or justified the initial shift in market expectations.[10]

The conceptual literature received further impetus from the 1997–98 crises in Asian emerging market economies. Consistent with the key feature of the first-generation models of speculative attacks, these were cases in which countries were clearly constrained by exhaustible supplies of

[8] See Group of Ten Deputies (1993) and Isard and Mussa (1993).

[9] Obstfeld (1996) and Ozkan and Sutherland (1998) made early contributions circulated in 1994. See also Isard (1994) and Jeanne (1997).

[10] Economists continue to debate the realism of models in which expectations can shift exogenously and give rise to multiple equilibria, as distinct from models with endogenous expectations and a single endogenously determined equilibrium that may be a discontinuous or highly nonlinear function of the state variables of the model.

foreign exchange reserves, and in which investors rushed for the exits in the expectation that those left behind would suffer large losses. They were also episodes in which large and volatile movements in exchange rates were widely linked to shifts in the expectations and uncertainties of market participants, and in which the policy responses attached considerable importance to restoring market confidence, consistent with the subset of second-generation models in which countries are vulnerable to multiple equilibria.[11]

But one prominent feature of the Asian episodes—that currency crises led to severe short-term declines in real output—was missing from, or not adequately captured by, the existing literature on speculative attacks. This phenomenon has been widely associated with so-called balance-sheet mismatches—in particular, the fact that the crisis-stricken countries had built up large stocks of short-term foreign-currency-denominated debts without comparable stocks of liquid foreign-currency-denominated assets.[12]

Formal analysis of the implications of balance-sheet mismatches has generated a variety of new currency-crisis models in recent years. Jeanne and Zettelmeyer (2002) provide an overview of the literature, distinguishing between two classes of models, as sketched in Box 4.2. In models with balance-sheet mismatches, events that begin to weaken confidence in a country's ability to meet its debt payment obligations can have spiraling effects on exchange rate expectations and the net worth of domestic residents, resulting in both substantial currency depreciation and output collapse.

Consistent with impressions that policymakers have drawn from experience, the new models of currency crises highlight several important points. First, crises are not entirely predictable. They can occur suddenly in situations in which they were not at all inevitable until something happened to trigger a shift in expectations. Second, although crises are not entirely predictable, they generally strike countries that have allowed vulnerabilities to build.[13] Third, balance-sheet mismatches limit the effectiveness of monetary and fiscal policies in mitigating the real costs of

[11] See Krugman (1998) on "the confidence game."

[12] See, for example, Dornbusch (1999) and Krugman (1999, 2003).

[13] Like the anecdotal evidence, the new currency crisis models underscore that for a given ex ante distribution of exogenous shocks, countries with relatively large external debts and relatively large balance-sheet mismatches are relatively vulnerable to crises.

BOX 4.2. Currency-crisis models with balance-sheet mismatches

As described in greater depth by Jeanne and Zettelmeyer (2002), the two classes of currency-crisis models with balance-sheet mismatches generally feature a two-way relationship, or "loop," between expectations about future exchange rates and the net worth of domestic residents, as well as a link between net worth and output, where net worth is measured in terms of purchasing power over goods at world market prices. One part of the loop simply reflects the definition of net worth, which is common to all models, depends on the prevailing exchange rate, and hence in turn reflects expectations about future exchange rates. The other part of the loop is what distinguishes the two classes of models. One class features a net worth constraint on investment: firms need capital to produce but cannot borrow more than a certain fraction of their net worth.[1] The second class features a link between net worth and banking crises: low net worth leads to the collapse of the banking system.[2] The models vary in how they complete the loop by linking the expected future exchange rate to investment declines or banking crises. Some models rely on changes in the relative price of tradable and nontradable goods; other models embody policy reaction functions.

[1] Examples include Krugman (1999); Aghion, Bacchetta, and Banerjee (2000, 2001); and Schneider and Tornell (2004).
[2] These models generally build on the closed-economy bank-run framework of Diamond and Dybvig (1983). Examples include Chang and Velasco (2000); Burnside, Eichenbaum, and Rebelo (2001a, 2001b); and Jeanne and Wyplosz (2003).

---

an adverse shift in expectations, which tends to strengthen the case for international crisis lending, other things being equal.[14]

In recognition of the second point, the literature on currency crises has distinguished between two types of phenomena that may have made residents of creditor countries less cautious in lending to emerging market countries during the early 1990s, thereby contributing to the buildup of vulnerability in the form of large external debts and balance-sheet mismatches in the latter group of countries. One view, associated with McKinnon and Pill (1997) and Dooley (2000a), emphasizes the role of implicit or explicit government guarantees. According to this view, the apparent commitment of governments to maintaining fixed exchange rates and to guaranteeing their banks against failure created moral hazard that

---

[14] See the analysis and discussion in Jeanne and Zettelmeyer (2002).

induced foreign capital to flood into the emerging Asian economies. Another view, associated with Calvo and Mendoza (2000a, 2000b), emphasizes the role of informational frictions in creating incentives for capital to charge into and out of emerging economies in a herd. The phenomena of moral hazard and informational frictions are discussed in Chapter 5.

4.2   Selected Crises of the 1990s: Contributing Factors and Initial Stages

In seeking a better understanding of how to prevent international financial crises or reduce their frequency, it is useful to reflect on the developments that led to a selected set of the recent crises, and on the initial reactions by national policy authorities and the international community. This section provides case-by-case reviews of the precipitating factors and initial stages of seven of the major crises that have occurred since the mid-1990s: Mexico, 1994–95; Thailand, 1997; Indonesia, 1997–98; Korea, 1997–98; Malaysia, 1997–98; Russia, 1998; and Brazil, 1998–99. The Argentine experience is addressed in a different context later in the chapter. Reflection on these episodes points to four types of causal factors: weaknesses in the monetary and fiscal policies and other macroeconomic fundamentals of the crisis-stricken countries; adverse economic or political shocks; imperfections in international capital markets; and deficiencies in the policy advice or persuasiveness of the IMF.

As elaborated in the descriptions that follow, in each of the seven selected cases market participants arguably had valid reasons for concern about the macroeconomic policies and other fundamentals of the crisis-stricken country.[15] Weaknesses in economic fundamentals included: relatively large current account deficits, often associated with pegged nominal exchange rates and a recent history of real exchange rate appreciation; relatively high fiscal deficits that were politically difficult to address; and relatively high levels of short-term foreign-currency-denominated debt along with serious weaknesses in financial and corporate sector balance sheets. Second, in most of the crisis-stricken countries, the deterioration of macroeconomic fundamentals could be attributed in part to adverse external shocks in the form of a rise in world interest rates, a weakening

---

[15] Some economists regard the speculative attack on the French franc during the 1992 European currency crisis as a case in which underlying economic fundamentals were sound, but this view has not gone unchallenged; see Isard and Mussa (1993).

of the economies of major trading partners, currency devaluation by major international competitors, or a decline in the relative price of exports. Among such external factors, Japan's prolonged economic recession significantly weakened a major export market of the Asian crisis countries. Third, signs of imperfectly functioning international capital markets were evident in the fact that a number of crises were triggered by contagion, or by shifts in market sentiment that did not coincide with any changes in underlying economic fundamentals. And fourth, abstracting from issues about the quality of the policy advice provided by the Fund after the crises erupted (see Chapter 5), one finds clear evidence that in several cases the Fund offered sound policy advice well in advance of the crises but was not effective in persuading countries to avert disaster by making appropriate policy adjustments.

The vulnerabilities created by weaknesses in macroeconomic policies and other fundamentals are emphasized in the following reviews of the seven selected crises, which also point to the roles of adverse external shocks. The effectiveness of the Fund's precrisis surveillance is considered later in the chapter. Chapter 5 addresses both the nature and consequences of imperfections in the international financial system and the controversies over the types of policies that the Fund advised countries to implement in response to the crises.

4.2.1   Mexico, 1994–1995[16]

Mexico's crisis erupted after six years of remarkable achievements under a stabilization program launched in December 1987. Through relatively tight fiscal and monetary policies, reliance on the exchange rate as a nominal anchor,[17] a temporary freezing of public sector prices and wages, further liberalization of the trade and financial sectors, and various other structural reforms, the rate of consumer price inflation had been reduced

---

[16] This section draws heavily on Savastano et al. (1995) and Ghosh, Lane, Schulze-Ghattas, Bulir et al. (2002).

[17] The peso was pegged to the U.S. dollar from March to December 1988 and then allowed to depreciate at a preannounced rate until November 1991. Thereafter, the authorities managed the rate within a publically announced intervention band that was allowed to widen gradually over time, from 1.5 percent at the end of 1991 to 9 percent at the end of 1993, through a policy of maintaining a fixed upper bound on the value of the peso while allowing the lower bound to depreciate at a predetermined rate.

TABLE 4.1. Output growth, inflation, and the current account before and after selected crises

	Crisis year, T	Year									
		T−7	T−6	T−5	T−4	T−3	T−2	T−1	T	T+1	T+2
Real GDP growth (percent)											
Mexico	1994	1.7	1.3	4.2	5.1	4.2	3.6	2.0	4.4	−6.2	5.2
Thailand	1997	11.6	8.1	8.1	8.3	9.0	9.2	5.9	−1.4	−10.5	4.4
Indonesia	1997	9.0	8.9	7.2	7.3	7.5	8.2	8.0	4.5	−13.1	0.8
Malaysia	1997	9.0	9.5	8.9	9.9	9.2	9.8	10.0	7.3	−7.4	6.1
Korea	1997	9.0	9.2	5.4	5.5	8.3	8.9	6.8	5.0	−6.7	10.9
Russia	1998	−5.0	−14.5	−8.7	−12.7	−4.1	−3.6	1.4	−5.3	6.3	10.0
Brazil	1998	1.0	−0.5	4.9	5.9	4.2	2.7	3.3	0.1	0.8	4.4
Consumer price inflation (percent)											
Mexico	1994	131.8	114.2	20.0	26.7	22.7	15.5	9.8	7.0	35.0	34.4
Thailand	1997	6.0	5.7	4.2	3.3	5.1	6.3	5.6	5.9	7.8	0.0
Indonesia	1997	7.9	9.4	7.5	9.7	8.5	9.4	7.9	6.2	58.0	20.7
Malaysia	1997	2.8	4.4	4.7	3.6	4.1	3.5	3.5	2.7	5.3	2.8
Korea	1997	8.6	9.3	6.2	4.8	6.3	4.5	4.9	4.4	7.5	0.8
Russia	1998	92.7	1734.7	878.8	307.5	198.0	47.9	14.7	27.8	85.7	20.8
Brazil	1998	477.4	1022.5	1927.4	2075.8	66.0	16.0	6.9	3.2	4.9	7.1
Current account balance (percent of GDP)											
Mexico	1994	3.1	−1.1	−2.6	−2.8	−4.7	−6.7	−5.8	−7.0	−0.6	−0.7
Thailand	1997	−8.3	−7.5	−5.5	−5.0	−5.4	−7.9	−7.9	−2.1	12.8	10.2
Indonesia	1997	−2.8	−3.4	−2.2	−1.5	−1.7	−3.4	−3.2	−1.8	4.2	4.1
Malaysia	1997	−2.1	−8.6	−3.7	−4.6	−7.6	−9.7	−4.4	−5.9	13.2	15.9
Korea	1997	−0.8	−2.8	−1.3	0.3	−1.0	−1.7	−4.4	−1.7	12.7	6.0
Russia	1998	0.5	−1.4	1.4	1.9	1.4	2.1	−0.6	−0.8	11.3	17.2
Brazil	1998	−0.3	1.6	−0.1	−0.3	−2.6	−3.0	−3.8	−4.2	−4.8	−4.0

Note: Based on annual data. Source: IMF, World Economic Outlook.

from more than 130 percent in 1987 to single digits in 1993–94, and real GDP growth had been raised from less than 2 percent in 1987 to an average of 4 percent from 1989–94 (Table 4.1). A key element in this effort was an explicit agreement on policies between labor, business, and the government—*the Pacto*—which was renewed periodically and remained in effect over the entire 1988–94 period. Financial liberalization proceeded rapidly during 1988–89 with the freeing of interest rates, the removal of credit controls and lending restrictions, and the abolishment of reserve requirements and compulsory liquidity ratios. This was followed, between mid-1990 and mid-1992, by the privatization of Mexico's eighteen commercial banks, which had been nationalized in 1982. Substantial trade reforms were also undertaken, consisting of unilateral tariff cuts and the negotiation of free trade agreements with several Western hemisphere countries, including the North American Free Trade Agreement (NAFTA) with the United States and Canada. Other structural reforms included the easing of restrictions on foreign investment and ownership, the deregulation of a number of key sectors of the economy (agriculture, mining, telecommunications, and transportation), and the privatization of large public enterprises.

The successful stabilization and structural reform efforts attracted large capital inflows, with the current account deficit averaging 6.25 percent of GDP in 1992–93.[18] Then, starting in early 1994, financial conditions began to tighten in a number of industrial economies, including the United States, where short-term interest rates were raised gradually but substantially during the year, beginning in February. In addition, Mexico experienced a succession of domestic political shocks—an uprising in the southern state of Chiapas during January, the assassinations of presidential candidate Colosio in March and of the secretary general of the ruling party in September, and a second Chiapas uprising in December. The March assassination was followed by an abrupt fall in capital inflows, a depreciation of the peso to the edge of its intervention band, and a large loss of foreign exchange reserves during April. The Mexican authorities let interest rates on short-term peso-denominated debt (*Cetes*) rise considerably, and they were able to keep pressures subdued from the end of April through early November. However, credit from the Bank of Mexico to the financial system, and from banks to the private sector, was allowed to expand rapidly during the year, and the current account deficit widened to 7 percent of GDP. Moreover, between March and October, the authorities effectively replaced a large amount of their outstanding Cetes debt with short-term instruments payable in pesos but indexed to the U.S.

---

[18] In real terms, the trade-weighted average value of the peso appreciated by more than 50 percent from the end of 1987 through the end of 1991, and by another 15 percent during 1992–93.

dollar (*Tesebonos*). In early December, shortly after President Zedillo was sworn into office, tensions in the Chiapas resumed; and on December 22, after experiencing a very large drop in foreign exchange reserves (from $25 billion in early November to $6 billion), the Mexican authorities abandoned their intervention band and allowed the peso to float. The peso depreciated sharply as market participants questioned Mexico's ability to service its short-term debt; by the end of January it was worth nearly 40 percent less (against both the U.S. dollar and on a trade-weighted basis) than it had been at the end of November.

Initial efforts to put together a financial rescue package led to the commitment of an $18.5 billion official line of credit on January 2. This failed to arrest market pressures, and negotiations over an adjustment program and financing continued until the end of the month. On January 31, with Mexico on the brink of default, the U.S. administration proposed a package of more than $50 billion from the U.S. Treasury, the IMF, the Bank for International Settlements, and private institutions. On February 1, by invoking an "exceptional circumstances clause," the IMF increased the amount of financing to be provided under its Stand-By Arrangement (SBA) from the initial statutory limit (300 percent of quota) to $17.8 billion (688 percent of quota), to be disbursed over an 18-month period.[19]

The Mexican experience supports the view that crises are often attributable to multiple factors. Mexico suffered a succession of adverse domestic political shocks and an external environment made increasingly difficult with the rise in dollar interest rates. The external debt position became progressively harder to sustain as the large current account deficit—already eliciting strong alarms from some widely respected economists in early 1994[20]—was allowed to persist, as short-term debts were increasingly indexed to the U.S. dollar, and as dollar interest rates rose and the peso depreciated. In addition, the Mexican authorities can be faulted for not tightening monetary policy more aggressively.[21]

---

[19] See Ghosh et al. (2002). A smaller successor stand-by-arrangement (SBA) was approved in July 1999, effectively enabling Mexico to stretch out the repayment of drawings under the 1995 SBA; by the end of August 2000, drawings under both SBAs had been fully repaid.

[20] See Dornbusch and Werner (1994).

[21] See the discussion in Savastano et al. (1995). The Mexican authorities were further criticized for not reporting key economic data to the IMF on a timely basis; see IMF (1995a: 45–6).

4.2.2 Thailand, 1997[22]

The first half of the 1990s was a period of remarkably rapid outward-oriented growth in the Asian developing economies. In Thailand, real GDP expanded by 9 percent per year on average during the 1990–95 period, while consumer price inflation averaged 5 percent per annum (Table 4.1). During the same period, the general government balance registered a surplus in every year, amounting to 3 percent of GDP on average. Not surprisingly, this unusually successful macroeconomic performance was associated with large inflows of foreign capital, which combined with a relatively high domestic saving rate (nearly 35 percent of GDP) to facilitate a rate of fixed capital formation that exceeded 40 percent of GDP. The capital inflows were intermediated primarily by commercial banks and finance companies.

The situation deteriorated considerably during 1996. Export growth slowed sharply, partly because the Thai economy lost competitiveness against Japan, a major trading partner. The erosion of competitiveness was a consequence of maintaining an effectively fixed exchange rate between the Thai baht and the U.S. dollar,[23] which had rebounded from pronounced weakness in the spring of 1995, appreciating by roughly 15 percent against the Japanese yen during the last three quarters of 1995 and nearly 15 percent more during 1996. Through its effect on the expected future profitability of Thailand's traded-goods sector, the loss of competitiveness vis-à-vis Japan also made investments in Thailand less attractive. As a result, equity values dropped steeply and property values also weakened. This seriously eroded the quality of balance sheets in the financial sector, which were largely unsupervised and vulnerable as a result of chaotic deregulation in the early 1990s.[24] Between mid-1996 and mid-1997, the government took over the Bangkok Bank of Commerce, the

---

[22] The material in this section draws heavily on IMF (1997) and Berg (1999).

[23] Although the baht was officially pegged to a basket of currencies, the methodology used by Reinhart and Rogoff (2004) characterizes it as de facto pegged to the U.S. dollar from March 1978 through July 1997.

[24] Among other things, the government had promoted the Bangkok International Banking Facility, which provided a channel for Thai banks to borrow abroad and onlend foreign currency to domestic customers. This led to a sharp rise in the foreign-currency liabilities of the Thai banking system, from about 5 percent of GDP in 1990–91 to 28 percent of GDP in 1995. See Eichengreen (1999b: 159), who cites Radelet and Sachs (1998).

largest Thai finance company was intervened and merged with a bank, and several finance companies experienced deposit runs. During the same period, several banks had their credit ratings downgraded, and Moody's lowered its ratings of both short-term and long-term government debt.

The shift in market sentiment and mounting concerns about financial sector soundness led to a series of increasingly intense speculative attacks on the baht after July 1996. Despite growing sentiment that the current account deficit was unsustainable and a series of IMF urgings to address the situation,[25] the Thai authorities resisted serious adjustment efforts. In early 1997, the Bank of Thailand began to support the currency largely through unreported foreign sales of baht, increasing its outstanding commitments to deliver foreign exchange forward from about $5 billion at the end of 1996 to $30 billion at the end of June. Meanwhile, the government spent several percent of GDP to support financial institutions. Short-term (three-month) interest rates, which had been kept at around 10 percent per annum during 1996 and the first half of 1997, were raised above 20 percent in late June. This, however, did not arrest the strong pressures on reserves and the exchange rate, and on July 2 the authorities allowed the baht to float.

Negotiations for a Fund program began during July, and it was not until late that month that the Thai authorities revealed the state of their reserves to the IMF.[26] The Fund insisted that Thailand start shutting down some insolvent finance companies, and following a heated debate within the Fund, a decision was made to provide a comprehensive guarantee of claims on the banks and finance companies that were to remain open.[27] On August 5 the Thai authorities suspended the operations of fifty-five finance companies and announced the comprehensive guarantee, and on August 20 the IMF's Executive Board approved a three-year SBA providing the equivalent of $4 billion (505 percent of quota), with additional financing of $13 billion to be provided by other sources.[28] At the insistence of the United States, approval of the SBA was conditional on the

---

[25] These urgings reportedly started at least a year in advance of the crisis; see Krueger (2003a: 344) and Blustein (2001: 60–4).

[26] See Blustein (2001: 72–3).

[27] See Blustein (2001: 75–6).

[28] Thailand completed repayment of the funds drawn under the SBA at the end of July 2003.

Thai authorities first making it publicly known that they had effectively depleted the country's reserves through forward commitments.[29] Following that revelation, the baht plummeted as market participants came to fear that the financial package was not enough.

Like other crisis cases, the Thai experience conveys the impression that the difficulties that afflicted the economy could have been lessened considerably if appropriate adjustment policies had been forcefully implemented at an earlier date, as the Fund had advised.[30] An appropriate adjustment strategy would have included exchange rate depreciation, undertaken at a stage when Thailand still had large holdings of foreign exchange reserves. Abandoning the exchange rate peg, however, would have run the risk of a loss of confidence and a self-reinforcing overreaction in foreign exchange and financial markets. For that reason, it would have been all the more important to combine the exchange rate depreciation with a program of actions to deal forcefully with Thailand's growing financial sector difficulties.

The development and mismanagement of the Thai crisis can be largely blamed on the fragility of the domestic political situation. Internal politics effectively prevented the finance minister and central bank governor from addressing financial sector problems, pressuring the authorities to continue to inject liquidity into unsound financial institutions, and thereby contributing to increasing market pessimism about Thailand's economic prospects.[31] Since November 1996, the country had been governed by a fragile six-party coalition, and several senior members of the second largest party had controlling interests in some of the most unhealthy finance companies. Rather than risking the collapse of his government, the prime minister gambled on compromise and delay. The finance minister, appointed in November, was blocked from addressing financial sector problems in even a modest way, and resigned in June 1997. The next finance minister, who was also blocked from following through on serious plans to address Thailand's economic and financial problems, resigned in mid-October, citing the need for a "genuinely independent, credible economic team."[32] When Standard & Poor's downgraded Thailand's credit rating in late October, it wrote that "patronage-based politics increasingly

---

[29] See Blustein (2001: 80–1).
[30] See the discussion in Mussa (1997).
[31] See Haggard (2000: 51–5).
[32] See Haggard (2000: 54).

has impaired the ability of technocrats to manage ongoing financial stress, while Thailand's fragmented political landscape offers little prospect of cohesive government in the near term."[33] By early November 1997 the prime minister had resigned. Although the successor government saw the return to power of a more reform-minded party, its ambitions were muted by the need to hold together a multiparty coalition, and the fractious nature of coalition politics continued to prevent Thailand from addressing its problems with force and rapidity.[34]

4.2.3   Indonesia, 1997–1998[35]

Like Thailand, the Indonesian economy performed remarkably well through the first half of the 1990s. Real GDP grew at an average annual rate of 8 percent during 1990–95, while consumer price inflation averaged close to 9 percent per year (Table 4.1). In several important respects, moreover, Indonesia seemed in better shape than Thailand at the beginning of 1997. The export slowdown had been less severe, real GDP growth had remained at 8 percent during 1996, and the current account deficit had averaged 2.5 percent of GDP during 1990–95—significantly lower than in Thailand—remaining around 3.2 percent during 1996.

However, as in Thailand and many other emerging market economies, the financial and corporate sectors posed major vulnerabilities. The stock of short-term external debt had risen to high levels, primarily through direct borrowing from foreigners by private nonfinancial corporations, rather than borrowing by the government or the banking system. The banking sector had engaged fairly heavily in property lending, and in the absence of aggressive bank closures, a number of insolvent institutions were continuing to function with central bank subsidies. Lack of reliable information, however, made it difficult for market participants and the authorities to gauge the scale of the problem:

Despite an improved regulatory framework, compliance with prudential regulations and credit guidelines was poor, and there were serious doubts on the accuracy and transparency of banks' financial statements—compounded by a tradition of

---

[33] See the *Far Eastern Economic Review*, November 6, 1997, p. 21, as cited by Haggard (2000: 54–5).
[34] See Haggard (2000: 92–100).
[35] This section draws heavily on Berg (1999) and Ghosh et al. (2002).

related-party lending, cross holdings of equities and loans, and liberal options for loan restructuring.[36]

Following Thailand's decision to float the baht on July 2, 1997, the rupiah came under strong downward pressure. The Indonesian authorities at first launched a vigorous interest rate defense, raising overnight rates to nearly 100 percent, but fears of a banking system collapse led the authorities to lower interest rates and float the rupiah on August 14.[37] Speculative pressures then subsided for several weeks, reemerging in October to push the rupiah to 30 percent below its prefloat level by month's end. Political uncertainties contributed significantly to the speculative pressures.[38] An election had been scheduled for early 1998, and it was not known whether President Suharto would seek another term. Furthermore, difficulties of restoring market confidence were compounded by the well-known fact that the President's relatives and friends had benefited enormously from the regime and would likely suffer substantially from serious efforts to restore macroeconomic stability.

In early November the IMF approved a three-year SBA equivalent to $10 billon (490 percent of quota), with additional commitments and pledges totaling $26 billion from other sources. This had a positive effect on market sentiment, but one that proved short lived. Unlike in Thailand (and Korea), where, after initial hesitations, monetary policy was tightened significantly and succeeded in stabilizing exchange rates and then allowing interest rates to be gradually lowered, in Indonesia

monetary policy veered widely off course soon after the IMF-supported program started . . . against a background of banking collapse and political turbulence. . . . [For two months] the central bank poured liquidity into the banking system, ostensibly to stave off its collapse in the face of bank runs.[39]

However, this policy failed to address the confidence problem, and bank runs continued until a strengthened program—including a blanket guarantee for bank liabilities—was announced in early January 1998.[40]

---

[36] See IMF (1998a: 152).

[37] Although officially pegged to a basket of undisclosed currencies, the rupiah behaved like a de facto crawling peg against the U.S. dollar from the late 1970s through July 1997; see Reinhart and Rogoff (2004).

[38] See Krueger (2003a).

[39] See Boorman, Lane, Schulze-Ghattas, Bulir et al. (2000: 32).

[40] Some members of the Fund staff had argued strongly for a blanket deposit guarantee during the negotiation period that preceded the November SBA, but they did not prevail

Meanwhile, speculative pressures resulted in a further precipitous drop in the rupiah.

For a variety of reasons—including continuing political uncertainties, the severity of the economic downturn, failure to move quickly to address the problems of corporate debt, and continuing rapid monetary growth fueled by liquidity support for failing financial institutions—the apparent restoration of confidence again proved short lived. Following the reelection of Suharto in March 1998 and the formation of a new government, an IMF review was completed in early May on the basis of another substantial modification of the program:

After a promising start, including successful talks with private creditors regarding the restructuring of corporate sector obligations and the rollover of short-term bank debt, the program was cast off track by severe civil unrest, which led to the resignation of President Suharto on May 21, 1998.[41]

By mid-June the rupiah was worth less than one-fifth of its precrisis value. This proved to be the trough, but in the context of continuing political and social unrest, the process of engineering an economic recovery proceeded very slowly.[42]

Analogous to the role that domestic political fragility played in the Thai crisis, the prevalence of cronyism had much to do with the development and mismanagement of the Indonesian crisis. Indonesia had a very strong government under Suharto, but it was widely recognized that his relatives and friends were benefiting enormously from the regime. Many bank loans to cronies were on nonperforming status, and business ventures involving friends and relatives were absorbing large subsidies, contributing to the

over those concerned with moral hazard. See Blustein (2001: 110), who provides the following statement by Michael Mussa, former Economic Counselor of the IMF: "there was not a clear and decisive strategy to deal with that problem [bank runs]" because "it was not well thought out in advance of the program, by us or by them." Related to this, the Independent Evaluation Office (2003b: 13) concludes that the "single greatest cause of the failure of the November 1997 program was the lack of a comprehensive bank restructuring strategy, which led to a rapid expansion of liquidity to support weak banks ... [that] in turn contributed to a weaker exchange rate and greater distress in the corporate sector."

[41] See Ghosh et al. (2002: 76).

[42] The November 1997 SBA was replaced by an Extended Fund Facility (EFF) in August 1998, which was in turn replaced by a second EFF in February 2000. As of the end of April 2004, Indonesia's outstanding drawings on the Fund were equivalent to nearly U.S.$10 billion or 324 percent of quota.

buildup of Indonesia's vulnerability.[43] In addition, the unwillingness or inability of the government to confront crony privilege made it difficult to shore up market confidence and arrest capital flight once the crisis began. In Indonesia's case, moreover, the confidence and capital flight problems were compounded by the age and declining health of the President, which created the prospect of major political change: "it was the crisis of the end of regime, with great uncertainty about what would come next, in a situation of ethnic tension."[44]

4.2.4   Korea, 1997–1998[45]

Another of the Asian miracle countries, Korea, had also achieved rapid GDP growth with single-digit inflation and relatively small current account deficits throughout the 1990–95 period (Table 4.1). Its vulnerability to crisis, like that of Indonesia, had little to do with macroeconomic imbalances and much to do with unsound financial and corporate sector balance sheets.[46]

Weaknesses in the corporate sector and the banking system became increasingly apparent during 1996 and the first half of 1997, as Korea's terms of trade worsened in the context of the won's appreciation against the yen,[47] and as GDP growth slowed. Years of bad lending practices and a weak supervisory and regulatory framework had left the banking system with heavy loan exposures to chaebols (industrial conglomerates). By the middle of 1997, six highly leveraged chaebols had gone bankrupt, and with increasing concerns about looming financial sector problems, external finance for Korea had begun to dry up even before the Thai crisis erupted. In late August the Korean authorities announced a package of measures aimed at increasing market confidence, but external financing conditions deteriorated further. Even so, the won remained essentially stable until late October, when a 6 percent devaluation of the Taiwan

---

[43] See Krueger (2003a), who provides additional background on the Indonesian crisis and the initial Fund program.

[44] See Fischer (2001c: 44).

[45] This section draws heavily on Berg (1999) and Ghosh et al. (2002).

[46] Krueger (2003a) provides perspectives on the crisis in the context of Korea's successful development strategy and the rise and fall of its industrial conglomerates (chaebols).

[47] According to the classification developed by Reinhart and Rogoff (2004), from December 1995 through November 1997, Korea maintained a de facto crawling peg between the won and the U.S. dollar. From mid-year 1995 to mid-year 1997, the won depreciated 15 percent against the dollar while appreciating 15 percent against the yen.

dollar and a successfully repelled attack on the Hong Kong dollar raised concerns about Korea's vulnerabilities, including its weakened competitiveness with Taiwan. In mid-November the trading band for the won was widened, and on November 21 the authorities officially requested a Fund program. By early December the won had depreciated more than 20 percent against the U.S. dollar, and usable foreign exchange reserves had declined to $6 billion (from about $30 billion at the end of 1996 and $22.5 billion at the end of October). On December 4 the IMF approved a three-year SBA, equivalent to about $21 billion (1939 percent of quota),[48] with additional financing totaling $37 billion. The positive announcement effect was soon overwhelmed, however, by a renewed erosion of confidence when the leading candidates for the mid-December presidential elections hesitated to publicly endorse the program, and when new information became available about the country's high level of short-term external debt and low level of usable reserves.[49] On December 24, with the won in free fall, with reserves nearly depleted, and with Korea on the brink of default,

> an eleventh-hour deal was concluded with major bank creditors to maintain their credit lines to Korea through March 1998; this arrangement was broadened at the end of January to a rescheduling of short-term claims by a larger group of bank creditors.[50]

By the beginning of February, early signs of stabilization had emerged.

Notably, the political environment in Korea after the December election contrasted sharply with the political situations in Thailand and Indonesia. Although the outgoing president and national legislature had refrained from seriously addressing the country's financial and corporate sector problems before the election, the newly elected president, Kim Dae

---

[48] Almost two-thirds of the Fund financing was provided under a one-year arrangement from the Supplemental Reserve Facility (SRF). Korea wound up drawing nearly the full $21 billion but completed the repayment of its borrowings ahead of schedule in August 2001.

[49] Unlike Thailand, which had effectively depleted its reserves through forward commitments, Korea had deposited most of its reserves in the overseas branches and affiliates of Korean banks, where they had either been used to meet debts falling due or could not be quickly withdrawn without undermining the banking system. Moreover, official figures on Korea's short-term external debt had failed to include the debts of overseas affiliates of Korean firms and banks and were thus understated by about $50 billion, which the IMF did not learn until late November. See Blustein (2001: 126–30).

[50] See Boorman et al. (2000: 29). Blustein (2001) provides additional background on the "eleventh-hour deal."

Jung, understood clearly that Korea had mismanaged liberalization and lost the confidence of foreign investors, and that it needed to implement structural reform policies consistent with the prevailing international environment.[51] Moreover, despite having won the election by only a narrow margin, President Kim "was able to make substantial progress on his [reform] program by exploiting the crisis and his political assets wisely at the outset of his administration," including during the two months between the election and his inauguration.[52] Perspectives on Korea's relatively successful recovery from crisis are provided in Chapter 5.

4.2.5   Malaysia, 1997–1998

The Malaysian economy had generated real GDP growth averaging nearly 9.5 percent per year over the 1990–95 period, with consumer price inflation averaging less than 4 percent annually (Table 4.1). Fiscal policy had remained prudent and the domestic savings rate was high. Moreover, there was little dependence on foreign capital, as short-term capital inflows were discouraged through strict controls on short-term borrowing, the net foreign exchange positions of banks, and off-balance-sheet activities. In addition, the reported stock of nonperforming loans in the financial system was relatively low (under 4 percent in 1996), capital adequacy ratios in the banking system appeared high, and the supervisory and regulatory framework was generally regarded as strong—though weaknesses in the domestic banking system would be revealed as the crisis developed.[53] This left the current account as the most prominent vulnerability in the picture. In the context of a gradual appreciation of the real effective exchange rate, the current account deficit had approached 10 percent of GDP in 1995, dropping back to less than 5 percent as the economy slowed slightly in 1996.

---

[51] See Haggard (2000: 100–7). As noted by Eichengreen (1999b: 158–9), Korea had liberalized its capital account "entirely backwards," maintaining strict controls on inflows of foreign direct investment, limiting opportunities for foreigners to purchase bonds and equities issued by Korean corporations, restricting the ability of Korean chaebols to borrow on international capital markets, and leaving Korean banks free to borrow abroad and onloan to the chaebols. This was the logical outgrowth of the government's cultivation of a bank-centered financial system, but it resulted in a stock of international debt that had a relatively short maturity, increasing the country's vulnerability to capital flow reversals.
[52] See Haggard (2000: 101).
[53] See Berg (1999: 52).

After Thailand abandoned its peg on July 2, 1997, the Malaysian ringgit came under strong pressure, along with a number of other Asian currencies. The Malaysian authorities initially resisted the pressure by raising overnight interest rates and tightening fiscal policy, but after a few weeks the interest rate hikes were largely reversed and the ringgit was allowed to float.[54] By mid-October, the ringgit had declined more than 20 percent against the U.S. dollar.

Unlike Thailand, Indonesia, and Korea, Malaysia did not seek to negotiate a program with the Fund. In early December, however, the government announced a series of economic policy measures, including sharp cuts in government spending, that came to be characterized as "an IMF package without the IMF."[55] Moreover, analogous to course corrections made in the Asian countries with IMF programs, macroeconomic policy was adjusted in early 1998 when, with real GDP contracting sharply, various measures were taken to direct credit to specific targeted sectors of the economy and fiscal policy was revised to a more expansionary stance.

The policy measures announced in early December 1997 also indicated the authorities' intention to pull the plug on insolvent firms, to tighten prudential regulation, and to consolidate vulnerable finance companies as a prelude to restructuring the entire banking system.[56] Between February and July, the government followed through with actions to strengthen corporate governance, to safeguard the soundness of the banking system, and to deal with nonperforming loans.[57] Moreover, early in 1998 the government announced a guarantee of deposits at all financial institutions.

On September 1, 1998, following the Russian default in August, the Malaysian authorities adopted a policy package designed to insulate monetary conditions from external financial volatility. The package included controls on capital outflows, the prohibition of offshore ringgit transactions, and the repegging of the ringgit against the U.S. dollar.[58]

---

[54] Although officially pegged to a basket of currencies, for many years prior to July 1997 the ringgit had been maintained within a de facto moving band against the U.S. dollar; see Reinhart and Rogoff (2004). From midyear 1995 through midyear 1997, the ringgit weakened by 3 percent against the dollar, which appreciated more than 30 percent against the yen.

[55] See Haggard (2000: 61).

[56] Ibid.

[57] See Meesook, Lee, Liu, Khatri et al. (2001).

[58] The World Bank subsequently worked with the Malaysian authorities to convert the capital controls into an exit tax, which has fewer adverse side effects than direct controls

These measures were complemented by fiscal stimulus and enabled the subsequent lowering of interest rates.

Whether Malaysia's heavy reliance on capital controls represented a more effective strategy than the policies adopted by other crisis-stricken Asian countries has been debated inconclusively.[59] Various factors make it difficult to compare the experiences of the different Asian crisis countries in a way that isolates the effect of Malaysia's controls or sheds clear light on their effectiveness relative to the effectiveness of adopting an IMF program. One of the difficulties is that the controls were not imposed until some fourteen months after the crisis erupted, by which time the ringgit had already depreciated substantially and a considerable volume of short-term capital may have left the country. Notably, Malaysia chose not to retain its controls on a permanent basis but rather eased and eventually removed them during the course of 1999–2001.[60]

4.2.6   Russia, 1998[61]

Russia's financial crisis can mainly be attributed to the failure of domestic policies, over many years, to deal effectively with the problem of large fiscal deficits:

The fiscal problems, in turn, originated in failure to reform the tax system, inadequate tax collection that formed part of a culture of nonpayment, lack of spending discipline in important areas, and slow progress in structural reform, including enterprise restructuring and the legal framework, which adversely affected the economy's performance more broadly.[62]

The history of large fiscal deficits had generated a continuing buildup in holdings of Russian government debt by domestic and foreign investors. With external debt at the end of 1997 more than 40 percent of GDP and rising, a series of domestic political shocks and external developments during the first half of 1998, including declining oil prices, led to increased

and can be lowered gradually to avoid a large disturbance when it is removed; see Stiglitz (2002b).
[59] See, for example, Sebastian Edwards (1999), Dornbusch (2002b), Kaplan and Rodrik (2002), and the summary discussion in Kenen (2001: 136–8).
[60] See Meesook et al. (2001).
[61] This section draws heavily on Fischer (2001c: 15–16) and IMF (1998c).
[62] See IMF (1998b: 7).

difficulties in selling ruble-denominated debt. Negotiations to augment Russia's financing from the IMF began in June, and a tentative agreement was reached in July. Because the government lacked a majority in parliament (the Duma), economic policy implementation during the 1990s had been largely by decree, and its effectiveness had suffered. This time the Fund insisted that the Duma would have to approve ten specific measures as prior conditions for the first installment of financing. When the government succeeded in passing only eight of the ten measures, the Fund reduced the amount of financing by nearly 15 percent, with the remainder to be disbursed in September if the other two measures had been passed by then. Meanwhile, difficulties were also encountered in securing debt restructuring agreements with private creditors, market pressures intensified, and the Russians requested more financing. To the surprise of market participants who had gambled that the international community would treat Russia as "too big or too nuclear to allow to fail," the request was refused. This led, over the weekend of August 14–16, to Russia's decision to, in effect, devalue the ruble and unilaterally restructure (i.e., default on) its debt.

The refusal to provide additional official financing to Russia, together with the actions announced by the Russian authorities, triggered dramatic and contagious reactions in financial markets. As a reflection of heightened risk perceptions (or intensified risk aversion), interest rate spreads on emerging market bonds rose very sharply, almost across the board, to an average in excess of 1,700 basis points in early September, compared with less than 600 basis points during most of 1997 and early 1998 (recall Figure 4.3). Equity prices fell sharply in both emerging market and industrial countries, and many emerging market currencies came under intensified downward pressures.[63] As a consequence of the simultaneous collapse of the prices of virtually all risky assets, many international investors and banks suffered large losses. One of the more prominent developments was the near failure of a major U.S. hedge fund, Long-Term Capital Management (LTCM), which had highly leveraged positions across a

---

[63] As reported by Blustein (2001: 276), clients listening to a Deutsche Bank conference call on August 26 were told that the decision to say no to Russia represented a change in the rules of the game, and that "anybody being caught this way in Brazil probably deserves all he gets."

broad range of markets and substantial links with a number of U.S. and European financial institutions.[64] "The widespread flight to quality and liquidity gave rise to a severe tightening of credit conditions, not only for emerging market borrowers, but also for non-prime corporate borrowers in some mature markets, especially the United States."[65] Policymakers around the world responded appropriately, however, lowering interest rates in most industrial countries; and by early October, the worst of the scare had passed.

4.2.7   Brazil, 1998–1999[66]

As in Russia, Brazil's financial crisis can be largely attributed to a history of public sector imbalances. The stabilization program that Brazil adopted in mid-1994 (the Real Plan) included a strong fiscal adjustment at its introduction and achieved great success in reducing inflation from quadruple-digit to single-digit levels (Table 4.1). However, the fiscal stance was subsequently loosened and the public sector borrowing requirement reached 6.3 percent of GDP in 1997. In addition, the fiscal deterioration, along with a 20 percent appreciation of the trade-weighted real exchange rate between the middle of 1994 and the end of 1997, contributed to a widening of the current account deficit, which reached nearly 4 percent of GDP in 1997.

These macroeconomic imbalances left Brazil vulnerable to contagion when other emerging markets experienced inflammations. Pressure mounted in October 1997 following the outbreak of the Asian crisis, and nearly $8 billion of Brazil's foreign exchange reserves drained away in a single month. The authorities responded by raising interest rates sharply and announcing a tightening of fiscal policy, which stopped the outflow of reserves and induced a resumption of capital inflows. By the fall of 1998, however, slippages in fiscal adjustment and the continued growth of the public debt had again become strong concerns, and Brazil was particularly hard hit by the contagion that followed the Russian default. The authorities again raised interest rates sharply and announced measures

---

[64] Failure was averted through a private rescue organized with the help of the New York Federal Reserve Bank. See Franklin Edwards (1999) for perspectives on hedge funds and the collapse of Long-Term Capital Management (LTCM).

[65] See IMF (1998c: 2).

[66] This section draws on IMF (1998c) and Ghosh et al. (2002).

to tighten the fiscal stance, which slowed the capital outflow. Discussions also began on a program with the Fund.

Having seen the global effects of the Russian default, the management of the IMF and the authorities of its leading creditor countries were petrified by the prospects of a similar default by Brazil, the world's eighth largest economy (as measured by GDP). This apparently put Brazil in a strong bargaining position, enabling it to resist pressures to devalue or speed up its rate of crawl and to reject the idea of combining official support with a private-sector bail in.[67] In early December, a three-year SBA was approved for about $18.1 billion (425 percent of quota), with an additional $23.7 billion to be provided from other sources.

The arrangement with the Fund eased the downward pressures on foreign exchange reserves, but not for long. Brazil's Congress defeated an important component of the fiscal package and delayed other measures included in the economic policy program; the governor of Brazil's second largest state (Minas Gerais) announced that it would not honor its debt to the federal government; and the central bank reduced interest rates rapidly and prematurely during December. Consequently, foreign bank creditors refused to roll over maturing credit lines and the real again came under intense pressure in late December and January. On January 15, after a one-day experiment with a wider currency band, the central bank was forced to let the exchange rate float and to seek to renegotiate and reinforce the IMF-supported program. By that time, however, the risks to the global financial system had greatly subsided, and in early March the IMF and the U.S. authorities indicated that new money hinged on Brazil's ability to obtain "voluntary commitments by their creditor banks."[68] The New York Federal Reserve Bank contributed to the effort to bail in the private sector by hosting a meeting of U.S. and Canadian banks, which agreed to maintain their credit lines until the end of August.[69] As a result, on March 30 the Fund approved the disbursement of a new installment of credit under a revised economic program.[70]

---

[67] See Blustein (2001: 338–48).

[68] See Blustein (2001: 366).

[69] See Blustein (2001) for additional background. As in the case of LTCM, Federal Reserve officials applied no explicit pressure on the banks in attendance, but as a regulator that approved bank mergers and other matters, the Fed clearly had the power to make life difficult for the parties represented at the meeting.

[70] The revised December 1998 SBA was succeeded by a second SBA of about $15.6 billion in September 2001, which was replaced in turn by a third SBA of about $30.4 billion

In contrast to currency depreciations in other crisis-stricken emerging market economies, Brazil's devaluation had very little impact on its banking system. One of the likely reasons was that Brazil's banking sector was relatively small as a result of past inflations and lower savings rates. In addition, Brazil's devaluation had been widely and long anticipated, providing time for market participants to adjust, facilitated by government sales of foreign exchange reserves and exchange-rate-linked instruments.[71]

4.2.8 Sources of vulnerability and common characteristics

Reflections on the emerging market crises of the 1990s point to several types of conditions that made countries vulnerable, as well as to some common features of crisis episodes. Summers (2000) lists seven somewhat-related sources of vulnerability: pegged exchange rates; large current account deficits; large fiscal deficits; high levels of short-term government debt; high levels of short-term foreign-currency-denominated debt; banking and financial sector weakness; and poor general governance. Table 4.2 identifies those sources of vulnerability that had become very serious concerns in each specific crisis episode, based on Summer's subjective assessments in six of the cases[72] and my own separate set of subjective assessments for Malaysia. These subjective assessments suggest that pegged exchange rates contributed very seriously to vulnerability in all seven cases[73]; that banking and financial sector weaknesses contributed very seriously in all cases except Brazil; that high levels of short-term foreign-currency-denominated debt were very serious sources of vulnerability in four cases (Thailand, Indonesia, Korea, and Russia); that large fiscal deficits were very serious concerns in two cases (Russia and Brazil); that high levels of short-term government debt were very serious factors in three cases (Mexico, Russia, and Brazil); that current account deficits contributed very seriously to vulnerability in four cases (Mexico, Thailand,

---

in September 2002. As of the end of April 2004, Brazil's outstanding drawings from the Fund were equivalent to roughly $26 billion, or nearly 600 percent of quota.

[71] See Fischer (2001c: 24).

[72] See Summers (2000, Table 2).

[73] Even though Indonesia let its currency float at a relatively early stage of the crisis rather than deplete its reserves to defend the exchange rate, Summers regards the inflexible exchange rate regime as a factor that played a major role in encouraging the large buildup of foreign currency debt in the private sector.

TABLE 4.2. Sources of vulnerability

Source of vulnerability	Country						
	Mexico	Thailand	Indonesia	Malaysia	Korea	Russia	Brazil
Pegged exchange rate	x	x	x	x	x	x	x
Weak banking and financial sectors	x	x	x	x	x	x	
High levels of short-term foreign currency debt		x	x		x	x	
Large fiscal deficits						x	x
High short-term government debt	x					x	x
Large current account deficit	x	x		x			x
Poor general governance			x			x	

Note: Sources of vulnerability reflect the subjective assessments in Summers (2000), Table 2, for all countries except Malaysia. An x indicates a very serious source of vulnerability.

Malaysia, and Brazil); and that poor general governance was a source of very serious concern in two cases (Indonesia and Russia).

Although the major crisis episodes did not all reflect the same mix of vulnerabilities and were touched off in different ways, their evolution had a number of features in common. In each case a period of substantial capital inflows was followed by a shift in market sentiment, giving rise to decisions by (foreign and domestic) market participants to reduce their financial claims on the country. These shifts in sentiment were not always triggered by changes in economic fundamentals, but in every case market participants had rational reasons to be strongly concerned about economic fundamentals, including the country's ability to meet its debt payment obligations and resist currency depreciation. In every case, at some point after capital had begun to flow out of the country, investors shifted their focus from evaluating the situation in the country to evaluating the behavior of other investors. The rate of withdrawal increased as a bank-run psychology took hold, and investors sought to avoid being the last ones in as they saw the country's reserves being depleted.[74]

Thus the process snowballed as a panic mentality developed, intensifying the pressures on reserves and the exchange rate and strengthening the rationale for capital flight in a vicious circle that further weakened economic fundamentals and validated the initial shift in market sentiment.

Such panic-driven rushes for the exit, along with the herd-driven surges in capital inflows that typically preceded them, are problematic features of the international financial system. So is the contagious spreading of crises from one country to another. These are subjects to which subsequent chapters return.

4.3   IMF Influence During Precrisis Periods

The large number of major emerging market crises that have erupted since the mid-1990s raises questions about the effectiveness of the IMF. Given the continuity of the Fund's surveillance, why hasn't it been more successful at influencing countries to adjust policies on a timely basis and thereby avoid becoming vulnerable to crises? The answer should distinguish between two separate issues. One issue pertains to the effectiveness of the Fund in detecting potential problems at an early stage and providing appropriate and timely policy advice. The second relates to countries' willingness and political capacity to heed the Fund's advice.

From a statistical perspective, economists have not yet succeeded in constructing an early warning system model that displays a high degree of accuracy in predicting currency crises on the basis of economic fundamentals.[75] In principle, however, the Fund should have been able to prevent or mitigate many of the financial crises of the past decade. As noted in Chapter 3, its failure to do so partly reflected a longstanding practice of paying limited attention to financial sector vulnerabilities—a practice that mirrored the focus of most academic courses in international economics and open-economy macroeconomics, but a practice that the

---

[74] See Summers (2000: 5).

[75] Berg and Pattillo (1999) show that the leading early warning models that economists had developed as of the late 1990s would have failed to provide useful or very informative forecasts of the Asian crisis had they been used in 1996.

Fund should have been savvy enough to abandon in light of the major roles that financial sector vulnerabilities had played in earlier crises in Argentina, Chile, and the Scandinavian countries.[76]

In a number of cases, however, several other factors contributed to the Fund's failure to prevent crises. In Mexico and Korea, the national authorities did not provide the Fund with timely data on international reserves and foreign debt, which impaired its ability to detect problems at an early stage.[77] In Thailand, Russia, and Brazil, the authorities failed to heed policy advice that the Fund offered well in advance of their crises.[78]

Why do some countries fail to heed the Fund's policy advice? One possibility is that they genuinely regard it as bad advice, but it would be difficult to defend this conjecture as a general explanation. Most of the economics profession agrees with the broad guidelines that shape the Fund's policy advice (as described in Chapter 3) and shares the Fund's views on the types of vulnerabilities that emerging market countries should be advised to guard against (as listed in the previous section). This, of course, is not to deny that the Fund has sometimes offered bad advice, or to overlook the major controversies that remain over some components of the policy advice that the Fund has offered in trying to resolve crises (as discussed in the next chapter).

Part of the reason that policymakers fail to follow good advice is that policies that would be beneficial for countries over the medium run and reduce the risks of crises often involve short-run costs that are politically difficult for national authorities to impose.[79] Indeed, in countries that are

---

[76] The report of the Independent Evaluation Office (2003b) notes that IMF surveillance pointed to financial sector weaknesses as sources of concern but did not sufficiently appreciate the large currency depreciations that might occur, the severe balance-sheet effects that might result, and hence the magnitude of the macroeconomic risks posed by financial sector weaknesses.

[77] As noted by Crow et al. (1999), this was particularly problematic in the case of Korea, where fiscal and current account deficits—the traditional vulnerability signals—were both relatively modest. Thailand also disguised the depleted state of its foreign exchange reserves, but the Fund, on the basis of other indicators, had begun to urge the Thai authorities to adjust policies at least a year in advance of the July 1997 crisis.

[78] The Indonesian and Malaysian crises took the Fund and most of the economics profession largely by surprise, mainly because both countries got caught in the contagion of the Thai crisis and their major sources of vulnerability were nontraditional—that is, financial sector weaknesses rather than large macroeconomic imbalances. As suggested in the previous paragraph, however, these are cases in which the Fund can be faulted for not paying more attention to financial sector vulnerabilities.

[79] In evaluating the effectiveness of Fund surveillance over four selected countries that went into crisis (Brazil, the Czech Republic, Indonesia, and Korea), Crow et al. (1999: 7)

heading for trouble, sound policy advice often involves a tightening of fiscal or monetary policies.[80]

How can the incentives of policymakers be changed to make them less inclined to pursue policies that are beneficial in the short run but costly over the medium run? One approach would be to strengthen the leverage exerted on countries by the international community—either directly or indirectly through financial markets. Consideration of this approach raises two additional questions. Does the Fund have adequate leverage to push its policy recommendations? And does the Fund need stronger incentives to use its leverage?

In reality, the Fund can usually exert significant leverage over the policies of countries that rely on it for financial assistance, but it does not have much direct leverage over the policies of other members. Thus, in a majority of cases, the Fund lacks the means to directly pressure member countries to adjust their policies. The industrial countries last made use of Fund credit in the mid-1980s, and over the past decade the Fund has had financial arrangements in place with no more than 40 percent of its other members at any point in time.[81]

Several indirect approaches can be used for trying to influence policies in countries that do not have a need for financial assistance. One approach relies on peer pressure, which the Fund can exert by virtue of the fact that its Executive Board represents its 184 member countries as a group and speaks for the international community. A second approach is to work toward establishing a closer relationship between the soundness of national policies and the interest rate premiums and other conditions that countries face in international financial markets—that is, to try to make it more costly or difficult for countries with unsound policies to borrow from private financial institutions. This approach involves efforts

judged that "the single most important factor limiting Fund impact was a difficult internal political situation."

[80] Drazen (2000b, Chapter 10) provides an analytical treatment of the various reasons that national authorities may fail to adopt socially beneficial policies.

[81] The number of arrangements in place at the end of the Fund's financial years peaked at sixty-two on April 30, 2001 and fell to forty-eight on April 30, 2004; see IMF (2003c, Table II.2) and www.imf.org. Of the forty-eight arrangements, eleven were SBAs, two were arrangements under the EFF, and thirty-five were arrangements under the Poverty Reduction and Growth Facility. Recall that an arrangement reaches completion (ceases to be in place) when disbursement of the final installment of credit has been approved; thus the number of arrangements in place does not correspond to the number of countries with outstanding debt to the Fund.

to keep private financial market participants better informed about countries' economic policies and performances, about their compliance with various standards and codes for the government and the financial and corporate sectors, and about the Fund's risk assessments and recommendations for policy adjustment. As noted in Chapter 3, the initiatives to strengthen Fund surveillance since the mid-1990s have given considerable emphasis to making relevant information available to market participants on a timely basis, and to increasing transparency about the Fund's assessments of members' policies and policy institutions.[82] Moreover, there is now some evidence that a country's compliance with standards and codes affects the spreads and credit ratings that it faces in international financial markets.[83] A third approach is to condition a country's eligibility for future financing from the Fund on the track record it establishes in strengthening institutions and market structures and in pursuing sound macroeconomic policies. This type of ex ante conditionality has been advocated by a number of economists[84] and is discussed further in Chapter 8.

The initiatives undertaken since the mid-1990s, including the major push for greater transparency, can be viewed as an effort to strengthen the Fund's indirect leverage over policies in member countries. A separate issue is whether the Fund has been making effective use of the direct leverage it already has.

If the Fund has been ineffective in trying to prevent crises, it is not for lack of the backbone to provide early and candid warnings to national authorities. In some cases, the failure to provide early warnings can be attributed to the fact that national authorities have not provided adequate information to the Fund on a timely basis. Indeed, as already noted, several of the countries that experienced major crises during the past decade concealed relevant information about reserve holdings or external debts until very late in the game; and a number of initiatives to address such

---

[82] The Fund has periodically wrestled with and rejected the idea of issuing public warnings when it believes a country is headed for serious trouble; see Fischer (2001c: 68). Like the early warning signals generated from econometric models, a practice of issuing summary evaluations would undoubtedly be prone to both Type 1 and Type 2 errors (i.e., issuance of unwarranted warnings and failure to issue warranted warnings). However, this does not argue against providing market participants with frank and transparent descriptions of the Fund's multidimensional assessments and policy advice.

[83] See Christofides et al. (2003).

[84] See for example, the Meltzer Commission (2000), Jeanne and Zettelmeyer (2001), and Kenen (2001).

problems have been launched since the mid-1990s. These cases aside, however, the perception from inside the Fund is that the "private dialog between the management and staff of the IMF and the officials of a country that we believe to be heading for trouble can be very frank indeed. Reporting to the Board is also typically very frank."[85]

It may be noted as well that, on many occasions, the Fund's policy recommendations have been followed by national authorities and have proven successful, though it is often difficult to determine whether the authorities would have arrived at the same decisions in the absence of discussions with the Fund. "[S]uccess has many parents, and since it is the authorities within the country who have responsibility for policy decisions, they rightly tend to take the credit."[86]

On numerous other occasions, however, countries have failed to heed the Fund's policy advice, leading to suggestions that the Fund has been too timid in using its direct leverage over national policies. Mussa (2002) voices such criticism with particular force in connection with Argentina's experience between 1991 and 2001—a case in which the failure to maintain consistency between the exchange rate and fiscal policy led from triumph to tragedy.

Argentina had fallen into deep recession at the end of the 1980s, experiencing financial instability that led to hyperinflation in 1990. As a major step toward addressing these problems, the Argentine government announced the Convertibility Plan in early 1991, fixing the exchange rate between the peso and the U.S. dollar and replacing the previous monetary policy regime with a currency board mechanism intended to keep the exchange rate credibly fixed.[87] These reforms, which were followed by important measures to ensure a sound banking system, achieved spectacular results. By 1993, inflation was down to low single-digit levels,

---

[85] See Fischer (2001c: 68). See also Crow et al. (1999: 6), who found that "in their own cases, member country authorities did not generally regard the Fund's bilateral surveillance advice as insufficiently frank and direct." In contrast, as noted by the Independent Evaluation Office (2003b), the public has often been kept in the dark about important concerns raised in Fund surveillance through a watering down of such concerns in documents that were intended for publication or that might be leaked.

[86] See Fischer (2001c: 69).

[87] As noted in Chapter 2, a currency-board mechanism is an institutional arrangement in which the exchange rate is fixed and the liabilities issued by the monetary authority (the monetary base) are rigidly linked to the monetary authority's holdings of foreign exchange. In general, the monetary base can only be increased through the acquisition of additional stocks of foreign exchange, which typically cover a large percent of the monetary base outstanding.

and, apart from a sharp but relatively brief recession triggered by contagion from the Mexican crisis of 1994–95, the economy grew quite rapidly through mid-1998.

Nevertheless, fiscal discipline was never established. In 1993, thanks to the earlier hyperinflation and substantial debt reduction under the Brady bond restructuring of early 1993, the ratio of government debt to GDP stood at roughly 29 percent. Five years later it had risen to 41 percent, despite GDP growth of 26 percent during the interim. The long recession that began in late 1998 then made it more difficult to rein in fiscal deficits. Sovereign debt continued to build, doubts about Argentina's ability to service its mounting debts continued to grow, new or renewed credits became progressively more difficult to obtain, and the macroeconomic situation spiraled out of control during the course of 2001. This led to the government's decision to close the banks in early December 2001, which essentially marked the end of the Convertibility Plan and the currency board arrangement.

Some of the lessons for policy remain under debate, as is discussed in subsequent chapters. In Mussa's view,

the failure of the Argentine government to maintain a sufficiently prudent fiscal policy . . . when the Argentine economy was performing well was surely a key—indeed, arguably the key—*avoidable* policy problem that ultimately contributed to the tragic collapse of Argentina's stabilization and reform efforts.[88]

However, Mussa also draws attention to the fact that Argentina's difficulties were exacerbated by the commitment to keep its exchange rate fixed against the U.S. dollar when the dollar strengthened markedly after mid-1995, and when the currency of an important trading partner depreciated significantly following the collapse of Brazil's crawling peg regime in early 1999. Argentina might have been much better able to manage the difficulties of 1999–2001 if it had decided to abandon the Convertibility Plan in 1997 or 1998, or if its labor and product markets had been sufficiently flexible to avoid the unemployment and associated fiscal costs and political pressures that an erosion of international competitiveness generally induces.

Argentina's experience does not represent a case in which the policies that led to the crisis were imposed by the Fund. Rather, both the

---

[88] See Mussa (2002: 19).

Convertibility Plan and Argentina's fiscal policies were designed and pursued by the Argentine government.

In Mussa's view, however, Argentina's ownership of its policies does not absolve the Fund from blame. Argentina was operating with financial support from the Fund throughout the period, and by failing to press hard enough and soon enough for fiscal discipline as a condition for its ongoing support, Mussa argues, the Fund committed a serious sin of omission and shares responsibility for the tragic outcome.[89] When the fiscal deficit began to exceed the ceilings set under the Fund-supported adjustment program during 1995, in the context of economic activity that proved weaker than expected because of spillover effects from the Mexican crisis, the Fund demonstrated flexibility in allowing an upward revision of the deficit ceiling. However, it did not press symmetrically for deficits well below the program ceilings during the three years of rapid recovery that began in late 1995, and it tended to cave in when deficits exceeded the ceilings:

[D]uring the period from 1995 through 1998, the deficit of the Argentine government was within the quarterly limits prescribed at the beginning of each year under the IMF-supported program less than half of the time. More than half of the time, waivers were granted for missed fiscal performance criteria, or these criteria were met but only after they had been revised upward, or the violations (at the ends of some years) were simply ignored by the Fund and effectively swept under the rug.[90]

What are the lessons for Fund surveillance? In contrast to its popular image as an institution that is overzealous in imposing fiscal austerity, the Fund can be faulted for being too lax in the case of Argentina. Mussa suggests that the internal practices and bureaucratic organization of the Fund contributes to such laxity by inducing a bias toward positive assessments of countries' economic performances and policies and a tendency to lean sympathetically toward the preferences of individual member countries.[91] This view leads to the suggestion that better mechanisms of decision making and accountability are needed:

[89] Alternatively, the Fund could have pressed Argentina to abandon its currency board and devalue, as Krugman (2002) would have advised, at least in retrospect.

[90] See Mussa (2002: 18–19).

[91] In a similar vein, the external evaluators of Fund surveillance concluded that there were "extremely strong incentives for the [Fund] staff to maintain a close relationship with country authorities" and noted that "countries tend to react badly to criticism, especially when they have difficulties." See Crow et al. (1999: 90).

mechanisms that provide more effective checks and balances to assure that decisions are made on the basis of the best possible analysis, not analysis that is biased by a desire to see things from the member's point of view; and mechanisms that provide for careful appraisal of the Fund's performance in critical cases and, when mistakes have been made, appropriately assess (in some detail) the responsibility for those mistakes.[92]

Argentina illustrates that the Fund's inherent laxity in imposing conditionality can eventually result in very high costs for the countries involved. "Even users of Fund resources must recognize that if the conditionality associated with Fund support is seen as a travesty, its value in helping to restore confidence will be seriously undermined."[93]

4.4 Concluding Perspectives

The three decades since the collapse of the Bretton Woods regime have given rise to large stocks of internationally mobile financial capital and regular international financial crises. These phenomena are not new to modern times. High levels of foreign capital stocks and fairly regular financial crises were also features of the international gold standard era. Nor are they phenomena that can easily be eliminated. As noted in Chapter 2, cross-border capital flows are difficult to control effectively, particularly after domestic financial markets have been liberalized; and even if international capital flows could be successfully controlled, the important role they play in contributing to longer-term economic growth should not be overlooked. Controls sufficiently strict to completely eliminate the prospect of international financial crises would likely reduce cross-border capital flows very substantially and be highly detrimental to prospects for sustained economic growth.

That being said, it is difficult to regard the status quo as either morally acceptable or politically sustainable. The costs of international financial crises—reflected in deep recessions and widespread economic hardship and social stress in crisis-stricken countries—are simply too high. Accordingly, the international community has been focusing on various ways to reduce the incidence and severity of financial crises within the context of a system of liberalized (or only moderately controlled) capital movements. This effort has recognized that the factors that make countries

---

[92] See Mussa (2002: 67–72).
[93] See Mussa (2002: 68).

vulnerable to crises include country-specific macroeconomic imbalances and structural weaknesses as well as various imperfections in the international financial system.

Partly as a result of the major crisis experiences of the 1990s, there is fairly wide agreement that for countries with significant involvement in international capital markets, the major types of country-specific vulnerabilities include fixed but adjustable exchange rate arrangements, high levels of short-term foreign-currency-denominated debt, weak banking and financial sectors, large fiscal deficits, high levels of short-term government debt, large current account deficits, and poor general governance. Among the seven major crisis episodes reviewed in Section 4.2—Mexico, Thailand, Indonesia, Korea, Malaysia, Russia, and Brazil—fixed but adjustable exchange rates were instrumental in all seven cases; short-term foreign-currency-denominated debts had reached high levels in four cases (Thailand, Indonesia, Korea, and Russia); banking and financial sector weaknesses created very serious vulnerability in all cases except Brazil; large fiscal deficits were major sources of vulnerability in two cases (Russia and Brazil); high levels of short-term government debt were prevalent in three cases (Mexico, Russia, and Brazil); current account deficits were large in four cases (Mexico, Thailand, Malaysia, and Brazil); and poor general governance was a source of very serious vulnerability in two cases (Indonesia and Russia).

The challenge of avoiding or correcting such country-specific vulnerabilities is largely a responsibility of individual countries. As noted in Chapter 3, however, the international community has been taking important steps to help lead and speed the way—including through the promulgation of standards and codes, the programs to assess financial sector soundness and review compliance with standards and codes, the general provision of technical assistance, and the emphasis on making more information publicly available to strengthen the incentives for countries to adopt sound policies and to move toward greater compliance with standards and codes. That being said, several of the crises experienced over the past decade, including those of Thailand and Argentina, provide support for the view that the steps taken by the international community to address country-specific vulnerabilities do not yet reflect an appropriate balance between "carrots" and "sticks," and that effective crisis prevention requires a larger tough-cop role for the IMF.

Needless to say, country-specific vulnerabilities are not solely responsible for the wave of financial crises that has washed over emerging market countries during the past decade. As elaborated in subsequent chapters, economists have emphasized various imperfections in the international financial system that can also be blamed for contributing to the buildup of vulnerabilities and for not facilitating a more rapid and less costly process of crisis resolution. Some of the imperfections are associated with weak property rights and a lack of well-defined processes for dealing with international debts in periods of economic distress. Such weak and uncertain mechanisms for protecting creditors' interests tend to bias the composition of international capital flows toward short-term foreign-currency-denominated debts, thereby contributing to the balance sheet mismatches that magnify the vulnerabilities of debtor countries. Moreover, in the absence of effective mechanisms for coordinating a country's creditors, the system lacks the ability to successfully dissuade agents from stampeding to move capital out of a country in situations in which economic or political developments raise concerns that may warrant a moderate reallocation of financial portfolios in the very short run, but that also warrant some time for policy authorities to address the fundamental sources of concern. Other imperfections arise from informational frictions. These include the fixed costs of collecting and processing information, together with factors that prevent agents from reaping the full benefits of incurring the fixed costs of assimilating information. They also include factors that distort the incentives of institutional investors, on the supply side of international capital flows, in providing and reacting to information. Another deficiency of the system is the absence of markets for contingent securities that emerging market countries could use to better insure against adverse macroeconomic shocks beyond their control—such as industrial-country recessions, commodity price shocks, or across-the-board increases in interest rate risk premia. These systemic imperfections and what can be done about them are discussed in subsequent chapters, especially Chapter 8.

5

The Effects of Crises and Controversies
Over How to Respond

This chapter considers the effects of financial crises and the issue of how to respond. It focuses first on two common and troublesome patterns in international capital flows: sudden stops, in which large volumes of capital inflows are followed by sharp reversals (Section 5.1), and contagion, in which a financial crisis in one country triggers substantial financial market turbulence or crises in other countries (Section 5.2). These phenomena can be attributed to a number of underlying factors, some of which reflect imperfections in the functioning of financial markets and call for reforms of the international financial system. The chapter next considers various controversies over how crisis-stricken countries and the international community should respond to financial crises, along with related criticisms of the IMF's policy advice. The topics covered include controversies about choices of exchange rate arrangements, appropriate monetary and fiscal policy responses, and the extent to which the IMF should require countries to implement structural reforms as a condition for financial assistance (Section 5.3), as well as controversies about the moral hazard that may be generated by the practice of providing IMF bailout loans (Section 5.4). After discussing the controversies, the chapter turns to lessons from the relatively successful adjustment policies pursued by Korea (Section 5.5), followed by concluding perspectives (Section 5.6).

5.1 The Sudden Stop Phenomenon

As described in Chapter 4, international financial crises are characterized by massive efforts to shift financial capital out of claims on countries that come to be regarded as vulnerable to debt payment problems, or to other macroeconomic or political developments that would lead creditors to suffer losses. Such episodes have often been preceded by a number of years of substantial net capital inflows. The turnaround can be triggered by domestic economic or political events, or by changes in the external environment. The triggering event sometimes generates only a small initial shift in market sentiment and a small initial response of capital flows. However, such initial developments tend to feed on themselves as capital flight intensifies concerns about prospective debt payment problems and capital losses, which in turn induce additional capital outflows that can snowball into a major rush for the exits.

Table 5.1 shows annual data on net private capital flows and real GDP growth for selected crisis-stricken countries during periods starting three years before and ending three years after the outbreak of each crisis. As one can see in the top panel, the crises were characterized by substantial reversals or declines in net private capital inflows in all cases except Brazil (recall also Figure 4.1). Shifts in net private capital flows from the year before to the year after the outbreak of crisis ranged from about 7 percent of GDP for Mexico, Korea, and Russia to 14 percent of GDP for Malaysia and 25 percent of GDP for Thailand. The relatively large declines over relatively short periods have led Calvo (1998) and others to refer to these events as sudden stops.[1]

A tragic feature of international financial crises is that they do not simply affect the financial institutions, firms, and individuals that have taken on debt or provided credit. Rather, the emerging market crises of the past decade—despite large-scale financial rescue packages from the international community—have had pervasive adverse effects on jobs, incomes, wealth, and living standards throughout the crisis-stricken countries, as well as in whatever other economies got caught in the contagion. The large reversals in capital flows have been reflected in sharp declines in output, high unemployment, and major adverse impacts on the plight of the poor. As indicated by the lower panel of Table 5.1, from the year before the crises to the year after, real GDP growth declined by 8 percentage points in Mexico, 13 percentage points in Korea, more than 15 percentage points in Thailand and Malaysia, and more than 20 percentage points in Indonesia. In Russia, GDP growth turned sharply negative during the crisis year but rebounded strongly thereafter, thanks to a sharp rise in

---

[1] The term *sudden stop* was introduced to the literature by Dornbusch, Goldfajn, and Valdes (1995). Analogously, Kindleberger's (1978) classic work on manias, panics, and crashes emphasizes the pronounced and often sudden reversals in market sentiment toward the assets involved.

TABLE 5.1. Capital flow reversals and output losses

	Crisis year, T	T−3	T−2	T−1	T	T+1	T+2	T+3	Change between T−1 and T+1
		Net private capital flows as a percent of GDP							
Mexico	1994	6.5	6.8	8.6	4.6	1.4	4.0	3.9	−7.2
Thailand	1997	8.2	13.0	10.5	−9.4	−14.3	−4.8	−6.4	−24.9
Indonesia	1997	3.9	6.2	6.3	7.1	−3.0	−9.2	−7.9	−9.3
Malaysia	1997	1.4	8.2	10.2	2.4	−3.8	−9.0	−6.5	−14.0
Korea	1997	2.7	2.1	4.2	−4.7	−2.8	3.4	2.2	−7.0
Russia	1998	2.5	−3.3	1.8	−0.3	−4.8	−6.3	−3.3	−6.6
Brazil	1998	4.3	4.4	3.0	3.5	4.0	5.0	3.5	1.0
		Real GDP growth rate in percent							
Mexico	1994	4.2	3.6	2.0	4.4	−6.2	5.2	6.8	−8.1
Thailand	1997	9.0	9.2	5.9	−1.4	−10.5	4.4	4.6	−16.4
Indonesia	1997	7.5	8.2	8.0	4.5	−13.1	0.8	4.9	−21.1
Malaysia	1997	9.2	9.8	10.0	7.3	−7.4	6.1	8.6	−17.4
Korea	1997	8.3	8.9	6.8	5.0	−6.7	10.9	9.3	−13.4
Russia	1998	−4.1	−3.6	1.4	−5.3	6.3	10.0	5.0	5.0
Brazil	1998	4.2	2.7	3.3	0.1	0.8	4.4	1.4	−2.5

Note: For net private captial flows, a positive sign indicates an inflow.
Source: IMF, *World Economic Outlook.*

world oil prices. In Brazil, which did not experience a reversal of net private capital flows, real GDP growth slowed considerably but remained positive.

The emerging market crises of the past decade are frequently referred to as *capital account crises*. Consistently, in developing frameworks for analyzing how such crises begin and spread, economists have gravitated toward focusing on large reversals in capital flows as a key phenomenon that drives many other aspects of the macroeconomic adjustment process.[2] Because the balance of private capital flows is equal—under balance of payments accounting definitions, and ignoring errors and omissions in measurement—to the current account position (i.e., the balance of trade in goods and services) plus the change in official holdings of foreign

[2] See, for example, Calvo (2003).

exchange reserves minus any increase in official liabilities to nonresidents, changes in net private capital flows are often associated with either current account adjustment or changes in official reserve holdings. Furthermore, because current account adjustment is greatly facilitated by exchange rate adjustment and difficult to achieve rapidly without either exchange rate adjustment or the introduction (modification) of trade restrictions, it is typical for sudden stops in capital flows to be accompanied by some combination of exchange rate adjustment and a change in reserves.[3]

The channels through which large reversals of capital inflows lead to collapses in output and employment are well known. A net withdrawal of financial capital curtails the availability of credit for purchasing the imported materials and intermediate goods that are necessary to produce output in the short run and for financing the investments needed to sustain output over the medium run. Moreover, in an economy that depends on financial intermediaries to provide domestic working capital, the curtailment of external credit to one group of economic participants can raise concerns about the balance-sheet positions of domestic financial intermediaries and impair the financial system's ability to continue to attract domestic savings and provide domestic working capital to support the output and incomes of other economic participants. Furthermore, in a Keynesian world, declines in output, incomes, and investment are exacerbated through multiplier effects.[4]

What makes countries susceptible to sudden stops? As discussed in Chapter 4, susceptibility depends on a number of factors (recall Table 4.2). Among these, high and growing levels of public or external debts can be major sources of vulnerability, particularly when much of the debt is short term and denominated in foreign currencies.

---

[3] As noted in Chapter 4, much of the empirical analysis of international financial crises defines a crisis event as an episode for which a weighted average of the change in the exchange rate and the change in foreign exchange reserves exceeds some threshold level.

[4] The factors contributing to the output collapse are mutually reinforcing and difficult to disentangle. A survey of 1,200 Thai manufacturing firms in late 1997 and early 1998 ranked the increase in input costs (resulting from exchange rate depreciation) and weak demand as the two leading reasons that firms reduced their production levels, with the high cost of capital and lack of access to credit ranked third and fourth; see Dollar and Hallward-Dreimeier (2000). One would presume, however, that lack of access to credit was a major factor for those small and medium-sized businesses that had traditionally relied on the fifty-five Thai finance companies that were shut down in August 1997 (recall Chapter 4, Subsection 4.2.2).

Economic theory does not provide much guidance on optimal debt–GDP ratios.[5] The convergence target established by the Maastricht Treaty as a criterion for joining the Euro Area—an upper limit of 60 percent of GDP—seems to have gained some status as a norm for the public debts of industrial countries. In that context, Fischer (2002) suggests that "if a 60 percent debt ratio is an appropriate upper limit for an industrialized country, the limit for most developing countries should be significantly lower, say around 40 percent."[6] In addition, the IMF (2003c) and Reinhart, Rogoff, and Savastano (2003b) suggest that, for emerging market countries on average, 35 to 40 percent is a prudent upper bound for ratios of external debt to GDP (see Chapter 7).

Rules of thumb may be useful as rough guidelines, but a country's ability to service its debt depends on future outcomes for many economic variables and other factors, and one cannot judge debt sustainability by simply comparing debt—GDP ratios with such suggested threshold values. The challenge of assessing debt sustainability is discussed in Chapter 7, but the pitfalls of relying on simple guidelines can be inferred from Table 5.2, which provides data on precrisis levels of public and external debts. In three of the selected crisis-stricken countries—Mexico, Korea, and Brazil—the stocks of both public debt and external debt were no greater than 35 percent of GDP at the start of the crisis year. Nevertheless, debt was becoming more difficult to sustain in each of these cases. Mexico was allowing a large current account deficit to persist, and it was increasingly indexing short-term debt to the U.S. dollar in an environment of rising dollar interest rates. Korea was encountering the bankruptcies of a number of highly leveraged industrial conglomerates, which threatened the solvency and debt-servicing capacities of its financial institutions. Brazil was plagued by a large fiscal deficit. And both Korea and Brazil were caught in the contagion from financial crises in other countries.

Although these experiences illustrate that debt sustainability can become a problem even when debt levels are relatively low, high levels of debt are particularly troublesome. Accordingly, it is relevant to ask why some

---

[5] As McKinnon and Pill (1997) implicitly emphasize, the optimal ratio of external debt to GDP depends on whether capital'inflows are used productively; in their view, some emerging market countries have at times allocated capital so poorly that the inflow may have reduced GDP growth rates.

[6] See Fischer (2002: 5). Among other things, Fischer's opinion takes account of the fact that the interest rates paid by emerging market countries are both higher and more variable than those paid by industrial countries.

TABLE 5.2. Public and external debts before selected crises

	Crisis year, T	Debt at end of year T−1	
		Public debt	External debt
Mexico	1994	30.9	32.7
Thailand	1997	14.5	59.8
Indonesia	1997	23.2	53.4
Malaysia	1997	50.0	38.4
Korea	1997	8.8	31.6
Russia	1998	52.4	41.3
Brazil	1998	35.2	24.8

Note: Public debt is total domestic and external holdings as percent of GDP. External debt is total private and public holdings as percent of GDP.
Source: IMF, *World Economic Outlook* (see September 2003 issue, Chapter 3, for background on the public debt data).

emerging market countries and their creditors have allowed high external debt ratios to develop. From the perspective of the debtors, part of the answer is that countries opened themselves to international capital flows without first putting in place sound prudential frameworks for supervising and regulating financial markets and collecting and monitoring data on external debt. Moreover, the authorities of some countries (Thailand and Korea) pursued policies explicitly designed to channel capital inflows through the banking system, which resulted in stocks of external debt that had relatively short maturities.

From the perspective of creditors, one possible explanation of the buildup of large holdings of emerging market debt, as alluded to in Chapter 4, is that investors perceived emerging market governments to be providing implicit guarantees for both the banking system and their (de facto fixed) exchange rates. Such perceptions, along with relatively high interest rates on emerging market debt, would presumably have led creditors to anticipate returns that looked very attractive relative to what they could expect to earn on other investments.[7]

[7] Dooley (2000a, 2000b) argues that the high output costs that debtor countries can expect to suffer if they renege on their implicit guarantees adds further to the perceived credibility of the guarantees and the inducement to capital inflows; see also Bulow and Rogoff (1989a). As a related point, Calvo et al. (1993, 1996) argue that surges in capital inflows to developing countries tend to be particularly prevalent when industrial-country interest rates are relatively low, other things being equal.

A second line of explanation of creditor behavior focuses on the role of informational imperfections in contributing to both surges in capital inflows and subsequent sharp reversals, and perhaps also to the phenomenon in which financial crises spread contagiously from one emerging market country to another (as discussed in the next section). As emphasized by Calvo and Mendoza (2000a, 2000b), there are fixed costs of collecting and processing the information relevant for assessing country risks, and there are limits on short positions that prevent investors from reaping the full benefits of assimilating costly information in states of the world in which doing so would require large short positions. The interaction of these factors provides incentives for market participants to become "divided between a small set of informed specialists and a sea of largely uninformed investors who either are clients of the specialists, mimic their behavior, or trade blindly on the basis of their prior distributions of asset returns."[8] This distinction between informed and uninformed investors is consistent with anecdotal evidence on the prominence of *herding behavior*, in which many investors take positions on the basis of what market leaders recommend or are observed to do, and *momentum strategies*, in which investors trade on the basis of recent price trends, buying assets whose prices have been rising and selling assets whose prices are on a downtrend.

As further perspectives on the incentives to invest with the herd rather than incur the costs of collecting and processing information, Calvo and Mendoza (2000b) emphasize that asymmetries in the remuneration structures of portfolio managers, under which below-average returns are penalized more heavily than above-average returns are rewarded, strengthen the incentive for investors to imitate each other. (Such distortions on the supply side of international capital flows are discussed in Chapter 8.) They also note that it is generally attractive to diversify portfolio positions through investments in many countries, given that country returns are less than perfectly correlated, so that the gain from assimilating information at a fixed cost—and thus the incentive not to follow the herd—declines

---

[8] See Calvo and Mendoza (2000a). Although such a division of market participants is standard in finance theory (see Grossman and Stiglitz, 1980, and Gennotte and Leland, 1990), the signal-extraction approach introduced by Calvo (1999) assumes that the uninformed extract information from noisy information about specialists' trades rather than information about prices.

with an increase in the number of countries where wealth can be invested (hence with globalization).[9]

A number of contributions to the literature have focused on the role of imperfect information without drawing sharp distinctions between informed and uninformed investors. No economic agent has perfect information about future policies, or about the prospective outcomes for the macroeconomic variables that it is relevant to consider when making investment decisions. Informational imperfections arise not only because facts are costly to obtain and evaluate but also because "[s]ome of the relevant 'data,' such as whether a government will follow through on reform and maintain its commitment to monetary and fiscal discipline, are unavoidably based on opinion and conjecture as much as hard evidence."[10] The lack of perfect foresight and perfect policy credibility provides portfolio investors with strong incentives to hold a relatively high proportion of their claims on emerging market countries in the form of short-term maturities denominated in foreign currencies, thereby contributing to the balance-sheet mismatches of emerging market countries.[11]

Debates in academic forums have sometimes cast implicit guarantees and informational imperfections as competing explanations for the large capital inflows to emerging market economies. A more appropriate view is that both phenomena have probably contributed importantly to the buildup of large investments in emerging market debt.

Similarly, although different conceptual models of currency crises or capital flow reversals are often cast as competing explanations, a more appropriate view is that different models emphasize different aspects of economic behavior, many of which may provide valid and complementary insights into the types of behavior and behavioral constraints that contribute to capital flow reversals. Thus, models that emphasize the role

---

[9] It may be noted, however, that greater portfolio diversification can lead to higher correlations. Indeed, Mauro, Sussman, and Yafey (2002) find that correlations between spreads on emerging market sovereign bonds were significantly highly in the 1990s than during the 1870–1913 period, and that it is difficult to attribute the entire change to an increase in cross-country correlations of economic fundamentals. The authors conjecture that much of the explanation lies in the change in institutional arrangements for investing in emerging markets—in particular, the decline in the prominence of individual investors and the rise of institutional investors that, among other things, hold more diversified portfolios.

[10] See Eichengreen (1999b: 3).

[11] See Jeanne (2003).

of herding behavior or momentum trading in contributing to currency crises should not be regarded as necessarily competing with models that emphasize the role of balance-sheet mismatches. The former models provide a framework for explaining why markets tend to overreact to various shocks, whereas the latter models (recall Chapter 4, Section 4.1) emphasize that balance-sheet mismatches contribute to the strength of capital flow reversals regardless of whether markets overreact to shocks. In reality, herding behavior and balance-sheet mismatches presumably reinforce each other in exacerbating the strength of capital flow reversals.[12]

The imperfect functioning of international financial markets has various implications for policy. Among other things, the presence of informational frictions and the prevalence of sharp reversals in capital flows provide a rationale for international financial institutions or creditor-country governments to serve as a safety net or lender of last resort by standing ready to provide funds to crisis-stricken countries.[13] In addition, the tendency of investors to rush for the exits once market sentiment starts to shift, and the devastating output costs that can be associated with sudden and widespread withdrawals of capital, point to the desirability of debt resolution mechanisms that can lead to better solutions for both crisis-stricken countries and investors as a group. Coordination mechanisms that eliminate or mitigate the incentives for investors to rush for the exits can buy time both for countries to make transparent their commitments to sound policies and for investors to collect and evaluate relevant information. In principle, accordingly, well-designed coordination mechanisms provide a vehicle for substantially reducing the severity of international financial crises for both debtor countries and creditors as a group. In practice, however, the effort to design and reach international agreement on such mechanisms poses major challenges, as discussed in Chapter 8.

---

[12] That being said, some of the distinctions between different conceptual models do reflect fundamentally competing views of the world. As noted by Mendoza (2002a), for example, many models of currency crises have the feature that credit constraints are always binding along the economy's equilibrium path, which distinguishes them fundamentally from models that account for abrupt output collapses as an atypical phenomenon nested within more regular business cycles. See Calvo (2003) for a model of the latter type, in which growth is a negative function of the debt burden and can switch discontinuously from high to low as the debt burden crosses a critical threshold.

[13] See Fischer (1999), Jeanne and Wyplosz (2003), Corsetti, Guimaraes, and Roubini (2003), and references therein on the case for an international lender of last resort, which is also discussed briefly in Chapter 8.

All in all, the important insights gained from recent contributions to the conceptual literature on currency crises have provided economists and policymakers with a broad understanding of the roles of implicit guarantees, informational imperfections, and inadequate coordination mechanisms in contributing to large reversals in capital flows. In that connection, a number of economists have argued that policymakers in the major creditor countries have tended to attribute the blame for financial crises disproportionately to the debtor countries, paying too little attention to their own responsibility for addressing deficiencies in the functioning of international financial markets, which are dominated by investors and financial institutions from their countries.[14] The widespread use of leverage in international financial markets is one of the practices that promotes the cascading of financial distress, and concerns have also been raised about the prevalence of transactions in derivatives (discussed in Chapter 7), which result in financial positions that are not reported on balance sheets and are therefore hard to monitor.[15]

Although conceptual and econometric analysis has led to an improved understanding of international financial crises, such disasters continue to occur. Moreover, as described in Chapter 8, although policymakers have taken a number of important steps to try to strengthen the functioning of the international financial system, there remain major problem areas in which policymakers and their economic advisors have not reached a consensus on what to do. This makes it all the more important for the conceptual literature to continue to pursue the challenge of obtaining a deeper understanding of the nature of financial market imperfections and how policy can effectively address them.

[14] See Radelet and Sachs (1998) and Dobson and Hufbauer (2001).

[15] Some implications of leverage and derivatives (e.g., options contracts) are described by Eichengreen (1999b: 164), who lists the following aspects of the scramble for cover and its contagious effects during the Asian crisis: the collapse of East Asian asset values and the fall of the Nikkei led already distressed Japanese banks to call in loans; once asset prices began to fall, hedge funds and other investors who had purchased emerging market securities on margin were forced to sell into a falling market, and the further the market fell, the more frequent the margin calls became; when Moody's downgraded the sovereign debts of Thailand, Korea, and Indonesia to below-investment-grade status, many portfolio managers were required to liquidate their holdings of these securities, and the assumption that sovereign debts are less risky than those of corporate and financial issuers then turned the latter into junk bonds as well; and a number of bond contracts contained provisions that gave creditors the option to call for immediate repayment in the event of downgrading.

5.2 Contagion

Experience over the past decade has created a widely held impression that international financial crises have a tendency to spread from one country to another. This tendency—particularly apparent following the 1994–95 crisis in Mexico, the 1997 crisis in Thailand, and the 1998 Russian crisis— has led to a literature on contagion.[16]

Economists have not reached consensus on either a precise definition of contagion or the most meaningful way to explore its presence, nature, and strength empirically. An early contribution by Eichengreen et al. (1996) defined contagion as existing when the probability of a crisis in one country is increased by the occurrence of a crisis elsewhere, but other studies have adopted different interpretations of the concept.[17] Some investigators have defined contagion as occurring when the volatility of asset prices spills over from the crisis country into higher volatility in other countries. Others have defined contagion as a significant increase in the co-movements across countries of asset prices and quantities (e.g., exchange rates, interest rate spreads, equity prices, and capital flows) following the occurrence of a crisis in one or more of the countries. Still others have interpreted contagion as a change in the transmission mechanism following the occurrence of a crisis, as would be reflected in an intensification of normal spillover effects or structural breaks in the data-generating process.

A synchronization or clustering of crises across different countries can have a number of possible explanations. Common global shocks—such as a change in commodity prices, a rise in U.S. interest rates (as in the run-up to the 1994–95 Mexican crisis), or a change in key-currency exchange rates (such as the appreciation of the U.S. dollar against the Japanese yen in the run-up to the 1997–98 Asian crisis)—are one type of contributing factor. Other possible explanations arise from the trade and financial linkages between countries, as well as from informational effects and political factors. Trade linkages operate through two important transmission mechanisms—income effects and relative price effects. By depressing aggregate demand, a major decline in economic activity and income in one country generally lowers its purchases of other countries' exports, thereby

---

[16] Literature surveys are provided by Pericola and Sbracia (2001); Dornbusch, Park, and Claessens (2000); and Kaminsky, Reinhart, and Vegh (2003).

[17] See the discussion and references in Pericola and Sbracia (2001).

also depressing economic activity elsewhere. In addition, a change in one country's exchange rate (or relative price level) generally tends to affect exports and economic activity in other countries with which it competes in producing for either own markets or third markets. Financial linkages also provide two channels through which shocks in one country can be transmitted internationally. These include wealth effects, whereby changes in one country's wealth influence its desired asset holdings in other countries, and market illiquidity, whereby significant losses in one market force highly leveraged investors to withdraw from other markets in order to meet margin calls and other demands for liquidity. Still other channels for contagion include informational imperfections that result in market participants failing to discriminate adequately among different countries based on fundamentals; wake-up calls, whereby a crisis in one country affects investors' expectations and perceptions about common structural conditions and vulnerabilities in other countries[18]; and political factors, whereby the prospective spillover effects operating through nonpolitical channels (e.g., trade and financial linkages) change the political calculus of national authorities and lead forward-looking market participants to speculate on exchange rate adjustments.[19]

Significant evidence of contagion has been found by a number of econometric studies, but without pinning down the relative importance of the different transmission channels (see Box 5.1). The anecdotal evidence makes it reasonable to presume, however, that common shocks, trade linkages, and financial linkages have all played important roles in the contagious propagation of crises. In addition, the anecdotal evidence strongly suggests that contagion isn't random but rather tends to strike countries with relatively large macroeconomic imbalances, financial sector weaknesses, or other vulnerabilities.[20]

Along with establishing the existence of contagion and investigating the channels through which it occurs, the literature has explored the questions of why contagion occurs in some cases but not in others, and why the contagion from some emerging market crises tends to be confined to countries in the same region of the world whereas in other cases contagion

---

[18] Summers (2000) regards wake-up calls as a particularly important channel for contagion in the crises of the 1990s, and Goldstein (1998) asserts its importance in the spread of the Asian crisis.

[19] See Drazen (2000a).

[20] See Kenen (2001: 70).

BOX 5.1. Selected econometric studies of contagion

Using quarterly data for the period 1959–93, Eichengreen et al. (1996) searched for evidence of contagion among twenty industrial countries. To identify crises, the authors used an index of exchange rate market pressure, measured as a weighted average of changes in a country's exchange rate, short-term interest rate, and stock of international reserves. They then constructed a dummy variable—equal to one when the index exceeded some threshold and zero otherwise—and estimated a probit model with various macroeconomic and political fundamentals included as independent variables. Their estimates suggested that a currency crisis elsewhere in the world increased the probability of a domestic currency crisis in the same calendar quarter by 8 percentage points, which was statistically significant. They also found evidence that international trade linkages tend to increase the magnitude of the contagion effect.

The approach used by Eichengreen et al. has stimulated a number of other studies. Among these, an investigation by Kaminsky and Reinhart (2000)—using the same definition of contagion, a broadly analogous definition of crises,[1] and monthly data for both industrial and developing countries over the period 1970–98–finds evidence that susceptibility to contagion is highly nonlinear. A single country in crisis is not a particularly good predictor of crises elsewhere, but the probability of crisis in any one country rises sharply with the number of other countries in crisis. Moreover, unlike Eichengreen et al., Kaminsky and Reinhart devote considerable attention to financial linkages along with trade linkages, noting that most countries that are linked in trade are also linked in finance, and conclude that it is difficult to pin down econometrically the relative importance of the two types of linkages in explaining contagion. Van Rijckeghem and Weder (1999) make essentially the same points in analyzing the transmission of spillover effects following the Mexican, Thai, and Russian crises. In particular, they note the high correlation of financial and trade linkages and find econometrically that financial linkages are almost always significant in explaining contagion when trade linkages are excluded, and vice versa.[2]

---

[1] Kaminsky and Reinhart excluded the interest rate change from their exchange market pressure index because many of the countries in their sample had regulated financial markets with no market-determined interest rates.

[2] Among more recent studies, Rigobon (2003) proposes new techniques for dealing with some of the methodological problems that can arise in econometric investigations, and Bayoumi, Fazio, Kumar, and MacDonald (2003) suggest a test that circumvents the problems.

also spreads to other regions. On the first question, anecdotal evidence suggests that episodes of fast and strong contagion tend to occur when the countries involved have common leveraged creditors.[21] On the second question, econometric evidence suggests that contagion tends to spread globally only when it affects asset markets in the world's financial centers; in particular, extreme equity price changes in one emerging market country tend not to be associated with extreme equity price changes in emerging markets in other regions of the world unless they are also associated with extreme equity price changes in the world's financial centers.[22]

The anecdotal evidence also suggests that contagion has been partly attributable to "wake-up calls." In particular, market commentary lends support to the views that the contagion observed after the Thai crisis to a large extent reflected an awakening of market participants to the risks implied by weak financial sectors, and contagion after the Russian crisis reflected an awakening to new information about the rules of the game regarding official bailouts. Market participants may well respond rationally to the information they have, but that does not imply that they are aware of all facts relevant to the decisions they make; and both the Thai crisis and the Russian default focused market participants on important new information.

5.3 Controversies Over the Macroeconomic and Structural Policy Responses

The official community's responses to the financial crises of the past decade have generated considerable controversy. In the Mexican case, the main controversy was over the size of the financial bailout package, which far exceeded the scale of previous rescue efforts. In the Asian crisis cases, strong controversies arose over the monetary, fiscal, and structural policy measures that countries were asked to implement as conditions for financial assistance from the Fund. This section discusses controversies over exchange rate arrangements, interest rate policies, fiscal adjustment, and the extent to which countries were required to take structural policy

---

[21] See Kaminsky et al. (2003).

[22] See Kaminsky and Reinhart (2003), who analyze daily changes in equity price indexes for thirty-five industrial and emerging market countries from January 1997 through August 1999.

actions as part of the conditionality attached to IMF lending. The next section turns to controversies over the scale of crisis lending.

5.3.1 Exchange rate arrangements

The Second Amendment of the Fund's Articles of Agreement gives countries the right to choose from among a wide variety of exchange rate arrangements.[23] That right has been respected by the Fund's Management and Executive Boards, which have generally accepted the choices of member countries; however, the Fund has the power to put countries seeking its financing under considerable pressure to avoid exchange rate arrangements that are widely regarded as unsustainable.[24]

The financial crises of the past decade have led most international economists to conclude that soft forms of fixed exchange rate arrangements—that is, fixed rate arrangements that can be overwhelmed relatively easily by speculative pressure—have been a major source of vulnerability for countries with substantial involvement in international capital markets. The distinguishing feature of soft arrangements is that the commitment to keep the exchange rate fixed is simply a statement by the policy authorities rather than a statement reinforced by institutional arrangements that would be hard to change. Consistently, expert opinion has shifted to the view that, abstracting from cases of high inflation, emerging market countries should either allow their exchange rates to fluctuate over fairly wide ranges or make hard commitments to fixed exchange rates. A hard commitment to a fixed exchange rate can be made either by adopting a currency board or by replacing the national currency with a major foreign currency as legal tender (e.g., "dollarizing" or "euroizing" the economy).

One danger of soft forms of fixed exchange rates is that a lack of exchange rate variability in normal times can foster complacency about exchange rate risks, contributing to a buildup of balance-sheet positions with currency mismatches as well as (other) unhedged commitments to

---

[23] Countries are required to keep the Fund informed of their exchange arrangements and are expected to reveal any intended changes when they apply for financial assistance.

[24] As an example of the Fund's respect for its members' right to choose, Mussa (2002) emphasizes that the IMF accepted Argentina's desire to establish a currency board in the early 1990s despite considerable skepticism about its desirability and sustainability. Similarly, as Blustein (2001) notes, in approving the December 1998 SBA for Brazil, the IMF accepted the Brazilian authorities' unwillingness to devalue or speed up the rate of crawl.

buy or sell foreign exchange, and leaving economic agents vulnerable to exchange rate adjustments that policymakers might subsequently come to regard as desirable. A related danger is that unless a country lets its exchange rate adjust at the first signs of emerging macroeconomic imbalances, forward-looking market participants may well begin to develop concerns about the sustainability of the (explicit or implicit) commitment to the exchange rate—at least in cases in which maintaining the exchange rate implies a drain of the country's foreign exchange reserves—and, in the absence of a very credible commitment to address macroeconomic imbalances through means other than exchange rate adjustment, such concerns can snowball into a currency crisis.

A soft exchange rate peg was one of the sources of vulnerability in each of the seven major crises cases reviewed in Chapter 4. In five of the cases, the pegs had collapsed before the countries requested assistance from the Fund.[25] In the other two cases—Russia and Brazil—the Fund was lending to help defend an exchange rate peg that had initially been adopted as part of a successful disinflation program; and in both of these cases, the pegs ultimately collapsed. In all seven cases the countries involved did not have much desire to try to establish new exchange rate pegs in the near term, so the choice of exchange rate regime was not a contentious issue.

The subject of exchange rate regimes is discussed at greater length in Chapter 7, but several additional points deserve emphasis here. First, the views of the Fund staff generally coincide with views that are widely held among the economics profession more broadly, which include the recognition that different exchange rate arrangements are appropriate for different types of countries, and that different arrangements may also be appropriate for the same country in different types of circumstances.[26] Among the wisdom gained from experience is the realization that an exchange rate anchor—more specifically, a commitment to a crawling exchange rate peg or band—can be very helpful for stabilizing from high inflation, but that such a commitment can be very risky without an exit strategy.[27]

---

[25] This includes the case of Malaysia, which never requested the Fund's assistance.

[26] See Mussa, Masson, Swoboda, Jadresic et al. (2000) for a description of prevailing views.

[27] See Fischer (2001c: 60). As Eichengreen (1999b) notes, the accepted wisdom on exiting from a fixed exchange rate regime is to do so before capital stops flowing in—that is, while the pressure is still for appreciation rather than depreciation. See also Eichengreen, Masson, Bredenkamp, Johnson et al. (1998) and Eichengreen, Masson, Savastano, and Sharma (1999).

The second point is that financial crises are not limited to countries with soft forms of fixed exchange rates. Crises can also occur under flexible rates, and, as demonstrated by Argentina's experience in recent years, even currency-board arrangements are not immune.

A third point, also illustrated by Argentina's experience with a currency board, is that the hardness of an exchange rate arrangement depends on other structural features of the economy. During 1995, in the wake of contagion from the Mexican crisis, the Fund negotiated a program that helped Argentina successfully defend its currency board. By 2001, however, the same currency board was no longer very hard in the sense that Argentina's commitment to defend it had lost much of its credibility, even in the context of ongoing and large-scale financial support from the international community. The loss of credibility, and the ultimate collapse of the currency board in December 2001, can be linked to a lack of political support within Argentina for the public sector wage adjustments and other fiscal austerity measures that would have been necessary to correct large and growing macroeconomic imbalances without exchange rate adjustment. Thus, as Argentina's experience underscores, the adoption of a currency board, or even the dollarization of an economy, does not by itself establish an exchange rate arrangement that market participants will automatically expect to remain sustainable over a long horizon. Real wage flexibility, especially in the public sector, and public support for other large fiscal adjustments when needed, appear to be very important preconditions for the sustainability of currency boards and dollarized economies.[28]

5.3.2 Interest rate policies

As a prerequisite for financial support from the IMF, crisis-stricken emerging market countries were generally pressured to raise nominal interest rates significantly at the outset of their adjustment programs. This so-called high interest rate prescription was allegedly the most controversial aspect of the Fund programs for the Asian emerging market countries.[29]

---

[28] See Calvo (2001). It is interesting to observe in this connection that Hong Kong's currency board is supported by the province's flexible labor markets, as well as by its extreme openness to international trade, a highly internationalized banking system, and a monetary authority that is insulated from political pressures; see the discussion in Eichengreen (1999b).

[29] See Fischer (2001c: 28).

Opponents argued that high interest rates typically generate recessions, emphasizing among other things that business failures can significantly increase the volume of nonperforming loans on the books of domestic financial institutions and cause them to curtail lending, and strongly suggesting that the high interest rate prescription was an important factor in weakening the economies and contributing to the high human costs of the crises.[30] One critic emphasized that the orthodox prescription for dealing with economic slumps is to lower interest rates and characterized the high interest rate policy as "a break with, even a betrayal of, a sort of deal that capitalism and its economists made with the public two generations ago."[31]

The Fund was very aware that high interest rates repress consumer demand and are damaging to businesses. However, it also faced the reality that financial institutions and corporations had taken on obligations to service large amounts of debt denominated in foreign currencies, and it was highly concerned that substantial currency depreciation—which would considerably increase the real burden, measured in domestically produced goods, of servicing and repaying foreign currency debts—could undermine the viability of the business and banking sectors, which would also be damaging to the economy.[32] The underlying premise was that high interest rates were needed to restore the attractiveness of holding domestic currency and to thereby arrest the capital outflow and reduce the extent of exchange rate depreciation. A related concern was that inflation could become a serious problem unless the currency was stabilized. Furthermore, in the Asian cases, by the time that the adjustment programs were being negotiated and the Fund and national authorities were weighing the costs of higher interest rates against the costs of currency depreciation, significant currency depreciations had already taken place. As noted by Fischer (2001c), raising interest rates was the traditional way of defending a currency, and experience in dealing with the Mexican crisis had reinforced the view that a high interest rate policy worked. Moreover, it seemed reasonable to assume that—provided the adjustment programs were viewed as sufficient to reestablish macroeconomic sustainability—interest rates would only have to be high temporarily to stem the capital outflows and restore confidence, and could then be reduced. This proved to be the case in both Korea and Thailand.

[30] See Furman and Stiglitz (1998), and Feldstein (1998).
[31] See Krugman (1998).
[32] See Fischer (2001c: 29).

The Fund has characterized the monetary policy prescriptions in its programs for the crisis-stricken Asian countries as trying "to walk a narrow line, seeking to resist downward pressure on the exchange rate while avoiding a crippling effect on the real economy."[33] It has also responded to critics by arguing that the data on real interest rates and money and credit suggest that monetary policy was not as tight as the critics seemed to think.[34] It has not denied that monetary tightening had a cost for the real economy, arguing that the alternative would have been more costly.

A key analytic point—essential for understanding the policy debate—is that the prevalence of large debts denominated in foreign currencies, particularly if the foreign currency debts have a large short-term component, can fundamentally alter the set of feasible outcomes for external and internal stability. Prior to the currency crises of the 1990s, it was traditional to base macroeconomic policy prescriptions on the paradigm of a simple trade-off between external and internal balance. In some countries, monetary policies were oriented primarily toward achieving stable economic growth with low inflation, with the recognition that moving interest rates up and down in pursuit of internal stability might exacerbate the variability of exchange rates and current account balances, other things being equal. In other countries, interest rate policy was oriented primarily toward stabilizing exchange rates, which could also serve to keep inflation low but was generally expected to be accompanied by greater variability in economic growth rates.

This traditional paradigm has now lost much of its relevance for emerging market countries and most of the major industrial countries—at least in times of financial market turbulence. As noted earlier, in the aftermath of the Summer 1992 European currency crisis, a new paradigm has emerged that recognizes the phenomenon of self-fulfilling or self-justifying speculative attacks. This paradigm emphasizes that a loss of confidence in a country's ability or willingness to prevent currency depreciation, however triggered, can produce an economic crisis that justifies the loss of confidence, and, for countries with large debts denominated in foreign currencies, also has large adverse effects on domestic economic activity, as elaborated in the next paragraph. Thus, in contrast to the traditional

[33] See Boorman et al. (2000: 31).
[34] See Lane, Ghosh, Hamaan, Phillips et al. (1999), and Boorman et al. (2000).

view that interest rate policy could be used to maintain either internal balance or external balance, the new paradigm suggests that interest rate policy will succeed in stabilizing neither the exchange rate nor domestic economic activity unless it succeeds in sustaining confidence in the currency.

The forces that cause a small loss of confidence to snowball into major downward pressures on foreign exchange reserves and the exchange rate are easy to understand in countries that have large short-term foreign-currency-denominated debt obligations or large unhedged commitments to make foreign currency payments for international trade transactions. In particular, with a large and inelastic demand to exchange domestic currency for foreign currency in the short term, a rush for the exits (herding) can be a rational form of behavior: a small shift in sentiment that leads some market participants to cover their foreign currency needs early can trigger a rush by other rational market participants to try to purchase foreign currency before the country's official reserves are depleted or the exchange rate moves adversely. Similarly, with large and inelastic demands for foreign exchange in the short run, it is not surprising that the currencies of crisis-stricken countries depreciated very substantially once they were set free to float.[35] Furthermore, because the effects of large capital flow reversals on credit availability and the costs of servicing existing debts sharply curtailed the ability of firms to finance production and investment, with associated sharp declines in output, many loans that looked reasonable before the crises suddenly became nonperforming afterward, thereby making the crises (or capital flow reversals) self-justifying. In Krugman's (1998) view, "whatever the sins of the Asian economies, it's important to understand that most of what [became] wrong with them is the consequence, not the cause, of their crisis."[36]

These points notwithstanding, the premise that high interest rates at the outset of Fund programs were necessary to maintain or reestablish confidence and to thereby mitigate capital flow reversals and currency depreciation remains an unsettled issue. Neither conceptual analysis nor empirical research has been helpful for resolving the debate. As Furman

---

[35] Kenen (2002a) emphasizes this point.

[36] In support of this view, Krugman (1998) estimates that a scaling up of Thailand's capital account reversal to the size of the U.S. economy would show net inflows of foreign investment of roughly $200 billion annually for a number of years followed by a net outflow of $1 trillion.

and Stiglitz (1998), Corden (1999), and others have noted, because an increase in interest rates has a contractionary effect on domestic demand, the extent to which it can succeed in moderating exchange rate depreciation is ambiguous in theory.[37] Interest rates sufficiently high to lead to deep recessions, domestic bankruptcies, and social unrest can erode market confidence about the government's ability to maintain macroeconomic stability, thereby further intensifying the desire to move capital out of the country and the associated downward pressure on the exchange rate. As an empirical question, moreover, there exists "exactly zero convincing evidence" on the effect of interest rates on the exchange rate, "forcing both the Fund and its critics to rest their cases on arguments rather than statistics."[38]

That being said, responsible economists advising crisis-stricken countries cannot ignore the fact that, by themselves, low interest rate policies are not conducive to rebuilding the confidence and creditworthiness that is necessary for continuing to attract the domestic savings and foreign capital needed to support production and investment. As Krugman (1998), Eichengreen (1999b), and Kenen (2001) have all noted, when a country has a large stock of foreign-currency-denominated debts and markets lack confidence in the country's ability to service its debts, the pursuit of a low-interest policy in hopes of stimulating domestic recovery can easily lead to a further erosion of confidence, steep currency depreciation, and thus an intensification of debt-servicing difficulties—unless the government suspends debt payments and imposes comprehensive capital controls. This

---

[37] See Jeanne and Zettelmeyer (2002) for formal models in which balance-sheet effects render monetary policy ineffective in offsetting adverse shifts in exchange rate expectations and protecting the economy from self-fulfilling crises with real costs.

[38] See Eichengreen (1999b: 112). See Kraay (2003) for an empirical study, Boorman et al. (2000) and Kenen (2001) for summary perspectives on the empirical literature, and Lahiri and Vegh (2002) for an analytical framework suggesting that the relationship between interest rates and exchange rates is inherently nonmonotonic. In a consistent manner, the report of the Independent Evaluation Office (2003b: 16) concludes that the experience of Indonesia, Korea, and Brazil "does not provide a definitive answer to the ongoing debate on the effectiveness of high interest rates in stabilizing the exchange rate." In contrast, Berg, Jarvis, Stone, and Zanello (2003) tabulate evidence from ten crisis cases—the seven discussed in Chapter 4 plus Bulgaria (1997), Ecuador (2000), and Turkey (2001)—and infer (p. 11) that "[t]he countries that floated and were most successful at ending quickly the period of volatility were those that tightened monetary policy early and sharply and that did not ease monetary policy until stability had been clearly restored.... Typically after an initial spike, nominal interest rates returned to pre-crisis levels or below in only a few months."

essentially raises a second question: should countries continue to allow capital to flow so freely? This issue is addressed in Chapters 7 and 8.

5.3.3   Fiscal adjustment

When the Fund makes adjustment loans to countries facing external financing difficulties, the conditions attached to the loans typically call for a tightening of fiscal policy. Sometimes fiscal tightening is prescribed as a direct response to high and potentially unsustainable levels of debt. Sometimes the justification is that the country's balance of payments deficit reflects an overheated economy, and that fiscal contraction is a sensible way to reduce excess aggregate demand. For several of the major financial crises of the 1990s–in particular, Mexico, Russia, and Brazil—the prescription of fiscal tightening was generally viewed as highly appropriate. By the same token, Argentina's failure to follow the Fund's prescription for fiscal tightening is widely viewed as one of the key factors that contributed to the crisis that erupted in 2001 (recall the discussion in Chapter 4).

The Fund also prescribed fiscal tightening in the initial programs it negotiated for Thailand, Indonesia, and Korea. In those cases the justification was less clear cut and the prescriptions elicited strong criticism. The Fund soon recognized and acknowledged the validity of the criticism and acted within a few months to modify the programs.

Fischer (2001c: 25–8) provides perspectives on both the thinking behind the fiscal prescriptions in the Asian crisis cases and on how the Fund adjusted its prescriptions over time. In the initial (August 1997) program for Thailand, the first of these cases to come to the Fund, fiscal tightening was prescribed for two reasons: to address the large current account deficit and to provide room for absorbing large anticipated fiscal costs of cleaning up the financial system. In addition, the prescription was conditional on a forecast that substantially overestimated the strength of aggregate demand and underestimated the degree to which imports would contract—errors common to virtually all official and private forecasts made at the time. By the end of October, when a Fund mission was sent to Thailand to conduct the first review of the program, it had become clear that aggregate demand and the current account deficit were contracting much more sharply than had previously been anticipated, and the mission was told to revise the program to let automatic stabilizers work and allow the fiscal deficit to widen.

The Indonesian and Korean cases also involved programs that initially called for moderate fiscal tightening but—as the macroeconomic outlooks deteriorated and outside criticism mounted[39]—were soon revised to allow for fiscal deficits. "By early 1998, . . . and through most of the rest of the crisis the Fund found itself in the unaccustomed position of criticizing the failure of the governments concerned to make deficits as large as targeted."[40] The fact that the Fund has acknowledged the errors in its initial fiscal policy prescriptions for the Asian crisis countries provides reason to believe that the same type of mistake will not be made again.

It is hard to know how much damage was caused by the initial fiscal tightening. Although the Fund realized its mistakes and adjusted its programs in a matter of months, it is generally accepted that macroeconomic crises develop in highly nonlinear and path-dependent manners.[41] Whether the initial fiscal tightening contributed significantly to the loss of confidence and rush for the exits is debatable; to the extent that it did, however, it would be misleading to suggest that the adverse effects of the initial tightening were substantially offset by the subsequent actions to reverse it.[42]

In a related but separate criticism of the Fund's fiscal policy prescriptions, Corden (1999) focuses on alternative possible uses of Fund credit and the trade-off between supporting fiscal stimulus and bailing out creditors. In his view, and consistent with the Fund's purpose of providing countries with "opportunity to . . . [avoid] measures destructive of national or international prosperity," the limited funds available from official institutions "should be used not for rescuing foreign creditors—nor for financing capital flight—but for financing compensating fiscal expansion."[43] A somewhat analogous opinion is that scarce foreign exchange should

---

[39] As with many other policy issues, there was also a vigorous debate within the Fund over the fiscal policy prescriptions, both among the staff and among Executive Directors.

[40] See Fischer (2001a: 27–8). Neither Thailand, Korea, nor Indonesia made full use of the room for fiscal expansion allowed during 1998 under the Fund programs, and Malaysia's budget outturn was also less expansionary than expected; see Boorman et al. (2000: 53).

[41] Sachs (2003a) emphasizes this point.

[42] The Independent Evaluation Office (2003a: 16) concludes that the initial fiscal tightening was not the cause of the output collapse in either Indonesia or Korea, the two Asian cases that it evaluates. The Independent Evaluation Office (2003b) provides a more extensive examination of the Fund's fiscal policy analysis and advice based on a large sample of programs and detailed studies of fifteen specific cases.

[43] See Corden (1999: 59).

be used to provide credit for exporting, which can have expansionary effects similar to fiscal measures. Such views, like the stand against high interest rate policies, implicitly presume that crisis-stricken countries would be willing to resort to capital controls and suspensions of debt payments (issues addressed in Chapters 7 and 8), and that the IMF and other official creditors would support such an approach.

5.3.4   Structural policies and the scope of conditionality

Are countries pressured to satisfy too many conditions as prerequisites for financing from the Fund? Does the Fund impose policy advice in areas where it has little expertise, or on issues that are unrelated to countries' macroeconomic problems? Is the Fund guilty of ignoring the social consequences of its policy advice? These questions lie at the heart of debates over the appropriate nature and scope of IMF conditionality.

Discussions of IMF conditionality often distinguish between macroeconomic policies and structural policies, where the latter refer to policies aimed at "either improving the efficiency of resource use or increasing the economy's productive capacity."[44] Structural policies are generally designed to reduce or dismantle government-imposed distortions or to put in place or strengthen various institutional underpinnings of a market-oriented economy. Such policies encompass, inter alia, the liberalization of restrictions on trade, capital flows, and foreign exchange transactions; the restructuring of taxes and fiscal expenditures; measures to reduce or eliminate wage and price rigidities and other labor and product market distortions; privatization and public enterprise policies; measures to strengthen the education system and improve public health; unemployment insurance, pension plans, and other social safety net policies; measures to strengthen financial sector institutions, corporate governance, and the prudential framework; and environmental policies.

Over the years, structural policy conditionality has become a much more significant component of Fund-supported economic stabilization programs. Part of the impetus came from developing countries in the 1970s, when it was argued that Fund programs were oriented too much toward demand management and short-run issues and paid too little

[44] See Goldstein (2003c: 366).

attention to the supply side and the medium-run prospects for economic growth. This led to the establishment of the Extended Fund Facility (EFF) in 1974, with the requirement that programs under the EFF must have a structural orientation. Attention to structural policies increased substantially further in the late 1980s and early 1990s, when the former Soviet bloc collapsed and the Fund was called on to design programs to help approximately two dozen central and eastern European countries make the transformation from centrally planned economies to market-oriented systems. The transformation process required countries to plan and prioritize an extensive list of structural changes, encompassing reforms of the price system, the fiscal sector, the financial sector, the trade and payments system, and the social security system, as well as a program for privatization.[45]

When the IMF produces tables or charts showing the number of conditions in its programs, it normally refers to the aggregate number of prior actions, performance criteria, and structural benchmarks.[46] Recall from Chapter 3 that prior actions are measures that must be taken as preconditions for approval of an adjustment program, whereas performance criteria apply to clearly defined measures that can be monitored objectively and that must be implemented within a specific time frame as conditions for continued credit drawings under the program. A structural benchmark comprises either a critical action that cannot be specified in terms that can be monitored objectively or an action that is intended to serve as a marker in assessing progress on critical structural reforms but for which nonimplementation would not, by itself, warrant an interruption

---

[45] The Fund and the World Bank were in positions to provide expert advice in a number of these areas, and in many countries the national authorities solicited and valued such advice. In such cases, it seemed desirable to make an intentional effort to help guide the process by providing each of the relevant economic agencies in the country with a prioritized list and suggested timetable for several structural adjustment measures. This at least was the strategy underlying the first IMF adjustment program for Lithuania, which I had the opportunity to help design in 1992. Accordingly, relevant structural measures were identified and prioritized in consultation with the national authorities, and the Fund also consulted closely with the World Bank in areas where the Fund had less expertise. Although the Fund sometimes required that one or more of the structural adjustment measures be completed as prior actions for the first installment of financial assistance, and identified several others as performance criteria or benchmarks that had to be met to qualify for future installments, the majority of the structural measures were regarded as actions planned by the government but not part of the formal conditionality of the programs.

[46] See IMF (2001b, 2002b).

of the scheduled disbursements of Fund financing.[47] To monitor the observance of performance criteria and structural benchmarks, the Fund conducts program reviews, normally every six months, and more frequently when there are substantial uncertainties about major economic prospects or policy implementation. When a country fails to meet a performance criterion, continued access to Fund financing requires a waiver from the Executive Board, which is typically granted if the delay or nonimplementation is not seen as overly detrimental to attaining the program's objectives or if adequate compensatory measures are taken. From that perspective, the choice of whether to list a critical structural policy action as a performance criterion or a benchmark does not necessarily make much difference for the implementation of the program, and in the past the Fund's practices have varied across programs and over time.[48]

Along with the three components of formal conditionality, IMF programs often include indicative targets for those segments of a program for which there is too much uncertainty to establish performance criteria. Variables for which indicative targets are specified at one stage of a program are often established as performance criteria at subsequent stages after uncertainty about economic trends has been reduced. In addition, prior to the decision to limit conditionality to measures of critical importance and the establishment of new guidelines for conditionality in 2002, Fund programs sometimes included lists of other structural measures that had no formal conditionality attached but that the Fund staff monitored and reported to the Executive Board when the programs were reviewed.

The Fund's programs for the crisis-stricken Asian economies included much larger numbers of structural measures than the norms that had emerged in programs for the transition economies.[49] On average, Fund

---

[47] Although delays in the implementation of individual benchmarks do not necessarily hold up the release of scheduled Fund financing, delays in a substantial number of benchmarks can lead the Executive Board to hold up disbursements.

[48] The Korea program included twenty-one structural performance criteria (an average of seven per year) along with a substantial number of structural benchmarks, whereas the programs for Thailand and Indonesia relied primarily on structural benchmarks. A few examples of measures that were listed as structural performance criteria in the May 1998 Letter of Intent for Korea, but that presumably would have also qualified as structural benchmarks, are: "Allow foreign banks and brokerage houses to establish subsidiaries," "Complete assessment of the recapitalization plans of commercial banks," and "Require listed companies to publish half yearly financial statements prepared and reviewed by external auditors in accordance with international standards."

[49] In this connection, Goldstein (2003c: fn. 22) notes that one of Russia's programs with the Fund may have included even more structural policy measures than the Asian programs.

SBAs for twenty-five transition economies over the 1989–97 period included thirteen structural policy conditions, whereas EFF arrangements for six transition economies over the same period included twenty-three.[50] By contrast, the number of structural policy measures in the IMF programs for crisis-stricken Asian countries reached peaks of 140 for Indonesia (in April 1998), 94 for Korea (in November 1999), and 73 for Thailand (in May 1998).[51]

The number of structural measures in the Asian crisis cases was strongly and widely criticized. Critics generally regarded the number of measures as excessive and questioned whether they were all important to the success of the programs. Some contended that the Fund's push for far-reaching structural reforms undermined the effort to restore confidence and stem the capital outflow by leading panicky investors to form exaggerated assessments of the severity of the structural problems, or to attach excessively low probabilities to the prospect that countries could meet the performance criteria and avoid an interruption of official financial assistance.[52] A related concern was that overly onerous programs could discourage adjustment efforts by the crisis-stricken countries and lead other countries to avoid or delay coming to the Fund for assistance. A third line of criticism was that the Fund lacked the expertise, and was overstepping its mandate, in a number of the structural policy areas.

It was also charged that some of the structural measures were politically motivated and represented an abuse of the power of the IMF and its largest member countries. In that regard, Feldstein (1998: 32) claimed that several features of the IMF plan for Korea were

replays of the policies that Japan and the United States have long been trying to get Korea to adopt. These included accelerating the previously agreed upon reductions of trade barriers to specific Japanese products and opening capital markets so that foreign investors can have majority ownership of Korean firms, engage in hostile takeovers opposed by local management, and expand direct participation in banking and other financial services.

Fischer (2001c: 34) notes that the inclusion of large numbers of structural measures in the Russian case was "intended to support an extensive program of structural reforms that our Russian counterparts hoped to implement in driving forward the faltering Russian reform process, intended to change the entire economic system."

[50] See Goldstein (2003c, Table 5.6), which is based on Mercer-Blackman and Unigovskaya (2000).

[51] See Goldstein (2003c, Table 5.5).

[52] See Feldstein (1998) and Radelet and Sachs (1998). See also the discussions in Goldstein (2003c) and Kenen (2001).

In Feldstein's view, the selection of specific reforms to include in an IMF program should be based on three questions. Is the reform really necessary to restore access to international capital markets? If the reform is a technical matter, does it interfere unnecessarily with the proper jurisdiction of a sovereign government? And would the Fund think it appropriate to impose a similar reform on a major industrial country?

Most of these criticisms elicited strong counterarguments. Concerns that the large number of structural measures exacerbated investor panic were countered in part by the view that the crises did not simply reflect liquidity problems. With financial sector weakness widely perceived as a major contributing factor, there seemed to be a strong case for addressing the structural weaknesses of the crisis-stricken Asian countries. In that connection, Fischer (2001c) pointed out that the structural policy measures in the programs for Thailand, Korea, and Indonesia largely involved financial sector conditions that "generally related to recapitalizing or closing bankrupt institutions, ensuring that equity holders took their losses, marking down assets and in some cases transferring those claims to other institutions, and deciding what to do with deposit claims."[53] In addition, the Indonesian program contained a number of structural measures that were related to governance—that is, corruption—such as ending the clove and plywood monopolies. Inclusion of these conditions reflected a belief that restoration of investor confidence required strong signals of a change in "the way of doing business in the country."[54] More generally, the focus on governance problems in Fund programs reflected the view that the Fund should not, and cannot afford, to lend money to a government that will not use it to address its country's problems effectively.

As counterarguments to other criticisms of the scope of the Fund's structural conditionality, it has been noted that the Fund does not have the leverage to apply meaningful conditionality ex ante, and that a Fund program represents the best chance that countries may have to make real progress in addressing structural weaknesses.[55] Moreover, with regard to the Fund's mandate and competency, the world has come to adopt an increasingly expansive view of the range of structural policies and institutions that are important for achieving macroeconomic goals, and the IMF has developed considerable expertise in dealing with financial sector issues

[53] See Fischer (2001c: 35).
[54] See Fischer (2001c: 34).
[55] See Geithner (2003).

and draws heavily on the World Bank and other international financial institutions in designing and monitoring structural policy conditionality in areas where it lacks expertise.

Although the Fund has now built up expertise in dealing with financial sector issues, some critics have argued that its approaches to restructuring the financial and corporate sectors in the Asian crisis cases contributed to the erosion of confidence and the depth of the crises. Some of these critics focus on issues of timing, agreeing with the need to address financial sector weaknesses and even close many banks over a three-year or five-year horizon, but objecting strongly to the closure of a significant number of financial institutions in the middle of a fragile situation.[56] The counterargument is that markets would not have been reassured by an IMF message that there was nothing to worry about, given the bad news that was emerging each day about the state of financial systems.[57] In Goldstein's view, the overriding challenge in resolving a crisis is

convincing market participants both that the structural weaknesses that played such a key role in motivating the crisis have permanently changed for the better and that the overhang of short-term debts of banks and corporations can be resolved in a satisfactory and reasonably expeditious way.[58]

Goldstein also regards the decision of how many banks to close in a crisis as a judgment call. A key objective is to convey the impression "that all the bad banks have been resolved, and that the ones remaining open are solid."[59] As noted by Fischer (2001c), moreover, there is a clear perception, fed by Japan's experience over the past decade, that unless financial sector difficulties are dealt with up front, they will almost certainly be detrimental to the restoration of confidence and the resumption of healthy macroeconomic performance.[60]

Beyond considerations of timing, a number of basic issues about the strategy for financial and corporate sector restructuring remain under

[56] See Sachs (2003a).
[57] See p. 357 of the "Discussion Summary" following Krueger (2003a).
[58] See Goldstein (1998: 37).
[59] See Goldstein (1998: 36). Citing Mussa, Goldstein notes the experience of the United States in 1933, when 7,000 of the nations 25,000 banks were closed in conjunction with other major policy actions, and the strongest cyclical recovery in U.S. history began a month later.
[60] As a related point, Dziobek and Pazarbasioglu (1997) studied twenty-four countries that experienced systemic bank restructurings and found that the countries quickest to act generally experienced the best recovery patterns.

considerable debate among experts in policymaking institutions and the academic and supervisory communities.[61] This makes it difficult to judge the extent to which the Fund's approaches may have contributed to the erosion of confidence and the depth of the crises in the Asian cases. On the basis of the discussion in Chapter 4, however, it seems reasonable to fault the Fund in the Indonesian case but not in the cases of Thailand and Korea. The initial program for Indonesia did not reflect a clear and decisive strategy to deal with bank runs, whereas the Thai program, in contrast, was preceded by actions to close insolvent finance companies and issue a comprehensive guarantee of deposits in the financial institutions that remained open. Moreover, in the Korean case, in which the authorities moved rapidly to address the country's structural problems, output bottomed out after two quarters and recovered sharply over the next two years (see Section 5.5).

Regarding the number of structural measures that countries have been pressured to accept, the Fund has admitted that some of its programs have been overloaded[62] and has moved in recent years to narrow the scope of its conditionality. Under revised guidelines adopted in September 2002, structural conditions are to be included only when they are regarded to be of critical importance for achieving the goals of the program, monitoring its implementation, or complying with specific provisions of the Fund's Articles of Agreement.[63] Whether the Fund's new guidelines will in fact result in a substantial streamlining of Fund conditionality will depend to some extent on whether they are effective in insulating the Fund from the various types of political pressures that member countries and public interest groups can exert. As Goldstein (2003c: 431) emphasizes,

[in part,] streamlining and improving Fund structural policy conditionality is about Fund management saying "no" more often than in the past—to requests for Fund assistance where the expectation is low that the country will actually implement Fund policy conditions, to G-7 governments when they propose new tasks for the Fund that go beyond the Fund's core competence, to NGOs that seek to use a country's Letter of Intent with the Fund to advance agendas (even if desirable) that lie outside the Fund's mandate and comparative advantage, and to

[61] See Hoelscher, Quintyn, et al. (2003) for Fund views on managing systemic banking crises. See also Dziobek and Pazarbasioglu (1997), Stone (2002), and Claessens, Klingebiel, and Laeven (2003) for perspectives on financial restructuring of the banking and corporate sectors.

[62] See Fischer (2001c: 36).

[63] See IMF (2002b).

developing-country finance ministries that want to use micro conditions in Fund programs to impose spending discipline on other government ministries that could not be obtained via their national legislatures.

It is well known, as alluded to indirectly by Feldstein (1998), that some of the structural measures included in the Korean and Indonesian programs resulted from pressures exerted by G-7 governments during program negotiations—pressures that would appear to have violated Article XII, Section IV of the Fund's charter, which requires members to "refrain from all attempts to influence any of the [Fund] staff in the discharge of [their] functions."[64] It is also a reality that the Congress of the Fund's largest shareholder—which has the power to block quota increases and other actions requiring parliamentary ratification in countries holding an 85 percent supermajority of the Fund's voting power—has enacted laws requiring the U.S. Treasury to instruct the U.S. Executive Director to the Fund to "vigorously promote" a long list of structural policy measures in IMF country programs and to send Congress regular reports on the actions taken to comply with such legislative mandates.[65] As Geithner (2003: 442) notes,

[t]he erosion of the traditional internationalist center in the U.S. political spectrum has left... [the U.S. administration and the Fund] more vulnerable to the demands of a coalition on the right and left, the price of whose support has been an escalating set of demands, on the one-hand for market-oriented reforms and liberalization and on the other hand for social equity and core labor standards.

Even so, the bulk of the structural measures in the Asian crisis programs cannot be attributed to political pressures from G-7 governments or other outside interest groups. Moreover, as Geithner suggests, the scope of structural conditionality is less worthy of concern than the major disagreements within the economics profession over the basic strategy of Fund programs for crisis-stricken countries. In particular:

The lack of consensus in the economic profession about the appropriate macro policy response to a confidence crisis in an economy with a healthy fiscal position but a terribly weak banking sector is fundamentally troubling. The extent of the debate within the Fund, between the Fund and the World Bank, and among the

---

[64] See Goldstein (2003c: 424). See also Blustein's (2001) description of the Fund's negotiations with Indonesia.

[65] See, for example, United States Department of the Treasury (2002).

experts in the supervisory community about the appropriate degree of forbearance and about strategies for intervention, recapitalization, resolution, and asset disposal in banking systems undergoing systemic failure is highly problematic and caused very damaging delays in the recent cases.[66]

There is also the issue of whether Fund programs give too little weight to the social costs of adjustment policies, or to the impacts on the poor. Several perspectives seem relevant here. First, virtually all Fund programs pay attention to safety nets. This includes attention to the overall fiscal consequences of existing social safety nets as well as some attention to possible modifications that would address country-specific needs. In some cases, attention focuses on strengthening the safety net from a social perspective, such as providing for the development of unemployment insurance schemes or pension systems in countries that previously had none. Although such measures might be included in Fund programs, their design and implementation would generally draw on the World Bank or other sources of expertise.[67]

That being said, most countries in need of Fund programs have fiscal imbalances that have to be addressed, which casts the Fund in the unenviable role of proposing ways to reduce the scope and cost of social safety nets. This might involve measures to rationalize the pension system, or to reduce the fiscal burden of popular subsidies that hold down the prices of necessities such as rice, bread, cooking oil, or energy. To a large extent, the degree of fiscal austerity built into a Fund program ultimately reflects the amount of financing that the international community is willing to make available. Thus, the view that Fund programs, as a matter of equity, should involve more financing and less adjustment is appropriately directed at the major creditor countries rather than the Fund staff and management. The choice of how to impose a given degree of fiscal austerity typically raises issues involving both intracountry equity and economic efficiency. Although it would be inappropriate for the Fund to impose its views on the equity aspects of these matters, it would also be inappropriate for the Fund to neglect the efficiency aspects. Accordingly, Fund programs often reflect compromises on issues involving subsidies.

---

[66] See Geithner (2003: 442).

[67] The program for Indonesia continued subsidies to prices of rice and cooking oil; the Thai program included public works spending to employ the poor; and the program for Korea focused on developing an unemployment insurance scheme. See Fischer (2001c: 35).

5.4 The Issue of Moral Hazard: Controversies Over Crisis Lending

Some critics of IMF programs have charged that large-scale lending, although helpful for restoring confidence and resolving financial crises in the short run, has the undesirable consequence of making countries more prone to crises over the longer run—the so-called moral hazard effect. By contributing to expectations that countries in financial crises will receive bailout loans, so the argument goes, the IMF encourages borrowers and lenders to behave in ways that make such crises more likely.[68] Through their effects on the incentives of both private financial market participants and policy authorities, prospects of bailouts can promote excessive risk taking, unproductive investment, and wasteful government spending, and they can also weaken the incentives for emerging market countries to maintain sound macroeconomic policies and undertake desirable structural reforms.

The term *moral hazard* is widely used in the literature on insurance, where it refers to the notion that the provision of insurance reduces the incentives for insured parties to take preventive actions, thereby raising the likelihood that the event being insured against will occur. It is accepted wisdom in the insurance literature that moral hazard is indeed a real world phenomenon, but that this does not preclude the case for insurance. Fire insurance is generally regarded as a socially beneficial product, even if its availability causes some people to be less cautious with matches. Similarly, crisis lending may be socially desirable even if its prospect induces more risky behavior and weakens incentives for implementing sound macroeconomic and structural policies. In general, the case for crisis lending depends on the degree to which its adverse consequences are outweighed by the benefits of financial rescue efforts. Moreover, as discussed later, recent contributions to the literature include proposals for improving the trade-off between the benefits and costs of crisis lending.

Standard insurance contracts provide transfer payments to insured parties when specified types of adverse events occur. Some economists have contended that international bailout loans involve analogous transfers to the bailed-out countries, with the burden ultimately falling on taxpayers in the IMF's creditor countries. A common view is that "[w]hat really

---

[68] Proponents of this view include Calomiris (1998b), Goldstein (1998), and Meltzer (1998).

happens is that the U.S. ends up subsidizing the IMF's growing practice of making large loans at low interest rates to very risky economies . . . and U.S. government money comes from taxpayers."[69]

This view is inconsistent with the evidence to date. As noted in Chapter 3, the repayment record on official international lending to emerging market countries—as distinct from highly indebted poor countries (HIPCs) with little access to international financial markets—has been very strong in the aggregate.[70] Moreover, the strong repayment record by the emerging market countries has not been a matter of gimmickry. Although repayment periods have been extended in some cases, the IMF has not been avoiding default by repeatedly relending, nor is there any apparent evidence that IMF loans have been repaid largely with funds borrowed from other official sources. Although the past is not necessarily a good predictor of the future, for cases in which crisis lending has gone hand in hand with the implementation of sound economic recovery programs, the repayment of IMF loans has not yet been a problem.[71]

The fact that official international bailout lending has not imposed a burden on taxpayers in creditor countries does not imply that it has not created moral hazard in the form of excessive risk taking by private international lenders or emerging market borrowers. To the extent that official bailout loans are eventually repaid with interest, however, the burden of any moral hazard associated with official bailout lending is ultimately borne either by private creditors or by the residents of the debtor countries.

With regard to contentions that the prospect of official crisis lending contributes to excessive risk taking by private financial market participants, there is strong anecdotal evidence that the precedent of large-scale crisis lending to Indonesia and Korea in late 1997 and early 1998 gave investors confidence that Russia would receive similar assistance. Indeed, investors who poured money into Russian GKOs (treasury bills with high interest rates) prior to mid-August 1998 actually referred to their investments as a "moral hazard play." It is also clear, however, that the Russian

---

[69] See the *Wall Street Journal* editorial column, April 23, 1998, as cited by Jeanne and Zettelmeyer (2001).

[70] See Jeanne and Zettelmeyer (2001), and Rogoff (2002a).

[71] A separate indication that significant burdens have not been imposed on creditor-country taxpayers can be found in the U.S. Treasury's reports to Congress on the "Financial Implications of U.S. Participation in the International Monetary Fund."

default changed investors' perceptions of the rules of the game regarding bailouts, and that in each of the financial crises of the past decade, many investors took large losses. These latter considerations provide some grounds for arguing that, whatever the motives for their past behavior, investors have presumably learned from experience and are unlikely to assume that official bailouts will generally enable them to avoid significant losses in the future.[72] At the same time, it remains important for the international community to make sure that future crisis lending is conducted in a manner that does not prevent private investors from suffering appropriate losses.

There is also the prospect that crisis lending might lead debtor-country governments to take excessive risks by weakening their incentives to implement sound macroeconomic and structural policies. Some have dismissed this possibility with arguments that policymakers generally do not welcome the need to call on the IMF, that central bank governors and finance ministers tend to lose their jobs when lax policies lead to financial crises, and that crisis-stricken countries suffer severely.[73] Others accept these points but counter that virtually all crisis-stricken countries have suffered from macroeconomic imbalances or structural weaknesses that policies did not adequately address ex ante. In that connection, one interesting proposal is to introduce prequalification requirements or ex ante conditionality for Fund lending—that is, to make the generosity of international bailouts in a crisis conditional on the quality of policies prior to the crisis.[74] Whether or not the prospect of crisis lending has weakened policy resolve in the past, linking the generosity of crisis lending in the future to the quality of policies ex ante could strengthen incentives for implementing sound macroeconomic policies and expediting structural reforms. This proposal is addressed in Chapter 8.

With regard to the overall case for international crisis lending, Mussa (1999) offers several relevant perspectives. First, it is important to understand that if the objective were to completely eliminate all instances of

---

[72] Consistently, in a study of interest rate spreads on emerging market sovereign bonds before and after August 1998, Dell'Ariccia, Schnable, and Zettelmeyer (2002) find that the "nonbailout" of Russia not only raised the general level of spreads but also increased their sensitivity to fundamentals and their cross-country dispersion.

[73] See Fischer (2001c: 41), who notes that for the six crisis cases that his study addresses—Mexico, Thailand, Indonesia, Korea, Russia, and Brazil—ten of the twelve central bank governors and finance ministers lost their jobs within weeks of the outbreaks of the crises.

[74] See Meltzer Commission (2000), Jeanne and Zettelmeyer (2001), and Kenen (2001).

moral hazard, it would be necessary to abolish national governments and central banks as well as the IMF and the World Bank. Second, the potential moral hazard directly generated by IMF bailout loans "is certainly far less than the moral hazard problems that are typically associated with interventions by national governments. The IMF gives loans that it firmly expects to be repaid."[75] Third, the solution to moral hazard concerns is to strike the right balance. International support packages are desirable to the extent that they reduce the overall economic losses suffered from financial crises. Fourth, because different financial crises are triggered by different types of events and reflect different types of underlying problems, "we cannot, should not, and do not have a system in which in every . . . [financial crisis] creditors are expected to take losses or a system in which creditors never take losses. Either would be senseless."[76]

Although such perspectives undermine some of the criticisms of official international bailout lending, there remain legitimate concerns about the size of IMF support packages and ongoing discussions, within the international financial community, of the case for burdensharing by the private sector. These issues are discussed in Chapter 8.

5.5   What Worked Best? Impressions from Korea's Recovery

Attempts to assess and compare the successes and failures of countries' crisis recovery efforts confront two major problems. The first is the difficulty of disentangling the many factors that contributed to the onset and recovery from individual crises. The second is the necessity of adjusting for the different initial conditions and external factors faced by the different crisis-stricken countries, which is particularly difficult in a comparison of crises that occurred at different times and in different regions of the world.

That being said, there is a fairly widespread impression that Korea's recovery was more successful than those of the other crisis-stricken Asian countries, and that it also compared favorably to the recoveries from the Mexican, Russian, and Brazilian crises.[77] Korea's economy bottomed out

---

[75] See Mussa (1999: 385).
[76] See Mussa (1999: 388).
[77] Collyns and Kincaid, eds. (2003), provide a much more extensive discussion, by members of the Fund staff, of the lessons that have been drawn from recent experiences of managing financial crises.

in the second quarter of 1998, two quarters after the onset of the crisis, with real GDP subsequently expanding at a 10 percent average annual rate during 1999–2000 to reach a level, according to some estimates, that slightly exceeded potential output during 2000.[78] This relatively favorable performance makes it especially relevant to consider the main factors that contributed to Korea's recovery.

Five factors stand out as particularly important elements in Korea's recovery: a strong political commitment to move rapidly in addressing the country's structural problems; an early and successful effort to reschedule the country's short-term external debts; an expansionary stance of fiscal policy, facilitated by a low initial level of government debt; a successful effort at persuading workers to accept lower wages and higher unemployment, which was instrumental in preventing the emergence of inflation following the large exchange rate depreciation; and the success in creating an environment, largely as a result of the previous factors, in which low inflation and the restoration of confidence allowed monetary policy to be eased at a fairly early stage.

The first factor—strong political commitment to move rapidly in addressing the country's structural problems—is described by Haggard (2000). Soon after the election of Kim Dae Jung as Korea's new leader on December 18, 1998, and two months before his inauguration, the new president met with the outgoing president to form an Emergency Economic Committee, comprised of six members each from the outgoing and incoming governments, that began to serve as a de facto economic cabinet under the effective control of the president-elect. Many reforms were then passed in special legislative sessions held during the transition period, including the establishment of a new Financial Supervisory Institution with substantial powers and the revision of nearly two dozen laws governing the financial and corporate sectors. The new president also met with the heads of thirty-five chaebol to outline an agreement on five principles of corporate restructuring. In addition, he convened a Tripartite Commission of labor unions, business associations, and government officials that proved effective in guiding the process of increasing the flexibility of the labor market while guaranteeing an adequate social safety net for adversely affected workers.

---

[78] See Chopra, Kang, Karasulu, Liang et al. (2002), who arrive at similar estimates of potential output by using three different techniques.

For its part, the Fund played a major role in helping to formulate a detailed plan and timetable for addressing financial and corporate sector problems, and in closely monitoring the process of structural reform. As noted earlier, the Korea program included an extensive number of structural policy measures, most of which were concentrated in the two core areas of financial and corporate sector restructuring. Following approval of the program on December 4, 1997, there were two biweekly program reviews in mid-December and early January and five quarterly reviews during 1998 and early 1999, after which the frequency of program reviews was reduced to six-month intervals. In addition to monitoring progress on well-defined structural measures, the reviews provided a vehicle for filling out the agenda in areas that were difficult to define ex ante. As noted by Chopra et al. (2002: 51), the frequent monitoring

provided an opportunity to adapt the structural reform agenda and make mid-course corrections to policies in light of developments (e.g., the tightening of regulations on provisioning for exposure to companies undergoing workouts, and defining a strategy for bank privatization). Although this sometimes meant expanding the agenda in response to emerging problems, it also allowed refocusing, with some reforms that were no longer seen as important being dropped from the agenda.

The second key factor in Korea's recovery was the early restructuring of its short-term external debts, which eliminated the specter of ongoing downward pressures on foreign exchange reserves and the exchange rate and the prospect of imminent default. The rescheduling process went through several stages.[79] On December 24, 1997, following strong pressures exerted by national authorities, a temporary agreement was reached with U.S. banks to maintain their credit lines to Korean banks at existing levels. Negotiations were then initiated on a more comprehensive rescheduling of bank debt maturing during 1998, with agreement in principle reached on January 16 followed by a longer-term restructuring agreement in March. An important factor in resolving the collective action problem and obtaining agreement was a debt-monitoring system that the Fund and the Bank of Korea set up for enforcing the agreement. Unlike in other countries, moreover, comprehensive monitoring of Korea's external debt was greatly facilitated by the facts that the debts were owed to a relatively small number of foreign banks, and that Korea had restricted its

[79] See Chopra et al. (2002: 34–5).

corporations to borrowing from domestic banks.[80] It is arguable whether the agreement can be regarded as voluntary, but ex post assessment suggests that it was creditor friendly: "[b]anks that agreed to coordinated rollovers incurred no losses, and in exchange for their claims on Korean banks received government-guaranteed claims carrying generous interest rates."[81]

Expansionary fiscal policy, facilitated by a low initial level of government debt (less than 10 percent of GDP at the end of 1996), was a third important factor. The original budget for 1998, passed in November 1997, had targeted a small fiscal surplus based on an assumption that real GDP would expand by 6 percent. By early 1998, partly in response to the sharply deteriorated outlook and partly because it had been swayed by outside criticism (recall the discussion in Subsection 5.3.3), the Fund was "urging" the Korean government to change the direction of its fiscal policy.[82] In February and March the government took measures to increase unemployment-related spending and other social safety net spending, and for the year as a whole the budget outturn was a deficit of 4.2 percent of GDP, compared with a cyclically neutral deficit of 1.5 percent of GDP.

The fourth key factor was the successful effort to reach a social accord under which workers were willing to accept lower wages and higher unemployment—an effort in which the Tripartite Commission played an important role. Because business enterprises have traditionally been the major provider of social benefits in Korea, the prospect of corporate restructuring and increased unemployment posed a significant threat to the social safety net, and workers were essentially willing to accept wage and job cuts in exchange for retraining benefits and other measures to strengthen social benefits.

A fifth factor was the fairly early easing of monetary policy, which was facilitated by the environment established through the early actions to alleviate concerns about default (through debt restructuring) and maintain low inflation (through the labor agreements worked out by the Tripartite Commission). By June 1998, about seven months after the start of the crisis, overnight interest rates (adjusted for inflation) had been brought

[80] Kenen (2001: 142) argues that, in part for this reason, the Korean restructuring could not readily be replicated in other countries.
[81] See Chopra et al. (2002: 35).
[82] See Chopra et al. (2002: 41–5).

back down to the average level that prevailed during the twelve-month period prior to the crisis.[83]

5.6 Concluding Perspectives

Events of the past decade have forced economists to continue to reexamine and refine the way they think about currency crises. As described in Chapter 4, the conceptual frameworks that had emerged during the 1970s and 1980s emphasized that, in a world of rational forward-looking market participants, a country that is expected to eventually run out of foreign exchange reserves will inevitably confront a speculative attack—in some cases well before its reserves are depleted. Thus, countries in which macroeconomic policies induce market participants to develop expectations of large and persistent current account deficits are asking for trouble. A second insight, which gained prominence during the early 1990s in the wake of the turmoil in European exchange markets, is that countries in which prevailing exchange rates imply domestic macroeconomic conditions that are politically unsustainable are also vulnerable to speculative attacks by forward-looking market participants. By the same token, in a world with large stocks of internationally mobile private funds, an adverse shift in market sentiment about the sustainability of an exchange rate can trigger large capital flows and become self-justifying, because the domestic macroeconomic costs implied by the policies required to defend against large capital flows can erode political support for such policies and force the authorities to let the exchange rate adjust.

Additional perspectives have been provided by the currency crises that have stricken emerging market countries since the mid-1990s. As discussed in this chapter, two common features of these episodes—namely, that many of the crises have been preceded by periods of large capital inflows, and that they have also been contagious, tending to spill over from one country to another—have focused economists on the major role that financial market imperfections play in contributing to crises. Among other things, these insights imply that the devastating effects of emerging market currency crises cannot be attributed entirely to unsound macroeconomic policies or weak institutions in the emerging market countries. Rather, a large share of the blame stems from deficiencies in the functioning

---

[83] See Chopra et al. (2002, Table 2).

of international financial markets, which are dominated by financial institutions and other investors from the major industrial countries. Various proposals for mitigating imperfections in the international financial system are discussed in Chapter 8.

Although the current functioning of international financial markets is a source of major concern, it is important to stay focused on the fact that countries with sound macroeconomic policies and relatively strong institutions have fared much better than countries with weaker policies and institutions. In this vein, the experience of the past decade suggests that an emerging market country that chooses to maintain a fixed exchange rate (either de jure or de facto) is particularly prone to currency crisis unless it goes to the extreme of dollarizing its economy or adopting and maintaining a highly credible currency-board arrangement.

The policies that the Fund has pressured emerging market countries to adopt in responding to attacks on their currencies have generated considerable controversy. One major source of controversy is the strong emphasis that IMF programs have placed on tightening monetary policy at the outset of a crisis. Although monetary tightening is contractionary in a country such as the United States, which conducts most of its international borrowing and lending in its own currency, the so-called balance-sheet effects of currency depreciation can also be contractionary in a country with large stocks of foreign-currency-denominated debt. Such balance-sheet effects provide the motivation for raising interest rates to try to restore confidence and arrest currency depreciation. However, as critics of the Fund's policy prescription have argued, raising interest rates may not actually have the intended effect of supporting the exchange rate if it heightens fears of recession, erodes market confidence in the government's ability to maintain economic stability, and further intensifies the desire to move capital out of the country. The effect of the interest rate on the exchange rate is thus a matter of debate, and the debate has not been resolved to date by either conceptual or empirical analysis. In short, the current state of wisdom on this issue does not extend much beyond a vague recognition that the effectiveness of a high interest rate policy in strengthening the exchange rate or, more generally, the desirability of raising interest rates at the outset of a crisis, depends on both the economy's balance-sheet structure and a number of other factors that are not clearly understood. That being said, however, it remains highly plausible—and many would say highly likely—that when markets already lack confidence in a country's ability to meet scheduled payments on its debts, a low interest rate policy aimed at stimulating economic recovery will lead to a further erosion of confidence and steep currency depreciation unless the government also suspends debt payments and imposes comprehensive controls on capital outflows.

IMF programs have traditionally called for fiscal tightening. Often this is because the balance of payments financing difficulties that have to be corrected can be attributed to overheated economies, and fiscal contraction is a sensible way to reduce excess aggregate demand. In other cases fiscal tightening is prescribed as a direct response to high and potentially unsustainable levels of government debt. Neither of these considerations was relevant for the Asian crisis countries, and the Fund's call for fiscal tightening in those cases, though reversed before many months had passed, was widely recognized as a mistake. Indeed, given that monetary policy was being tightened, many critics would have advocated an easing of fiscal policy in the Asian crisis countries. Although the Fund is not likely to repeat the same mistake in similar circumstances, history suggests that fiscal tightening will continue to be an appropriate policy recommendation for the majority of countries that request financing from the Fund. Moreover, given the experiences of Argentina, Brazil, Russia, and a number of other countries, many would argue that the Fund could make its crisis prevention efforts more effective by taking a tougher stance on fiscal deficits.

The Fund has also been strongly and widely criticized for pushing the Asian crisis countries to implement a large number of structural measures as conditions for obtaining official financing. Some have contended that insistence on far-reaching reforms fueled investor panic by creating exaggerated impressions of the severity of structural problems as well as a sense that countries would have difficulty satisfying the conditionality and therefore faced the prospect of a suspension or interruption of Fund financing. A related concern was that excessively burdensome conditions would discourage program countries from attempting to meet their performance criteria and discourage other countries from seeking the Fund's assistance. A third line of criticism was that some of the structural policy measures overstepped the Fund's mandate or fell outside the Fund's areas of competence. Yet another charge was that some of the structural measures were politically motivated and represented an abuse of power by the Fund and its major shareholders.

Much of this criticism has been strongly contested. Concerns that structural measures exacerbated investor panic have been countered with the view that each of the crisis-stricken countries suffered from serious financial sector problems, that most of the structural measures were aimed at addressing those problems, and that investors would not have received much comfort from being told that there was little to worry about when bad news about the financial sector was surfacing every day. There was a strong perception in many circles, fed by Japan's experience since the early 1990s, that unless financial sector difficulties were dealt with up front, they would almost certainly be detrimental to the restoration of confidence and the resumption of healthy macroeconomic growth. Concerns that structural measures would discourage adjustment efforts were countered with the point that the Fund does not have much leverage to overcome political obstacles to meaningful structural adjustment in normal times, and that a Fund program may represent the best chance that countries have to make real progress in addressing structural weaknesses. Concerns that the Fund was overstepping its mandate and competencies were met with the response that the world has come to adopt an increasingly expansive view of the range of structural policies and institutions that are important for achieving macroeconomic goals, that the Fund has now developed considerable expertise in financial sector issues, and that the Fund follows a practice of drawing on the World Bank and other international financial institutions on issues outside its areas of expertise.

Notwithstanding these counterarguments, the Fund has responded to the criticism by narrowing the scope of its conditionality, guided by the view that structural conditions should be included only when they are essential for achieving macroeconomic goals. Whether earlier application of such a criterion would have made a large dent in the number of structural measures included in programs for the Asian crisis countries is arguable. There is considerable support for the view that the key challenge in seeking to restore confidence and promote recovery in those cases was to convince market participants that the problems of unhealthy financial institutions were being resolved, that the financial institutions remaining open were healthy, and that the way of doing business in the country was changing for the better. Consistently, most of the structural measures in those cases were designed to resolve financial sector problems and address crony capitalism with reasonable speed in hopes of restoring confidence and thereby promoting the macroeconomic goals of the programs.

Perhaps the solution lies in reducing the extent of formal conditionality—that is, conditions that must be met to avoid an interruption or suspension of financing—without reducing the scope of the Fund's policy advice. It is worth emphasizing in this regard that for countries that genuinely seek to strengthen their institutional structures and achieve greater compliance with internationally accepted standards and codes, progress can often be greatly facilitated by having a fairly detailed plan and tentative timetable for structural actions.

Some critics of IMF programs have charged that large-scale official lending, although potentially helpful for restoring confidence and resolving financial crises in the short run, has the undesirable moral hazard effect of making countries more prone to crisis over the longer run. This contention has to be framed against the following perspectives. The first point is that official bailout loans are somewhat analogous to auto or fire insurance, which can be socially desirable even if it makes some people less cautious when driving or using matches. Point two is that the evidence on official loan repayments refutes the notion that large-scale bailouts have imposed costs on the taxpayers of creditor countries. IMF loans to crisis-stricken countries are provided at market-related interest rates, in some cases with penalty charges, and—in contrast to the IMF's concessional lending to low-income countries, which is funded out of a different pot—the repayment record to date has been very good. The third point is that the very good repayment record on official loans does not refute contentions that the practice of official bailouts leads to excessive risk taking by private international lenders or weakens incentives for borrowing countries to implement sound macroeconomic and structural policies. It simply implies that the burden of any moral hazard associated with official bailouts has been borne in the past by either private creditors or the residents of the debtor countries. Point four is that many private international investors have suffered large losses from currency crises, and those that engaged in moral hazard plays before the Russian default have learned a costly lesson. Point five is that there nevertheless remain strong concerns about the size of IMF support packages and the prospect that moral hazard may impose burdens on creditor-country taxpayers in the future, let alone the very high costs that financial crises impose on debtor countries, which may or may not be exacerbated by moral hazard. Such concerns have led to considerable attention within the international policy community to the issue of burdensharing by private creditors—a topic that is discussed in Chapter 8.

Attempts to assess and compare the successes and failures of countries' crisis recovery efforts are fraught with both the complication of disentangling the many factors that contributed to the onset and recovery from individual crises and the difficulty of adjusting for the different initial conditions and external environments faced by the different crisis-stricken countries. Those difficulties notwithstanding, the Korean recovery stands out as a relatively successful example. Reflection on the Korean case points to five factors that were particularly important elements of the recovery: a strong political commitment to move rapidly in addressing the country's structural problems; an early and successful effort to reschedule the country's short-term external debts; an expansionary stance of fiscal policy, facilitated by a low initial level of government debt; a successful effort at persuading workers to accept lower wages and higher unemployment, which was instrumental in preventing the emergence of inflation following the large exchange rate depreciation; and the success in creating an environment, largely as a result of the previous factors, in which low inflation and the restoration of confidence allowed monetary policy to be eased at a fairly early stage.

6

Perspectives on Economic Growth and Poverty Reduction

Chapters 4 and 5 have addressed the causes and effects of international financial crises, and Chapters 7 and 8 will discuss how various country-specific and systemic reforms can make the international financial system more effective in preventing, mitigating, and managing crises. An evaluation of the strengths and weaknesses of the international financial system should also assess the support it provides to countries in their pursuit of higher standards of living and the reduction of poverty over the longer run. Accordingly, this chapter provides an overview of what economists know and don't know about the factors that contribute to economic growth and poverty reduction.

Figure 6.1 provides two different perspectives on how rapidly standards of living have been rising since 1980.[1] The two plots contrast the cumulative distributions of developing countries and their aggregate population by average growth rates of countries' real per capita GDPs. Each diamond (in the lower plot) or square (in the upper plot) corresponds to an individual country, with the corresponding distance along the horizontal axis indicating the average growth rate of the country's per capita GDP over the period 1980–2002. Thus, the leftmost diamond and square correspond to the developing country with the lowest (i.e., most negative) average growth rate. For each square the vertical distance shows the proportion of developing countries with average per capita growth rates equal to or below that shown on the horizontal axis, whereas for each diamond the vertical dimension corresponds to the proportion of

---

[1] This figure is based on a chart provided to me by Bernard Wasow of The Century Foundation.

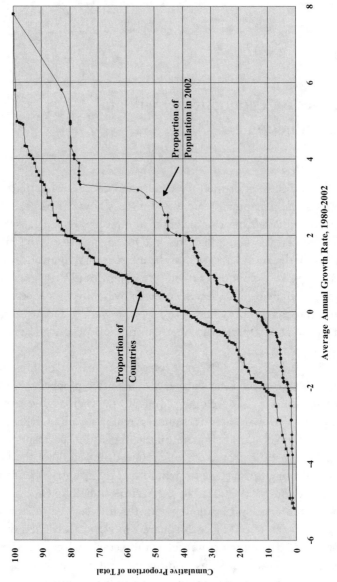

Figure 6.1. Distributions of developing countries and their population by per capita output growth. *Source: IMF, World Economic Outlook.*

208

the aggregate population of developing countries that reside in countries with average per capita growth rates equal to or below that shown on the horizontal axis. The two large jumps in the vertical dimension of the sequence of diamonds correspond to India and China, which have large populations and also experienced relatively high rates of GDP growth. The intersections with the vertical axis indicate that about 40 percent of the developing countries experienced zero or negative growth in per capita GDP over the 1980–2002 period, whereas only 15 percent of the developing-country population lives in countries that failed to achieve positive per capita GDP growth. At the other end of the distributions, only 12 percent of developing countries experienced average annual per capita GDP growth in excess of 3 percent, whereas roughly half of the developing-country population lives in countries in which per capita output grew faster than 3 percent.

Although the two plots in Figure 6.1 paint very different pictures of the historical record in raising per capita incomes, the difference essentially boils down to the fact that the developing world has had the good fortune of having its population concentrated in countries that have succeeded in generating relatively rapid growth since 1980. That major element of good fortune, however, should not divert attention from the large number of countries that have failed to grow, and from the need to develop a better understanding of how countries can achieve and sustain high rates of economic growth.

In focusing on the determinants of economic growth, this chapter first reviews the progress that economists have made in accounting for growth in terms of a set of three proximate determinants: physical capital accumulation, human capital building through education and skill-enhancing work experience, and productivity growth through technological progress (Section 6.1). It then describes efforts to relate economic growth to a set of deeper determinants—in particular, institutions and incentives, openness to international trade and capital movements, and geography (Section 6.2). Next the chapter reviews how economists think about poverty and the factors that contribute to reducing poverty (Section 6.3). Following that, it turns to lessons that have been gleaned from the experience of providing financial development aid (Section 6.4) and ends with concluding perspectives (Section 6.5).

6.1   Proximate Determinants of Growth: Physical Capital, Human Capital, and Technology[2]

The conceptual literature on economic growth has relied heavily on two simple frameworks: the Harrod–Domar model and the Solow model.[3] In its skeletal form, the Harrod–Domar model posits that the expansion of output is linearly related to the increase in the stock of physical capital. In contrast, in the skeletal form of the Solow model, output growth depends on three factors: the expansion of the physical capital stock, the growth of the effective labor force, and the rate of technological progress, where the latter is generally taken to correspond to the rate of increase in total factor productivity (i.e., the productivity of capital and labor combined).

In addition to facilitating advances in the conceptual analysis of the economic growth process, each of these models has played an important role in empirical analysis. Although repudiated as a prescriptive framework by Domar (1957), the Harrod–Domar model, with its assumption of a constant incremental capital–output ratio, has often been used to calculate the amount of investment required—or the financing gap that must be filled—to generate a target amount of output growth. Such back-of-the-envelope calculations have served a useful purpose on many occasions. However, as Easterly (2002) emphasizes, there is no evidence that investment is either a necessary or a sufficient condition for economic growth, and the resort to simple calculations of investment needs and financing gaps has had the counterproductive effect of diverting economists' attention from the deeper determinants of economic growth.

Unlike the prescriptive uses of the Harrod–Domar framework, empirical applications of the Solow model have been oriented primarily toward decomposing observed rates of economic growth into amounts that can be accounted for by investment in physical capital, human capital formation, and technological change. In seeking to account for growth over the medium run, these applications focus on a different time horizon than Solow (1957), whose pathbreaking insight, based on steady-state analysis, was that technological change (i.e., productivity growth) was the only possible source of per capita output growth in the long run. Solow emphasized that although countries with relatively high saving rates would

---

[2] This section draws heavily on Easterly (2002).
[3] Seminal contributions include those by Harrod (1939), Domar (1946), and Solow (1957).

have relatively high levels of capital per worker and output per capita, no country would be able to sustain growth in its per capita output over the long run without growth in productivity.

In analyzing the historical record of output growth, economists have reasoned that if all countries had access to the same technology, the Solow model combined with the assumption of diminishing returns to capital would provide incentives for relatively high levels of investment in countries with relatively small initial capital stocks, implying that standards of living should normally rise faster in capital-poor countries than in capital-rich countries. This proposition, however, finds little support in the data.[4] Indeed, Pritchett (1997) has estimated that living standards around the world have diverged "big time" over the past century and a quarter. On the basis of available data and an estimate of the lowest level of GDP per capita that could have sustained life in 1870, Pritchett estimates that the ratio of real per capita incomes in the world's richest and poorest countries increased by roughly a factor of five between 1870 and 1990.

Needless to say, some developing countries have managed to grow significantly faster than the world's most advanced economies during recent decades, creating considerable interest in the factors that contributed to their success. An initial set of accounting exercises for the so-called Gang of Four Asian tigers (Korea, Taiwan, Singapore, and Hong Kong) attributed much of their rapid economic growth to capital accumulation per worker and relatively little to technological change.[5] This impression was revised, however, when the exercise was modified to take into account estimates of the extent to which capital accumulation was itself driven by, and attributable to, technological change.[6]

As discussed in the next section, subsequent econometric studies have also established explicitly that technological change is not an exogenous process,[7] and that both the adoption of new technologies and the accumulation of physical and human capital are only proximate determinants of growth. Technological change and factor accumulation respond

---

[4] Romer (1987) was influential in rejecting the proposition, using data from the United Nations' International Comparisons Project on purchasing-power-parity-adjusted levels of per capita incomes for more than 100 countries over the period 1960–81.

[5] See Young (1992, 1995).

[6] See Klenow and Rodriguez-Clare (1997), who credit Barro and Sala-i-Martin (1995) for also emphasizing the need to recognize that capital accumulation may partly be an endogenous response to technological progress.

[7] See, for example, Bernanke and Gurkaynak (2002).

endogenously to deeper determinants, such as the institutions that define and protect property rights and provide incentives for entrepreneurship and innovation, the openness of economies to international trade and foreign direct investment, and various geographical characteristics.

With regard to proximate determinants, however, there is now a broad consensus among economists that technological change not only holds the key to economic growth in theoretical models of the long-run steady state, as emphasized by Solow, but also is fundamental to an understanding of historically observed growth experiences. In particular, analysis of the variation in living standards across countries suggests that most of the variation can be explained by differences in technology or productivity, with considerably less attributable to differences in physical capital per worker and educational attainment.[8]

The perception that technological change is the most important proximate determinant of economic growth is consistent with Schumpeter's (1911) view that "creative destruction" is the main economic force driving the growth of output. As Easterly (2002) stresses, however, the process of creative destruction depends critically on whether people have incentives to adopt new technologies. Many factors can undermine such incentives, including vested interests in old technologies or the lack of economic and legal systems that enable innovators to reap adequate benefits from their innovations.[9]

6.2   Deeper Determinants of Growth

Economists will never have a complete explanation of economic growth. As Easterly (2002) emphasizes, technological change—the key proximate determinant of growth in the Solow framework—involves significant elements of path dependence and luck. An example of its path dependence is provided by the history of transportation. Camel transportation made sense in the Middle East and North Africa because it conserved

[8] See Hall and Jones (1999), who estimate, for example, that of the thirty-five-fold difference in output per worker between the United States and Niger in 1988, a factor of 1.5 was explained by differences in physical capital per worker, 3.1 by differences in educational attainment per worker, and 7.7 by the productivity residual.
[9] Governments can strengthen incentives for innovation in various ways, such as subsidizing private research and development and the adoption of best-practice technologies, encouraging foreign direct investment, and establishing a system of intellectual property rights that allows inventors to keep a substantial share of the profits from their inventions.

resources that would otherwise have been spent building and maintaining roads. Wheel transportation made more sense in the West, however, and it was the latter path that led to major innovation—the railroad.[10] In addition, technological change can involve important complementarities (e.g., between the Internet and the personal computer) as well as fortuitous discoveries that defy attempts to provide a simple explanation of the process.

Despite the difficulties of providing complete explanations of technological change and economic growth, economists can point to a number of deeper determinants of growth, which in turn provide valuable perspectives on what policymakers can do to promote the process. The recognition that technological change (or increasing productivity) contributes importantly to the growth of per capita output emphasizes the role of incentives for entrepreneurship and innovation, along with the institutions that define and protect property rights and shape economic incentives, as deeper determinants of economic growth. The perception that countries that have pursued export-oriented development strategies have fared relatively well suggests that trade openness is another deeper determinant of economic growth, which in turn raises the controversial question of whether openness to international capital flows is also conducive to growth. Other deeper determinants include various geographical characteristics that influence the incentives for economic activity and technological change, such as climate, the disease environment, and distance from markets.

Although the recent economics literature has focused on institutions, trade openness, and geography as key considerations in attempts to explain growth, there are difficulties in identifying the separate influences of the three factors. Neither institutional quality nor trade openness is completely exogenous; both are influenced to some extent by geography. Moreover, there is some evidence of a two-way relationship between trade openness and institutional quality; better institutions result in more trade,[11] and more openness to trade leads to higher-quality institutions.[12] To complicate matters further, there is two-way causation between growth and its deeper determinants, with growth tending to contribute to better

[10] See Easterly (2002: 187–8).
[11] See Anderson and Marcouiller (2002).
[12] See Wei (2000c).

institutions and greater trade openness while also tending to change the importance of given geographical characteristics.

These difficulties notwithstanding, economists have made significant advances in using econometric methodologies to analyze growth; see Box 6.1. Additional perspectives have been gained from case studies of country experiences with growth. The two approaches should be viewed as complementary. In principle, hypotheses based on case studies that do not find support in cross-country regressions should be viewed as suspect, as should findings from cross-country regressions that cannot be meaningfully verified from case studies. In reality, however, the growth experiences of individual countries have typically been influenced importantly by idiosyncratic factors,[13] which makes it difficult to generalize and has left economists with different opinions about what it is valid to conclude from the combination of cross-country regressions and country narratives. One set of views is that, in general: (i) the quality of institutions is key; (ii) government policy toward trade does not play nearly as important a role as the institutional setting; (iii) geography is not destiny; (iv) good institutions can be acquired, but doing so often requires experimentation, willingness to depart from orthodoxy, and attention to local conditions; (v) the onset of economic growth does not require deep and extensive institutional reform; but (vi) sustaining high growth in the face of adverse circumstances requires ever stronger institutions.[14]

6.2.1 Institutions and incentives

As defined by North (1994: 360):

Institutions are the humanly devised constraints that structure human interaction. They are made up of formal constraints (e.g., rules, laws, constitutions), informal constraints (e.g., norms of behavior, conventions, self-imposed codes of conduct), and their enforcement characteristics. Together they define the incentive structure of societies and specifically economies.

This definition distinguishes institutions from organizations (i.e., groups of individuals bound together by common purposes), although in most countries various organizations warrant inclusion among the important institutions that define the incentive structures of economic agents. The definition also implicitly emphasizes, in the spirit of Coase (1960,

[13] See, for example, Subramanian and Roy (2003) on the Mauritian Miracle.
[14] These views are the inferences that Rodrik (2003b) draws from country narratives; each of the six points reflects his wording.

BOX 6.1. Cross-country growth regressions

A number of econometric studies have looked for statistically significant links between the levels or growth rates of per capita incomes and measures of institutional quality, trade openness, and certain geographical characteristics.[1] These studies represent important advances over earlier attempts to account for growth simply in terms of physical and human capital formation and technological change. Although the regression model is "worryingly oversimplified"[2] and the econometric methodology remains subject to strong criticism, the regression results tend to confirm widespread impressions of the importance of institutional quality—at least as reflected in survey data that capture subjective perceptions of the protection afforded to property rights and the strength of the rule of law. These studies also suggest that geography has both direct effects on cross-country patterns of income and indirect effects operating through the influence of geographical characteristics on colonization and institutional quality. In addition, they provide mixed evidence on the significance of trade openness, which appears to be sensitive to how trade openness is measured.

As noted in the text, neither institutional quality nor trade openness is a truly exogenous variable. Accordingly, one of the methodological challenges in estimating growth regressions is to find measures of exogenous cross-country variation in institutional quality and trade openness. Following Acemoglu et al. (2001), a number of studies have relied on colonial legacy, in turn linked to variation in settler mortality rates, as an instrument for isolating an exogenous component of institutional quality.[3] Similarly, following Frankel and Romer (1999), the literature has used geographical characteristics (e.g., sizes of countries, distances between countries, whether countries share a border, and whether countries are landlocked) to construct measures of exogenous variation in bilateral and aggregate trade flows. One of the remaining difficulties, emphasized by Dollar and Kraay (2003), is that the instrument for institutional quality also tends to have good explanatory power for trade, and the instrument for trade openness has good explanatory power for institutional quality. Thus, although the two instruments perform well in their respective univariate applications, they are not sufficient to isolate the partial effects of institutional quality and trade openness.

[1] The many contributions include those by Sachs and Warner (1995); Hall and Jones (1999); Frankel and Romer (1999); Acemoglu, Johnson, and Robinson (2001, 2002); Rodriguez and Rodrik (2001); Easterly and Levine (2002); Rodrik, Subramanian, and Trebbi (2002); Warner (2003); and Sachs (2003b).

[2] See Sachs (2003b).

[3] As Acemoglu et al. (2001) argue, this approach exploits the fact that, where settler mortality rates were high, European powers set up "extractive states" that were largely designed to transfer resources to the colonizer and did not provide much protection for property rights or checks and balances against government expropriation. Where settler mortality rates were low, many Europeans migrated and tried to replicate European institutions with strong emphasis on private property and checks against government power.

1992), that institutions have an important bearing on the transactions costs of producing output. Economists schooled in neoclassical theory often tend to overlook the costs of arranging economic transactions and enforcing agreements, which in reality can be very substantial.[15] Although economists have a very limited understanding of the way that institutions evolve as the complexity of the economic environment increases, it seems clear that success in sustaining economic growth depends critically on how well institutions adapt to permit low-cost transactions in the impersonal markets that characterize productive economies. "It is adaptive rather than allocative efficiency which is the key to long-run growth."[16]

Economists have long emphasized the allocative efficiency associated with market systems. Decision making based on the prices that equilibrate supply and demand in competitive markets can provide an efficient way of allocating resources in economies composed of many heterogeneous individuals and firms.[17] Market mechanisms allow workers with different skills and firms managed by different individuals to pursue their comparative advantages in production. Markets also allow households with different consumption preferences to purchase different combinations of goods and services such that each household can maximize the utility it obtains with the money it spends.

However, experience has also demonstrated that market systems in which many economic agents have opportunities and incentives to innovate provide a relatively high degree of adaptive efficiency. Support for this view was reinforced during the 1980s and early 1990s by the breakdown of central planning systems in the former Soviet Union and a number of other economies of central and eastern Europe after decades of relatively poor economic performances. That being said, however, there is also strong awareness that to adapt efficiently and function well in generating economic growth, market economies require various types of institutions and a significant amount of public sector involvement.

Rodrik (2003a) divides institutions into four types—market creating, market regulating, market stabilizing, and market legitimizing—and suggests that each type is important for sustaining economic growth. In particular, growth requires institutions that create markets by defining

---

[15] In an empirical study of the U.S. economy, Wallis and North (1986) estimate that transactions costs accounted for 45 percent of GDP in 1970.

[16] See North (1994: 367).

[17] See Smith (1776), Hayek (1941), and Arrow and Debreu (1954).

property rights and enforcing contracts; institutions that regulate markets and correct market failures; institutions for stabilizing markets through the exercise of monetary and fiscal policies and through prudential regulation and supervision; and institutions for legitimizing markets through the provision of political voice and social safety nets.[18]

Rodrik also argues that "[m]ost first-order economic principles come institution free."[19] In particular, economic principles suggest that productive efficiency requires clear and enforceable property rights and the rule of law; that macroeconomic and financial stability requires sound money, fiscal sustainability, and appropriate prudential regulation and supervision; and that distributive justice and poverty alleviation require the targeting and incentive compatibility of redistributive programs. However, these principles do not dictate the specific forms that institutions must take to provide an environment that is highly conducive to economic growth.[20]

In general, the most relevant institution-building priorities and forms of institutions are country specific. Whereas most countries can benefit from many types of institutional reforms, governments face difficult choices over how to deploy resources. Moreover, as emphasized by North (1994), because countries have different informal norms and enforcement mechanisms, the formal institutional structures that work well for one country may not adapt very well to others.

Can the recognition that formal institutional structures may not adapt well from country to country be reconciled with the international community's initiative to provide and encourage compliance with standards and codes for various types of institutional arrangements? Presumably yes, but only if the orientation of the standards and codes exercise is to induce countries to adopt sound institutional arrangements without also insisting on narrowly specified forms of such arrangements.

Various studies have documented that investment and growth can be undermined by corruption[21] and thus encouraged by institutional

[18] See also the extensive discussion in World Bank (2001).
[19] See Rodrik (2003a: 22).
[20] For example, although there is now fairly strong econometric evidence (discussed later in this chapter) that economic growth is promoted when investors believe their property rights are protected, such evidence does not provide clear implications about the form that property rights should take. In that connection, Rodrik et al. (2002) argue that establishing credibility that property rights will be protected (as in China) is more important than having laws that establish a formal property rights regime (as in Russia).
[21] See Mauro (1995), Wei (2000a, 2000b), and Wei and Sievers (2000).

arrangements that guard against corruption by promoting transparency and accountability. Other important steps for avoiding corruption are to eliminate red tape, to establish the practice of honoring government contracts and not exploiting the private sector, and to create a meritocratic civil service.[22] It is also widely recognized, more generally, that even non-corrupt governments can undermine growth in numerous ways, including through failure to invest adequately in public services and infrastructure and through failure to adopt institutional arrangements that guard against high budget deficits, high inflation, and negative real interest rates.

Although experience has demonstrated that growth is promoted by market systems and institutional arrangements that provide widespread opportunities and strong incentives for innovation, well-functioning market systems rest on very fragile political foundations, as emphasized by Rajan and Zingales (2003). One threat comes from the prospect that the government will be captured by vested interests—that is, that policymakers will succumb to political pressures from established groups of firms or workers whose agenda is to protect the status quo from the creative destruction that competitive markets unleash. Thus, the effectiveness of governance in promoting technological innovation and growth depends on institutional arrangements that guard against excessive concentration of economic power and that prevent government from degenerating into a system that primarily serves the interests of the rich. A second and somewhat related threat comes from the prospect that large groups of citizens may become disillusioned with the system. Withstanding this threat requires not only level playing fields on which everybody has a fair chance of participating but also a social safety net that adequately insures people against the hardships associated with creative destruction. The social safety net should be designed to support people directly rather than to protect existing firms against the failures that are essential to the process of creative destruction.[23]

Research over the past decade has provided fairly convincing evidence of the importance of financial development in promoting economic growth—and hence of the importance of institutional arrangements that

---

[22] See the discussion in Easterly (2002).

[23] Rajan and Zingales (2003) suggest that there is a widespread need to rethink the focus of social safety net programs, which have been mainly designed to guard against acute poverty and the temporary dislocation caused by business cycles, rather than to facilitate adjustment to the structural change associated with economic growth.

create an environment favorable to the development of well-functioning financial markets.[24] As emphasized in the conceptual literature, financial instruments and markets perform various functions that promote capital accumulation, technological change, and economic growth. These functions include reducing transactions and information costs[25]; mobilizing savings; allocating credit; facilitating the trading, hedging, and diversification or pooling of various risks; and easing the trading of goods, services, and financial contracts.

A strong empirical association between financial development and economic development was established in a seminal contribution by Goldsmith (1969), who analyzed data on thirty-five countries from 1860 to 1963. However, Goldsmith emphasized that his findings only established a positive correlation and said nothing about the direction of causation. Thus, until economists began to address the relationship with more penetrating econometric methodologies, spurred by King and Levine (1993), some members of the profession continued to view financial development as a sideshow that simply accompanied economic development.[26]

King and Levine (1993) examined four measures of financial development: the liquid liabilities of the financial system as a ratio to GDP; the ratio of bank credit to the sum of bank credit plus central bank domestic assets; the ratio of credit allocated to private enterprises to total domestic credit excluding credit to banks; and credit to private enterprises as a ratio to GDP. They found strong positive correlations between each of the four measures of financial development (averaged over 1960–89) and three growth indicators—real per capita growth, capital accumulation, and productivity growth averaged over 1960–89—after they controlled for initial income per capita, initial secondary school enrollment, the ratio of government spending to GDP, inflation, and the ratio of exports plus imports to GDP. They also showed that the initial 1960 value of the first

---

[24] The role of financial development in promoting economic growth has been debated since at least the time of Schumpeter (1911). See Levine (1997) and Rajan and Zingales (2001) for surveys of the academic literature and Rajan and Zingales (2003) for a comprehensive discussion that draws on both econometric and anecdotal evidence.

[25] Transactions and information costs include the costs of acquiring information, enforcing contracts, and exchanging goods and financial claims. As Levine (1997) emphasizes, any theory of the role of financial systems in economic growth must implicitly or explicitly add some kind of frictions—such as transactions and information costs—to the Arrow–Debreu (1954) framework of state-contingent claims.

[26] See, for example, Robinson (1952: 86), as cited by Rajan and Zingales (2001).

of the four measures of financial development predicted the three growth indicators over 1960–89.[27]

Although King and Levine suggested a direction of causation running from financial development to growth, two considerations challenged that conclusion.[28] One possibility was that financial development and economic growth were both driven by a common omitted variable; the second was that the financial development indicators expanded in anticipation of economic growth. Evidence that largely dismisses these two possibilities has now been provided by Jayaratne and Strahan (1996) and Rajan and Zingales (1998). Thus, "[t]heory and evidence make it difficult to conclude that the financial system merely—and automatically—responds to industrialization and economic activity, or that financial development is an inconsequential addendum to the process of economic growth."[29] Although it is clear that financial crises are highly disruptive to the growth process, the link between the financial system and growth goes beyond the relationship between finance and shorter-term fluctuations.[30]

6.2.2 Openness to international trade

Notwithstanding the mixed evidence from econometric studies, most economists believe that growth can be promoted by opening economies to international trade and foreign direct investment. In praising open trade policies, economists emphasize that the gains from trade come through multiple channels. In particular, the benefits come from competition that forces weak firms to close while inducing new firms to take hold, sometimes in the same industry; from reducing the price and increasing the quality of imported consumer goods and inputs to production; and from the expansion of markets, which facilitates increased specialization.[31] Opening to foreign direct investment can also bring important benefits, including knowledge about technologies and markets and an upgrading of the skills of domestic workers.

---

[27] They did not have enough observations on initial 1960 values to investigate this for the other three financial development variables.

[28] See the discussion in Rajan and Zingales (2001).

[29] See Levine (1997: 720).

[30] Stimulated by the general consensus that financial development has a first-order influence on economic growth, a new literature has begun to explore the role of legal institutions in explaining differences in financial systems. See the survey by Beck and Levine (2003).

[31] See Irwin (2002).

Evidence suggestive of a relationship between trade openness and growth comes from examining the trade performances of two groups of countries: those that have achieved high average rates of per capita GDP growth over prolonged periods, and those that have failed to grow. Panagariya (2003) conducts such an exercise for two different periods: 1961–80 and 1980–99. He finds for each period that both export and import growth rates were relatively high in most of the cases of rapid GDP growth and relatively low for most countries that failed to grow. Although such evidence does not imply that trade openness is either strictly necessary or sufficient for rapid GDP growth, it does reveal that few countries have been able to sustain rapid GDP growth without also being open to a rapid expansion of trade.

Unfortunately, discussions of trade openness have not distinguished carefully between extreme positions and what economists actually believe. With regard to the free-trade extreme, almost all economists accept that the theoretical case for unrestricted trade is ambiguous in the presence of market imperfections, and few if any believe that economic growth can be guaranteed by simply lowering trade barriers. With regard to the opposite extreme, those economists who advise caution in opening up to trade also recognize that world markets are a source of technology and capital, and that "[n]o country has developed successfully by turning its back on international trade and long-term capital flows."[32]

Although it is widely perceived today that outward-oriented trade policies are conducive to economic growth, economists held radically different views during the 1950s and 1960s.[33] Among the premises that influenced thinking during that period were the views that developing countries were heavily engaged in the production of primary commodities, that a low elasticity of demand for primary products presented a pessimistic outlook for standards of living unless countries developed manufacturing industries, and that the development of manufacturing required protection from imports while domestic industries were in their infancy stages.[34] These views led countries to pursue import substitution industrialization strategies supported by trade protection. Beginning in the mid-1960s, however, the case for import substitution strategies was challenged from

[32] See Rodrik (2001a: 23).
[33] See Krueger (1997) and Baldwin (2004) for discussions of how and why economists' views on the relationship between trade and growth have evolved.
[34] Among others, Prebisch (1950) gave prominence to such arguments.

several directions. First, contributions to the pure theory of trade policies questioned the wisdom of import protection. Second, the development of the theory of effective protection, and its application, opened economists' eyes to wide disparities in effective protection that the prevailing import-substitution policies were according to different industries. Third, the examination of how import-substitution policies worked in practice drew attention to the prominence of rent-seeking activities and the buildup of vested interests. Fourth, a number of East Asian countries began to grow rapidly under export-oriented development strategies.

Despite these challenges to the strategy of pursuing economic development through import protection, in Krueger's (1997) view the case for outward-oriented development strategies did not become "unarguable" until the early 1980s. Following the 1979 oil price shock, the 1980–82 world recession, and the accompanying developing-country debt problems, many heavily indebted countries were unable to service their debts and encountered prolonged crises. In contrast, growth resumed rapidly in the net-importing countries of East Asia, which had debt–GDP ratios similar to those of other heavily indebted developing countries. What differed significantly between the two sets of countries were their debt–export ratios and the related fact that larger export volumes and the greater flexibility of their economies allowed the East Asian countries to maintain debt service.[35]

Although a fairly broad consensus has emerged in favor of outward-oriented development strategies, there is less agreement on whether countries should move rapidly to liberalize their barriers to imports. Berg and Krueger (2003) argue that there are few preconditions for trade openness and hence a case for opening markets to trade early in the development process. Others have emphasized that most of today's rich countries embarked on growth behind protective barriers and other policies to promote development objectives (e.g., temporary monopolies, subsidized credits, and tax incentives), that rapid trade liberalization can cause severe dislocations to affected sectors of the economy, and that trade policies should be designed as part of a fairly comprehensive development strategy.[36]

Warner (2003) draws distinctions between a number of propositions about trade openness. Empirical evidence supports the contentions that

---

[35] Krueger credits Sachs (1985) for drawing early attention to this distinction.
[36] See Rodrik (2001a).

economies open to trade tended to avoid negative growth disasters between 1970 and 1990 (prior to the major financial crises of the 1990s)
and also tended to grow faster than economies closed to trade over the
same period. Empirical evidence also refutes the contentions that open
trade policies guarantee positive growth and that countries closed to trade
never achieve positive growth. But there remain several important unresolved issues on which future research is desirable, including whether
open trade policies only help growth when they are combined with good
institutions; whether open trade policies help growth but only at the cost
of greater economic instability; whether completely free trade is better
than moderately free trade in promoting growth; and whether passive
trade liberalization works to ensure moderate growth while fast growth
requires more active liberalization—that is, policies that actively promote
exports rather than simply creating and enabling an open environment
for trade.

6.2.3   Openness to international capital flows

In theory, access to foreign capital creates the potential for faster economic
growth and allows countries to smooth their consumption and investment
expenditures relative to domestic production. In practice, however, the
experience with international capital flows has been very volatile, with
numerous cases of surges in capital inflows followed by sudden stops and
financial crises. The extremely high costs of these crises have contributed
to the widely held view that countries should not liberalize financial markets and capital flows before strengthening their financial institutions and
establishing sound systems of prudential regulation and supervision.

The output collapses associated with the crises that have often followed
financial liberalization have also led economists to consider more carefully
whether capital account liberalization—even when properly sequenced—
is conducive to economic growth over the long run. Although it is generally agreed that the development of domestic financial markets is conducive to growth, as already noted, there is currently less agreement
on whether openness to international finance is also advantageous for
growth.

In addressing this issue, economists have distinguished between different types of international capital flows. Among these, inflows of foreign direct investment (FDI) have generally been regarded as particularly

conducive to growth over the long run. FDI not only adds to a country's capital stock but can also give rise to the introduction of new technologies, expanded access to foreign markets, and opportunities for the domestic labor force to develop new skills and managerial know-how.[37]

Although technological advance, skill and managerial development, and expanded market access generally yield major benefits, recent econometric work does not support the view that either FDI or portfolio capital flows have had a quantitatively significant impact on economic growth; see Box 6.2. This finding has to be interpreted carefully, however. As Prasad, Rogoff, Wei, and Kose (2003) have noted, the lack of evidence may reflect the difficulties of detecting relationships econometrically; there are reasons to believe that any relationship is complicated by nonlinearities or threshold effects (as suggested by Borensztein, De Gregorio, and Lee, 1998); most countries that have encouraged international capital flows have continued to do so, despite the setbacks; and theories suggesting that openness to international capital flows is conducive to growth are not necessarily wrong, provided that countries have established disciplined macroeconomic policies and a core set of sound institutions before opening up to foreign capital.[38]

Although many economists share the view that countries should not liberalize international capital flows before establishing a core set of sound institutions, some have emphasized that opening up to foreign capital provides countries with incentives for strengthening financial sector institutions and can be important in overcoming resistance to financial sector reform. Thus, Rajan and Zingales (2003: 124) disagree with the prescription that "countries with a weak institutional environment should postpone financial sector liberalization till they strengthen their institutions." In their view, access to finance is particularly important for spreading economic opportunity and promoting growth, and opening up to foreign

---

[37] In this connection, it is fairly clear that the pure allocative efficiency gains from reallocating capital internationally are a relatively minor component of the benefits from foreign direct investment (FDI) compared with the gains from the diffusion of new technologies, skills, and know-how. See Gourinchas and Jeanne (2003), who infer that "emerging economies do not benefit greatly from international financial integration if the latter does not increase their productivity at the same time that it reallocates capital internationally."

[38] Prasad et al. (2003) also list the fastest and slowest growing countries over the period 1980–2000 and establish that openness to international capital flows is neither a necessary condition for fast growth nor a sufficient condition for avoiding slow growth.

BOX 6.2. Selected studies of the impact of international capital flows on economic growth

Using a data set for sixty-nine developing countries over the period 1970–89, Borensztein et al. (1998) find that FDI contributes relatively more to growth than domestic investment, but only when the host country has a minimum threshold stock of human capital. This result suggests that FDI is beneficial to growth only when the host country has sufficient capacity to absorb advanced technologies. Moreover, in a subsequent study based on a data set for more than seventy industrial and developing countries over the period 1960–95, Carkovic and Levine (2002, p. 3) find that "after controlling for the joint determination of growth, foreign capital flows, country-specific factors, and other growth determinants, the data do not suggest a strong independent influence of FDI on growth." Although the latter finding does not dispute the positive association between growth and FDI, and may or may not stand up to further econometric scrutiny, it suggests that the link between growth and FDI is simply attributable to the fact that the types of policies and institutions that are conducive to growth are also conducive to FDI.[1] Similar findings emerge from a study by Edison Levine, Ricci, and Slok (2002), who focus on both stock and flow data for portfolio capital and for FDI.

Rather than focusing directly on growth, some econometric studies have focused on the relationship between long-term capital inflows and domestic investment; see, for example, Bosworth and Collins (1999) and Mody and Murshid (2002). The latter study, based on a sample of sixty developing countries during the 1980s and 1990s, finds evidence that FDI has had a large and statistically significant impact on domestic investment, whereas portfolio flows and bank loans have not. Mody and Murshid also find that the impact of long-term capital flows was smaller during the 1990s than during the 1980s, consistent with the increasing share of portfolio flows during the 1990s and evidence that an increasing proportion of FDI was channeled into acquisitions of existing productive capacity rather than investments in new productive capacity. And consistent with the findings of Carkovic and Levine (2002) and Edison et al. (2002), when Mody and Murshid augment their regression to include terms in both FDI and the interaction of FDI with the World Bank's Country Policy Institutional Assessment Index, the interaction term is statistical significant whereas the former term is not.

[1] Carkovic and Levine rely on a methodology that extracts the exogenous component of FDI without investigating the specific determinants of FDI.

capital is a particularly important vehicle for inducing change in institutional environments that suppress financial market competition and limit access to finance. Analogously, Gourinchas and Jeanne (2003), although not addressing the issue of how rapidly countries should open up to international capital flows, suggest that economists may be paying too much attention to the fact that market imperfections and financial crises deprive countries of the full benefits of international financial integration and insufficient attention to the ways that international financial integration affects domestic engines of growth and development.

Other relevant perspectives come from reflecting on various development experiences. Stiglitz (2002a) notes that FDI has played an important role in many, but not all, of the most successful growth stories. Some downsides to FDI are that foreign businesses often destroy local competitors, with competitive advantages sometimes arising in part from special privileges extracted from the government; that the inflow of FDI may be oriented toward appropriating the income associated with natural resources rather than creating wealth; and that inflows of FDI into industries intensive in natural resources can bring the so-called Dutch disease, giving rise to exchange rate appreciation and undermining the competitiveness of other industries. Stiglitz cites Japan and Korea as examples of remarkably successful growth experiences in which FDI played a very small role. In contrast, China, Malaysia, and Singapore have benefited significantly from the access that FDI has given them to markets and new technology while also managing to keep the abuses of FDI in check.

Needless to say, the subject of opening economies to international capital flows warrants more attention than this section has given it. Additional discussion is provided in Chapter 7.

6.3   Poverty

Although many individual countries have established their own national thresholds for measuring poverty, most of the literature on the extent of world poverty has used the World Bank's international poverty lines of one and two dollars a day when income or consumption is measured in terms of 1993 international purchasing power parity (PPP) prices. The one-dollar-a-day line happens to correspond approximately to the national poverty lines of a number of the poorest countries[39] and is also the criterion used in the millennium development goal of cutting in half, between 1990 and 2015, the proportion of people who are living in poverty.[40]

Even under a common definition of what constitutes poverty, there are major disagreements about the extent of poverty and how much it has changed over time. Bhalla (2002) estimates that the proportion of the world's population living in poverty declined from 30 percent in 1987 to 13.1 percent in 2000, whereas Sala-i-Martin (2002) focuses on the longer time period 1970–98 and also finds a substantial decline in poverty on a worldwide basis. In contrast, the World Bank estimates a much slower decline in poverty, from 28.7 percent of the world's population in 1987 to 22.7 percent in 1999.[41]

What are the difficulties in estimating poverty levels and why is there such a wide range of estimates?[42] Some of the difficulties are associated with the PPP price indices used to convert incomes from local currency into international prices. In addition to the general conceptual problems that arise in constructing PPP price indices, the data on international prices that are available from the International Comparisons Project are not designed to focus explicitly on the consumption bundles of the poor, and updates of the project's data (based on periodic benchmark surveys) have resulted in some very large changes in poverty counts compared with earlier counts.

Another difficulty is associated with the choice between two methodologies for calculating the percentage of a nation's population that is living in poverty. One method combines data on the distribution of incomes or consumption levels within the country, typically from household surveys,

---

[39] See Deaton (2003).

[40] The well-being of the poor depends importantly on education and health as well as income or consumption, and in addition to including goals for an income-oriented measure of poverty, the millennium development initiative (see Section 6.4) includes goals for education, health, gender equality, and the environment.

[41] See Chen and Ravallion (2001) and Ravallion (2003) for World Bank estimates and perspectives. One fact not in dispute is that, on a regional basis, the growth of per capita income and consumption during the past two decades has been close to zero in all parts of the developing world except Asia, which accounts for most of the world's population (both poor and nonpoor) and has grown rapidly.

[42] Deaton (2003) lucidly discusses the statistical and methodological difficulties in arriving at poverty estimates, and Zettelmeyer (2003a) provides an insightful reconciliation of the contrasting estimates by Bhalla (2002) and the World Bank.

with national income and product account (NIPA) measures of aggregate national consumption or income. The second method relies on household survey data for both the distribution and the aggregate national levels of income or consumption. Although the household survey data focus on less comprehensive measures of income and consumption than NIPA data and also tend to miss relatively large proportions of people at both ends of the income distribution—because rich people are often hard to reach or noncooperative whereas relatively large numbers of the poor do not live in households and are also hard to reach—they have the merit of capturing more of the informal component of income-generating activity, which in many countries is very substantial relative to the activity that gets captured in the NIPA statistics.

As it turns out, the two methodologies lead to considerably different calculations. Estimates based on NIPA data, such as those provided by Bhalla (2002) and Sala-i-Martin (2002), suggest that the percentage of the world population living in poverty has declined much more substantially during recent decades than survey-based estimates, such as those produced by the World Bank.

Which estimates are right? Deaton (2003) argues that survey-based methodologies are more appropriate than NIPA-based methods. One element in his reasoning is that the components of consumption that are missed by the household surveys have little relevance for the poor. Another consideration is that the share of unmeasured income-generating activities presumably declines significantly as economies develop, implying that measured GDP growth rates tend to be overstated, with ratios of survey-measured consumption to NIPA-measured consumption declining as economies develop. Deaton also emphasizes, however, that until the World Bank provides better documentation and availability of either the survey data or summary statistics derived from them, "the (flawed) methodology used by Bhalla and Sala-i-Martin is the *only* way that outsiders can calculate world poverty estimates."[43]

In analyzing the factors that affect poverty levels over time, economists have found systematic evidence that the growth of GDP per capita tends to reduce poverty. Growth helps absorb the poor into gainful employment, rapidly growing economies generate fiscal resources that allow governments to undertake targeted antipoverty programs, and, by making it

---

[43] See Deaton (2003: 22).

less difficult to earn income, growth can also make it more feasible for poor families to avail themselves of public services such as health care and education.[44] At the same time, economists have not uncovered much evidence that macroeconomic policies reduce poverty over and above the important effects that operate through growth,[45] nor is there empirical evidence of a systematic relationship between trade openness and poverty other than the relationship that operates through growth.[46]

These considerations do not imply that economic growth is the only means to poverty reduction, or that the relationship between poverty and growth is simple to describe. However, the fact that growth is a key channel for alleviating poverty has a number of implications. One that has been clearly evident over the past decade is that financial crises tend to have major adverse consequences for poverty.[47] Another implication is that institutions for creating, regulating, stabilizing, and legitimizing markets are of central importance not only for sustaining economic growth but also in determining outcomes for the poor.

Despite the systematic evidence that growth is a key channel for poverty reduction, there remains strong disagreement over how to pursue the goal of alleviating poverty. Kanbur (2001) attributes much of the disagreement to differences in perspectives and analytic frameworks regarding the nature of the relationship between poverty and growth and the types of policy packages that are conducive to growth. For purposes of simplification, he distinguishes between two different sets of perspectives, one of which tends to be held by finance ministers, the staff of the international financial institutions, the financial press, and academic economists trained in the Anglo-Saxon tradition, whereas the other tends to be held by members

---

[44] See Panagariya (2003) and Bhagwati and Srinivasan (2002).

[45] See Cashin, Mauro, Pattillo, and Sahay (2001).

[46] See Berg and Krueger (2003). As Panagariya (2003) notes, however, one would expect trade liberalization to directly affect poverty through two channels. The first is the Stolper–Samuelson effect: removal of trade barriers stimulates exports of the goods that are intensive in the country's relatively abundant factor, which for low-income countries is generally unskilled labor. Second, protectionist policies typically discriminate against agriculture, which employs the bulk of the poor.

[47] Baldacci, de Mello, and Inchauste (2002a, 2002b) emphasize three channels through which crises tend to affect income inequality and increase poverty. Weaker economic activity affects jobs in both the formal and informal sectors; currency depreciations tend to reduce the relative prices of nontradables, raise the relative price of imported foods, and hurt the poor, who spend much of their incomes on food; and fiscal retrenchment often leads to cuts in public outlays on social programs, transfers to households, and wages and salaries.

of advocacy groups and operational nongovernmental organizations (NGOs). In Kanbur's view, the main differences between the two sets of perspectives are associated with aggregation, time horizon, and market structure (monopoly power). On aggregation, the first group tends to emphasize income measures of welfare and the percentage of the population below a poverty line, whereas the second group focuses more on the prospects that public services for the poor can worsen considerably but not show up in income-based measures of poverty, or that the absolute numbers of the poor can increase with population growth even though the percentage in poverty is declining. On time horizon, the first group tends to focus on the medium run whereas the second is more concerned about the short run (and for some issues, such as the environment, the very long run). On market structure, the first group tends to analyze issues in the context of competitive markets in which agents have little market power, whereas the second group has an instinctive picture of economies populated by agents with considerable market power (including big corporations, governments, and local moneylenders).

Kanbur does not hold out hope that the two different sets of perspectives can be reconciled, but he does suggest that recognizing and trying to understand legitimate alternative views on economic policy, and being open and careful in presenting policy messages, is both good analytics and good politics. "When the . . . [World Bank] whose self-stated mission is to eradicate poverty can only hold its Annual Meetings under siege from those who believe its mission is to further the cause of the rich and powerful, there is clearly a gap to be bridged."[48]

6.4   Aid and Debt Relief

How much can growth be promoted through foreign aid and debt relief? Should the member countries of the Organization for Economic Cooperation and Development (OECD) be implored to be more generous in providing development assistance, or is fifty years of foreign aid enough? Although foreign assistance has at times been associated with helping countries move from economic crisis to rapid development,[49] the preponderance of econometric evidence suggests that development aid has not

---

[48] See Kanbur (2001: 16).
[49] Success stories include the European recipients of Marshall Plan aid following the Second World War, Taiwan in the 1950s, Botswana and Korea in the 1960s, Indonesia in the 1970s, Bolivia and Ghana in the late 1980s, and Uganda and Vietnam in the 1990s.

had a significant impact on economic growth.[50] The idea that countries can be lifted out of poverty simply by giving them sufficient financial aid belies half a century of experience.[51]

In evaluating why aid has not been very effective in promoting growth, two relevant issues are whether aid has led to an increase in investment, and how the size of the increase in investment compares with the amount of aid. In that regard, Easterly (2002) reports that for eighty-eight countries for which data are available spanning the three decades 1965–95, the correlation between aid and investment was positive in just seventeen cases, and investment increased at least one for one with aid (i.e., aid was not associated with a decline in domestic savings) in only six of the seventeen cases. In numerous instances aid has given rise to increases in government consumption or unproductive investments, or has relieved pressures for countries to strengthen macroeconomic policies and pursue desirable institutional reforms. And in some cases, aid has been used to enhance the comforts and amass the personal fortunes of corrupt national leaders.

The provision of foreign aid gained prevalence during the 1950s and 1960s. For Western countries the motivation was a combination of altruism and self-interest. Aid was viewed not only as a means to raise living standards in recipient countries from a humanitarian perspective but also as a way to promote the political and strategic interests of donor countries. Thus, substantial amounts of aid went to countries that were political allies of the major powers. The volume of official development assistance (ODA) trended upward through the 1980s, but it peaked in 1991 and began a gradual decline as its strategic importance waned following the end of the Cold War.[52]

Between 1950 and 1995, the OECD countries provided about $1 trillion of ODA (measured in 1985 dollars).[53] As a consequence of the

---

[50] See Tsikata (1998). The view that aid has a positive impact on growth in countries with sound fiscal, monetary, and trade policies—after account is taken of the independent effects of good policies, sound institutions, and the like—is supported in an influential paper by Burnside and Dollar (2000); however, the specific econometric evidence provided by Burnside and Dollar has subsequently been challenged by Easterly, Levine, and Roodman (2003).

[51] See Panagariya (2002) and Berg (2003).

[52] See World Bank (1998). It may be noted that the decline in ODA after 1991 coincided with a sharp rise in private financial flows to developing countries.

[53] See Easterly (2002: 33). The most common definition of aid is the OECD measure, ODA, which comprises grants, debt forgiveness, and concessional loans at interest rates that imply a grant element of at least 25 percent. The grant element of a concessional

upward trend in ODA and its limited effectiveness in promoting growth, many low- and middle-income countries have become significantly more aid dependent. Indeed, among a sample of fifty-six aid recipients, the median ratio of aid to GDP increased from about 6 percent to roughly 11 percent between the second half of the 1970s and the first half of the 1990s, and the mean increased from 9 percent to 16 percent.[54] On a regional basis, the mean aid–GDP ratios during 1991–95 were 7.4 percent in the Asia and Pacific region (five countries), 4.5 percent in the Middle East and North Africa (eight countries), 21.2 percent in Sub-Saharan Africa (thirty-four countries), and 10.5 percent in the Western Hemisphere (nine countries).

Despite the history of aid ineffectiveness and growing aid dependence, development assistance continues to be viewed as an important vehicle for reducing poverty, which many regard as one of the most daunting problems that the world faces in the new century. That being said, the past decade has brought a number of changes in the international community's approach to development assistance. First, countries have established an ambitious but limited set of development goals—in particular, the Millennium Development Goals, announced at the United Nations Millennium Summit in September 2000, which built on discussions at a number of international conferences and summits during the 1990s.[55] Second, there has been increased focus on the idea of allocating development aid in a manner that rewards better performance—and of not allocating aid to countries characterized by poor governance (i.e., by the lack of the rule

loan is calculated using a discount rate of 10 percent. Roughly one-third of ODA has been channeled through and administered by multilateral agencies such as the United Nations Development Program and the World Bank, and the remainder has been provided directly as so-called bilateral aid from developed-country governments. The term *official development finance*, a broader concept than ODA, refers to all financing that flows to developing countries from developed-country governments and multilateral agencies, some of which is loaned at interest rates close to market levels.

[54] See Tsikata (1998: 7 and Appendix). The sample includes low- and middle-income countries for which the aid–GDP ratio exceeded 5 percent in at least one year during 1975–95. It excludes the transition economies, countries that did not exist in 1975, and countries with populations below 1 million.

[55] The Millennium Development Goals, which in most cases apply to the period through 2015, set targets for reducing poverty; achieving universal primary education; promoting gender equality and empowering women; reducing child mortality; improving maternal health; combating HIV–AIDS, malaria, and other diseases; ensuring environmental sustainability; and developing a global partnership for development. It may be noted that the case for promoting gender equality rests not only on moral grounds but also on evidence that increasing the economic opportunities for women helps to slow population growth.

of law or enforceable contracts and by the prevalence of corruption)—along with some initial steps toward implementing this idea.[56] Third, there has been more explicit recognition that development strategies and targets should be "owned" by the individual countries involved and should emerge from a broad participatory process involving open and collaborative dialogue between national authorities and relevant economic and social groups.[57] And fourth, there has also been more explicit recognition of the fact that many low-income countries have become caught in debt-related poverty traps, with dim prospects for growth as long as they are burdened with high levels of debt relative to GDP.

The increased awareness of debt-related poverty traps has led to coordinated action by the international community to encourage low-income countries to develop strategies for poverty reduction and growth, and to support such country-owned strategies by providing debt relief through the Heavily Indebted Poor Countries (HIPC) Initiative.[58] The challenge of releasing countries from poverty traps and achieving the Millennium Development Goals is likely to require substantial amounts of external finance, and debt relief is potentially a very important mechanism for overcoming poverty traps and giving countries a fresh start. In addition, some economists have stressed the importance of providing future development finance mainly in the form of grants rather than loans, so that countries do not once again get caught in debt traps.

Although it seems clear that substantial amounts of financial assistance will be needed to achieve the Millennium Development Goals, history suggests that it is crucial to avoid allocating aid in the same manner that has been ineffective in the past. Some have argued, accordingly, that debt relief and other forms of aid should be conditioned on country performance

---

[56] Increased attention to the idea, which dates back at least to Chenery and Strout (1996), is apparent, for example, in the assessment of aid effectiveness by the World Bank (1998). A recent step toward implementation is the U.S. administration's initiative to provide some of its bilateral aid through a new Millennium Challenge Account. Under this initiative, aid is to be allocated on the basis of a list of indicators relating to the quality of governance, such as civil liberties, political rights, voice and accountability, government effectiveness, rule of law, and control of corruption; the strength of the effort to invest in people, such as immunization rates, the completion rate for primary education, public spending on health as a percent of GDP, and public spending on primary education as a percent of GDP; and the quality of macroeconomic and regulatory policies, such as country credit rating, inflation, the budget deficit as a ratio to GDP, days to start a business, trade policy, and regulatory quality rating. See Taylor (2003).

[57] See OECD Development Assistance Committee (1996) and IMF (2000).

[58] See IMF (2003i). Recall the discussion in Chapter 3, Subsection 3.3.2.

and the quality of the policy environment, and not simply on promises of macroeconomic adjustment and other growth-promoting actions. As Easterly (2002) has stressed, donors in the past have often been overly eager to lend and hence have been ineffective in ensuring that financial assistance leads to growth-promoting actions. Such ineffectiveness has reflected a combination of factors, including genuine concerns about the poor, incentives to protect budget allocations by staying loaned out, and incentives to window dress financial accounts by providing countries with new loans to avoid defaults on old loans. In Easterly's view, the poor in recipient countries would be better off, paradoxically, if aid disbursement decisions were allocated to a hard-hearted agency that didn't care about poverty.

Berg (2003) provides a different set of views, arguing that it is not helpful to frame the aid effectiveness debate as a general problem; that aid effectiveness problems are most severe in countries with very weak institutional capacities; that most bilateral aid—which constitutes roughly two-thirds of total ODA—is motivated by humanitarian concerns (disaster relief), historical or cultural ties between countries, or the pursuit of national economic or political goals (drug, immigration, or pollution control and trade expansion) and hence is not readily amenable to reallocation; that except at the extremes, it is almost impossible to distinguish good and bad policy environments in a politically (or even analytically) convincing way; and that much of the responsibility for aid failures should be attributed to the donors. In criticizing donor practices, Berg notes that the problems include ill-conceived and poorly supervised projects and programs, the adoption of unsuitable approaches, complex accounting requirements, and a propensity of donors to impose their own (frequently changing) priorities and agendas. He also emphasizes that aid-related visiting missions and management tasks absorb huge amounts of the time and energy of local officials, and that aid projects sometimes displace local expertise or preempt local entrepreneurship and draw away civil servants to administer aid-funded programs.

Consistent with the notion that institutional quality plays a major role in underpinning economic growth, a fundamental challenge is to provide financial aid and technical assistance in a manner that helps countries strengthen their institutional capacities. This is particularly the case in the least developed countries, which are typically characterized by thin cadres of skilled and educated people, organizational disarray in the public sector, and small and neglected or discouraged private sectors. An implication, in Berg's (2003) view, is that financial aid and technical assistance should be provided in a manner that has much less of a donor-driven character than has traditionally been the case, and that gives local agencies much greater scope to choose and design projects on their own on the basis of their capacities to implement. Donor concerns should focus less on what should be done and more on how projects can be implemented in a manner that builds institutional capacities and achieves effective results.

In addition to allocating aid in a manner that helps build institutional capacities, it is important to guard against certain macroeconomic difficulties that aid has sometimes generated.[59] One potential problem is that large inflows of external resources may lead to excess demand for domestic goods or otherwise strain a country's absorptive capacity. Another difficulty is that uncertainty about future aid flows complicates fiscal planning.[60] In principle, each of these difficulties can be largely resolved by phasing aid in a careful and predictable manner.

Aid can also bring a third difficulty—Dutch disease—if the official financing leads to exchange rate appreciation and erodes the profit margins and international competitiveness of some of the established primary-product and industrial sectors. However, to the extent that exchange rate appreciation is a likely consequence of using aid to build the recipient country's productive capacity and strengthen the profitability and competitiveness of certain other sectors, Dutch disease should not be regarded as an unwelcome phenomenon for the country as a whole. Moreover, the distributional issues that arise are also present in other contexts—for example, in considering the effects of opening the economy to trade and FDI. Whether spurred by financial aid, trade liberalization, or institution building, the growth process is bound to have uneven effects on different sectors and regions of the economy. Lustig (2001) notes, for example, that the gains to Mexico from NAFTA have been concentrated in firms set up in border states to supply the U.S. market, and that traditional agriculture in Mexico, as well as regions relatively far from the U.S. border, have been hurt. Part of the solution for mitigating or avoiding a rise in inequality—and for addressing, more generally, the disruptions associated with the process of creative destruction—is to strengthen social

[59] See Heller and Gupta (2002).
[60] Fiscal difficulties can also arise from in-kind aid that creates additional spending needs, as when nurses are required to administer drugs donated as in-kind aid.

safety nets and upgrade the skills of the population. In addition, various country-specific measures to support lagging sectors or regions may be desirable on grounds of equity or political economy.

6.5   Concluding Perspectives

In discussing ways to strengthen the architecture of the international financial system, the academic and policymaking communities have devoted considerable attention to the challenges of preventing and resolving financial crises. It is also important to focus the architecture agenda on the longer-run objectives of raising living standards and reducing poverty. Accordingly, this chapter has considered the factors that contribute to economic growth and poverty reduction.

Much of the relevant academic literature has focused on three proximate determinants of economic growth: physical capital formation, human capital formation, and technological change. This literature emanated from a pathbreaking conceptual contribution by Solow (1957), who emphasized that in the hypothetical long-run steady state, technological change (i.e., productivity growth) is the only possible source of growth in per capita output. Countries with relatively high rates of saving will have relatively high steady-state levels of capital per worker and output per capita, but no country will be able to sustain steady-state growth in per capita output without growth in productivity.

Although initially designed for conceptual analysis of economies in long-run equilibrium, the model developed by Solow has also provided the basis for empirical studies of the proximate determinants of economic growth over medium-run horizons. Such studies suggest that most of the variation in living standards across countries can be attributed to differences in technology or productivity, with considerably less explained by differences in physical capital per worker or education levels. This finding is consistent with Schumpeter's (1911) view that output growth is achieved primarily through a process of creative destruction.

The process of creative destruction depends critically on whether people have opportunities and incentives to innovate and adopt new technologies or more productive ways of organizing economic activity. Many factors can undermine such opportunities and incentives, including vested interests in old technologies or the lack of economic and legal systems that enable innovators to reap adequate benefits from their innovations.

The latter perspectives have focused attention on deeper determinants of technological change and economic growth, with particular attention to the importance of institutions and the stimulus that can potentially be provided by openness to international trade and capital flows. The discussion of the deeper determinants of growth has also recognized the influence of certain geographical characteristics, such as climate, the disease environment, and distance from markets.

Economists use the term *institutions* to refer to the combination of formal constraints, informal norms or conventions, and enforcement characteristics that shape the incentive structure for societies and, in particular, for economic behavior. In this way, the concept of institutions is much broader than the concept of organizations (i.e., groups of individuals bound together by common functions or purposes). Various types of institutions are required to enable a market economy to perform effectively in stimulating innovation and sustaining growth. One taxonomy distinguishes between four types of institutions: market creating, market regulating, market stabilizing, and market legitimizing. This taxonomy recognizes that innovation and growth require institutions to create markets by defining property rights and enforcing contracts, to regulate markets and correct market failures, to stabilize markets through the exercise of monetary and fiscal policies and through prudential regulation and supervision, and to legitimize markets through the provision of political voice and social safety nets.

Although economists have a limited understanding of how institutions evolve as the complexity of the economic environment increases, the role of innovation and creative destruction makes it clear that success in sustaining economic growth depends critically on how institutions develop and adapt. Adaptive efficiency, more so than allocative efficiency, appears to be the key to raising standards of living over time.

Because countries have different informal norms and enforcement characteristics for governing economic behavior, the formal institutional arrangements that are effective in one country may be ineffective in others. Moreover, the most essential institutional features—including clear and enforceable property rights, the rule of law, sound money, a well-disciplined fiscal process, appropriate prudential regulation and supervision, and distributive justice—can be provided through various forms of institutional arrangements. This has implications for the effort to induce countries to comply with standards and codes for various types of institutions. On the one hand, it is clear that the need for well-functioning institutions provides an essential role for government in a market economy, and it is equally clear from experience that governments can undermine growth in numerous ways, including through failure to adopt institutional arrangements that provide and protect property rights, exercise appropriate prudential supervision, and guard against high budget deficits, high inflation, and negative real interest rates. Thus, compliance with standards and codes for various institutional features is important for growth. On the other hand, it is also important that the standard and codes exercise leave ample scope for countries to achieve compliance through specific institutional forms that are suitable to their own individual country circumstances.

Some economists have emphasized that well-functioning market systems rest on very fragile political foundations. The preservation of an environment that provides widespread opportunities and incentives to innovate requires institutional arrangements that prevent the government from degenerating into a system that primarily serves the interests of the wealthiest members of society or of other vested interest groups. In addition, social safety nets that insure people adequately against the hardships associated with creative destruction are important for withstanding the prospect that large groups of citizens may become disillusioned with the system.

Extensive anecdotal evidence suggests that opportunities to innovate can be substantially enhanced through access to finance. Consistently, formal econometric research has provided fairly convincing evidence of the importance of financial sector development in promoting economic growth. Thus, institutions that are conducive to the development of well-functioning financial markets have a particularly important role to play in the process of economic growth.

Most economists are persuaded that growth can be promoted by opening economies to international trade and foreign direct investment. The benefits come through multiple channels, including from the competition that drives inefficient firms out of business while inducing efficient firms to emerge and expand; from reducing the price and increasing the quality of the goods available to domestic firms and consumers; from the expansion of markets and the increased scope to specialize and reap economies of scale; and from the international transmission of knowledge and skills that are relevant to production and marketing. That being said, there remain significant differences of opinion on how rapidly countries should liberalize trade, with some economists emphasizing that most of today's rich countries embarked on development behind protective trade barriers and arguing that less advanced countries should design their trade and foreign direct investment policies in the context of fairly comprehensive development strategies.

The financial crises of the past decade have left economists very aware of the dangers of opening economies prematurely to international capital flows. Indeed, the IMF and its major creditor countries have been strongly criticized for not adequately recognizing and warning countries of the dangers of liberalizing domestic financial markets and international capital flows before they have strengthened financial institutions and established sound systems of prudential regulation and supervision. There are significant differences of opinion, however, on whether countries should be prepared to spend a prolonged period trying to strengthen financial sector institutions before opening up to foreign capital. Some economists argue that an open and competitive financial sector is fundamentally important in setting the stage for growth, that a sheltered domestic financial sector is likely to be resistant to serious institutional reform, and that it is inadvisable to wait too long before liberalizing restrictions that have sheltered the domestic financial sector, even if removing them leads to financial crisis in the short run.

Discussions of poverty and the challenge of meeting the Millennium Development Goal for its alleviation have been clouded by disagreements over measurement issues. A clear analytical point, however, is that the most effective vehicle for reducing poverty is economic growth. This does not imply that economic growth is the only means to poverty reduction, but it does imply that institutions for creating, regulating, stabilizing, and legitimizing markets are of central importance not only for sustaining growth but also in determining outcomes for the poor.

The international community has become increasingly aware over the past decade that many low-income countries have gotten caught in poverty traps, with dim prospects for economic growth as long as they are burdened with high levels of debt relative to GDP. This has led to the HIPC initiative for relieving the debts of heavily-indebted poor countries that develop programs for poverty reduction and growth that command the support of the IMF and World Bank, and that establish track records of reform and sound policies under those programs. To a large extent, the decision to restrict debt relief to countries that have established track records of reform and sound policies reflects the fact that, for various reasons, official development assistance has not been very effective as a vehicle for promoting growth over the past half century. This has led some to conclude that debt relief and other forms of development assistance are unlikely to be effective in promoting growth in the future unless they are administered in a hard-hearted manner that allocates aid primarily to countries with track records of strong performance and that withholds aid from countries characterized by poor governance. Others have attributed some of the blame to donor practices, emphasizing the need for donors to provide financial aid and technical assistance in a manner that is much more oriented than in the past toward building institutional capacities in recipient countries.

PART THREE

The Agenda for Reform

7

What Can Individual Countries Do

In considering what has been wrong with the globalization process from an economic welfare perspective, Part Two has focused on two major concerns about the performance of the global economy in recent decades: the fairly frequent occurrence of severe financial crises, and the fact that many countries have experienced inadequate growth and excessive poverty. A key objective was to lay the groundwork for developing a list of country-specific and systemic problems that influence the prevalence and severity of financial crises and growth failures.

Drawing on Part Two, this chapter and the next identify a number of problems that contribute to the onset of international financial crises, that impede the resolution and increase the depth of crises, or that create obstacles to economic growth and poverty reduction. The list distinguishes between those problems that are country specific in nature and those that relate to the general functioning of the international financial system. The chapters then describe the main ideas that economists and policymaking institutions have put forth for addressing each of the problem areas, focusing in this chapter on what countries can do individually to mitigate crises and stimulate growth and, in Chapter 8, on directions for systemic reform.

There is no way to completely prevent financial crises or eliminate growth failures. As Volcker (1999: 255) has observed:

International financial crises ... are built into the human genome. When we map the whole thing, we will find something called greed and something called fear and something called hubris. That is all you need to produce international financial crises in the future.

Nevertheless, the countries that have experienced major financial crises over the past decade have not been selected at random; each of them suffered from significant macroeconomic imbalances or financial sector vulnerabilities. Similarly, countries that have experienced economic stagnation or relatively low growth tend to have institutional structures that limit the opportunities or incentives for entrepreneurship and technological innovation. Thus, although some of the problems that contribute to financial crises and growth disappointments relate to human nature and the imperfect functioning of the international financial system, others are country specific.

As emphasized in Chapter 2, the sophistication of international financial markets and the current lack of political support for relinquishing monetary policy autonomy in the key-currency countries suggest that the world is stuck with the prevailing international monetary system for the foreseeable future. So revolutionary change is not in the cards. However, given the significant number of problems that adversely affect the functioning of the global economy, serious pursuit of well-designed evolutionary measures for addressing these problems can plausibly deliver considerable benefits. As discussed in previous chapters, some of these evolutionary changes are already underway.

Box 7.1 lists five types of country-specific problems that have contributed to the frequency and severity of financial crises and growth failures. The list is arranged in an order in which it is convenient to discuss the problems, not in an order that judges their relative importance. The associated agenda for individual countries—a set of fairly extensive and ongoing challenges—includes: devising a sensible strategy for controlling and liberalizing domestic financial markets and international capital flows (Section 7.1); strengthening institutions, information, and the financial and corporate sectors (Section 7.2); adopting sustainable exchange rate arrangements (Section 7.3); maintaining discipline over macroeconomic policies and the levels of public and external debt, and expeditiously addressing any financial sector problems or other developments that threaten to erode market confidence (Section 7.4); and opening the economy to international trade and foreign direct investment (FDI) in a manner that exploits opportunities for growth-enhancing activities (Section 7.5). As noted in the concluding perspectives (Section 7.6), although economists generally agree on a broad characterization of what countries should try to achieve under each item on the agenda, in most cases countries can benefit from devising their own specific approaches, although experience provides considerable guidance on useful directions to take and pitfalls to avoid.

BOX 7.1. Country-specific problems

1. Some countries have liberalized their policies toward domestic financial markets and international capital inflows without adequately strengthening their financial sectors and prudential structures.
2. In many developing countries the institutions required to support well-functioning markets are underdeveloped, the provision of economic data is inadequate in scope or timeliness, and the financial or corporate sectors are vulnerable to balance-sheet problems. Institutional structures are also deficient in some advanced economies, where weaknesses in accounting, auditing, and corporate governance have led to a significant erosion of trust in the financial reporting framework.
3. Some countries that are open to international capital flows maintain exchange rate arrangements that do not adequately protect against destabilizing speculation—that is, they attempt to keep their exchange rates fixed within narrow ranges without making credible commitments to avoid realignments by adopting institutional arrangements that make exchange rate adjustment very hard.
4. Some countries make inadequate efforts to maintain debt discipline and sound macroeconomic policies, or they fail to respond expeditiously to financial sector problems or other developments that pose threats to market confidence.
5. Some countries open up to international trade and FDI without strategies that adequately exploit opportunities for growth-enhancing investment, production, and institution building.

7.1   Devise a Sensible Strategy for Liberalizing Domestic Financial Markets and International Capital Flows

The frequency and high costs of financial crises during the past decade have led to a general reevaluation of the case for liberalizing domestic financial markets and international capital flows, along with the related case for imposing controls on capital flows that are currently unrestricted.[1] Two of the factors highlighted in previous chapters have been

---

[1] Dooley (1996), Eichengreen, Mussa, Dell'Ariccia, Detragiache et al. (1998), Neely (1999), and Cooper (1999b) provide surveys of the theoretical and practical cases for capital controls. Rogoff (2002b) presents an overview of some key issues and Ariyoshi, Habermeier, Laurens, Otker-Robe et al. (2000) provide an extensive study of the use and liberalization of capital controls in fourteen selected countries.

particularly instrumental in precipitating this reevaluation. First, the typical emerging market crisis has been associated with a surge in capital inflows followed by a sharp reversal or sudden stop. Second, the increased frequency of international financial crises since the mid-1990s was preceded by a substantial liberalization of domestic financial markets and international capital flows by emerging market countries in the late 1980s and early 1990s.

The main arguments against capital controls, or against any other distortions of the market allocation of resources, are based on both economic theory and historical experience. Theory suggests that markets driven by the profit incentives of firms and the income—consumption desires of worker—households can provide a relatively efficient system for allocating resources. Moreover, experience suggests that such systems are relatively efficient in encouraging technological innovation and economic growth over time, a view that was strongly reinforced by the extensive breakdown of central planning systems in the former Soviet Union and elsewhere during the 1980s and early 1990s. Among other things, experience teaches that relying on governments to control the allocation of resources has often led to corruption and the financing of unproductive activities, and that capital controls, like other regulations, have also led to the development of vested interests that obstruct the removal of the controls after they have served their original purposes. In addition, controls can have the counterproductive effect of providing leeway for governments to delay or try to avoid the fiscal or monetary policy actions that are appropriate for addressing serious macroeconomic imbalances.[2]

These arguments against capital controls have to be weighed against the prospect that the market allocation of resources may be distorted by factors other than government controls or may fail to make appropriate allowance for various forms of public goods. In concept, the case for capital controls—or, more generally, for controls on domestic financial markets and international capital flows—rests on the theory of the second best. If the allocation of resources in financial markets suffers from some distortion that cannot be eliminated, it may be possible to improve welfare through a second-best approach of judiciously imposing another

---

[2] By the same token, a number of conceptual models have developed the point that the liberalization of controls can signal that policymakers are committed to maintaining sound macroeconomic policies, thereby influencing the expectations and behavior of market participants in potentially helpful ways; see, for example, Bartolini and Drazen (1997).

distortion. From this perspective, controls on domestic financial markets and international capital flows can be justified, at least in principle, on the basis of several different types of distortions.

One justification is that inefficiencies arise in financial markets because of informational frictions. In particular, the costs of screening borrowers and monitoring their behavior, and various factors that limit the ability of agents to reap the full benefits of incurring such costs, lead economic agents to participate in financial markets on the basis of incomplete and asymmetric information.[3] This can result in adverse selection of borrowers, partly because lenders have incomplete information and partly because some borrowers may have incentives to gamble for redemption by investing in projects that offer the prospect of high payoffs but are also highly risky. Similarly, asymmetric information can allow borrowers, once loans have been made, to alter their behavior in ways that increase the risks of default. In addition, asymmetric information can lead to excessive volatility in financial markets as a result of the related phenomena of herding behavior, in which many investors take positions largely on the basis of the recommendations or behavior of market leaders, and momentum trading, in which investors buy and sell assets largely on the basis of recent trends in asset prices. As argued by Calvo and Mendoza (2000a) and discussed in Chapter 5, such informational frictions may figure importantly in explaining the phenomena of sudden stops and contagion in international capital flows, which are two prominent features of emerging market financial crises.

Another justification for capital controls comes from the orientation of governments toward providing macroeconomic stability, which leads them both to accumulate foreign exchange reserves as a device for smoothing national consumption (as national output varies over the business cycle) and to provide explicit or implicit insurance to the domestic financial system. As emphasized by Dooley (2000a) and Dooley and Walsh (2003), these factors create expectations that governments will spend some of their foreign exchange reserves to avert defaults by the domestic financial system, which may induce private creditors to lend countries more than is socially optimal.

Proponents of capital controls have further emphasized that financial markets act from a fundamentally different perspective than the policy

---

[3] See the discussions in Bryant (2003), Stiglitz (2004), and Eichengreen, Mussa et al. (1998).

authorities entrusted to promote national welfare. Even if policy authorities have no better information than financial market participants, a case for controls can be based on the fact that financial market behavior is myopic and motivated by "greed and fear."[4] It has also been argued, from a somewhat related perspective, that controls during times of market stress can buy governments breathing room to coordinate a resolution of panics exacerbated by the uncoordinated behavior of financial market participants, to address any underlying macroeconomic problems, and through such actions to alleviate the fears of financial market participants and avoid the high economic and social costs of financial crises.[5]

From a somewhat different perspective, the challenges of stimulating and sustaining economic growth also provide justification for emerging market countries to maintain controls on domestic financial markets and international capital flows. Many economists have emphasized that no country has developed successfully without taking advantage of international trade and long-term capital flows, It is important, however, for countries to open themselves to trade and foreign capital in a manner that is consistent with a coherent strategy for domestic investment, institution building, and economic growth. As discussed in Chapter 6, it is now widely recognized that the ability of market economies to sustain growth depends on the strength of various types of institutions: institutions that create markets by establishing property rights and enforcing contracts; institutions and mechanisms for regulating markets and correcting market failures; institutions for stabilizing markets through the application of monetary and fiscal policies and prudential regulation and supervision; and institutions that legitimatize market outcomes by providing political voice and social protection and insurance. Such institutions take time to build and strengthen, and, in the interim, uncontrolled financial markets appear to be a major source of instability. Just as today's industrial countries relied on various restrictions on domestic financial markets and international capital flows for several decades after World War II, a case can be made—at least in principle—for today's emerging market economies to rely on financial market restrictions and capital controls until relevant institutions have been strengthened substantially further. In contrast, as

---

[4] See Cooper (1998).
[5] A similar perspective, in models or discussions that feature multiple equilibria, is that controls can potentially guide an economy to a good equilibrium or prevent movement from a good equilibrium to a bad equilibrium.

noted in Chapter 6, some economists argue that a sheltered domestic financial sector can be an obstacle to serious institutional reforms and a major handicap to growth, and that it can be counterproductive to wait too long before exposing the domestic financial sector to foreign competition.[6]

The case for capital controls must be based not only on principle but also on whether they can be implemented effectively in practice. A large body of empirical and anecdotal evidence suggests that the effectiveness of capital controls in practice depends on both the state of the country's financial markets and the nature of the controls. As emphasized in Chapter 2, the revolution in electronic communications and computer technology has made it easy for sophisticated market participants to evade financial market restrictions by shifting the geographical location of financial transactions and repackaging financial products, and the experience of industrial countries since the 1970s confirms that capital controls are no longer effective for highly developed market economies. Moreover, industrial-country banks and other financial institutions that play large roles in international financial markets are adept at evading capital controls imposed by emerging market economies, and in also helping residents of those economies evade controls. Nevertheless, empirical evidence suggests that controls on domestic financial markets and international capital flows continue to have significant effectiveness in countries without highly developed financial sectors and, as discussed later, that certain types of market-based controls may be useful, on a temporary basis, for helping emerging market countries resist surges in short-term capital inflows. At the same time, most economists recognize that capital controls are likely to become progressively less effective and more counterproductive the longer they are in place.[7]

For countries that have not yet liberalized restrictions on domestic financial markets and international capital flows, the consensus advice is to open up to capital flows carefully, replacing controls with effective prudential regulation, and making sure that macroeconomic stability is well established.[8] As characterized by Garber (1998a:29):

[6] See Rajan and Zingales (2003).

[7] It is interesting to note in this connection that most of the controls imposed by Malaysia in September 1998 were removed after one or two years, and that the widely cited controls imposed by Chile in 1991 (as described later) were removed in 1998.

[8] Among economists who have been strongly critical of the push for developing countries to liberalize domestic financial markets and international capital flows, Bhagwati (1998)

According to this prescription, if the phased opening to competition from foreign financial institutions to the unhindered movement of capital is accompanied by a simultaneous push to world-class risk control and a supervisory environment, the ad-on costs of capital-market opening can be minimized or avoided. Thus, a snapshot of the first-class financial systems suggests that countries opening their capital account should strengthen the capital base of their financial institutions and improve supervision and prudential standards. These improvements include upgrades of supervisory personnel, senior and risk-control management in the financial institutions, accounting systems to make capital requirements meaningful, provisioning rules, and legal systems governing bankruptcy. In addition, connected lending should be limited and insolvent institutions speedily eliminated, however politically unpalatable the process.

Even with this prescription, however, the historical experience of most emerging market countries and many industrial countries has led some to conclude that for cases in which domestic financial sectors have been strongly sheltered from competition, the probability of a crisis-free transition is not very high.[9] The liberalization of financial restrictions generally makes markets more competitive, squeezes the profit margins of previously sheltered financial institutions, and leaves less leeway for poor loan and management practices.[10] In addition, liberalization generally gives financial institutions more scope to take risks, as well as more scope to engage in off-balance-sheet transactions that stretch the capacity of regulators to monitor financial activities and risk positions. In Garber's view,

advocates the encouragement of inward FDI flows but would not move to liberalize restrictions on other capital flows rapidly until a country had gained "political stability, economic prosperity and substantial macroeconomic expertise." Rodrik (1998: 60), who elsewhere emphasizes that countries cannot develop successfully by remaining closed to international trade and long-term capital flows, regards "capital flows as a medicine with occasionally horrific side effects" and suggests that it is not good regulatory policy "to remove controls on the sale and use of such a medicine."

[9] U.S. experience provides a classic example of the dangers. As a response to the serious financial difficulties that the savings and loan (S&L) industry encountered toward the end of the 1970s, exacerbated by a sharp rise in U.S. interest rates during 1979, the U.S. authorities substantially deregulated the industry in the early 1980s, allowing S&Ls to engage in more risky activities. Moreover, prudential regulation and supervision were weakened rather than strengthened, and federal deposit insurance gave depositors little incentive to monitor the thrifts; see Kane (1985). The liberalization of deposit interest rates allowed insolvent S&Ls to continue attracting funds and gamble for redemption by investing in commercial real estate ventures with high prospective yields but also high risks. More than 1,000 S&Ls failed between 1980 and 1992, with the deposit guarantee costing the federal government an estimated $127 billion, or 2.3 percent of 1990 GDP. See Lindgren et al. (1996).

[10] See Eichengreen, Mussa et al. (1998).

liberalizing restrictions that have sheltered the domestic financial sector "will almost inevitably lead to a financial crisis," and policymakers should realize this ex ante and "decide that it is worth recognizing and filling a hole in bank balance sheets amounting to 15 percent or more of gross domestic product now in order to gain a better mechanism to allocate capital in the long term."[11] Others seem less pessimistic,[12] but all share the view that financial crises are bound to occur from time to time, and most emphasize the dangers of removing restrictions on capital account transactions before major problems in the financial system are addressed and a sound prudential framework is in place, and before macroeconomic stability is well established.

Discussions of capital controls often distinguish between the different forms of capital flows. Recall that capital flows are often decomposed into banking flows, portfolio flows, and direct investment; banking flows are defined as purchases or sales of claims on banks, portfolio flows encompass purchases or sales of bonds and equities, and direct investment includes the purchase or sale of real estate and production facilities.[13] Distinctions are also made between short-term and longer-term flows. FDI flows are generally regarded as longer-term flows that can serve as an important vehicle for stimulating growth. FDI flows are also generally regarded as not very volatile, which is consistent with recorded data (recall Figure 2.9), although the recorded data may be somewhat misleading because off-balance-sheet derivative transactions (e.g., forward contracts, swaps, and options—see the paragraphs that follow) allow direct investments to be effectively reversed or offset just as readily as portfolio investments. Even so, abstracting from possible political concerns about foreign ownership, economists widely regard the liberalization of inward direct investment as one of the first measures that countries should take in opening up to international capital flows. As a complementary measure for attracting inward FDI flows, countries are generally advised to liberalize restrictions on the repatriation of earnings. In addition, as discussed in Chapter 8, some economists favor the liberalization of equity flows ahead of debt flows on the view that the former have better risk-sharing

---

[11] See Garber (1998a: 29–30).
[12] See Eichengreen, Mussa et al. (1998).
[13] Investments in the equities or bonds of a firm in which the investor holds at least 10 percent of the equity is also recorded as direct investment under international statistical conventions.

properties whereas the latter pose a greater threat to international financial stability.

As discussed in Chapter 4, it is also widely perceived that a large buildup of short-term external debt leaves a country more vulnerable to crisis than a comparable buildup of longer-term external debt and, accordingly, that controls on short-term inflows should be favored over controls on longer-term inflows.[14] However, differential controls or prudential regulations on short-term and longer-term instruments are often evaded through the use of derivative transactions that effectively transform long-term instruments into short-term instruments, or vice versa.[15]

Investors can change the maturity profiles, currency exposures, and, more generally, the overall risks and expected returns associated with their investment positions through transactions in derivative products.[16] It is not surprising, accordingly, that the rapid growth of recorded cross-border capital flows has been paralleled by an explosive growth of derivative transactions over the past two decades (Figure 7.1). The most widely used derivatives are fairly simple, consisting mainly of forward contracts, swaps, and basic options contracts. A forward contract is an arrangement to exchange two assets on some fixed date in the future at an exchange rate (or other terms) specified by the contract. A swap involves an exchange of assets today along with an agreement to reverse the exchange at some specified future date. Options contracts give their owners the right, but not the obligation, to deliver or receive assets—either on a pre-specified future date (European options) or at any time prior to a specific date (American options)—under the terms and contingencies agreed by the parties entering into the contract. Although a substantial volume of derivative transactions are conducted on organized exchanges in which people get together to trade futures and options contracts, most derivative transactions are arranged through the phone and computer network of

[14] Concerns about the potential volatility of short-run flows should not be misinterpreted as suggestions that all short-term capital flows are bad. As emphasized by Rogoff (2002b), short-term credits are the lifeblood of international trade, and short-term instruments are important for enabling producers and investors to hedge.

[15] Moreover, for reasons emphasized by Jeanne (2000b, 2003) and Tirole (2002) and discussed in Chapter 8, effective controls on short-term inflows might well result in a substantial reduction in total capital inflows rather than a substantial substitution of long-term flows for short-term flows. See Cordella (2003), however, for a counterargument.

[16] See the discussion in Garber (1998b).

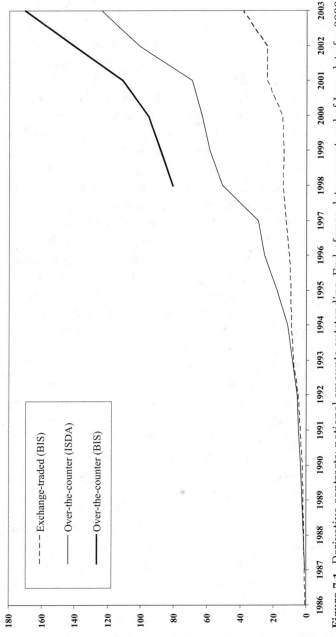

Figure 7.1. Derivative contracts: notional amounts outstanding, End-of-year data, except end of June data for 2003 (In trillions of U.S. dollars). *Sources:* Bank for International Settlements (BIS) *Quarterly Review*, various issues, and International Swaps and Derivatives Association Inc. (ISDA). The ISDA data include interest rate swaps and options and cross-currency swaps. The BIS data for over-the-counter instruments, which start in 1998, include foreign exchange, interest rate, equity linked, commodity linked, and other contracts. The BIS data on exchange-traded instruments include foreign exchange, interest rate, and equity index futures and options.

over-the-counter trading among financial institutions and other market participants dispersed around the globe.

The availability of derivative products for managing investors' risk exposures can induce gross capital flows that would not otherwise occur. Moreover, to the extent that derivative transactions result in off-balance-sheet exposures rather than changes in recorded balance-sheet positions, they can also confound the nature of the cross-border flows that occur and greatly complicate the tasks of prudential regulation and supervision. For example, if a country decided to impose a tax on short-term borrowing from abroad but exempted longer-term borrowing from the tax, banks desiring funds for only a month could reduce their tax burden by borrowing long term and entering an off-balance-sheet forward contract to repay the funds in thirty days. Alternatively if the country prohibited nonresidents from purchasing equity in domestic firms, a nonresident might be able to purchase a structured note from a resident, arranged by an offshore intermediary that delivered the purchasing price of equity shares to the resident and promised to deliver back to the nonresident the value of the equity at some agreed date in the future (or perhaps gave the nonresident the option of when to cash the structured note for the value of the equity). As another example, residents wishing to speculate in foreign currency can evade restrictions on currency conversions in the home foreign exchange market by contracting with an offshore bank for a nondeliverable forward contract—that is, a contract that requires no physical delivery of currencies upon purchase and is settled at maturity by delivering the difference between the agreed price and the realized price, where the price is linked to the exchange rate. Similarly, limits on open foreign exchange positions may be ineffective when banks can use offshore subsidiaries or derivative instruments to circumvent them.

This emphasis on channels for evading capital controls should not obscure the fact that financial derivatives also provide very important vehicles for market participants to hedge against the financial risks associated with international trade and investment. More generally, by providing more complete markets, financial derivatives play a significant role in promoting a more efficient allocation of the world's productive resources, in spreading the risks associated with technological innovations, and, consequently, in contributing to a stronger rise in incomes and consumption. Nevertheless, it is well to bear in mind that "financial engineering houses are designed to pick apart and arbitrage capital-flow channels that are not airtight"[17]—that is, to design derivative contracts that are effective for evading capital controls.

There are different forms of capital controls and reasonably broad agreement that some forms are more attractive than others. Market-based controls, such as interest rate ceilings or reserve requirements, are generally favored over quotas, licenses, or other controls that require administration, because the latter types tend to provide strong incentives for bribery and to result in less productive allocations of capital.

Distinctions are also drawn between controls on capital inflows and controls on capital outflows. Empirical studies appear to support the view that controls on capital inflows can have significant effects while also apparently suggesting that controls designed to inhibit capital outflows have not been very effective, especially when devaluation is anticipated.[18] That being noted, however, the case for temporary standstills on capital outflows remains an important issue for debate in the context of proposals for systemic reform (see Chapter 8).

One widely cited proposal for discouraging short-term capital inflows is the Tobin tax. Under the original proposal by Tobin (1978), a small percentage of all foreign exchange transactions would be taxed away, implying a relatively high effective tax rate on funds moved across currencies for only short periods of time and a negligible effective tax rate on long-term capital movements. In theory, this would throw "sand in the wheels" of short-term speculative capital movements. In practice, however, it would only work if all countries agreed to adopt it and no country sought to profit as a haven in which foreign exchange transactions could avoid the tax.

An alternative way of throwing sand in the wheels of short-term capital movements, similar in spirit to the Tobin tax, is to impose an unremunerated reserve requirement of fixed duration on all capital inflows. Such an experiment was conducted by Chile between 1991 and 1998. In particular, banking and portfolio flows were subjected to a one-year mandatory non-interest-paying deposit—the *encaje*—which was initially set at 20 percent of principal and increased to 30 percent in 1992.[19] Studies of the Chilean controls tend to conclude that the encaje did not

---

[17] See Garber (1998a: 33).
[18] See Eichengreen, Mussa et al. (1998) and IMF (1995b).
[19] The word *encaje* means strongbox in Spanish. See Kenen (2001), Neely (1999), and Agosin and Ffrench-Davis (1997) for descriptions of the Chilean controls.

have a significant impact on the overall volume of capital inflows but did shift the composition away from short-term inflows.[20] Moreover, financial engineering research efforts did not figure out how to circumvent the encaje through derivative transactions,[21] suggesting that the recorded shift in composition away from short-term inflows was probably not an illusion. However, the Chilean regime left open some loopholes, at least temporarily,[22] and as Sebastian Edwards (1999) emphasizes, the controls were unable to insulate Chile from the Asian crisis. Furthermore, the controls imposed particularly strong financial constraints on small-sized firms, which some regard as important sources of job creation and growth in emerging market countries.[23]

These many considerations lead to several conclusions.

First, because there are large potential long-run benefits from liberalizing financial market restrictions and capital controls, because attempts to retain restrictions are likely to lose their effectiveness and become counterproductive over time, and because there are clear dangers to liberalizing capital controls before major problems in the financial system are addressed, it is highly undesirable to leave the task of strengthening the financial sector and prudential framework until late in the development process.[24]

Second, because FDI can be particularly beneficial for long-run growth whereas excessive short-term debt can leave countries particularly vulnerable to financial crises, the sequencing of financial liberalization should

[20] See Kenen (2001: 134). Montiel and Reinhart (1999) report a similar finding—that controls on short-term or portfolio capital inflows affect the composition but not the overall volume of capital flows—based on a panel of fifteen emerging market countries during 1990–96.

[21] See Garber (1998b: fn. 15).

[22] See Forbes (2003).

[23] See Forbes (2003), who suggests that smallness made firms less able to obtain long-term finance, more dependent on funding from banks (which had little scope to avoid the encaje), and poorly positioned to take advantage of the loopholes that remained open.

[24] A somewhat related issue is whether the IMF's jurisdiction should be extended, as proposed by the Interim Committee in September 1997, through an amendment to the Fund's Articles that requires member countries to assume "carefully designed and consistently applied obligations" with regard to capital account liberalization. The issue has faded in the aftermath of the Asian currency crises, but the views of eight leading experts are collected in a volume edited by Kenen (1998). Fischer (1998) argues in favor of such an amendment, Polak (1998) maintains that an amendment is unnecessary and would lead to a significant unproductive reallocation of Fund resources, and Rodrik (1998: 65) worries that "canonizing capital-account convertibility . . . would leave the typical 'emerging market' hostage to the whims and fancies of . . . country analysts in London, Frankfurt, and New York."

aim to open the economy to inward direct investment flows relatively early while moving much more cautiously to liberalize restrictions on inflows of short-term debt.

Third, temporary reliance on Chilean-style controls appears to be a relatively attractive way of responding to strong inflows of short-term debt, provided the controls can be enforced transparently and without corruption.

7.2   Strengthen Institutions, Information, and the Financial and Corporate Sectors

As emphasized in the first conclusion to the Section 7.1, it is important for countries to move expeditiously in addressing the challenges of strengthening their financial sectors, including their frameworks for prudential regulation and supervision.[25] The virulence of the crises that struck Thailand, Korea, and Indonesia brought a new appreciation of the vulnerabilities that can breed in the financial sector. Possible sources of vulnerability include foreign currency borrowing without adequate hedging; accumulating short-term debts when assets are longer term; poor credit allocation; weak risk management practices more generally; ineffective financial supervision and regulation; and booms in equity and real estate prices.[26]

Needless to say, the focus on strengthening institutions and market structures should not be concentrated solely on the financial sector. The

[25] Caprio and Honohan (1999) provide general perspectives on banking problems and regulation issues, and Barth, Caprio, and Levine (2002) provide empirical findings on what works best in bank regulation and supervision. Caprio and Honohan (2002) note that the presence of foreign-owned banks can mitigate the trade-off between dampening short-run volatility and promoting the longer-run health of the banking sector and the economy.

[26] On the basis of recommendations of the Financial Stability Forum's Working Group on Capital Flows, Kenen (2001: 132) suggests that the set of prudential regulations for guarding against excessive liquidity and foreign currency exposures might include limits on banks' open foreign currency positions; special reserve requirements on foreign currency funding; higher reserve or liquidity requirements on banks' short-term foreign currency debts than on their long-term foreign currency debts; and requiring banks to condition loans with the stipulation that borrowers hedge their foreign currency positions. As a mechanism to provide stronger incentives for market discipline, Calomiris (1998a, 1999) would require banks to maintain at least a minimal ratio of subordinated debt to risk-weighted assets (see the discussion in Chapter 8). Such measures would induce substitution of short-term corporate borrowing for bank-related inflows, but maintaining a healthy banking sector—which plays a particularly large role in the allocation of capital and is underpinned by the state—is an important objective.

potential for economic growth depends on the quality of the many types of institutions or institutional mechanisms that are relevant for creating, regulating, stabilizing, and legitimizing markets. Legal institutions can contribute importantly to the stimulation and expansion of economic activity by clarifying property rights, enforcing contracts, and thereby strengthening the incentives and prospects for entrepreneurship.[27] Regulatory bodies and other mechanisms are important for monitoring the behavior of market participants and for addressing market failures to ensure that the behavior of markets is consistent with the public interest. Macroeconomic policy authorities are important, along with prudential supervisors for the financial sector, for stabilizing the economy and controlling the monetary system and the public sector accounts. In addition, the quality of macroeconomic stabilization policy requires institutional arrangements for collecting and disseminating economic statistics. And public support for policies that are conducive to creative destruction and growth can be significantly enhanced through institutional arrangements that provide individuals with adequate social safety nets.

Although it is clear that markets won't work well in the absence of relevant institutional structures, comparisons of different market economies indicate that different types of institutional arrangements can succeed in supporting markets, and that the required degree of institutional sophistication depends on the stage of market development. Indeed, because different countries have different informal norms of behavior and enforcement mechanisms, formal institutional structures that work well in one country may not work well in others.[28] That being recognized, however, the international community has launched a major initiative to develop standards and codes that can serve as minimal requirements or benchmarks for various types of institutional structures, to help countries assess how well their institutions comply with the benchmarks, and to provide technical assistance to countries seeking to strengthen their institutional structures.

As part of this effort to help countries strengthen protection against financial crises and lay the foundations for sustainable growth, the IMF

---

[27] De Soto (2000, 2001) argues that entrepreneurship in developing countries is severely constrained by a lack of institutional mechanisms that would make it feasible for residents to harness the potential of their real estate assets to serve as collateral for start-up and working capital.

[28] See North (1994).

and World Bank have been focusing, in collaboration, on the areas of improving information and strengthening the financial and corporate sectors. Recall from Chapter 3 that twelve standards have been designated as particularly relevant in these areas—specifically, three transparency standards (data dissemination, monetary and financial policy transparency, and fiscal transparency), five financial sector standards (banking supervision, securities regulation, insurance supervision, payment and settlement, and combating money laundering and terrorist financing) and four corporate sector standards (corporate governance, accounting, auditing, and insolvency).

Recall also from Chapter 3 that the Fund and the Bank have launched two somewhat interrelated assessment programs—a Financial Sector Assessment Program (FSAP) and an initiative to generate Reports on the Observance of Standards and Codes (ROSCs). Countries that request to participate in the FSAP receive comprehensive diagnoses of potential financial sector vulnerabilities, covering a range of institutions (including banks, mutual funds, and insurance companies) and financial markets (money markets, securities markets, and foreign exchange markets), as well as the payments systems and the regulatory, supervisory, and legal frameworks that underpin the financial institutions and markets. The depth and scope of coverage is tailored to country-specific circumstances. The assessments focus inter alia on stress tests, compliance with relevant standards and codes, and priorities for reform and development. ROSCs involve smaller-scale assessments, looking at compliance with individual standards or codes. ROSCs relating to financial sector standards are often conducted in the context of a financial sector assessment (FSA). Although FSAs and ROSCs are conducted jointly by the IMF and World Bank, they draw on the knowledge of experts from a range of cooperating central banks, supervisory agencies, standard setting bodies, and other institutions. Participation in FSAs and ROSCs is voluntary. Whether or not to make public the associated reports is also left for individual countries to decide. Regardless of the choice, the reports in many cases raise issues that are important to macroeconomic objectives or policies and feed into Fund and Bank surveillance.

Participation in assessment programs is only a first step. Once financial sector vulnerabilities and any deficiencies in meeting standards and codes have been diagnosed and priorities established, countries face the challenge of addressing the various weaknesses. In many cases this requires technical assistance from the Fund, the Bank, or a country with established expertise; and in all cases it takes time. Progress will depend importantly on the seriousness and speed with which national authorities seek to benefit from the programs. It will also depend importantly on the quantity and quality of the experts from the international community who are available to participate in providing assessments and technical assistance, on the financial resources that are allocated to support the programs, and in some cases on whether the international community chooses to change the incentives of national authorities (see Chapter 8).

The need for strengthening institutions, information, and the financial and corporate sectors is by no means confined to the emerging market countries and other developing economies. The unexpected collapse of Enron (a giant U.S. energy corporation) toward the end of 2001, along with other subsequent corporate failures, have pointed to weaknesses in accounting, auditing, and corporate governance and have led to a significant erosion of trust in the financial reporting framework in the United States. Addressing these problems, and restoring and maintaining confidence in the quality and integrity of external audits, remains a major challenge for the United States and other industrial countries.

7.3   Adopt Sustainable Exchange Rate Arrangements

The late Henry Wallich, after many years of studying international financial markets from the vantage points of Yale University and the Board of Governors of the Federal Reserve System, came to the view that although economists did not know the right levels for exchange rates, they could often tell a wrong exchange rate when they saw one. A similar observation can be made about exchange rate arrangements.

Economists continue to debate what type of exchange rate arrangement is right for emerging market countries, but they are broadly agreed that for a country open to a substantial volume of international capital flows, a pegged exchange rate is strongly inadvisable unless institutional arrangements are adopted that make the exchange rate impossible or extremely hard to change.[29] One way to establish a hard peg is to effectively get rid

---

[29] See Obstfeld and Rogoff (1995), Cooper (1999a), Frankel (1999), Edwards and Savastano (2000), Mussa, Masson et al. (2000), Reinhart (2000), Fischer (2001b), Corden (2002), Calvo and Mishkin (2003), Rogoff et al. (2004), and Tavlas (2003) for recent discussions of issues relating to exchange rates and the choice of exchange rate regime.

of the exchange rate altogether by replacing the national currency with a foreign currency as legal tender—often referred to as dollarizing the economy. As a variant on this approach, countries can create a new common currency and pool their monetary autonomy in a common central bank, as the Euro Area countries have done. Another approach is to institute a currency-board arrangement under which the monetary authority is only allowed to issue new monetary liabilities through purchases of eligible foreign-currency-denominated assets at a predetermined and rigidly fixed exchange rate. Because changes in the monetary authority's liabilities (the supply of base money) must be fully backed by changes in its foreign exchange assets, currency-board arrangements are perceived as considerably less likely to lead to concerns about monetary policy credibility than regimes under which the monetary authority has broad discretion over the money supply and can be put under strong political pressures to use its discretion. Accordingly, currency-board arrangements have also generally been referred to as hard exchange rate pegs. In contrast, the traditional form of pegged exchange rate arrangement, where the monetary authority is only committed to maintain the rate within a narrow fluctuation range, is regarded as a soft peg.

Soft exchange rate pegs provide invitations for speculative attacks when large volumes of domestic and international liquidity can be shifted rapidly from one currency to another. This lesson has now been driven home by the breakdown of the Bretton Woods system in the early 1970s, by the repeated crises within the European Monetary System between its inception in 1979 and the substantial widening of its fluctuation margins in 1993, and by the emerging market crises of the past decade. Indeed, a pegged exchange rate arrangement (either de jure or de facto) was one of the sources of vulnerability in each of the seven crisis episodes reviewed in Chapter 4.

The vulnerability of a soft peg regime stems from the fact that the monetary authority's commitment to keep the exchange rate pegged within narrow margins establishes a presumption that it will react to economic shocks in ways that prevent the exchange rate from changing. Such a presumption can reduce and distort the exchange rate risk that domestic economic agents perceive when they borrow in foreign currency. Under such a regime, if macroeconomic policies and market pressures in a country experiencing relatively strong economic expansion lead to a positive differential between domestic currency interest rates and foreign currency interest rates, the combination of the interest differential and perceptions of relatively low exchange rate risk can give domestic residents an incentive to borrow in foreign currency rather than domestic currency. Moreover, the buildup of foreign currency debt is likely to be most prominent at short maturities, as short-term international credit tends to be more readily and cheaply available than longer-term debt. Should subsequent developments eventually lead to a recession in output or a contraction of export earnings, a large stock of short-term foreign-currency-denominated debt can raise doubts about the county's ability to meet payments on its external debt. This creates a dilemma for the monetary authorities, who may be reluctant to resist the downward currency pressures by raising interest rates and further depressing output and, in any case, are likely to come under political pressure to refrain from raising interest rates during a recession. In turn, as market participants come to perceive the policy dilemma, they will begin to attach significant probability to the prospect that the authorities will abandon the exchange rate peg—a shift in expectations that, for a country with substantial involvement in international capital markets, can easily feed on itself and develop into a full-scale self-justifying speculative attack.

Although soft forms of pegged exchange rates with narrow fluctuation margins are highly inadvisable for countries with substantial involvement in international capital markets, the case against soft pegs has often been overstated or misrepresented as a case against a wider range of exchange rate regimes. There is little support for the extreme form of the "bipolar view"—namely, that emerging market countries have the choice of hard forms of fixed exchange rates or freely floating rates, with a hollow middle ground. Relatively attractive intermediate choices include fixed or crawling exchange rate arrangements with wide fluctuation bands, as well as managed floating arrangements. Moreover, the case against soft exchange rate pegs does not apply to all countries. Roughly 130 of the Fund's 184 member countries are not extensively involved in international capital markets, and pegged exchange rates are an attractive option for many of these countries.[30] Furthermore, it would not be valid to suggest that

---

[30] Econometric work reported by Rogoff et al. (2004) suggests that, in developing countries with limited access to external capital, de facto pegged exchange rates and other limited flexibility arrangements (using the Reinhart–Rogoff (2004) classification) have been associated with lower inflation without any apparent reduction in GDP growth rates or increase in the volatility of GDP growth.

pegged exchange rate regimes have been the ultimate causes of international financial crises, or that countries with other types of exchange rate regimes are immune from crises. Consistent with this view, a number of economists have argued that well-functioning fiscal, financial, and monetary policy institutions are more important than the choice of exchange rate regime.[31]

Concerns about soft peg regimes for emerging market countries (or countries about to open up to capital flows) raise the questions of how and when to exit from such regimes. Historical experience suggests that most exits from currency pegs have occurred under unfavorable circumstances and have not had happy results.[32] This has been blamed in part on a tendency of policymakers to wait too long before exiting, reflecting either incentives to postpone the day of reckoning or hopes that underlying macroeconomic problems can be resolved without unpegging the currency. The seven crisis episodes reviewed in Chapter 4 provide cases in point. In each of the seven episodes, the exit from a de facto pegged exchange rate regime was essentially forced by market pressures (the draining of foreign exchange reserves) and resulted in unwanted large-scale currency depreciation.

In contrast, a number of countries (including Israel, Poland, Uruguay, Nicaragua, and Croatia) have had successful experiences in exiting from soft pegs or crawling peg regimes after relying on such exchange rate arrangements as nominal anchors for adjusting from high inflation.[33] These experiences have led to the accepted wisdom that exit is best undertaken when a currency is not under downward pressure, and that it is desirable to proceed gradually if possible, typically by widening the fluctuation margins in several steps.[34] Israel, for example, exited gradually from a pegged arrangement against the U.S. dollar, widening the fluctuation margins to plus or minus 3 percent in March 1990, replacing the fixed band with a plus or minus 5 percent crawling band in December 1991, further widening the band to plus or minus 7 percent in May 1995, and subsequently moving to an even wider crawling band arrangement against a basket of currencies (the U.S. dollar, the euro, the U.K. pound, and the yen). Moreover, Israel implemented these changes during

---

[31] See, for example, Calvo and Mishkin (2003).
[32] See Eichengreen (1999a) and Eichengreen, Masson et al. (1998, 1999).
[33] See Mussa, Masson et al. (2000, Appendix III).
[34] See Eichengreen (1999a) and Eichengreen, Masson et al. (1998, 1999).

a period of substantial capital inflows and progressive capital account liberalization.

By exiting gradually from soft peg arrangements and thus remaining committed during the process to managing the exchange rate to a considerable extent if need be, policymakers can avoid abruptly increasing the amount of exchange rate uncertainty to which market participants are exposed. Such an approach attempts to strike a balance between the goal of inducing market participants to pay more attention to hedging their foreign currency exposures and the objective of giving them time to learn to hedge and adjust their behavior. Two other elements of accepted wisdom are that it is important to adopt an inflation target or some alternative monetary policy strategy that can replace the exchange rate peg as a nominal anchor, and that the anti-inflation credibility of the new monetary policy regime may also require a strengthening of fiscal policies and institutions.[35]

In debating the appropriate choice of exchange rate regimes for emerging market countries, few if any economists advocate completely free floating. It is widely perceived that free floating would likely imply considerable exchange rate volatility for countries without extensively developed capital markets. Moreover, there is strong empirical evidence that emerging market countries have a "fear of floating"[36] and, by implication, a relatively strong distaste for exchange rate volatility. As noted in Chapter 2, even the key currencies of the system are subjected to strong pressures in international financial markets and are not left to float completely freely.[37] In contrast, exchange rate arrangements at the other pole—hard fixes—have strong advocates and have been implemented by a number of countries. There is also considerable support for intermediate regimes of either managed floating or wide-band arrangements that allow exchange rates to fluctuate moderately in both directions and thereby preserve a

---

[35] See Eichengreen (1999a) and Eichengreen, Masson et al. (1998, 1999).

[36] See Calvo and Reinhart (2002) and Hausmann, Panizza, and Stein (2000).

[37] Bergsten (1999: 124–5) argues that past experience with free floating by the United States under the first Reagan Administration (with "benign neglect" of the very substantial appreciation of the U.S. dollar between late 1980 and early 1985) had "enormous costs"—in particular, "the prolongation of recession for much of American manufacturing and agriculture . . . ; the substantial threat to the global trading system that ensued from the resultant outbreak of American protectionism . . . ; the shift of the United States from the world's largest creditor to the world's largest debtor country . . . ; and the several near misses of a 'hard landing' due to the sharp decline in the dollar that occurred in 1987."

moderate degree of two-sided uncertainty.[38] Furthermore, it is accepted wisdom that no type of exchange rate regime is right for all countries at all times.[39]

Whatever a country's choice of exchange rate arrangement, relevant measures should be taken to improve its sustainability. By the same token, the choice of exchange rate arrangement should depend on the country's political and institutional capacity to sustain it.[40] On the one hand, the intermediate arrangements of managed floats or fixed rates with wide bands require the capacity to conduct monetary policy in a more sophisticated manner than a narrow-margin peg demands. Moreover, for countries that have built up large net external debts denominated in foreign currencies, the monetary policy flexibility provided by managed floats or wide-band arrangements may not be very effective for controlling output and inflation, because the traditional Keynesian effects of interest rate adjustments may be largely offset by balance-sheet effects.[41] On the other hand, dollarized economies are prone to relatively severe business cycles unless wages and prices show a high degree of flexibility—including, especially, public sector wages and regulated prices.[42] Social safety nets can make any type of exchange rate regime more sustainable.

With regard to hard forms of fixed exchange rates, the collapse of Argentina's exchange rate regime in December 2001 destroyed any impressions that currency-board arrangements can easily survive times of severe economic austerity. In the Argentine case, the economic and political costs of foregoing exchange rate adjustment had eventually become unsustainable in the face of adverse external shocks and the country's inability to rein in its fiscal deficit and its rising debt–GDP ratio. Even so, the currency-board arrangement, following its establishment in early

---

[38] See Williamson (2000) and Goldstein (2002).

[39] See Frankel (1999) and Mussa, Masson et al. (2000).

[40] See Calvo and Mendoza (2000a), Mendoza (2002b), and Calvo and Mishkin (2003). See also Reinhart and Reinhart (2003a) on the credibility problems associated with both pure floats and tight pegs.

[41] See Hausmann, Gavin, Pages-Serra, and Stein (1999); Frankel, Schmukler, and Serven (2000); Borensztein, Zettelmeyer, and Philippon (2001); Berg, Borensztein, and Mauro (2002); and Jeanne and Zettelmeyer (2002) for perspectives on this issue.

[42] Reinhart, Rogoff, and Savastano (2003a) present empirical evidence that highly dollarized economies have experienced higher rates of pass-through from exchange rates into domestic prices than less dollarized economies, along with higher and more volatile inflation rates. At the same time, however, they find little empirical support for the view that dollarization hinders the effectiveness of monetary policy or adds complexity to the links between output, price levels, and the instruments of monetary policy.

1991, played a central role in Argentina's successful experience of stabilizing from hyperinflation (recall Chapter 4). Thus, the Argentine experience does not imply that dollarization should be given preference over currency-board arrangements. Currency boards remain a potentially useful mechanism for stabilizing from high inflation, although in the absence of a high degree of wage and price flexibility and fiscal control, it is important to have an exit strategy and to implement the exit before trouble develops.[43]

Perspectives on the pros and cons of dollarization are likely to be sharpened by the results of several recently initiated experiments. Ecuador dollarized abruptly in the midst of a crisis in January 2000,[44] and El Salvador and Guatemala made the U.S dollar legal tender during 2001. A few other countries have also had dollarized economies for some time; in particular, Edwards and Magendzo (2001) list fourteen independent countries and fifteen nonindependent territories—all very small economies—that used another country's currency as legal tender during the 1971–1998 period. Although dollarization is costly to reverse, it is by no means impossible to abandon such arrangements. Liberia is a country that once had a dollarized economy but chose to begin issuing its own currency, and the countries that emerged from the breakup of the former Soviet Union provide other examples of nations that have abandoned former currencies and issued their own new currencies.

Among arguments in favor of dollarization, theory emphasizes two channels through which such arrangements might be expected to have a positive impact on growth. By eliminating currency risk, dollarization allows countries to benefit from lower interest rates and higher investment, which promotes growth[45]; and the elimination of exchange rate risk also encourages international trade, which tends to promote growth.[46] In support of such theories, moreover, empirical studies have found strong

---

[43] Ghosh, Gulde, and Wolf (2000) analyze the historical performances of currency-board arrangements.

[44] Fischer (2001a) describes the events leading up to Ecuador's decision, which was taken in desperation. Writing five months after the event, Fischer noted that the Fund, if consulted, would probably have said that the preconditions for successful dollarization were not in place, but the early success of the experience required the Fund to reconsider its views on preconditions.

[45] See Dornbusch (2001).

[46] Calvo and Reinhart (2001a, 2001b) and Mendoza (2002b) argue that dollarization also helps countries reduce macroeconomic variability.

evidence that common currencies promote trade and growth.[47] Neverthe-less, the positive effect on growth is not confirmed in studies that concen-trate on the set of very small economies that have either adopted another country's currency as legal tender or created a new currency that is com-mon to the group.[48]

With regard to intermediate arrangements, Williamson (2000) describes a class of wide-band arrangements, and Dooley, Dornbusch, and Park (2002) suggest how monetary policy might be operated under a managed float. Williamson's so-called basket-band-crawl arrangements have three important features. First and foremost, in order to maintain competitive-ness, the central rate is adjusted over time at a crawl that approximately offsets the country's inflation differential. Second, for a country that has no dominant trading partner, the central rate is defined in terms of a basket of currencies rather than a single currency. Third, the fluctuation margins are defined by a wide band, for which Williamson recommends a 7 to 10 percent range on each side of the central parity.

By contrast, Dooley et al. advocate a framework for monetary and exchange rate policy that gives the authorities considerable discretion in managing the exchange rate without establishing a central parity or band. Their proposal also has three main features. First, monetary policy would be guided by a flexible inflation-targeting framework, with the short-term interest rate used as the policy instrument for pursuing announced infla-tion objectives over time, but in a manner that stabilizes output in the short run.[49] Second, sterilized intervention—that is, changes in the com-position of the central bank's assets between domestic assets and foreign currency holdings—would be relied on to moderate the daily volatility of the exchange rate (vis-à-vis a basket of the dollar, the euro, and the

---

[47] See Rose (2000, 2002) and Alesina et al. (2003) for evidence that currency unions promote trade, and Frankel and Rose (2002) for evidence that this also promotes growth. See Clark et al. (2004) for perspectives on the relationship between exchange rate stability and trade.

[48] Edwards and Magendzo (2001, 2003) find that these economies have enjoyed signif-icantly lower rates of inflation than countries with their own currencies, but that they have also experienced higher rates of macroeconomic volatility and have not experienced significantly different rates of per capita GDP growth. See Ghosh, Gulde, Ostry, and Wolf (1997) and Levi-Yeyati and Sturzenegger (2001, 2003b) for other studies of the effects of exchange rate regimes on GDP growth and inflation.

[49] Goldstein (2002) also advocates managed floating cum inflation targeting. Fraga, Gold-fajn, and Minella (2004) reflect on the Brazilian experience with inflation targeting and provide a prescription for other emerging market countries.

yen). Such intervention could be guided, for example, by an objective of constraining daily fluctuations to no more than 3 percent and weekly movements to no more than 6 percent. Third, cumulative sterilized intervention over time would be constrained by a target level for net foreign assets (i.e., foreign exchange reserves net of foreign currency liabilities and derivative positions), with the aim of eliminating deviations between the actual and target levels of net foreign assets over a six-month period. The latter target serves to make transparent the medium-run orientation of the country's exchange rate and reserve accumulation policies in a manner that preempts any tendency to stabilize the level of the exchange rate over the medium run and also leaves scope for the country to build its gross foreign exchange reserves to whatever level it desires. As discussed in the next section, however, a target for the economy's net external debt (as a ratio to GDP) might be a more appealing anchor than a target for the central bank's net foreign assets.

7.4 Maintain Debt Discipline, Sound Macroeconomic Policies, and Market Confidence

The previous sections have emphasized that countries seeking to benefit from the globalization process need to devise sensible strategies for controlling and liberalizing domestic financial markets and international capital flows, to address weaknesses in the institutional structures and information bases of their economies and the soundness of their financial and corporate sectors, and to adopt sustainable exchange rate arrangements. In addition, countries need to promote macroeconomic stability by maintaining their debts at sustainable levels, by conducting sound monetary and fiscal policies, and by reacting expeditiously and effectively to any economic or political shocks that threaten to erode market confidence.

There are no unique formulas for maintaining debt discipline, conducting sound macroeconomic policies, and inspiring market confidence. Meeting these challenges is largely a matter of judgment, but there is a good bit of collected wisdom to draw upon.

A key prerequisite for maintaining debt discipline is to establish institutional arrangements for the timely collection and ongoing monitoring and forecasting of relevant debt statistics. Relevant information includes data on the levels of government debt and the country's external debt, and on the currency and maturity composition of these debts. It is also important to try to develop as clear a picture as possible of the levels and compositions of the net and gross debts of the financial and corporate sectors. Needless to say, the picture will be somewhat blurred by the difficulties of assessing the off-balance-sheet positions of the private sector and the contingent liabilities of governments.

Because a country's ability to service its external and public debts depends on the future evolution of variables that can take on a range of values, one cannot judge the sustainability of given levels of debt simply by comparing debt–GDP ratios with some well-defined threshold values. Accordingly, to maintain debt discipline, countries should start by assessing how the stocks of external and public debts would be likely to evolve, relative to the country's and government's abilities to pay, under a range of different assumptions about future growth rates, interest rates, and exchange rates.

A country's ability to pay depends on both its debts and its assets. Thus, debt management goes hand in hand with the management of foreign exchange reserves. Building up a fairly substantial stock of liquid foreign exchange reserves may be important for maintaining monetary policy flexibility and market confidence, because countries occasionally experience large unanticipated deteriorations in their current account positions and—until the nature of the underlying shock is understood and appropriate policy adjustments are underway—may not be able to finance their current account deficits by further increasing their gross external debts.[50]

Exercises to assess the sustainability of a country's external debt typically relate implicitly to levels of net external debt and should include a focus on worst-case assumptions. The usefulness of running such debt-dynamics scenarios and stress tests does not depend on having a highly sophisticated forecasting model.[51] Although it is certainly desirable for models to be reasonably accurate in describing macroeconomic behavior, the primary purpose of the scenario analysis is to work through the implications of the national income accounting identities, including the international balance of payments identity, under various assumptions about

---

[50] See Aizenman and Marion (2004) for an analysis of optimal reserve holdings in the presence of sovereign risk and costly tax collection.

[51] Indeed, economists have not yet succeeded in developing models that have much accuracy in explaining or facilitating exchange rates and interest rate premiums—two variables that are crucial to debt-sustainability exercises and for which such exercises should input fairly wide ranges of possible values.

key macroeconomic variables, including worst-case assumptions.[52] Such exercises can help policymakers form judgments about the levels of public and external debts that they can comfortably assume the economy will be able to sustain. A second purpose is to assess the vulnerabilities that the current levels and compositions of debts pose for the financial and corporate sectors.[53]

Judgments about the levels of external and public debts that can prudently be maintained will vary from country to country. Rules of thumb are nevertheless of some interest. One study suggests that, for external debt, a 40 percent ratio to GDP is a prudent upper bound for emerging market economies on average.[54] The study also suggests that somewhat lower thresholds seem prudent for emerging market economies with relatively low export–GDP ratios, and somewhat higher thresholds for countries with relatively high export–GDP ratios.[55]

Once a country has formed judgments about prudent targets or upper bounds for its external and public debt ratios, it is important to conduct monetary and fiscal policies in a manner that is consistent with achieving these targets (or remaining within the bounds) over the medium run. A target for net external debt could be pursued through a framework for monetary and exchange rate policy that combines an approach of flexible inflation targeting and managed floating with a target level for the net

[52] For some countries, the worst case might involve a complete loss of access to new external credit.

[53] See IMF (2003b) for a discussion of the techniques of scenario analysis and stress testing in the context of the Financial Sector Assessment Program. See Goldstein (2003b) for a discussion of various pitfalls in "standard" debt-sustainability exercises.

[54] See IMF (2002a, Appendix I). The study focuses on data for the 1979–2001 period and looks at the distribution of the external debt ratios at which countries either went into arrears on principal or interest to commercial creditors (Case A) or undertook or experienced sharp declines or corrections of their debt to GDP ratios (Case B). In each case the sample excludes both the advanced countries and the low-income HIPCs that rely primarily on official financing, and, in each case, the analysis points to a 40 percent ratio as an appealing threshold. For countries with debt levels below the 40 percent threshold, the historical probability of arrears or a debt correction was in the neighborhood of 2 to 5 percent on average, whereas for countries above the threshold the historical probability of arrears or a debt correction was about 15 to 20 percent on average.

[55] In another study that takes into account the complete set of external debt defaults or restructurings during the period 1970–2001, Reinhart, Rogoff, and Savastano (2003b) offer the judgment that 35 percent is a reasonable debt threshold for developing countries, noting that one-half of the default or restructuring events took place at debt–GNP ratios below 60 percent in the year of the event, and that for the group of developing countries that entirely avoided defaults or restructurings, slightly over half of the annual observations of debt–GNP ratios were below 35 percent. See also IMF (2003b).

external debt of the economy—a variant of the Dooley et al. (2002) proposal described in the previous section.[56] The presumption here is that the
monetary authorities have control over at least two policy instruments—a
short-term interest rate, the relative proportions of domestic and foreign
assets on their balance sheet (as influenced through sterilized intervention
in the foreign exchange market), and perhaps the level of a Chilean-style
nonremunerated reserve requirement on capital inflows. Thus, the net
external debt ratio can be pushed toward its target by means of policy
actions that seek to influence the current account balance (i.e., the change
in net external debt) in one of two ways: either through sterilized intervention to influence the exchange rate, or through changes in the reserve
requirement to influence the desired level of capital flows.

Consistency with a target (or upper bound) for the public debt ratio has
to be maintained through disciplined fiscal policy. Moreover, countries are
well advised to establish medium-run targets for public debt ratios that
are low enough to allow considerable scope for fiscal stimulus during
recessions. By the same token, countries are well advised to adopt budgetary procedures and control mechanisms that are conducive to running
fiscal surpluses during expansionary times in order to accommodate fiscal
deficits during recessions.

A source of major difficulty in maintaining discipline over the fiscal balance is the so-called common pool problem. An increase in government
spending on a particular project often conveys its full benefits to only a segment of the population, whereas the collection of tax revenues to finance
the government generally imposes burdens that are much more broadly
dispersed. Accordingly, various interest groups compete for larger budget
allocations than they would choose if they had to fully internalize the
costs of the additional spending, which can lead to excessive government
spending and deficits.

Thus, merely establishing a public debt target is not likely to lead to
effective debt discipline; some type of coordination mechanism is also
required to ensure that the parties involved in the budget process appropriately internalize the full social costs of government spending. One
approach to achieving effective discipline over the budget process is to cen-
tralize control over spending levels in a single decision maker. A second

---

[56] Unless the initial net external debt position is close to the target ratio, policymakers would
also require guidance on how rapidly they should aim to induce adjustment toward the
target net debt ratio.

approach is to negotiate a consistent set of spending targets early in the process, and to establish an effective mechanism for inducing all parties involved to stick to those targets.[57]

Countries also stand to benefit significantly when monetary policy is effective in establishing a track record of low and stable inflation. A low-inflation environment is generally regarded as conducive to economic growth. Moreover, recent conceptual and empirical analysis suggests that such an environment also plays a key role in enabling emerging market countries to develop a domestic market for long-term domestic-currency-denominated debt and thus to reduce their reliance on foreign-currency-denominated debt issued abroad.[58] Accordingly, countries are well advised to establish institutional arrangements that allow monetary policy to operate effectively.[59]

Even with sound debt management and monetary and fiscal policies, macroeconomic stability can be undermined by sudden unanticipated events—for example, a sharp drop in consumption or investment spending triggered by a sudden adverse change in economic agents' expectations or uncertainties about the outlook for the economy. Thus, the preservation of macroeconomic stability requires policymakers to react quickly and effectively to events that threaten to seriously erode market confidence. In reacting to a crisis, policymakers must provide confidence to markets that a credible path out of the crisis exists and will be followed.[60] Similarly, in reacting to adverse developments that pose major threats to macroeconomic stability, policymakers must provide confidence that a credible solution for avoiding a crisis exists and will be followed.

One of the implications is that policy authorities must be prepared to react quickly and effectively to bank runs and other types of problems with major financial institutions. An announced or imagined problem with a specific financial institution can snowball into crisis unless actions are taken to protect the payments system and to ease fears of a widespread drain of liquidity from the financial sector. Irrespective of the causes, the

---

[57] See, for example, Poterba and von Hagen, eds. (1999), Alesina and Perotti (1996), and Daban, Detragiache, di Bella, Milesi-Ferretti et al. (2003) for insights on fiscal institutions and fiscal performance.

[58] See Jeanne (2003), Burger and Warnock (2003), Ize and Levi-Yeyati (2003), and Ize and Parrado (2002).

[59] Fraga et al. (2004) provide a prescription for inflation-targeting design in emerging market countries.

[60] See Summers (2000).

first step should be to provide sufficient liquidity to stop depositor and creditor runs and protect the payment system; the authorities should also move quickly to determine the nature of the problem and to design an appropriate policy response.[61] Authorities can often strengthen market confidence by providing the public with clear and consistent information about their strategy for resolving the situation. Other lessons from experience are that the resolution or recapitalization of weak banks must be handled without undermining broader public confidence in the banking system; that blanket deposit guarantees may be important for maintaining confidence while banks are being restructured; and that speedy resolution of debt workouts appears to be a key determinant of the pace of recovery from crisis.[62]

7.5 Open the Economy to Trade and FDI in a Manner That Results in Growth-Enhancing Activities

Although there is broad agreement that outward-oriented trade policies are conducive to economic growth, historical experience provides reason to question whether trade liberalization by itself is very effective in promoting growth. Is it sufficient to simply get relative prices right by liberalizing trade restrictions? None of today's industrial economies achieved their relatively high standards of living by moving quickly to completely remove trade barriers and eliminate government subsidies to favored sectors of their economies. Moreover, all of the Asian developing countries that have grown rapidly during recent decades under outward-oriented trade policies have relied on a mix of market forces and government guidance.

Such observations suggest that the government has an important role to play in controlling the manner in which the economy is opened and, more generally, in guiding the process of resource allocation and capital accumulation in ways that promote economic growth. There is also considerable anecdotal and econometric evidence, however, that government policies have contributed to "killing growth" in many countries.[63] Among other evidence, the experiences with central planning in the former Soviet

---

[61] See Dziobek and Pazarbasioglu (1997) and Hoelscher et al. (2003) for views on how to manage systemic banking crises.
[62] See Burton (2002).
[63] See Easterly (2002).

Union and elsewhere argue strongly against the approach of correcting market failures by replacing markets with government planners, and many other slow-growth experiences point to the corruption and rent-seeking activities that can suppress economic development when the government assumes an active role in the allocation of resources. Thus, the perspective that governments have played important roles in most, if not all, of the successful growth stories has to be weighed against the perspective that governments have also played highly counterproductive roles in many other cases. "The appropriate question to be asked is not whether government should play a role, but what role and how it can be performed most effectively."[64] In concept, the case for government interventions at early stages of development can be justified on various grounds, including the facts that the ability to raise capital and hedge against risk is limited by underdeveloped financial markets, and that technological and marketing knowledge have important public goods elements and are in short supply.

When considering the appropriate role for governments, particular interest attaches to the experiences of the emerging market economies in East Asia—the countries that largely inspired today's strong consensus in favor of outward-oriented development strategies. By most interpretations, the scope of government intervention in resource allocation was fairly extensive in those cases, involving "a range of policies that included credit subsidies and tax incentives, educational policies, establishment of public enterprises, export inducements, duty-free access to inputs and capital goods and actual government coordination of investment plans."[65] A comparison of one aspect of the Korean and Mexican strategies for opening to trade and FDI reveals a striking contrast. As a result of various performance requirements imposed on exporters and foreign investors, Korea catalyzed a relatively extensive stimulus to local industry, boosting the local input content of goods produced in its export processing zone at Masan from 3 percent of export value in the early 1970s to nearly 50 percent ten years later. By contrast, although Mexico has been assembling goods for the U.S. market since the mid-1960s and has progressed from assembling clothing to assembling high-tech goods, its government never required companies to transfer technology or purchase inputs from local

[64] See Stiglitz (1996: 155).
[65] See Rodrik (2001a: 18–19).

sources, and, as of the mid-1990s, 97 percent of the components used in Mexico's assembly industry were still imported.[66]

Why was government-guided resource allocation so successful in the East Asian countries? One account characterizes the government interventions as "a coherent strategy of raising the return to private investment."[67] Another account emphasizes that the interventions were designed to promote and use markets and not thwart the development of private entrepreneurship; were carefully balanced and adaptable to changing circumstances; were based on extensive consultation between government and business; were more focused on identifying market failures than on picking winners; provided businesses with a performance-based reward structure; and were accompanied by steps to develop a civil service based on merit.[68] Such explanations, however, do not provide a clear understanding of why politicians and bureaucrats in the East Asian countries did not subvert the government interventions much more extensively for their own self-interest.[69] And absent such an understanding, strong concerns about the prospects for corruption and rent-seeking activities leave economists generally hesitant to encourage the governments of other developing countries to intervene extensively in the resource allocation process.

For those who conclude from historical experiences that rapid growth requires a significant amount of government involvement in guiding the process of resource allocation and capital accumulation, one inference is that strong institutional mechanisms for discouraging corruption and rent-seeking activities are very important prerequisites for successful economic development. This adds an additional perspective to the earlier discussion of the important role that institutions play in contributing to economic growth. As discussed in Chapter 8, the international community can provide countries with stronger incentives to discourage corruption and promote effective institutions and resource allocation by strengthening the links between official development assistance (including debt

---

[66] See Rosenberg (2002).

[67] See Rodrik (2001a: 18).

[68] See Stiglitz (1996: 155–62). See also the discussion of appropriately designed "industrial policies" in Stiglitz (2002b), who emphasizes that government interventions to address market failures and provide public goods have played a major role in promoting technological advance and economic growth in the United States.

[69] Indeed, Stiglitz (1996: 174) suggests that the East Asian success story may have been more of a political miracle than an economic miracle.

relief) and the track records of countries in developing strong institutions and generating growth.

Along with the importance of institutional mechanisms to guard against corruption, several points stand out from the history of successful growth experiences. First, the development paths of the industrial countries and the East Asian developing countries generally involved significant government interventions and a fairly gradual liberalization of trade restrictions. Second, the countries that succeeded in sustaining growth devised their own approaches for opening their economies, just as they have followed different approaches in designing institutions for creating, regulating, and stabilizing markets—and in addressing distributional effects that raise concerns about equity and can threaten the political support for market economies.[70] Third, a reading of the East Asian experiences suggests that rather than seeking to replace markets or pick winning economic activities on their own, governments succeeded in promoting growth by relying heavily on markets—in particular, by shaping their strategies in consultation with the businesses that operated in markets, by implementing reward structures based on market performance, and by providing widespread opportunities for private entrepreneurship.

In designing strategies for opening up their economies, developing countries are significantly more constrained today than they were several decades ago. In particular, present international treaties prohibit various elements of the development strategies pursued by the East Asian countries. The North American Free Trade Agreement (NAFTA) does not permit Mexico to require a significant transfer of technology from foreign direct investors, and the rules of the World Trade Organization (WTO) also limit or preclude a number of types of government interventions, such as subsidies, the reengineering of foreign products, and various requirements that might be imposed on inflows of foreign direct investment.[71] This has led some economists to urge the international community to thoroughly review the developmental consequences of its trade agreements,

[70] As noted in Chapter 6, the process of creative destruction and economic growth is bound to have uneven effects on different sectors and regions of the economy. Part of the solution is to strengthen social safety nets and upgrade the skills of the population, and various other measures to support lagging sectors or regions may be desirable on grounds of equity or political economy.

[71] See Rodrik (2001b).

including the capacity of the WTO to promote global development under its current rules and governance arrangements.[72]

7.6 Concluding Perspectives

In beginning to consider how to strengthen the performance of the world economy and make the globalization process work better, this chapter has focused on an agenda for individual countries. Using a list of five broad types of country-specific problems that contribute to the incidence and intensity of financial crises or pose impediments to economic growth and poverty reduction, it has defined a corresponding five-part agenda of broad challenges for countries to pursue. These include: devising a sensible strategy for liberalizing domestic financial markets and international capital flows; strengthening institutions, information, and the financial and corporate sectors; adopting sustainable exchange rate arrangements; maintaining debt discipline, sound macroeconomic policies, and market confidence; and opening the economy to trade and foreign direct investment in a manner that results in growth-enhancing activities. The agenda is arranged in an order in which it is convenient to address the issues, not in an order that judges their relative importance. Economists generally agree on a broad characterization of what countries should try to achieve under each component of the agenda, and although there is no single road map that countries need to follow to meet the challenges, experience provides a considerable amount of guidance on useful directions to follow and mistakes to avoid.

Many economists have argued that the movement by emerging market countries to liberalize their domestic financial markets and international capital flows in the late 1980s and early 1990s played a leading role in setting the stage for the international financial crises of the past decade. This movement, which was welcomed (even if not actively encouraged) by the IMF and many of its creditor countries, is now widely regarded as a major policy error, given that countries had not taken adequate steps to strengthen their financial sectors and prudential frameworks.

Against that background, one of the important challenges for developing countries is to devise more sensible strategies for liberalizing domestic

---

[72] See Helleiner (2000). Others have advocated collusion by developing countries to insist on more favorable treatment in negotiated trade arrangements.

financial markets and international capital flows—strategies that reduce their vulnerability to crises without unduly sacrificing their prospects for economic growth. An obvious point, given the large potential long-run benefits from liberalizing financial markets and capital controls, is that countries should move expeditiously to strengthen their financial sectors and prudential frameworks. This is not a task that should be postponed until a late stage of development. A second point is that foreign direct investment can be particularly beneficial for growth whereas short-term external debt can leave countries particularly vulnerable to financial crises. Accordingly, countries should aim to open their economies to direct investment inflows relatively early and move much more cautiously in liberalizing restrictions on inflows of short-term debt.

Justifications for imposing or retaining controls on financial markets and capital flows are based on the theory of the second best—that is, the notion that if the allocation of resources in financial markets suffers from some distortion that cannot be eliminated, it may be possible to improve welfare through a second-best approach of judiciously imposing another distortion. A number of different theoretical justifications can be invoked, but in practice the case for capital controls must also be based on whether the controls can be implemented effectively. Sophisticated market participants, aided by advances in electronic communications and computer technology, have become adept at evading capital controls by shifting the geographical location of financial transactions and by repackaging financial products. Among other things, market participants can change the effective maturity profiles and currency exposures of their investment positions by engaging in derivative transactions (such as forward contracts, swaps, and options); consequently, many of the mechanisms that authorities might be tempted to rely on in seeking to influence maturity profiles or currency exposures can be effectively evaded. It appears, however, that financial engineering houses have not yet figured out a way to avoid Chilean-style effective taxes on capital inflows—that is, unremunerated reserve requirements aimed at discouraging short-term capital inflows by effectively taxing all capital inflows at a rate inversely related to their time to repatriation. Thus, for countries with reasons for concern about strong capital inflows and their external debt positions, temporary recourse to Chilean-style controls appears to be a relatively attractive way of trying to discourage inflows of short-term debt, provided the controls can be enforced transparently and without corruption.

It is now widely perceived that economic growth depends importantly on technological progress (productivity growth), that technological progress is best promoted in well-functioning market economies that provide incentives and widespread opportunities for innovation, and, accordingly, that growth depends importantly on the quality of a range of market-sustaining institutions. This presents a second major challenge for countries that have not yet developed institutions that are strong enough to support well-functioning market economies. Institutions that define property rights and enforce contracts are important for creating markets; regulatory bodies and other mechanisms are important for addressing market failures and keeping the behavior of financial intermediaries and other firms consistent with the public interest; macroeconomic policy institutions as well as prudential supervisors are important for stabilizing markets; and adequate social safety nets are important for maintaining political support for markets. Because countries have established different informal behavioral norms and rely on different enforcement mechanisms, the formal institutional arrangements that work well in one country may not adapt well to others.

To assist countries in meeting the challenge of strengthening institutions, the international community has launched a major initiative to develop standards and codes for various types of institutional structures, to provide assessments (when requested) of how well countries' institutions comply with relevant standards and codes, and to provide technical assistance to countries in their efforts to achieve compliance with the standards and codes. As discussed further in Chapter 8, progress in strengthening institutions will depend in an important way on the amounts of human expertise and financial resources that the international community makes available to support the standards and codes initiative, and on the incentives that the international community provides to countries to bring their institutions into compliance with relevant standards and codes.

A third challenge that countries face is to avoid the temptation to try to defend unsustainable exchange rate arrangements. Countries have a wide variety of exchange rate arrangements among which to choose, and it is generally recognized that different types of arrangements can work equally well for different countries at similar stages of development. It is also recognized that an exchange arrangement that works well for an individual country during one period of time is not necessarily the best arrangement for that country during subsequent periods. Consistently, many economists have emphasized that a country's choice of exchange regime has a second-order influence on its macroeconomic performance in comparison with the soundness of its monetary and fiscal institutions and the flexibility of its labor and product markets.

That being said, most economists agree that soft exchange rate pegs are highly inadvisable arrangements for countries that are open to a substantial volume of international capital flows. The propensity for such arrangements to lead to financial crises has now been demonstrated by the breakdown of the Bretton Woods system, by the repeated crises within the European Monetary System between its inception in 1979 and the substantial widening of its fluctuation margins in 1993, and by the many emerging market crises of the past decade. The case against soft pegs does not apply to all countries, however. Indeed, most member countries of the IMF are not yet extensively involved in international capital markets, and pegged exchange rates may be attractive options for many of them, provided they develop and implement exit strategies before they become highly exposed to private international capital flows.

The argument that countries open to international capital flows should avoid soft pegs has sometimes been interpreted as an argument in favor of either freely floating exchange rates or hard forms of fixed exchange rates. This interpretation can be highly misleading, however, as few economists support such an extreme characterization of the bipolar view. In particular, few economists advocate the benign neglect of the exchange rate that characterizes the freely floating pole, and there is widespread support for intermediate regimes that involve either managed floating or wide-band arrangements.

A fourth major challenge that countries face is to promote macroeconomic stability by maintaining their external and public debts at sustainable levels, by conducting sound monetary and fiscal policies, and by reacting expeditiously to developments that threaten to erode market confidence. Although there is no single road map for meeting these challenges, there is a good bit of collective wisdom on which countries can draw.

The financial crises of the past decade have underscored that high levels of external or public debt are a major source of vulnerability. Countries will not be magically protected from crises if they simply keep their debt–GDP ratios below some well-defined thresholds, but several studies support the judgment that emerging market countries are well advised to hold their external debt levels below 35 or 40 percent of their GDPs. A key prerequisite for maintaining debt discipline is to establish reliable mechanisms for the timely collection and ongoing monitoring of relevant debt statistics. Moreover, because countries are exposed to considerable uncertainty about variables that affect both the burden of meeting payments on their existing debts and the rate at which they accumulate additional external debt through current account deficits, it is important to form judgments about the sustainability of their external debts by running debt-dynamics scenarios under a fairly wide range of different assumptions—including worst-case assumptions—about interest rates, exchange rates, and other key variables.

Along with maintaining sustainable levels of external debt, countries must establish control over fiscal deficits and the levels of their public sector debt. This requires strong institutional mechanisms for coordinating the parties involved in the budget process in a manner that achieves effective discipline. In addition to establishing fiscal control, countries should set objectives for public debt–GDP ratios that are low enough to allow considerable scope for fiscal stimulus (at least through automatic stabilizing mechanisms) during recessions. It is thus important to adopt budgetary procedures and control mechanisms that are conducive to running fiscal surpluses during expansionary times, thereby accommodating fiscal deficits during recessions. Countries can also benefit substantially from institutional arrangements that allow monetary policy to be effective in establishing a track record of low and stable inflation, which is conducive both to economic growth and to reducing a country's reliance on foreign-currency-denominated forms of debt.

Countries also need to be prepared to react expeditiously and effectively to financial sector difficulties and any other economic or political shocks that threaten to erode market confidence. This requires the development and implementation of effective action plans, including effective communication strategies. When national authorities have devised coherent and potentially effective plans, they can generally shore up confidence by providing the public with clear and consistent information about the measures they are taking to deal with threats to macroeconomic stability.

The fifth challenge on the agenda for individual countries is to devise strategies for opening their economies in a manner that promotes growth-enhancing activities. Several perspectives can be drawn from the experiences of the East Asian developing countries—whose rapid growth has largely inspired today's consensus in favor of outward-oriented development strategies—as well as from the experiences of developed economies. First, the development strategies of today's developed countries and the East Asian developing countries have generally involved significant government interventions and a fairly gradual liberalization of trade restrictions. Second, these countries have taken different approaches to opening their economies, just as they have followed different approaches in designing institutions for creating, regulating, and stabilizing markets. Third, a reading of the East Asian experiences suggests that rather than attempting to replace markets or pick winning economic activities on their own, governments succeeded in promoting growth by relying heavily on markets—in particular, by shaping their strategies in consultation with the businesses that operated in markets, by implementing reward structures based on market performance, and by providing widespread opportunities for private entrepreneurship. Fourth, for countries that rely heavily on government interventions in opening up their economies, institutional mechanisms that guard effectively against corruption and rent-seeking activities are extremely important.

Taken together, the five broad challenges present a very large agenda for countries to pursue. The breadth of the agenda, and the fact that in many areas there is not a well-defined road map, make it clear that establishing and maintaining the conditions for sustained growth and poverty reduction is a major multifaceted ongoing task, and that it is very difficult, if not impossible, to avoid financial crises along the way. It is also clear, however, that despite the scope of the task, some countries have achieved remarkable success in generating economic growth, albeit with major setbacks along the way. These success stories provide grounds for optimism, and some possibly adaptable pieces of road maps, for other countries with competent and dedicated policy authorities. Nevertheless, the future growth prospects for individual countries depends in an important way as well on the international financial environment in which they operate, and hence on the efforts of the international community to pursue an appropriate agenda for strengthening the international environment. An agenda for reforming the international financial system is the subject of the next chapter.

8

How Can the International Financial System Be Reformed?

The previous chapter has focused on what countries can do individually to reduce their vulnerabilities to international financial crises and enhance their prospects for economic growth. This chapter now considers ways of reforming the international financial system that could help make the process of economic globalization work better.

The chapter is organized around a list of six systemic problems (see Box 8.1). The ideas that economists have proposed for addressing these problems are grouped under the following headings: strengthening the quality and impact of IMF surveillance (Section 8.1); inducing changes in the composition of international capital flows (Section 8.2); introducing contingent debt contracts or other mechanisms for hedging against macroeconomic risks (Section 8.3); addressing informational imperfections and distorted incentives on the supply side of international capital flows (Section 8.4); revamping debt resolution procedures (Section 8.5); and strengthening the frameworks for development aid and official non-concessional lending (Section 8.6). As noted in the concluding perspectives (Section 8.7), significant progress has been made in addressing several components of this agenda, whereas proposals for advancement in other areas remain either insufficiently well defined or too controversial to receive the support of the policymaking community.

8.1 Strengthen the Quality and Impact of IMF Surveillance

Discussions of Fund surveillance have distinguished between a number of ingredients on which effectiveness depends. Key factors include timely, comprehensive, and accurate information; first-rate analysis that takes account of all relevant perspectives; the scope and depth of coverage; effective communication with national authorities; and the willingness

BOX 8.1. Systemic problems

1. The quality of IMF surveillance has not always been first rate, and the impact has suffered from the IMF's limited leverage for inducing countries to pursue structural reforms and maintain sound macroeconomic policies.
2. International capital movements are biased toward debt-creating flows and away from equity flows, and the composition of debt flows has involved a large component of short-term foreign-currency-denominated debt.
3. Countries lack good financial instruments for hedging against macroeconomic risks that are beyond their control.
4. Informational imperfections contribute to surges and sharp reversals in capital flows, and also to contagion; and prevailing compensation systems distort the incentives of financial analysts and money market managers on the supply side of international capital flows.
5. Procedures for resolving difficulties with international debts to private creditors are plagued by the lack of effective coordination mechanisms; and the ability of countries to support exports and output is severely weakened in the absence of provisions for sustaining trade credit during the debt resolution process.
6. Historical experience suggests that development aid has not been sufficiently effective in promoting economic growth, and crisis lending has neither been conditioned in a manner that provides strong incentives for preventive actions ex ante nor always adequate to sustain market confidence when warranted.

and political capacity of the authorities to act on good policy advice.[1] It is convenient in this section to regard the first four of these factors as having relevance to the quality of Fund surveillance, and the last factor as relevant to the impact of Fund surveillance. In practice, quality and impact are interrelated: other things being equal, the higher the quality the greater the likely impact, and the lower the prospective impact the smaller the incentive to generate high quality. For present purposes, however, quality and impact are discussed separately.

In considering how to improve the quality of Fund surveillance, the central issue is what can be done to ensure that the Fund's analysis and policy advice are first rate. There is little mystery about how to address

---

[1] IMF (2003e) provides a similar list of factors.

the other aspects of quality, and steps recommended in recent reviews of Fund surveillance have already been taken or are well underway. In particular, important progress has been made during recent years in improving the timeliness, comprehensiveness, and accuracy of the information provided to the Fund by member countries, and the scope of surveillance—as distinct from the scope of conditionality—has been expanded to pay more attention to financial sector and capital account issues. Moreover, the Fund has remained frank and candid in its confidential communications with national authorities. It has also been making a major effort to make its activities and analysis more transparent to the public,[2] although further steps could be taken in this direction. In this connection, the Independent Evaluation Office (2003b) recommends that the publication of Staff Reports for Article IV consultations should be mandatory,[3] that Fund programs should routinely include agreed strategies for communicating the logic of the programs and any subsequent program-related information to the public, and that the Fund should develop "modalities for escalated signaling" when countries fail to address key identified vulnerabilities over several rounds of surveillance.

As noted in Chapter 3, the quality of the Fund's analysis and policy advice is limited by economists' existing knowledge and the best judgments that can be drawn from cumulative experience. The analysis of specific types of situations or problems tends to improve over time as experience points to areas of deficient knowledge, as theorists and empirical researchers succeed in defining and analyzing relevant questions, and as the interaction of research findings with additional experience adds to accumulated knowledge and improved best judgments. However, new problems continue to emerge as time passes and the global environment evolves, creating situations in which past experience provides limited guidance.

Interaction between the Fund staff and the research communities in academia and other policymaking institutions can be very constructive in keeping the Fund's analysis and advice closely aligned with the best analysis available, and in pointing those communities to areas in which

---

[2] Indeed, I found the Fund's public website an extremely valuable source of information in writing this book.

[3] As noted in Chapter 3, following a review of its transparency policy in June 2003, the Fund's Executive Board took a step in that direction by agreeing to move from a policy of voluntary publication of Article IV Staff Reports to a policy of presumed publication.

additional research could lead to significant improvements in policy analysis. Over the past two decades, the level of this interaction has been high and increasing. It has been promoted, inter alia, by the appointment of established and widely respected academic researchers to head the IMF's Research Department and serve as Economic Counsellor to the Fund; by well-funded visiting scholar, conference, and seminar programs at the Fund; by an active internal reeducation program that brings numerous academics and other outside experts to the Fund each year to provide half-day seminars and multiday courses on recent developments in fields of relevance to the Fund staff; by encouraging the Fund staff to conduct research and participate in outside conferences; and by institutional arrangements that promote the internal dissemination of policy-relevant perspectives through staff mobility and ongoing interactions between the different departments of the Fund.

The impact of Fund surveillance depends not only on the quality of the Fund's advice but also on the incentives that countries have to follow it. In turn, countries' incentives to follow the Fund's advice depend in part on their perceptions of the quality of the advice. Accordingly, although success in generating high-quality advice depends in a very important way on continuing efforts to shed light on controversial issues through ongoing debate among academics and policymakers, unwarranted criticism of the Fund that distorts perceptions of the quality of its advice can be detrimental to the effort to make Fund surveillance more effective.

For the most part, interactions between the Fund and the academic and outside policymaking communities have been very constructive in recent years. Outside criticism has played an important role in identifying cases of bad policy advice and, in such instances, catalyzing adjustments in the Fund's policy positions. An example here is the role that outside criticism played in leading the Fund to reverse its initial push for fiscal tightening at the outset of the Asian crisis. Nevertheless, on a number of specific policy issues on which the Fund is responsible for providing advice, the academic and outside policymaking communities do not have a consensus view; an example here is the Fund's push for higher interest rates at the outset of the Asian crisis—advice that had both strong supporters and strong critics among the community of outside experts. Moreover, in many controversial cases, those who disagree with the Fund's advice also disagree among each other, for example, on the issues of capital controls, the scale of Fund lending, and the desirable degree of exchange rate flexibility.[4]

To the extent that the effectiveness of Fund surveillance can be weakened by distorted perceptions of the quality of its policy advice, it is not constructive to slander the competence of the Fund when the debate outside the Fund is largely unresolved. Nor is it helpful that policymakers in debtor countries often use the Fund as a scapegoat to blame for the unpopular actions required to clean up the economic problems that have been allowed to develop on their watches. And perceptions of the quality of the Fund's advice can also be distorted by inadequate outside recognition that the Fund and other international organizations are "merely ancillary extensions of the national governments who planted them," with a significant part of their shortcomings attributable to the fact that "the governments of the major nations have failed to demand and support the appropriate policies."[5]

Although distorted perceptions of the quality of the Fund's analysis are not helpful, most discussions of the limited impact of Fund surveillance point to lack of leverage as the main underlying problem. Consistent with this view, proposals for strengthening the international financial system have included suggestions for giving IMF surveillance "more punch,"[6] arguing that the IMF should become "less of a fireman and more of a policeman."[7] At present, as Boorman (2002) and Geithner (2003) emphasize, the Fund lacks the capacity to provide meaningful conditionality ex ante and, in seeking to create incentives for meaningful reforms, must therefore rely heavily on program conditionality ex post. However, as demonstrated by the programs designed for the Asian crisis countries, this situation can lead to a heavy dose of ex post conditionality, and, as noted in Chapter 5, the burdensome nature of the Asian crisis programs has resulted in an effort to streamline program conditionality.

[4] Frankel and Roubini (2003) provide a longer list.
[5] See Bryant (2003: 14). As a somewhat related point, much of the general criticism of Fund austerity casts aspersion on the quality of the Fund's policy advice when more attractive alternatives are often precluded by two factors beyond the Fund's control—in particular, by the failure of national policymakers to take earlier actions to prevent their economies from deteriorating, and by the limited pool of financial resources that the international community has made available for the Fund to lend.
[6] See Goldstein (1998).
[7] See Eichengreen (1999b: 16).

An appealing way to strengthen countries' incentives to implement meaningful reforms is to condition access to Fund resources on the extent of the reform efforts that countries have taken ex ante.[8] The implementation of such ex ante conditionality or prequalification requirements would not necessarily imply that the Fund should refuse to make any credit available to countries without an established track record of sound macroeconomic policies and serious efforts at strengthening institutions and market structures. As Fischer (2001c) has commented, it may be too draconian to refuse to lend to countries with poor track records; this punishes the entire population for the behavior of policymakers who in many cases will have already lost their jobs. Moreover, as others have stressed, there is a need for some flexibility in Fund lending.[9] However, incentives for reform could be significantly improved if greater access to Fund credit (or more favorable credit terms) was provided to countries that had established strong track records of following sound policy advice from the international community.

A first attempt at imposing prequalification requirements has already fallen flat in the context of the Contingent Credit Line (CCL) facility. The purpose of the CCL, created in 1999, was to give countries incentives to strengthen policies by providing assurances to members with strong policies that Fund financial support would be available in the event of contagion from external events. The design of the CCL required countries to apply and be prescreened for eligibility, but no country chose to apply and the facility was allowed to expire at the end of November 2003. Potentially eligible countries apparently feared that a CCL would be viewed as a sign of weakness rather than strength, and that there might be negative fallout should they later be reevaluated as ineligible.[10] This experience suggests a need to redesign the implementation of prequalification requirements, perhaps by routinely evaluating every country's track record in the course of regular Article IV consultations. An approach that evaluated all countries routinely rather than relying on countries to apply for prequalification could avoid the stigma associated with the CCL.

---

[8] Such an approach is recommended by the Meltzer Commission (2000) and the Council on Foreign Relations (1999). See also Jeanne and Zettelmeyer (2001), Kenen (2001), and Geithner (2003).

[9] Kenen (2001: 152) takes this position but argues that it should be rule-based flexibility and that the Fund should be required to justify any and all departures from normal quota-based limits on access to Fund credit.

[10] See IMF (2003n).

The case for prequalification is strengthened by several developments: the increasing recognition that success in avoiding macroeconomic instability and generating sustained economic growth depends importantly on the quality of a country's institutions; the strong criticism that the Fund encountered when it included many elements of structural conditionality in its programs for the Asian crisis countries; and, partly in response to such criticism, the policy decision by the Fund to scale back the (ex post) conditionality attached to its lending. Indeed, unless accompanied by ex ante conditionality or other measures to provide countries with greater incentives to strengthen their institutions, the scaling back of the structural conditionality in IMF programs may well weaken the effectiveness of Fund surveillance.[11]

The implementation of ex ante conditionality would have to be based on an explicit description of how ex ante performance would be evaluated. A vehicle for evaluation could be created by pursuing Kenen's (2001) proposal to establish contracts between individual member countries and the Fund that spell out agendas and timetables for addressing macroeconomic and structural policy issues over medium-run horizons (perhaps five to seven years). Ideally, such formal contracts would embody IMF policy advice while also defining agendas that were owned by member countries—that is, that members perceived to be in their own genuine interests. Contracts that provided short menus of priorities for most of each country's economic ministries and agencies would presumably be more effective than contracts that provided long menus for a few ministries and agencies. However, one of the important lessons of the past decade of financial crises is that the challenges of strengthening financial sector institutions and the prudential framework should not be left until late in the development process, so it would be desirable for contracts to give particular emphasis to pursuing the recommendations that emerge from countries' participation in the Financial Sector Assessment Program (FSAP) and Reports on Observance of Standards and Codes (ROSCs).[12] Needless to say, the scope for drawing on financial sector assessments

---

[11] See Geithner (2003).

[12] Kenen (2001: 154) suggests that access to large-scale Fund credit should also be made conditional on whether countries have introduced collective action clauses and 90-day rollover options into debt contracts (issues discussed in Section 8.5), and also on whether the countries have heeded any urgings from the Fund about needs for macroeconomic policy adjustment.

(FSAs) and ROSCs would hinge on the adequacy of the human and financial resources available for conducting them. On average, FSAs for industrial and emerging market countries have absorbed 3 person years of resources, those for countries with less developed financial sectors have required about 2.5 person years, and the program is currently stretched thin.[13]

The effectiveness of such an approach—or of any other form of ex ante conditionality or prequalification requirements—would also depend on the credibility of the Fund's lending policies.[14] As discussed in Chapter 4, the anecdotal evidence suggests that the IMF Executive Board has had great difficulty suspending loan disbursements, or refusing to provide new money, to countries in which the major creditor countries of the Fund have substantial economic or strategic interests. This difficulty could potentially undermine the effectiveness of prequalification requirements as a mechanism for enhancing countries' incentives to strengthen their policies and institutional structures ex ante. Thus, the case for prequalification requirements would depend on whether the Fund's Executive Directors, in concluding Article IV consultations, could shed their past ambivalence about whether they want the Fund to exercise firm surveillance and be willing to declare countries as not qualified for financial support (or for more than a minimal amount of Fund credit) over the period until their next Article IV assessment.[15]

One mechanism for dealing with the Fund's credibility problem would be to rely on evaluation teams that operated independently of both the IMF and the countries involved. Although this might seem less efficient than having the Fund staff evaluate countries' track records in the course of regular Article IV consultations, reliance on independent evaluation teams and well-defined rules that linked access to Fund financing to countries' evaluation ratings might help overcome the political pressures that

---

[13] As noted in Chapter 3, as of March 2004, nearly five years after the initiation of the program, financial sector assessments (FSAs) had been completed for sixty-one countries and were underway for another twenty-eight countries. FSAs had been requested but not yet scheduled for eighteen countries, and the remaining seventy-seven members of the Fund had not yet requested FSAs; see IMF (2004, Table 2), as updated.

[14] Aizenman (2004) emphasizes this point.

[15] A provision for overriding such a declaration of ineligibility through a supermajority vote could be added as a safety valve for situations that posed grave threats to the international financial system. A provision could also be added to allow ineligibility to be reversed on the basis of concrete actions and reassessments prior to subsequent Article IV consultations.

sometimes make it difficult for the Fund to turn down credit requests from countries that are not committed to strong policy programs.[16]

Countries' incentives to pursue serious policy programs could be further strengthened by having the independent evaluation teams (or the Fund staff) periodically provide public report cards that graded both the quality of the contracts and the track records that countries had achieved. This would affect the incentives of national authorities by influencing the interest rate premia that their countries faced in international capital markets and, in countries with elected leaders, by providing information relevant to the performance evaluations of voters.

8.2 Induce Changes in the Composition of International Capital Flows

A number of proposals for systemic reform have focused on ways of inducing changes in the composition of international capital flows to make emerging market countries less vulnerable to financial crises. Some of these proposals are aimed at inducing a shift from debt-creating flows to equity flows.

The accumulation of a large volume of external debt leaves a country much more vulnerable to adverse macroeconomic or political developments, other things being equal, than an equivalent capital inflow channeled into foreign direct investment (FDI) or equity purchases. Indeed, all of the international financial crises experienced by emerging market countries since the early 1980s can essentially be regarded as international debt crises. Each of these episodes gravitated from adversity to crisis largely because of the way that debt holders reacted to fears that the debtor country would be unable (or unwilling) to meet its debt payment obligations. Such fears tend to make foreign banks and other lenders unwilling to roll over credits or extend new credits, leading to a liquidity shortage that makes it even more difficult for the debtor country to meet its payment obligations, and can thereby contribute to a vicious spiral of intensifying fear and liquidity shortage. In contrast, FDI and equity purchases do not carry fixed payment obligations, and a rush for the exits by equity holders

---

[16] Adherence to rule-based access for all financing would not be desirable, partly because failure to provide financing in some cases could pose systemic risks. The availability of financing in the form of General Arrangements or New Arrangements to Borrow in situations that threaten the international financial system would remain very important.

leads primarily to equity price changes without generating the intense liquidity problems created by a sharp curtailment of credit.

The discussion of factors contributing to currency crises has focused extensively on the vulnerabilities of the crisis-stricken countries, with much less attention to the supply-side dimension of international capital flows.[17] The supplies of bank loans and portfolio capital (funds invested in bonds and equities) to emerging market countries come predominantly from fewer than 200 large commercial banks and institutional investors (i.e., investment banks, insurance companies, mutual funds, pension plans, and hedge funds) in twelve industrial countries (the eleven G-10 countries plus Spain).[18] Accordingly, any effort to change the composition of international capital flows should take into account the incentives and investment practices of these different types of financial players.[19]

Creditors to emerging market countries are often perceived as having relatively weak legal recourse over a foreign government or private entity that repudiates its debts. They have nevertheless been willing to lend on a fairly large scale, at least during noncrisis periods, presumably because they perceive that emerging market countries have strong incentives to repay. This has led some economists to challenge the view that creditors have weak legal recourse, noting that foreign sovereign immunity laws do not preclude the possibility of international litigation in creditor-country courts and that such litigation poses a significant threat to the debtor country's ability to obtain trade finance.[20] Others emphasize, more generally, that creditors have reduced the incentives for debtors to default by structuring debt contracts in ways that imply large output losses for defaulting countries.[21] Consistently, casual observation suggests that governments

---

[17] In contrast, Dobson and Hufbauer (2001) concentrate on the supply side.

[18] See Dobson and Hufbauer (2001).

[19] This point is emphasized by Jeanne (2000b) and Tirole (2002).

[20] See Bulow and Rogoff (1989a) and Singh (2003). In most countries, foreign sovereign immunity law extends immunity to foreign sovereigns only for public acts and not for acts arising out of a state's strictly commercial or private activities. This implies that litigation can be pursued in creditor-country courts for defaults by either sovereign or private foreign entities. Furthermore, under continental European law, a creditor in a non-European country has scope to attach the European assets of a defaulting non-European sovereign or to prevent the sovereign from settling any payments through Euroclear. Thus, as documented by Singh, purchasers of distressed developing-country debt have earned very high rates of return, over and above legal costs, by persistently pursuing international litigation through channels that would impose very high costs on countries that failed to settle.

[21] See Dooley (2000a, 2000b). Recall Figure 5.1.

will go to great lengths to avoid imposing nonvoluntary restructurings of external debts,[22] and explicit statements by policy authorities confirm that the perceived costs of default are very high.[23]

Although creditors have been willing to lend to emerging market countries on a fairly large scale, only a small share of the lending has been denominated in the currencies of the emerging market countries, and much of the lending has been short term. The likely explanation is that creditors perceive that short-term foreign-currency-denominated assets are less apt to have their real values eroded by the policies and macroeconomic performances of debtor countries. Uncertainty about the monetary authority's ability to hold down inflation and prevent currency depreciation can contribute to the strong tendency to denominate debt in a major foreign currency; and general uncertainty about macroeconomic prospects can contribute to the prevalence of short-term maturities, which give creditors a better exit option than longer-term debt.[24] These considerations suggest that, in theory, emerging market countries can reduce their reliance on short-term foreign-currency-denominated debts through actions to make creditors less fearful of holding longer-term local currency debts—in particular, by establishing track records of consistently low inflation and by reinforcing policy credibility through institutional reforms.[25] That being said, the historical experiences of industrial countries in issuing long-term external debts denominated in their own currencies does not provide any basis for expecting quick results from such efforts.[26] And from the perspective of international investors, it is not clear whether the diversification benefits of adding additional currencies to financial portfolios outweigh the transactions and management costs.[27] Nevertheless, there is evidence that, for some emerging market countries with well-developed currency hedging facilities (e.g., South Africa, Hong Kong, and Poland),

[22] See Fischer (2003), who attributes such reluctance, among other things, to the fact that restructuring a government's external debt generally also requires restructuring the domestic financial system, because domestic financial institutions typically have large holdings of government debt.

[23] Bulow and Rogoff (1989b: fns. 40 and 41) provide quotes to this effect from Silva Herzog, Finance Minister of Mexico during the 1982 debt crisis, and Corazon Aquino, former President of the Philippines.

[24] See Jeanne (2000b) and Tirole (2002).

[25] Jeanne (2003) and Burger and Warnock (2003) argue that the stock of foreign-currency-denominated external debt depends importantly on the overall size of the domestic bond market, which they show to be sensitive to the level and volatility of historical inflation.

[26] See Bordo, Meissner, and Redish (2003).

[27] See Eichengreen, Hausmann, and Panizza (2003).

significant shares of external debts are already denominated in domestic currencies.[28]

The fact that creditors have a strong rationale for holding claims on emerging market countries in short-term foreign-currency-denominated forms has to be taken into account when considering the likely effects of proposals aimed at discouraging short-term foreign-currency-denominated capital inflows. Even if measures aimed at changing the composition of international capital flows were successful in making emerging market countries significantly less vulnerable to financial crises, they might also result in a significant reduction in the total volume of international capital flows, for better or for worse. This would seem to be a particularly likely implication of measures designed to curtail short-term foreign-currency-denominated flows, which provide creditors with relatively attractive protection.[29] Alternatively, such measures might primarily have window-dressing effects on balance sheets, inducing shifts from short-term to long-term international lending while also inducing creditors to offset the changes in their risk exposures—and hence in the counterpart risk exposures of the emerging market countries—through off-balance-sheet derivative transactions (e.g., forward foreign exchange transactions).

Another consideration is that choking off capital inflows to domestic banks—which predominantly take the form of short-term credits—can have adverse consequences for growth. Curtailing capital inflows to domestic banks can make it particularly difficult to sustain economic activity in countries where corporate governance is in its infancy and bankruptcy laws are virtually nonexistent, and where domestic banks, with their specific expertise in exercising power over local borrowers, are particularly important for financing economic activity.[30]

Along with the various uncertainties that contribute to the relative attractiveness of holding external debt in the form of short-term foreign-currency-denominated maturities, a number of other factors influence investor preferences for debt relative to equities. These factors, which are somewhat interrelated, include deposit insurance in both debtor and creditor countries; the prospect that countries experiencing debt problems will receive official bailout loans; the tendency to litigate international debt

---

[28] See Goldstein (2002).
[29] See Dooley (2000b) and Jeanne (2000b).
[30] See Diamond and Rajan (2001).

problems in creditor-country courts; and the relatively limited development of equity markets in emerging market countries.[31] Although deposit
insurance has considerable social value, by helping banks attract funds it
contributes indirectly to the scale of their international lending and may
increase the pressures for official bailouts of countries that encounter debt
problems. More generally, the risks that banks and non-banks encounter
in lending to emerging market countries are mitigated by the prospect that
countries facing external financing difficulties will receive official bailout
loans, and also by opportunities to recover losses through litigation in
creditor-country courts. By favoring debt flows, these factors indirectly
discourage equity flows into emerging market countries, adding to the
direct discouragement that comes from the limited development of equity
markets.

Several types of initiatives have been proposed for enhancing the attractiveness of equity investments relative to debt flows and thereby inducing
a shift in capital flows toward a composition that would leave countries
less vulnerable to international financial crises. Such proposals include
efforts to promote the development of equity markets, steps to reduce
the information costs and risks associated with equity investments,[32] and
changes in the provisions of debt contracts that increase the risks borne by
creditors. The latter changes could include the introduction of contractual
provisions or statutory arrangements that remove or limit the option for
litigation in creditor-country courts.[33]

Other proposals for changing the composition of international capital flows have focused on mechanisms for reducing their volatility. One
course of action—motivated by the view that changing the rules of
the game in creditor countries is at least as important as building institutions and reforming behavior in debtor countries—would seek to
strengthen the regulation and supervision of banks and other large international investors in the industrial countries, with particular attention to
hedge funds and other highly leveraged investors. Dobson and Hufbauer
(2001) suggest that such an effort should focus not only on changing the

---

[31] See Rogoff (1999a).

[32] Gelos and Wei (2002) focus on various indices of government and corporate
transparency—that is, summary measures of the availability and quality of information—
and find that institutional investors tend to have larger holdings of equity in countries
that have greater levels of transparency, other things being equal.

[33] See Rogoff (1999a).

incentives and behavior of banks and institutional investors but also on strengthening the incentive structures and resources of the G-10 financial supervisors.[34] This issue arises again in Section 8.4.

A second proposal, advocated by Calomiris (1998a, 1999), would create incentives for stronger private sector monitoring of banks throughout the world by requiring the banks of all IMF member countries to maintain at least a minimal ratio (e.g., 2 percent) of subordinated debt to risk-weighted assets.[35] To ensure that such junior debt would be held at arm's length and serve the purpose of inducing market discipline, Calomiris suggests that the debt be nontradable and held only by a group of approved and registered investors; more specifically, each bank's set of qualified holders would be a group of foreign financial institutions that had no other financial transactions with the issuing bank and were chosen, with the approval of both the domestic regulator and the IMF, from a common set of perhaps fifty reputable and well-diversified institutions. To ensure frequent but limited rollovers, the debt might be issued as two-year maturities in twenty-four equal monthly installments. To induce adjustment to signals of alarm from the holders of subordinated debt, banks would be constrained from issuing such debt at yields in excess of some ceiling,[36] thus forcing them, should it become impossible to market new debt at rates below the ceiling, to contract their risk-weighted assets to meet the minimum subordinated debt requirement.

A third proposal is to make seniority rights on sovereign debt more explicit.[37] This would address distortions that arise when a country issuing

---

[34] Among other things, Dobson and Hufbauer argue that financial supervisors need to pay more attention to systemic risks, coordinate more closely, and be held publicly accountable for spotting and resolving problems.

[35] Calomiris (1998a) credits the basic idea to proposals by two Federal Reserve System economists, Keehn (1989) and Wall (1989), in the context of the U.S. savings and loan and banking crises of the 1980s. He notes, in addition, that subordinated debt is much more straightforward to measure than the book value of equity, and its yield is observable.

[36] Calomiris suggests setting the ceiling at a fixed height above the yield on comparable maturity treasury instruments. Such a formula could prove highly undesirable, however, during periods of high uncertainty about the global economic outlook—such as periods following the outbreak of wars or major economic disasters—which are often characterized by strong increases in the demand for very-low-risk assets (treasury securities) and generalized increases in the interest premiums on all other assets. Policymakers might address this concern by defining the ceiling in relation to the average interest rate premium on subordinated bank debt, perhaps also taking account of the standard deviation.

[37] Zettelmeyer (2004) summarizes the literature and develops the case further. The seniority structure of corporate debt is already fairly well established through the practice of issuing different classes of debt (secured, ordinary, or subordinated) with a clear order of

debt today cannot make a credible commitment not to issue additional debt in the future—the so-called debt dilution or nonexclusivity problem.[38] Conceptual analysis has established that the prospect of debt dilution tends not only to raise the costs of borrowing ex ante but also to affect the composition of debt in a manner that results in higher costs of default ex post.[39] In particular, the prospect of debt dilution gives lenders incentives to try to protect themselves by issuing relatively short maturities; and to the extent that defaults are correlated with currency depreciation, it also gives lenders incentives to issue debt in foreign-currency-denominated forms. In addition, insofar as debts that are relatively easy to restructure are likely to suffer first in times of distress, the prospect of dilution can induce a composition of debt that mainly includes hard-to-restructure instruments.

The adverse effects of the dilution problem on the composition of debt could be mitigated by a mechanism that gave older debt explicit seniority over newer debt, with possible exceptions for trade credit and priority financing, in any debt restructurings. Zettelmeyer (2004) notes that the seniority of older debt over newer debt could be established through contractual covenants that prohibited debtors from issuing any subsequent debt unless it was contractually subordinated to previously issued debts.[40] The implementation of explicit seniority in debt restructuring would also require mechanisms for monitoring debt contracts and enforcing their seniority provisions. Zettelmeyer suggests that the first requirement could be met through the creation of a global registry of sovereign debt, as has been periodically proposed since the debt crisis of the early 1980s. He further argues that the second requirement could be met, without any actions that conflict with the sovereignty of debtors, if courts forced junior creditors to surrender any payments received in contravention of the subordination stipulated in the debt contracts.

Yet another proposal, suggested by Eichengreen and Hausmann (2002), is for the World Bank, other international financial institutions, and

---

priority for asset holders in the event of insolvency. See also Borensztein, Mauro, Jeanne, Zettelmeyer et al. (2004).

[38] The argument for explicit legal seniority to address the debt dilution problem dates back to at least the early 1970s. Zettelmeyer credits Kletzer (1984) with first drawing attention to the debt dilution problem in the sovereign debt literature.

[39] See Bolton and Jeanne (2004), Chamon (2002), and Lipworth and Nysted (2001).

[40] Bolton and Skeel (2003) emphasize the desirability of embedding explicit seniority within any statutory mechanism that might be established for sovereign debt restructuring.

industrial country governments to start issuing debts denominated in a new unit of account—the EM index, based on a diversified set of emerging market currencies—and to eliminate their currency mismatches by converting their loans to emerging market countries from dollars into emerging market currencies. On the surface, this would indirectly reduce the vulnerabilities of emerging market countries to adverse macroeconomic developments by reducing their stocks of dollar-denominated debts. However, although private holders of long-term claims on the World Bank presumably would not require a high premium for credit risk, it seems likely that they would require an interest rate premium to hold EM-denominated assets (at the expense of the World Bank and other issuers), or that they would seek to cover their holdings of EM-denominated assets through derivative transactions that would end up having emerging market counterparties,[41] thereby essentially offsetting the effects of the redenomination of the balance-sheet positions of emerging market countries.

8.3 Introduce Contingent Debt Contracts or Other Mechanisms for Hedging Against Macroeconomic Risks

Some proposals for systemic reform have focused on the introduction of new types of financial instruments as another way of influencing the composition of international capital flows in a manner designed to make emerging market countries less vulnerable to financial crises. Such proposals are oriented toward shifting the composition of emerging market debt toward claims that provide a hedge against macroeconomic risks— in particular, by making payment streams contingent on variables that affect the debtor country's ability to pay. In that spirit, Borensztein and Mauro (2002) revive the case for issuing GDP-indexed bonds, and Caballero (2003) suggests that each country should issue debt with payments contingent on a short list of external factors that have a critical bearing on its macroeconomic performance, including key commodity prices. Such proposals have a fairly long history.[42]

---

[41] They might do this, for example, through forward contracts that provided private investors with short positions in the EM component currencies and left emerging market countries obligated to deliver dollars in exchange for their currencies when the forward contracts matured.

[42] Shiller (1993) has been particularly influential in arguing the case for markets that provide insurance against macroeconomic risks; see Athanasoulis, Shiller and van Wincoop

In proposing that debt be indexed to GDP, Borensztein and Mauro are motivated in part by the fact that the ratio of external debt to GDP has been a significant and robust predictor of external debt crises.[43] This suggests that hedging against adverse outcomes for GDP is a relatively attractive way to reduce vulnerabilities (in comparison with hedging against adverse outcomes for some other summary statistic).[44] They also contend that GDP-indexed bonds could be created simply by adding a clause to standard sovereign debt contracts and piggybacking on existing markets for government bonds.[45] A GDP-indexed bond would be equivalent to the combination of a so-called plain vanilla bond and a security indexed to the country's GDP—that is, equivalent to a government bond with standard nominal coupon payments plus a security that promised payments proportional to the difference between actual GDP growth and some prespecified norm—and a market would presumably develop for the stripped-off indexed component.

Caballero's proposal is also motivated by the view that the output losses of crisis-stricken emerging market countries have been amplified by lack of appropriate instruments for insuring against macroeconomic risks. "Even in the best managed emerging economies, aggregate risk management is being done with stone-age instruments and methods."[46] Unlike Borensztein and Mauro, however, Caballero would not constrain hedging instruments to be defined in terms of a single variable and would restrict the list to variables that were largely exogenous to the country and readily observable. For Chile, payments on the new debt instrument could be made contingent on the outcomes for the price of copper (Chile's main export) as well as an average interest rate spread on the debts of emerging market countries. For Mexico, key variables might be the price of oil, U.S. GDP, and an emerging market bond spread.

In addition to considering the attractiveness of such hedging instruments from the perspective of the countries issuing them, it is relevant to

---

(1999) for an overview. See Borenzstein and Mauro (2002) for references to recent and past proposals in the context of developing countries.

[43] See Detragiache and Spilimbergo (2001).

[44] Borensztein and Mauro doubt that governments would be tempted to understate GDP growth. They further suggest that exports are likely to be more sensitive to government policies than GDP and, from that perspective, provide a less desirable summary statistic for debt indexation.

[45] By contrast, Shiller's (1993) proposal envisages the creation of markets for perpetual claims to a fraction of countries' GDPs.

[46] See Caballero (2003: 9).

ask whether and why they might be attractive to prospective investors. In the opinion of Borensztein and Mauro, GDP-indexed bonds, or their stripped indexed components,

> would create an altogether new opportunity for investors to take a view on a country's economic growth prospects. This would be particularly attractive in the case of emerging market countries where the stock market is not well diversified and where stock market fluctuations may have little to do with the country's fundamental growth prospects.[47]

In contrast, debt instruments with payoffs contingent on outcomes for several different variables would create a relatively complicated form of contingent claim that might well be less attractive to private investors in its unbundled state. Moreover, it might be relatively difficult for financial intermediaries to repackage the debt instruments to separate the risks and to then market the different components successfully. Accordingly, in comparison with GDP-indexed bonds, the types of contingent claims proposed by Caballero would likely be significantly more difficult to market unless they were limited to insuring against a single contingency or could be sold to international financial institutions and creditor-country governments.

Needless to say, the potential benefits of such contingent claims would depend on whether they were introduced in substantial volume. Introducing the instruments on a large scale could provide a substantial hedge against macroeconomic risks and might be important for jump starting a market. From these perspectives, it has been suggested that large-scale debt restructurings provide appealing occasions for introducing such instruments.[48]

It has also been suggested that international financial institutions or other official entities may have a role to play in fostering markets for such contingent claims. Among other reasons, there is a public goods element of markets for new securities: historical experience suggests that when a financial firm incurs the fixed costs of successfully developing a new product or market, competitors typically introduce similar products or

[47] See Borensztein and Mauro (2002: 18).
[48] Borensztein and Mauro (2002) note that Costa Rica, Bulgaria, and Bosnia and Herzegovina have all issued bonds containing an element of GDP indexation in the context of restructuring agreements. In the case of Bulgaria, however, the motivation was to sweeten the agreement for creditors by providing a kicker if GDP growth was relatively high.

enter the market within a few months, preventing the innovating firm from reaping the full returns on the costs it incurs.[49]

The development of markets for contingent claims is not the only way to provide emerging market countries with a hedge against macro risks. As one alternative, Calvo (2002) has suggested that creditor-country governments endow an Emerging Market Fund that would intervene, when warranted by established guidelines, to purchase emerging market debt and thereby help protect against contagion in special circumstances— for example, if an index of emerging market bond prices began to fall precipitously.

8.4 Address Informational Imperfections and Distorted Incentives on the Supply Side of International Capital Flows

Investment decisions are generally based on a set of expectations surrounded by considerable uncertainty. Correspondingly, volatility in asset prices or investment flows can generally be attributed to new information that leads investors to revise their expectations or that resolves or adds to their uncertainties. By the same token, efforts to improve the scope and quality of the information available to market participants ex ante can reduce the subsequent flow of new information and thereby reduce the volatility of asset prices and investment flows.

As discussed in Chapter 5, international capital flows to emerging market countries have been particularly volatile. Many emerging market countries have experienced surges in capital inflows, often followed by sharp reversals ('sudden stops') and the onset of financial crises. This pattern—along with the tendency for crises to spread contagiously from one country to another—has been partly attributed to informational imperfections. Accordingly, efforts to improve the information available to participants in international capital markets could help reduce the vulnerability of emerging market countries to volatile capital flows and financial crises.

The effort to address informational imperfections is an appropriate and important task for the public sector. One justification is that there are fixed costs of collecting and processing information along with various factors that prevent private firms and individuals from reaping the full benefits

---

[49] See Athanasoulis et al. (1999).

of incurring the fixed costs.[50] Thus, the private sector lacks the incentives to collect and disseminate the socially optimal amount of information. A related justification is that crisis avoidance or mitigation is a public good, and improved information has the potential to reduce the volatility of international capital flows and the frequency and severity of financial crises.

In fact, recent years have brought significant progress in improving the scope, quality, and timeliness of the data available to investors in emerging market countries. As discussed in Chapter 3, many emerging market countries have subscribed to the Fund's Special Data Dissemination Standard (SDDS), which now requires, inter alia, (i) comprehensive information on international reserves and other foreign currency assets, as well as net foreign currency claims against those resources, and (ii) information on the external debt of the general government, the monetary authorities, the banking sector, and other sectors, broken down by maturity and by instrument.[51] These steps to improve the availability of relevant information will presumably help dampen the surges in capital inflows that have contributed in the past to countries' net external debt positions and vulnerabilities to crises. As may be recalled from Chapter 4, a number of the emerging market countries that suffered financial crises during the past decade—including Mexico, Thailand, and Korea—did not provide the Fund or private market participants with complete and timely information on their international reserves and short-term external debts during the run-ups to their crises.

Improvements in the scope, accuracy, and timeliness of information on countries' international reserves and external debts are conducive not only to sound international portfolio and direct investment decisions by market participants but also to sound macroeconomic policymaking and financial supervision by national authorities. Indeed, the most important benefits of the SDDS may come from the steps that individual countries take to monitor their net external debt positions more comprehensively and continuously and to gear their macroeconomic policies and financial supervision and regulation toward avoiding a buildup of vulnerabilities.

---

[50] Calvo and Mendoza (2000a, 2000b) emphasize the role of margin requirements and short-selling constraints. Another factor is the difficulty of preventing information from leaking or being inferred by others.

[51] See IMF (2003f, 2003o). The transition period for providing reserves data ended in 2000, and that for providing external debt statistics ended in March 2003. Countries are also encouraged, but not required, to provide data on prospective debt service schedules.

The effort to improve data availability can also contribute to improving economists' conceptual analysis of crisis vulnerability and debt sustainability. In particular, it can lead to a deeper understanding of these concepts by forcing economists to focus more explicitly on what types of data are relevant for assessing them empirically.

The Fund's data dissemination standards are by no means the only initiatives that the international community has taken in recent years to improve the public's awareness of countries' economic developments and prospects. Other important initiatives include the practice of encouraging member countries to publish Fund surveillance reports, including regular Article IV Staff Reports, the reports generated in connection with the FSAP, and the ROSCs.[52]

A question that surfaces periodically is whether the Fund should warn the public whenever it regards a country as moderately or highly likely to experience a financial crisis. Fischer (2001c) notes that the case for such a system of "yellow and red cards" is arguable, particularly because all early warning system models are highly imperfect, generating both Type 1 and Type 2 errors (i.e., the errors of generating false alarms and of failing to sound appropriate alarms). To date, the IMF Executive Board has opposed the idea of the Fund becoming a rating agency, but this is an argument against characterizing the Fund's views in the form of a single summary rating, not an argument against providing market participants with more frank and transparent multidimensional assessments.

In addition to being influenced by the types of informational imperfections discussed earlier, international capital flows are affected by compensation systems that distort the incentives of financial analysts and investors in providing and responding to information. At least two distorting factors have received attention.[53] Investment banks in the major creditor countries earn large underwriting fees from being lead managers of bond sales, and strong links between the compensation of their employees (which can

---

[52] As noted in Chapter 3, the Fund published about 75 percent of the Staff Reports that were prepared during the eighteen months through August 2003 and has since moved from a policy of voluntary publication to one of presumed publication of Article IV reports. The Fund has also been publishing about two-thirds of both ROSCs and the reports on FSAPs; see IMF (2003q). The United States General Accounting Office (2003) recommends a substantial expansion of this source of information. In particular, it encourages the Fund to increase member countries' participation in the assessment programs; to improve the timeliness of FSAP and ROSC reports; to expand the coverage, frequency, and publication of reports on member countries' progress in implementing the recommendations of the assessment teams; and to consider making it mandatory to publish the reports.

[53] See Blustein (2003) and Calvo and Mendoza (2000b).

involve large bonuses in addition to salaries) and the underwriting income
of the firm create incentives for their financial analysts to provide clients
with overly rosy assessments of the macroeconomic prospects of debt-
issuing countries. Moreover, managers of many mutual funds are judged
by how well their portfolios perform in relative terms—for example, in
comparison with some benchmark index—rather than in absolute terms.
This provides managers of emerging market bond funds with incentives
to maintain portfolios with country shares that do not deviate very far
from those in the benchmark portfolio, thereby contributing to herding
behavior and distorting the response of capital flows to new information
about the macroeconomic prospects of emerging market countries.

Such distortions point to deficiencies in the financial regulation and
supervision of large institutional investors, which mainly reside in the
G-10 countries. This contributes to the case, argued by Dobson and Hufbauer (2001), for G-10 finance ministers and parliamentary committees
to review the instructions and incentives of financial supervisors with the
purpose of addressing factors that distort the behavior of international
capital flows on the supply side.

As Calvo and Mendoza emphasize, informational frictions can be
addressed not only through efforts aimed at improving the quality of
information and eliminating factors that distort market responses to information, but also by giving serious consideration to institutional arrangements that require less information.[54] Institutional arrangements
that economize on the information-gathering requirements of financial
market participants include dollarization, which reduces the need for information about a country's monetary and exchange rate policies, and
reliance on foreign banks, which can reduce the relevance of information
about domestic financial institutions.

8.5 Revamp Debt Resolution Procedures

The propagation and severity of financial crises can depend critically on
whether an effective mechanism is in place for coordinating the behavior
of individual creditors and debtors. Without such a mechanism, a moderate weakening of confidence about a country's ability to meet its scheduled
debt payments can snowball into a panic-driven rush for the exits, leading

---

[54] See Calvo and Mendoza (2000a) and Mendoza (2002b).

to an outcome that is not in the collective best interests of either creditors or the debtor country. Systemic reforms aimed at establishing more
effective mechanisms for dealing with collective action problems or coordination failures have the potential to substantially reduce the financial
losses and macroeconomic costs of financial crises.

There are several different types of situations in which it is important
to elicit cooperation from private creditors and debtors. As Kenen (2001)
notes, coordination mechanisms are important not only for mitigating
simple creditor panics but also for addressing the types of debt-related
problems encountered by Ukraine (which faced a bulge in redemption
payments due), Pakistan (which was told to restructure its debts to private
creditors as a condition for a Paris Club restructuring of debts to official
creditors), and Ecuador (where the president announced a decision to
withhold interest payments due on Brady bonds because the country faced
serious economic problems).[55]

The issue of how to design more effective mechanisms for debt resolution has generated considerable debate in recent years. To a large extent,
the debate was triggered by widespread concerns over the size of the official financial support packages that the international community wound
up providing to Mexico and the crisis-stricken Asian countries, and by
the global financial disorder that followed the decision to limit official
funding to Russia in August 1998. As an alternative to official bailouts
of debtor countries and their creditors, attention began to focus more
intensely on orderly ways of bailing in the private sector. There was a
strong consensus among economists and creditor-country policymakers
that the official sector should not shoulder all the consequences of failed
contractual arrangements between private creditors and emerging market borrowers, and that private sector involvement in taking losses was
important. It was also recognized, however, that the nature of private sector involvement has to be carefully designed so as not to induce private
capital to rush more quickly for the exits.[56]

In general, the case for mechanisms to elicit cooperation from creditors
and debtors comes from the fact that the resolution of debt problems is

---

[55] IMF (2003m) discusses shortcomings in the existing process of sovereign debt restructurings and provides summary descriptions of recent cases.

[56] Frankel and Roubini (2003) describe the evolution of official views on private sector involvement, its application to specific cases, and a number of unresolved and controversial
issues.

a path-dependent process and not a zero-sum game. Speedy resolution of debt problems can limit the adverse consequences for debtor countries and their creditors. "The potential benefits of moving rapidly to restructure debt while there is money on the table and before economic dislocation has taken hold is widely recognized in credit markets."[57] A well-defined resolution process can also have an important bearing on the pressures for official lending and on the effectiveness of official lending. Without an orderly procedure for resolving liquidity crises, the IMF can get caught in a "time consistency trap" and forced, de facto, to bail out countries in trouble.[58] Moreover, without a mechanism for stopping debt payments until debt problems have been resolved, a policy of limited official lending may be inherently ineffective. As Williamson (2000: 17) sees it:

Not all contingencies are foreseeable, and hence, no matter how conscientious the debtor, contingencies may arise in which it is something between unreasonably costly and totally impossible for the debtor to maintain debt service according to the original contractual terms. This is now widely acknowledged, but its corollary is not. The corollary is that any creditor that suspects restructuring to be a possibility has an incentive to liquidate its claim while that remains possible. Limited official loans will simply allow more creditors to get out rather than encourage them to stay in. The choice is between unlimited loans (a real lender of last resort...) and restructuring the debt....If one worries about...[the moral hazard associated with unlimited official lending], the logical conclusion is that the IMF should never undertake crisis lending except in the context of a standstill.[59]

Despite the strength of the general case for cooperative solutions to debt resolution problems, efforts to design mechanisms for achieving cooperation confront a number of complicated issues. Moreover, there remain strong concerns that the establishment of well-defined cooperative mechanisms for resolving debt problems ex post may have counterproductive effects on the behavior of debtors and creditors ex ante.

The debate over how to strengthen debt resolution procedures has focused on several different approaches. One approach is to design debt contracts to contain a set of collective action clauses that prevent debt

---

[57] See Krueger (2003b: 14).

[58] See Miller and Zhang (2000).

[59] As a related perspective, Boorman and Allen (2000) and Kenen (2001) emphasize that a policy of limited lending is "precariously balanced." The size of the financing gap (or the amount of official financing needed under a given adjustment effort) depends on success in stemming creditor panic, and success in stemming creditor panic depends on the amount of official financing provided.

workouts from being held up by various contingencies or obstructed by minority groups of creditors. A second approach is to pursue a statutory path for bringing more order to the debt resolution process through international agreement on bankruptcy procedures and debt-restructuring mechanisms. A third approach is to rely on contractual standstill provisions—that is, to insert clauses in debt contracts that provide for a temporary suspension of debt payments combined with a stay of litigation—as distinct from imposing standstills as part of a statutory debt resolution process. A fourth approach (already discussed in Section 8.2) is to establish explicit seniority rights for the restructuring of sovereign debt.

Discussions of collective action clauses have distinguished between several different collective action problems. As characterized by Roubini (2002), these comprise the rush to the exits, whereby investors attempt to unload their claims on the debtor; the rush to the courthouse, or grab race, whereby creditors initiate litigation to attach the debtor's assets; and the free rider or rogue creditor problem, whereby a minority of creditors may scuttle a restructuring agreement by holding out for more favorable terms. Various types of provisions can be inserted into debt contracts to facilitate the speedy and orderly resolution of any debt payment difficulties that might arise.[60] Among the most useful collective action clauses are majority restructuring provisions, which enable a qualified majority of bond holders to bind all holders of the same bond instrument to the financial terms of a restructuring, both before and after a default, and majority enforcement provisions, which prevent a minority of creditors from pursuing disruptive legal action after a default and prior to reaching a restructuring agreement. In combination, such provisions—also referred to as collective representation clauses and majority voting and sharing provisions—can prevent the debt-restructuring process from being obstructed by isolated creditors or by vulture groups that resort to lawsuits and other ways of holding out for favorable terms that are not in the interests of the majority of creditors. The appointment of standing committees of representatives of the various classes of creditors (e.g., bondholders, banks, and hedge funds), or the inclusion of engagement provisions in bond contracts, can also play a useful role in facilitating

---

[60] See Eichengreen (1999b) and IMF (2003d). Kletzer (2003) provides a formal model of sovereign debt renegotiation in which collective action clauses lead to efficient outcomes.

communication between creditors and debtors and in jump starting negotiations.

Most international sovereign bonds are issued in either the United States (governed by New York law) or the United Kingdom. Collective action clauses have long been present in bonds issued in the United Kingdom, but they have typically not been included in bond contracts governed by New York law. As of February 2003, collective action clauses were present in roughly one-third of the international sovereign bonds outstanding.[61] Empirical studies have found little support for the view that the inclusion of collective action clauses in bond contracts increases the interest rate spreads that borrowers must pay to market new debt.[62]

Partly as an effort to lead by example, a number of industrial countries—in particular, the United Kingdom, Canada, and the EU countries—have recently taken steps to begin introducing collective action clauses into their international sovereign bonds on a regular basis.[63] Moreover, in March 2003, Mexico took the lead for emerging market countries by issuing a bond containing collective action clauses in the U.S. market, and several other emerging market countries followed soon thereafter.[64]

One of the unresolved questions brought to the fore by differences among recent bond issues is whether a standardization of collective action clauses would be desirable, particularly with regard to the size of the qualified majority required to make a restructuring agreement binding. The British tradition uses a 75 percent threshold, but applies it to the amount of principal that is represented at relevant meetings of bondholders, as distinct from the total outstanding principal.[65] Another difficult issue is how collective action clauses might be designed to provide for

---

[61] See IMF (2003d: 15). Eichengreen, Kletzer, and Mody (2004) surmise that if collective action clauses were included in all new issues going forward, it would take the better part of a decade to complete the process of eliminating emerging market debt without collective action provisions.

[62] See, for example, Becker, Richards, and Thaicharoen (2001) and the references cited in IMF (2003d). By contrast, Eichengreen and Mody (2000) conclude that collective action clauses raise spreads for low-quality borrowers (perhaps by exacerbating moral hazard) but lower spreads for high-quality borrowers (perhaps because they facilitate restructurings where moral hazard is not a concern).

[63] See IMF (2003d).

[64] Although Mexico's move received considerable attention, Lebanon, Qatar, and Egypt had previously issued bonds with collective action clauses during 2000 and 2001.

[65] This approach, which prevents a restructuring agreement from being frustrated because a critical mass of bondholders fails to cast a vote, is important in Britain, where bond

aggregation across different debt instruments, including the set of debt instruments that do not contain collective action clauses.[66]

The approach of simply encouraging countries to add collective action clauses to debt contracts—the current policy of the IMF[67]—has the appeal of being only a small step away from laissez faire. A larger step would be to mandate that countries must include collective action clauses in all new bond contracts as a precondition for financial assistance from the IMF, or perhaps as a precondition for official authorization to issue debt in the United States, the United Kingdom, and other bond markets.

Starting in November 2001, along side the push for collective action clauses, the international community began to actively consider the case for a statutory sovereign debt-restructuring mechanism (SDRM). The initiative was catalyzed by Krueger (2001), who proposed several principles and pointed to a number of questions that had to be addressed. The questions concerned: (i) the legal basis on which an SDRM would rest; (ii) the locus of responsibility for operating the mechanism; (iii) the determinants of if and when the mechanism should be formally set in motion; (iv) how to ensure that the debtor behaved appropriately while under protection from its creditors; (v) what financing the IMF should provide; and (vi) the types of debt that should be covered by the stay and binding-in of minority creditors.

Proposals for international bankruptcy courts or other statutory arrangements for sovereign debt restructuring have a long history.[68] There has not been any precedent, however, for the recent effort to actually hammer out a set of arrangements on which the international community could agree. The effort to shape an SDRM—which benefited from extensive dialog with the private financial community, debt workout professionals, lawyers, academics, and the official community—was high on the Fund's agenda during the eighteen months through April 2003, when the Managing Director of the Fund presented a specific proposal to the International Monetary and Financial Committee (IMFC).[69] Although

---

holding is widely dispersed. It is less important in the United States, where bonds are held largely by mutual funds and other institutional investors.

[66] Eichengreen et al. (2003) and IMF (2003m) discuss a number of issues that bear on the effectiveness of collective action clauses, including the aggregation problem and various ideas that have been advanced for addressing it.

[67] See IMF (2003d).

[68] See the survey by Rogoff and Zettelmeyer (2002).

[69] See IMF (2003l).

BOX 8.2. Principles of the Proposed SDRM[1]

- The mechanism should only be used to restructure debt that is judged to be unsustainable by the debtor. It should neither increase the likelihood of restructuring nor encourage defaults.
- In circumstances in which a member's debt is unsustainable, the mechanism should be designed to catalyze rapid restructuring, both in terms of when it is initiated and, once initiated, when it is completed.
- Any interference with contractual relations should be limited to those measures that are needed to resolve the most important collective action problems.
- The framework should be designed in a manner that promotes greater transparency in the restructuring process.
- The mechanism should encourage early and active creditor participation during the restructuring process.
- The mechanism should not interfere with the sovereignty of debtors.
- The framework should establish incentives for negotiation—not a detailed blueprint for restructuring.
- The framework should be sufficiently flexible—and simple—to accommodate the operation and evolution of capital markets.
- Because the framework is intended to fill a gap within the existing financial architecture, it should not displace existing statutory frameworks.
- The integrity of the decision-making process under the mechanism should be safeguarded by an efficient and impartial dispute resolution process.
- The formal role of the Fund under the SDRM should be limited.

[1] As listed in IMF (2003l).

---

considerable agreement was eventually reached on a set of principals (Box 8.2) and details, as well as agreement on the approach of using an amendment to the Fund's Articles to establish a statutory framework, the level of support was not as high as the 85 percent supermajority required to move ahead. Accordingly, the IMFC recognized in April 2003 "that it is not feasible now to move forward to establish the SDRM" but agreed "that work should continue on issues raised in its development that are of general relevance to the orderly resolution of financial crises."[70] It subsequently encouraged sovereign debtors and private creditors, in

[70] See IMFC (2003a).

conjunction with the IMF, to work on developing a voluntary code of good conduct that could contribute to the orderly resolution of financial crises.

Proponents of an SDRM have argued that the orderly functioning of international capital markets requires "a strong, centralized legal framework to support its operation,"[71] and that collective action clauses are not adequate by themselves. Whether this view proves correct remains to be seen.[72] Should interest in an SDRM intensify again, the April 2003 proposal would provide a useful starting point for further deliberation, along with the proposal to make seniority rights explicit.[73] The main features of the April 2003 proposal were the following[74]: (i) It would protect the debtor from disruptive legal action by creditors while negotiations were underway, with provision for a temporary suspension (stay) of debt payments if approved by a supermajority of creditors. (ii) Creditors would have assurances that the debtor would negotiate in good faith and pursue sound economic policies that help protect the value of creditor claims; strong incentives would be provided to the debtor by the conditionality that the Fund imposes when it lends to a country that is in arrears. (iii) Creditors could agree to give seniority and protection from restructuring to new trade credits or other new lending to support economic activity (analogous to debtor in possession financing). (iv) A supermajority of creditors could make a restructuring agreement binding on all creditors, and minority groups of creditors would be prevented from pursuing disruptive legal action. And (v) an independent and impartial dispute resolution forum would be established to verify claims, ensure the integrity of the voting process, and adjudicate disputes that might arise.

The third provision, which would subordinate old debt to new trade credits, would help address the criticism that IMF programs impose too much austerity.[75] Some form of debtor-in-possession financing, aimed at giving firms the ability to continue to operate and preserve their going-concern value, is a common feature of corporate bankruptcy procedures

---

[71] See Krueger (2003b: 11).

[72] Stiglitz (2002b) notes that each of the advanced industrial countries has taken a statutory approach to debt restructuring rather than relying on market mechanisms augmented by collective action clauses or other contractual provisions.

[73] See Bolton and Skeel (2003).

[74] See Boorman (2003) and IMF (2003l).

[75] See Corden (1999). Recall Box 3.1, Criticism 4.

throughout the world,[76] but current national and international laws do not give countries analogous scope to maintain trade and production.

Another approach for resolving debt problems would rely on contractual standstill arrangements. Unlike collective action clauses, which facilitate voluntary debt workouts, standstill provisions give the debtor the option of imposing an involuntary solution—effectively a forced rollover of debts—for a temporary period. Unlike the standstill provisions of a statutory restructuring mechanism, contractual standstill arrangements could only be effective in forcing rollovers and protecting against litigation on new debt, because they could not be inserted into existing debt contracts.

The idea of adding standstill provisions to debt contracts began to surface in the late 1990s.[77] Among the advocates, Buiter and Siebert (1999) suggest that countries should require all debt contracts denominated in foreign currency to include a Universal Debt Rollover Option with a Penalty (UDROP). The option would entitle the borrower to extend the contract for a specified period at a penalty interest rate, but would only allow for a single extension; the implicit price of the option would be determined in the market by the contracting parties; subsequent derivatives trading would not be able to undo the rollover (standstill) provision because contingent liabilities would also have to carry the option; so all creditors would be automatically bailed in.

In a joint proposal by staff at the Bank of Canada and Bank of England, Haldane and Kruger (2001) argue that standstills can serve as a useful "backdrop measure to provide debtors and creditors with a breathing space to arrive at a co-operative outcome,"[78] but they also emphasize that it is important for the parties involved to know that the official sector will behave predictably and that official monies are limited. They further argue that standstills should be governed by guidelines that (i) set explicit time limits on the standstills; (ii) promote transparency, good-faith bargaining by debtors, and equal treatment of creditors as far as possible; and (iii) grant net new money seniority over existing claims, with particular attention to attracting trade credit that helps maintain production.

Kenen (2001, 2002b) proposes that the Fund encourage countries to adopt legislation requiring the inclusion of 90-day rollover options in all

[76] See Bolton (2003) for a survey of corporate bankruptcy practices in selected countries.
[77] See Kenen (2001: 147).
[78] See Haldane and Kruger (2001: 10).

foreign-currency-denominated obligations, public and private. He also argues that the power to trigger the rollover options should be vested with national authorities, not with individual debtors. In his view, procedures and guidelines should be put in place for national authorities to decide whether and when to impose an involuntary rollover, and, upon a decision to do so, for requiring all debtors to exercise their options simultaneously.

Opponents of standstill clauses have raised a number of objections, arguing that they undermine the primacy of contracts, may encourage debtors to default, may encourage creditors to rush for the exits, and may be difficult to enforce without comprehensive controls on purchases of foreign exchange. Each of these arguments has been countered.[79] The Fund can use the conditionality associated with its lending into arrears to motivate countries to adhere to various rules and procedures, including rules governing the provision of information on their aggregate debt positions and rules and procedures designed to prevent debtor countries from opportunistically exploiting the exercise of standstill provisions. Thus, by using its leverage effectively, the Fund can give countries strong incentives to honor their contracts in full and on time, and hence to avoid defaults, except when faced with a situation in which it is unreasonably costly or totally impossible to maintain debt service according to the original contractual terms. Moreover, relative to the situation in their absence, standstill provisions could have the effect of slowing the rush for the exits—and hence also easing the demand to purchase foreign exchange—if they were perceived as more effective in resolving collective action problems than attempts to organize rollovers in other ways.[80]

At the time of the Fund's Fall 2003 Annual Meetings, the push for statutory standstill provisions had given way to a request for further analysis of "issues of general relevance to the orderly resolution of financial crises, including transparency and disclosure, aggregation and inter-creditor equity," along with encouraging sovereign debtors and private creditors to

[79] See Haldane and Kruger (2001) and Kenen (2002b).
[80] Kenen (2002b) would minimize abuse of the contractual rollover option by allowing it to be exercised no more than once during the life of any debt contract and by requiring the country, before exercising it, to obtain a finding of fact from the IMF. Insofar as a 90-day period might not buy enough time in some cases that required debts to be restructured, Kenen would include a clause authorizing a supermajority of a sovereign's creditors to extend the initial rollover for additional 90-day periods. He would also encourage countries to include collective action clauses and rollover options in debt contracts by declaring that countries that do not adopt legislation requiring such clauses would suffer a reduction in their access to Fund credit after, say, a five-year period.

develop a voluntary code of conduct for resolving crises.[81] The controversial issues involved in debt restructuring, together with both the progress made in promoting collective action clauses and the fact that several countries have recently succeeded in negotiating debt restructurings without prolonged delays,[82] raise questions about the desirability of formal standstill provisions.

Quite apart from the debate over collective action clauses and standstill provisions, there remains strong concern about another aspect of the debt resolution process. In particular, there is strong concern that debtor countries and their private creditors will continue to game the IMF into large bailout loans, and that the debt resolution process will be unnecessarily complicated and prolonged by a lack of transparent and time-consistent behavior on the part of the IMF and the governments of its major creditor countries. In that context, a number of economists view strict limits on Fund lending as a sine qua non for making significant progress in inducing more orderly debt resolution procedures.[83]

8.6   Strengthen the Frameworks for Development Aid and Official Nonconcessional Lending

As noted in Chapter 6, the preponderance of econometric and anecdotal evidence suggests that for many recipient countries, development aid has not had a significant impact on economic growth over the past several decades. Similarly, considerable anecdotal evidence suggests that in many countries, the IMF's nonconcessional lending activities have not been sufficiently successful in inducing the policy reforms and generating the market confidence required to prevent or mitigate financial crises and sustain economic growth. Thus, two related challenges are to strengthen the frameworks for development aid (including concessional lending) to low-income countries and for crisis lending or other extensions of nonconcessional Fund credit to other countries with temporary financing needs.

In addressing the challenge of making development aid more effective, the international community has begun to pursue the idea of conditioning aid allocations on the track records that countries have established in either achieving economic growth or building institutions and

---

[81] See IMFC (2003b).
[82] See IMF (2003m).
[83] See Goldstein (2003b).

implementing policies that are conducive to future economic growth. It is clear that many low-income countries will not be able to break out of poverty traps without substantial volumes of debt forgiveness or other forms of aid, but in light of the history of aid ineffectiveness, there is also growing sentiment that the allocation of aid should be tied to past country performance rather than promises of adjustment. As discussed in Chapter 6, the HIPC initiative has taken steps in this direction by making debt relief conditional on both the preparation of strategies for poverty reduction and growth and an established track record of implementing such strategies. Similarly, in establishing the Millennium Challenge Account, the United States has taken steps to condition some of its bilateral aid on observable indicators of the quality of governance, the strength of the effort to invest in people, and the quality of macroeconomic and regulatory policies.

Although much of the recent discussion has focused on conditioning aid allocations on countries' track records in taking actions that are conducive to economic growth, another idea is to condition aid on countries' track records on matters that create major externalities for the rest of the world. In that vein, Bulow and Rogoff (1990) suggest that aid could be allocated in ways that encourage responsible policies toward the environment, population growth, or drug eradication—providing incentives, for example, to reduce deforestation, the burning of fossil fuels, or the production of chlorofluorocarbons. They also make the parallel suggestion that the amounts of aid that the international community asks individual donor countries to provide should depend on the donor countries' track records in areas that create important externalities.

An important variant of the idea of conditioning aid on track records is to establish aid contests—or to force countries to compete for a given volume of aid.[84] Low-income countries will not succeed in growing out of poverty traps unless the industrial countries are both generous in the total volume of aid they provide and hard hearted in allocating the aid in a manner that provides strong incentives for recipient countries to use it effectively. Competition for aid allocations, if appropriately designed, could provide incentives for recipient countries to use resources effectively, and clear evidence that aid was effective would tend, in turn, to make the industrial countries more willing to provide generous amounts of aid.

---

[84] See Easterly (2002).

Although the idea of conditioning aid on track records is appealing in principle, several considerations suggest that the scope for high pay-offs may be limited. Some economists have argued that a large share of development aid is not amenable to reallocation and that, except at the extremes, it can be very difficult to distinguish good and bad policy environments in a convincing way.[85] Roughly two-thirds of development aid is extended in bilateral form, and much of that is motivated by humanitarian concerns (disaster relief), historical and cultural ties, or the pursuit of specific goals of the donor countries (e.g., drug, immigration, or pollution control and trade expansion). In addition, it is analytically difficult to determine whether aid has been used productively when financial resources are highly fungible, and it is generally difficult to say no to prospective aid recipients in the absence of convincing evidence that resources have been squandered. Moreover, the problem is magnified by the fact that the major industrial countries have great difficulty taking a hard-hearted position with regard to those developing countries in which they have substantial economic or strategic interests, and the latter group includes most of the developing countries with relatively large populations and resource needs.

A second approach for trying to make aid more effective in promoting growth is to seek to improve the practices of aid donors. Critics of donor practices in providing financial and technical assistance cite ill-conceived and poorly supervised projects and programs, the adoption of unsuitable approaches, complex accounting requirements, the propensity of donors to impose their own priorities and agendas, the huge amounts of time and energy that local officials must devote to visiting aid missions and management tasks, and in some cases a tendency of aid projects to drain local expertise or displace local entrepreneurship.[86] These critics argue that the fundamental challenge is to provide aid in a manner that helps countries strengthen their institutional capacities, recognizing that the least developed countries are typically characterized by a scarcity of skilled and educated people, organizational disarray in the public sector, and small and neglected or discouraged private sectors. According to this view, aid effectiveness can be enhanced by providing financial and technical assistance in a manner that has much less of a donor-driven character

[85] See Berg (2003).
[86] See Berg (2003).

than has traditionally been the case, that gives local agencies much greater scope to design projects on the basis of their capacities to implement them, but that is also constructive in helping countries strengthen and build their institutional capacities.

In considering how to strengthen the framework for nonconcessional IMF lending, it is relevant to distinguish two objectives: increasing the incentives for countries to reform macroeconomic policies and build institutional capacities, and providing confidence to market participants. Both factors are important for preventing and resolving financial crises and sustaining economic growth. And even though success in motivating countries to adopt sound policies and build institutions can contribute importantly to sustaining market confidence, it does not eliminate the need to address the second objective.

As already discussed in Section 8.2, one approach for strengthening countries' incentives would be to link the degree of access to Fund credit to countries' track records in maintaining sound macroeconomic policies and pursuing structural reforms ex ante. As has also been emphasized, however, the effectiveness of such a system of prequalification requirements would require the Fund's Executive Directors and the authorities of the major creditor countries to consistently demonstrate an ability and resolve to say no to countries with poor track records. Indeed, many would argue that demonstrating a strong resolve to be a tough cop when warranted would do much more to strengthen the Fund's effectiveness than implementing a system of prequalification requirements.

Many economists and policymakers have come to the view that the international financial system cannot function effectively unless emerging market countries have access to a large volume of official credit that can be mobilized quickly, thereby meeting the objective of providing confidence that financial crises can be prevented or mitigated. This raises the issue of the extent to which the Fund (or some group of major creditor countries) should act as an international lender of last resort (LOLR).[87] One consideration is whether an international LOLR would strengthen the international financial system or worsen moral hazard problems and add to its fragility.[88] Another consideration is size: how large would an international LOLR have to be to function effectively? In the formal literature,

---

[87] For relevant literature, see Fischer (1999), Jeanne and Wyplosz (2003), Corsetti et al. (2003), and references therein.

[88] Recall the discussion of moral hazard in Chapter 5.

effectiveness is defined in terms of whether the LOLR can stop a panic from driving a country from a good equilibrium to a bad equilibrium; a distinction is drawn between an international LOLR that injects resources into the market and an international LOLR that uses its resources to back domestic banking safety nets; and some conceptual frameworks suggest that the latter type of LOLR may not have to be unrealistically large to function effectively.[89]

From an operational perspective, much of the discussion of crisis lending within the international policymaking community has focused not on the creation or funding of an international LOLR per se but rather on the terms and conditions under which countries should be granted exceptionally large access to IMF credit, and on the procedures that should be followed in making decisions on crisis lending. In September 2002 the Fund's Executive Board agreed that, at a minimum, four criteria would have to be met to justify lending in excess of the Fund's normal access limits. The four necessary conditions are: that the country is experiencing exceptional balance of payments pressures; that "rigorous and systematic analysis indicates that there is a high probability that debt will remain sustainable"; that the country has "good prospects" of regaining access to private capital markets within the time that the Fund's resources would be outstanding; and that the country's policy program provides "a reasonably strong prospect of success," when institutional and political capacities are taken into account.[90] As stated, these necessary conditions for crisis lending leave considerable scope for interpretive discretion, and it remains to be seen whether the new criteria and procedures for crisis lending will make the Fund more effective in functioning as a de facto international LOLR.

8.7 Concluding Perspectives

In continuing the discussion of what can be done to improve the performance of the world economy and make the globalization process work better, this chapter has turned from the challenges for countries to address on as individual basis to the various ideas that economists have put forth for reforming the international financial system as a whole. Starting from

[89] See Jeanne and Wyplosz (2003) and Corsetti et al. (2003).
[90] See IMF (2003h).

a list of six types of systemic problems that have contributed to the frequency and magnitude of financial crises or posed obstacles to economic growth and poverty reduction, it has defined a corresponding six-part agenda for systemic reform. The agenda includes strengthening the quality and impact of IMF surveillance; inducing changes in the composition of international capital flows; introducing contingent debt contracts or other mechanisms for hedging against macroeconomic risks; addressing informational imperfections and distorted incentives on the supply side of international capital flows; revamping debt resolution procedures; and strengthening the frameworks for development aid and crisis lending.[91]

As noted at the outset of Chapter 7, it is not feasible to completely prevent financial crises or eliminate obstacles to growth and poverty reduction. Moreover, because international financial markets are too large and sophisticated to control very effectively under the democratic and market-oriented political–economic systems of the industrial countries, and because there is little political support for abandoning those systems or for relinquishing monetary policy autonomy in the key-currency countries, revolutionary change is not in the cards. However, the pursuit of evolutionary changes across a broad agenda can plausibly deliver considerable benefits, and economists have identified fairly extensive agendas for individual countries and the international community. At present, proposals for pursuing reforms in some of the problem areas are still either insufficiently well defined or too controversial to receive the support of the international policymaking community, but significant steps are being taken to advance other parts of the agenda, and there are grounds for optimism that continuing progress will substantially strengthen the functioning of the international financial system.

One direction for strengthening the international financial system is through improvements in the quality and impact of IMF surveillance. The quality of the Fund's policy advice is inherently limited by existing knowledge and the best judgments that can be drawn from cumulative experience. Accordingly, fairly extensive interaction between the Fund staff and the research communities in academia and other policymaking institutions—through conferences, seminars, visiting scholar programs, collaborative research projects, and other mechanisms—can be very

---

[91] As in Chapter 7, the items on the agenda are listed in an order in which it is convenient to discuss them, without implying any judgments about their relative importance.

constructive in keeping the Fund's thinking and advice closely aligned with the best analysis available, and in pointing those communities to areas in which additional research could lead to significant improvements in policy analysis. As a consequence of both ongoing research and policy experience, economists and policymakers today have significantly deeper and broader perspectives than they did a decade ago on the determinants of economic growth and the factors that contribute to financial crises. At the same time, there remain strong disagreements among economists on a number of key policy issues on which the Fund cannot avoid taking a stand.

The impact of the Fund's surveillance depends not only on the quality of its analysis and policy advice but also on countries' incentives to follow the Fund's advice. National authorities are generally reluctant to impose unpopular policies in the short run, and countries with large fiscal or external deficits frequently turn a deaf ear when the Fund advises them to address such deficits. Moreover, the Fund has little leverage over countries that are not desperate to borrow. As a consequence, many countries delay making unpopular policy adjustments until their fiscal or external debts have grown to levels that are difficult to sustain and have made their economies highly vulnerable to crisis.

Because much of the challenge is to motivate countries to implement macroeconomic policies and structural reforms that will help them prevent crises, sustain growth, and avoid the need for Fund credit, a key to strengthening incentives is to link countries' prospective access to Fund credit—should they ever need it—to their track records in policy implementation and institution building prior to any requests for Fund credit. However, such ex ante conditionality, or prequalification requirements, may lack credibility and effectiveness in strengthening incentives unless the major industrial countries—speaking through their representatives on the IMF Executive Board—become significantly more hard-hearted and willing to say no to requests for credit drawings by countries with poor track records in policy implementation and institution building.

A second direction for strengthening the international financial system is to induce changes in the composition of capital flows. High levels of international debt make countries vulnerable to financial crises, so a shift from debt-creating inflows to inflows of foreign direct investment or equity purchases would have the desirable effect of leaving countries less vulnerable to crises, other things being equal. Moreover, inflows of foreign direct investment have the potential to be relatively conducive to economic growth. Short-term foreign-currency-denominated debts make countries particularly vulnerable to crises, so a shift in the composition of external debts toward longer-term maturities and domestic-currency-denominated instruments would also be desirable, other things being equal.

The important qualifier is that other things may not be equal. Given the risks they face, creditors have a strong rationale for holding claims on emerging market countries in short-term foreign-currency-denominated forms, because short-term maturities provide better exit vehicles and foreign currency denominations provide better protection against inflation and exchange rate depreciation. Some of the rationale comes from the fact that borrowers cannot commit *not* to issue new debt, which provides creditors with incentives to protect themselves against debt dilution by extending credit in short-term foreign-currency-denominated maturities as well as in other forms that are costly to restructure. A potentially effective way to address these incentives and mitigate their undesirable effects on the composition of debt would be to give older claims explicit seniority over newer claims in debt restructurings. In contrast, measures that attempted to curtail short-term foreign-currency-denominated inflows without addressing the incentives that give rise to such flows would motivate foreign investors to try to circumvent the measures through the use of derivative transactions (e.g., forward purchases of foreign currencies that effectively convert long-term domestic-currency-denominated claims into short-term foreign-currency-denominated claims). Moreover, measures that could not be circumvented might well induce a substantial contraction of aggregate capital inflows rather than a shift toward longer-term flows. Another relevant consideration is that short-term capital inflows serve valuable functions: they provide working capital that is needed to finance international trade; and they also provide liquidity to domestic banks, which have specific expertise in monitoring and wielding power over local borrowers and hence are particularly important for financing economic activity in countries that lack sound corporate governance and bankruptcy laws.

In addition to seeking to alter the composition of international debt in desirable ways, it may be useful to pursue a number of proposals aimed at shifting international capital flows away from debt-creating flows. Such proposals include efforts to promote the development of equity markets, steps to reduce the information costs and risks associated with foreign direct investments and equity holdings, and initiatives to revise foreign sovereign immunity laws or the provisions of debt contracts to prevent creditors from litigating debt defaults in creditor-country courts. It may also be useful to try to reduce the volatility of international capital flows by focusing, among other things, on proposals for strengthening the supervision of the financial institutions involved. This could be pursued by strengthening the incentive structures and resources of the G-10 financial supervisors and by establishing a subordinated debt requirement designed to create incentives for stronger private sector monitoring of banks.

A third item on the agenda for systemic reform is to create markets for contingent debt contracts or other mechanisms that can provide countries with better vehicles for hedging against macroeconomic risks. One proposal is to develop markets for GDP-indexed bonds, designed as the equivalent of plain vanilla government bonds with standard nominal coupon payments plus securities that promised payments proportional to the difference between actual GDP growth and some prespecified norm. A market for such contingent contracts could be piggybacked on existing markets for government securities. Another proposal would make debt payments contingent on outcomes for several different variables that were largely exogenous to the debtor country and readily observable—such as the prices of key commodity exports (such as copper for Chile or oil for Mexico), an average interest rate spread on emerging market debt, and perhaps the rate of GDP growth in major export markets. The potential benefits from such contingent claims would depend on whether they could be introduced in substantial volume, which has led to the suggestion that large-scale debt restructurings might provide appealing occasions for introducing such instruments. In addition, the demand for instruments with payment streams contingent on outcomes for more than one variable might depend on whether they could be easily repackaged by financial intermediaries into a bundle of separable contingent securities that each insured against a single type of risk.

The discussion of how to provide better mechanisms for insuring against macroeconomic risks has not focused solely on proposals for contingent securities. Another proposal is to create a pool of official funds that could be used to purchase emerging market debt and thereby help protect against contagion in certain circumstances—for example, if the average price of the bonds of a large number of emerging market countries began to fall precipitously.

A fourth focal point for systemic reform is the problem of informational imperfections. The fixed costs of acquiring and processing information, and various factors that prevent private firms and individuals from reaping the full benefits of incurring the fixed costs, contribute to the phenomena of herding behavior and momentum trading in financial markets. Together with unanticipated shocks and general uncertainties about future macroeconomic outcomes and policy actions, these phenomena give rise to patterns of international capital flows that have been associated with financial crises—namely, surges in capital inflows followed by sharp reversals (sudden stops), and contagion.

One direction for mitigating informational imperfections is to provide market participants with more extensive and more timely information. In that regard, recent years have brought significant progress in improving the scope, quality, and timeliness of the data available to investors in emerging market countries—including data on reserve holdings and external debts. In addition, the Fund now publishes much of the analysis generated in its surveillance of member countries, including about three-fourths of its regular Article IV Staff Reports and two-thirds of both the reports generated under the Financial Sector Assessment Program and the Reports on the Observance of Standards and Codes. There is scope to go further by extending the coverage of the assessment programs and eliminating the option for countries to block publication of surveillance reports. In general, although there are strong arguments against the idea of the Fund becoming a rating agency—because single summary ratings, like early warning indicators, are prone to the twin errors of generating false alarms and of failing to generate appropriate alarms—there are good arguments for providing market participants with frank and transparent multidimensional assessments.

Another direction for addressing informational imperfections is to focus on the supply side of international capital flows and the compensation systems that distort the incentives of financial analysts and investors in providing and responding to information. Such distortions point to deficiencies in the financial regulation and supervision of large institutional investors, which mainly reside in the G-10 countries. This reinforces the case for G-10 finance ministers and parliamentary committees to review the instructions and incentives of financial supervisors with the purpose of addressing factors that distort the behavior of international capital flows on the supply side.

A fifth item on the agenda for systemic reform is to revamp the procedures for resolving debt problems, which can be complicated substantially by collective action problems. Effective mechanisms for coordinating creditors and debtors is important for mitigating simple creditor panics, for addressing the types of temporary debt-servicing problems that can arise when debtors face a bulge in redemption payments, and for working out restructuring agreements when debtors encounter more fundamental difficulties in meeting their obligations to creditors. Experience has clearly illustrated that the resolution of debt problems is a path-dependent process and not a zero-sum game, and that mechanisms for eliciting speedy cooperation can limit the adverse consequences for both debtor countries and their creditors.

Discussions of how to strengthen debt resolution procedures have focused on four approaches: adding collective action clauses to debt contracts; establishing a statutory mechanism for restructuring debts; adding standstill provisions to debt contracts; and providing more explicit definitions of seniority rights in debt restructurings. Collective action clauses include provisions that enable a qualified majority of bond holders to bind all holders of the same bond instrument to the terms of a restructuring agreement, and that prevent a minority of creditors from acting disruptively. Most international sovereign bonds are issued in either the United States or the United Kingdom, and collective action clauses have long been present in sovereign bonds issued in the United Kingdom but typically not in those issued in the United States. This is beginning to change, however, as a number of emerging market countries, encouraged by the international community, have recently had successful experiences issuing sovereign bonds with collective action clauses in the United States. Nevertheless, the process of replacing existing debts without such clauses is inherently slow, so the progress that has been made in promoting collective action clauses will not result in significantly easier debt resolution for some time to come.

Along with efforts to promote collective action clauses, the international community has devoted considerable attention in recent years to designing a statutory mechanism for sovereign debt restructuring. Considerable progress was made toward agreement on the principles of such a mechanism, and a detailed proposal was prepared for consideration at the Spring 2003 meeting of the International Monetary and Financial

Committee, but the level of support was not as high as the 85 percent supermajority required to move ahead.

The third approach—encouraging the issuance of debt contracts with clauses that give debtors the option of imposing involuntary standstills in certain circumstances—has received much less consideration by the international community, in part because of the predominant focus on a statutory debt-restructuring mechanism, which would have included analogous standstill provisions. Unlike the provisions of a statutory debt-restructuring mechanism, contractual standstill provisions could only be effective in forcing rollovers and protecting against litigation on new debt, because they could not be inserted into existing debt contracts.

A sixth direction for systemic reform is to strengthen the frameworks for development aid to low-income countries and for crisis lending and other extensions of nonconcessional Fund credit to other countries with temporary financing needs. In considering these challenges, the idea of conditioning the allocation of aid and access to Fund credit on countries' established track records has gained increasing prominence. Low-income countries will not succeed in growing out of poverty traps unless rich countries are both generous in the amount of aid they provide and hard hearted in allocating the aid in a manner that creates strong incentives for recipient countries to use it effectively. Thus, part of the challenge is to establish a credible mechanism for saying no to prospective aid recipients—including countries in which the major powers have significant economic or strategic interests—in the absence of convincing evidence that aid resources will be used effectively. Similarly, the effectiveness of efforts to strengthen the impact of the Fund's policy advice may depend on whether countries come to perceive that unless they establish track records of sound macroeconomic policies and serious structural reforms ex ante, their access to Fund credit will be limited, should they ever request it.

In addition to depending on the strength of countries' commitments to use resources productively, as reflected in part by their track records, the effectiveness of aid can be influenced significantly by donor practices. Development aid could be made more effective if stronger efforts were made to provide financial and technical assistance in a manner that emphasizes the objective of helping countries build and strengthen their institutional capacities and has much less of a donor-driven character than has traditionally been the case.

The breadth of the agenda for systemic reform, together with the many ways in which countries can individually reduce their vulnerabilities to financial crises and improve their prospects for economic growth, provides the optimist with grounds for believing that the international financial system can be strengthened considerably without revolutionary change. Efforts to strengthen the international financial system since the late 1990s have achieved major advances on two items of the six-part agenda: the push to promote institutions conducive to economic growth and crisis prevention through the standards and codes initiative and the associated assessment and technical assistance programs, and the effort to address informational imperfections and to provide stronger incentives for sound policies through greater transparency. Significant progress has also been made on other parts of the agenda, but much more remains to be done.

References

Abiad, Abdul and Ashoka Mody 2003. "Financial Reform: What Shakes It? What Shapes It?," Working Paper WP/03/70, Washington, DC: International Monetary Fund.

Acemoglu, Daron, Simon Johnson, and James Robinson 2002. "Reversal of Fortune: Geography and Institutions in the Making of the Modern World Income Distribution," *Quarterly Journal of Economics* 117, 1231–94.

———, ———, and ——— 2001. "The Colonial Origins of Comparative Development: An Empirical Investigation," *American Economic Review* 91, 1369–1401.

Aghion, Philippe, Philippe Bacchetta, and Abhijit Banerjee 2001. "Currency Crises and Monetary Policy in an Economy with Credit Constraints," *European Economic Review* 45, 1121–50.

———, ———, and ——— 2000. "A Simple Model of Monetary Policy and Currency Crises," *European Economic Review* 44, 728–38.

Agosin, Manuel and Ricardo Ffrench-Davis 1997. "Managing Capital Inflows in Chile," *Estudios de Economia* 24, 297–321.

Aizenman, Joshua 2004. "Financial Opening: Evidence and Policy Options," in Robert Baldwin and Alan Winters, eds., *Challenges to Globalization: Analyzing the Economics*, Chicago: University of Chicago Press, forthcoming.

——— and Nancy Marion 2004. "International Reserve Holdings with Sovereign Risk and Costly Tax Collection," *Economic Journal*, forthcoming.

Alesina, Alberto and Robert Barro, eds. 2001. *Currency Unions*, Stanford, CA: Hoover Institution Press.

Alesina, Alberto, Robert Barro, and Sylvana Tenreyro 2003. "Optimal Currency Areas," in Mark Gertler and Kenneth Rogoff, eds., *NBER Macroeconomics Annual 2002*, Cambridge, MA: MIT Press, 301–45.

Alesina, Alberto and Roberto Perotti 1996. "Fiscal Discipline and the Budget Process," *American Economic Review* 86, 401–7.

Anderson, James and Douglas Marcouiller 2002. "Insecurity and the Pattern of Trade: An Empirical Investigation," *Review of Economics & Statistics* 84, 342–52.

Argy, Victor 1981. *The Post War International Monetary Crisis: An Analysis*, London: George Allen & Unwin.

Ariyoshi, Akiri, Karl Habermeier, Bernard Laurens, Inci Otker-Robe, Jorge Ivan Canales-Kriljenko, and Andrei Kirilenko 2000. *Capital Controls: Country Experiences with Their Use and Liberalization*, Occasional Paper 190, Washington, DC: International Monetary Fund.

Arrow, Kenneth and Gerard Debreu 1954. "Existence of an Equilibrium for a Competitive Economy," *Econometrica* 22, 265–90.

Artis, Michael and Mark Taylor 1994. "The Stabilizing Effect of the ERM on Exchange Rates and Interest Rates: An Empirical Investigation," *IMF Staff Papers* 41, 123–48.

Athanasoulis, Stefano, Robert Shiller, and Eric van Wincoop 1999. "Macro Markets and Financial Security," *Economic Policy Review* 5, 21–39. New York: Federal Reserve Bank of New York.

Bakker, Age and Bryan Chapple 2002. *Advanced Country Experiences with Capital Account Liberalization*, Occasional Paper 214, Washington, DC: International Monetary Fund.

Baldacci, Emanuele, Luiz de Mello, and Gabriela Inchauste 2002a. "Financial Crises, Poverty, and Income Distribution," Working Paper WP/02/4, Washington, DC: International Monetary Fund.

——, ——, and —— 2002b. "Financial Crises, Poverty, and Income Distribution," *Finance and Development* 39 (June), 24–7.

Baldwin, Robert 2004. "Openness and Growth: What's the Empirical Relationship?" in Robert Baldwin and Alan Winters, eds., *Challenges to Globalization: Analyzing the Economics*, Chicago: University of Chicago Press, forthcoming.

Baldwin, Robert and Alan Winters, eds. 2004. *Challenges to Globalization: Analyzing the Economics*, Chicago: University of Chicago Press, forthcoming.

Barro, Robert and Xavier Sala-i-Martin 1995. *Economic Growth*, New York: McGraw-Hill.

Barth, James, Gerard Caprio, and Ross Levine 2002. "Bank Regulation and Supervision: What Works Best?," Working Paper 9323, Cambridge, MA: National Bureau of Economic Research.

Bartolini, Leonardo and Allan Drazen 1997. "Capital Account Liberalization as a Signal," *American Economic Review* 87, 138–54.

Basel Committee on Banking Supervision 1997. *Core Principles for Effective Banking Supervision*, Basel, Switzerland: Basel Committee on Banking Supervision.

Baxter, Marianne and Alan Stockman 1989. "Business Cycles and the Exchange Rate Regime: Some International Evidence," *Journal of Monetary Economics* 23, 377–400.

Bayoumi, Tamim, Giorgio Fazio, Manmohan Kumar, and Ronald MacDonald 2003. "Fatal Attraction: A New Measure of Contagion," Working Paper WP/03/80, Washington, DC: International Monetary Fund.

Beck, Thorsten and Ross Levine 2003. "Legal Institutions and Financial Development," Working Paper 10126, Cambridge, MA: National Bureau of Economic Research.

Becker, Torbjorn, Anthony Richards, and Yungyong Thaicharoen 2001. "Bond Restructuring with Moral Hazard: Are Collective Action Clauses Costly?," Working Paper WP/01/92, Washington, DC: International Monetary Fund.

Berg, Andrew 1999. "The Asian Crisis: Causes, Policy Responses, and Outcomes," Working Paper WP/99/138, Washington, DC: International Monetary Fund.

Berg, Andrew, Eduardo Borensztein, and Paolo Mauro 2002. "An Evaluation of Monetary Regime Options for Latin America," Working Paper WP/02/211, Washington, DC: International Monetary Fund.

Berg, Andrew, Eduardo Borensztein, Gian Maria Milesi-Ferretti, and Catherine Pattillo 2000. *Anticipating Balance of Payments Crises: The Role of Early Warning Systems*, Occasional Paper 186, Washington, DC: International Monetary Fund.

Berg, Andrew, Eduardo Borensztein, and Catherine Pattillo 2004. "Assessing Early Warning Systems: How Have They Worked in Practice?," Working Paper WP/04/52, Washington, DC: International Monetary Fund.

Berg, Andrew, Christopher Jarvis, Mark Stone, and Alessandro Zanello 2003. "Re-Establishing Credible Nominal Anchors After a Financial Crisis: A Review of Recent Experience," Working Paper WP/03/76, Washington, DC: International Monetary Fund.

Berg, Andrew and Anne Krueger 2003. "Trade, Growth and Poverty: A Selective Survey," Working Paper WP/03/30, Washington, DC: International Monetary Fund.

Berg, Andrew and Catherine Pattillo 1999. "Are Currency Crises Predictable: A Test," *IMF Staff Papers* 46, 107–38.

Berg, Elliot 2003. "Increasing the Effectiveness of Aid: A Critique of Some Current Views," *Revue d'Economie du Developpement*, Special Issue: *Essais en l'Honneur d'Elliot Berg*, forthcoming.

Bergsten, Fred 1999. "Exchange Rate Choices: Discussion," in *Rethinking the International Monetary System*, Conference Series No. 43, Boston: Federal Reserve Bank of Boston, 124–7.

Bernanke, Ben and Refet Gurkaynak 2002. "Is Growth Exogenous? Taking Mankew, Romer, and Weil Seriously," in Ben Bernanke and Kenneth Rogoff, eds., *NBER Macroeconomics Annual 2001*, Cambridge, MA: MIT Press, 11–57.

Bhagwati, Jagdish 2004. *In Defense of Globalization*, New York: Oxford University Press.

——— 1998. "Why Free Capital Mobility may be Hazardous to Your Health: Lessons from the Latest Financial Crisis," remarks prepared for November 7, 1998 NBER Conference on Capital Controls (available at www.columbia.edu/~jb38/papers/NBER_comments.pdf).

Bhagwati, Jagdish and T. N. Srinivasan 2002. "Trade and Poverty in the Poor Countries," *American Economic Review* 92, 180–3.

Bhalla, Surjit 2002. *Imagine There's No Country: Poverty, Inequality, and Growth in the Era of Globalization*, Washington, DC: Institute for International Economics.

Blustein, Paul 2003. "Argentina Didn't Fall on Its Own," *The Washington Post* (August 3), Section A, 1.

———— 2001. *The Chastening*, New York: Public Affairs.

Board of Governors of the Federal Reserve System 1943. *Banking and Monetary Statistics*, Washington, DC.

Bolton, Patrick 2003. "Toward a Statutory Approach to Sovereign Debt Restructuring: Lessons from Corporate Bankruptcy Practice Around the World," *IMF Staff Papers* 50 (Special Issue), 41–71.

Bolton, Patrick and Olivier Jeanne 2004. "Structuring and Restructuring Sovereign Debt: The Role of Seniority," draft, Washington, DC: International Monetary Fund.

Bolton, Patrick and David Skeel 2003. "Inside the Black Box: How Should a Sovereign Bankruptcy Framework be Structured?" draft, Princeton, NJ: Princeton University, Department of Economics.

Boorman, Jack 2003. "Dealing Justly with Debt," speech to the Carnegie Council on Ethics and International Affairs, New York (April 30, available at www.imf.org).

———— 2002. "Interview," *IMF Survey* 31 (August 5), Washington, DC: International Monetary Fund.

Boorman, Jack and Mark Allen 2000. "A New Framework for Private Sector Involvement in Crisis Prevention and Crisis Management," in Jan Joost Teunissen, ed., *Reforming the International Financial System: Crisis Prevention and Response*, The Hague: Forum on Debt and Development.

Boorman, Jack, Timothy Lane, Marianne Schulze-Ghattas, Ales Bulir, Atish Ghosh, Javier Hamann, Alex Mourmouras, and Steven Phillips 2000. "Managing Financial Crises: The Experience in East Asia," *Carnegie-Rochester Conference Series on Public Policy* 53, 1–67.

Bordo, Michael, Barry Eichengreen, and Douglas Irwin 1999. "Is Globalization Today Really Different From Globalization a Hundred Years Ago?" *Brookings Trade Forum 1999*, Washington, DC: Brookings Institution Press, 1–50.

Bordo, Michael and Harold James 2000. "The International Monetary Fund: Its Present Role in Historical Perspective," *Greek Economic Review* 20 (Autumn), 43–76.

Bordo, Michael, Christopher Meissner, and Angela Redish 2003. "How 'Original Sin' was Overcome: The Evolution of External Debt Denominated in Domestic Currencies in the United States and the British Dominions 1800–2000," Working Paper 9841, Cambridge, MA: National Bureau of Economic Research.

Bordo, Michael and Anna Schwartz 1996. "Why Clashes Between Internal and External Stability Goals End in Currency Crises, 1797–1994," *Open Economies Review* 7, 437–68.

Bordo, Michael, Alan Taylor, and Jeffrey Williamson, eds. 2003. *Globalization in Historical Perspective*, Chicago: University of Chicago Press.

Borensztein, Eduardo, Jose De Gregorio, and Jong-Wha Lee 1998. "How Does Foreign Direct Investment Affect Economic Growth?," *Journal of International Economics* 45, 115–35.

Borensztein, Eduardo and Paolo Mauro 2002. "Reviving the Case for GDP-Indexed Bonds," Policy Discussion Paper PDP/02/10, Washington, DC: International Monetary Fund.

Borensztein, Eduardo, Paolo Mauro, Olivier Jeanne, Jeromin Zettelmeyer, and Marcos Chamon, 2004. Sovereign Debt Structure for Crisis Prevention, Occasional Paper, Washington DC: International Monetary Fund, forthcoming.

Borensztein, Eduardo, Jeromin Zettelmeyer, and Thomas Philippon 2001. "Monetary Independence in Emerging Markets: Does the Exchange Rate Regime Make a Difference?," Working Paper WP/01/1, Washington, DC: International Monetary Fund.

Bosworth, Barry and Susan Collins 1999. "Capital Flows to Developing Economies: Implications for Saving and Investment," *Brookings Papers on Economic Activity* 1, 143–69.

Botman, Dennis and Henk Jager 2002. "Coordination of Speculation," *Journal of International Economics* 58, 159–75.

Boughton, James 2001. *Silent Revolution: The International Monetary Fund 1979–1989*, Washington, DC: International Monetary Fund.

Breuer, Janice 1994. "An Assessment of the Evidence on Purchasing Power Parity," in John Williamson, ed., *Estimating Equilibrium Exchange Rates*, Washington, DC: Institute for International Economics, 245–77.

Brown, William Adams Jr. 1940. *The International Gold Standard Reinterpreted, 1914–1934*, New York: National Bureau of Economic Research.

Bryant, Ralph 2003. *Turbulent Waters: Cross-Border Finance and International Governance*, Washington, DC: Brookings Institution Press.

Buiter, Willem and Anne Siebert 1999. "UDROP: A Contribution to the New International Financial Architecture," *International Finance* 2, 227–47.

Bulow, Jeremy and Kenneth Rogoff 1990. "Cleaning up Third World Debt Without Getting Taken to the Cleaners," *Journal of Economic Perspectives* 4, 31–42.

——— and ——— 1989a. "A Constant Recontracting Model of Sovereign Debt," *Journal of Political Economy* 97, 166–77.

——— and ——— 1989b. "Sovereign Debt: Is to Forgive to Forget?" *American Economic Review* 79, 43–50.

Burger, John and Francis Warnock 2003. "Diversification, Original Sin, and International Bond Portfolios," International Finance Discussion Papers No. 755, Washington, DC: Federal Reserve Board.

Burnside, Craig and David Dollar 2000. "Aid, Policies, and Growth," *American Economic Review* 90, 847–68.

Burnside, Craig, Martin Eichenbaum, and Sergio Rebelo 2001a. "Hedging and Financial Fragility in Fixed Exchange Rate Regimes," *European Economic Review* 45, 1151–93.

——, ——, and —— 2001b. "Prospective Deficits and the Asian Currency Crisis," *Journal of Political Economy* 109, 1155–97.

Burton, David 2002. "The Asian Crisis—Lessons and Challenges Ahead," unpublished note (December 18), Washington, DC: International Monetary Fund.

Caballero, Ricardo 2003. "On the International Financial Architecture: Insuring Emerging Markets," NBER Working Paper 9570, Cambridge, MA: National Bureau of Economic Research.

Calomiris, Charles 1999. "Moral Hazard is Avoidable," in William Hunter, George Kaufman, and Thomas Krueger, eds., *The Asian Financial Crisis: Origins, Implications, and Solutions*, Boston: Kluwer Academic, 379–84.

—— 1998a. "Blueprints for a New Global Financial Architecture," speech, Washington: American Enterprise Institute (October 1, available at www.aei.org).

—— 1998b. "The IMF's Imprudent Role as Lender of Last Resort," *The Cato Journal* 17, 275–94.

Calvo, Guillermo 2003. "Explaining Sudden Stop, Growth Collapse, and BOP Crisis: The Case of Distortionary Output Taxes" (Mundell-Fleming Lecture), *IMF Staff Papers* 50 (Special Issue), 1–20.

—— 2002. "Globalization Hazard and Delayed Reform in Emerging Markets," *Economia* 2, 1–29.

—— 2001. "The Case for Hard Pegs in the Brave New World of Global Finance," in Jorge Braga de Macedo, Daniel Cohen, and Helmut Reisen, eds., *Don't Fix, Don't Float*, Paris: Organization for Economic Cooperation and Development.

—— 1999. "Contagion in Emerging Markets: When Wall Street is a Carrier," paper presented at the twelfth Congress of the International Economic Association Congress, Buenos Aires, Argentina (available at http://www.bsos.umd.edu/econ/ciecrp8.pdf).

—— 1998. "Capital Flows and Capital-Market Crises: The Simple Economics of Sudden Stops," *Journal of Applied Economics* 1, 35–54.

Calvo, Guillermo, Leo Leiderman, and Carmen Reinhart 1996. "Inflows of Capital to Developing Countries in the 1990s," *Journal of Economic Perspectives* 10, 123–39.

——, ——, and —— 1993. "Capital Inflows and Real Exchange Rate Appreciation in Latin America: The Role of External Factors," *IMF Staff Papers* 40, 108–51.

Calvo, Guillermo and Enrique Mendoza 2000a. "Capital Market Crises and Economic Collapse in Emerging Markets: An Informational-Frictions Approach," *American Economic Review, Papers and Proceedings* 90, 59–64.

—— and —— 2000b. "Rational Contagion and the Globalization of Securities Markets," *Journal of International Economics* 51, 79–113.

Calvo, Guillermo and Frederic Mishkin 2003. "The Mirage of Exchange Rate Regimes for Emerging Market Countries," *Journal of Economic Perspectives* 17, 99–118.

Calvo, Guillermo and Carmen Reinhart 2002. "Fear of Floating," *Quarterly Journal of Economics* 117, 379–408.

—— and —— 2001a. "Fixing for Your Life," in Susan Collins and Dani Rodrik, eds., *Brookings Trade Forum 2000: Policy Challenges in the Next Millennium*, Washington, DC: Brookings Institution Press, 1–39.

—— and —— 2001b. "Reflections on Dollarization," in Alberto Alesina and Robert Barro, eds., *Currency Unions*, Stanford, CA: Hoover Institution Press, 39–47.

Caprio, Gerard, Izak Atiyas, and James Hanson 1993. "Financial Reform: Lessons and Strategy," in Shakil Faruki, ed., *Financial Sector Reforms in Asian and Latin American Countries: Lessons of Comparative Experience*, Washington, DC: World Bank, 67–92.

Caprio, Gerard and Patrick Honohan 2002. "Banking Policy and Macroeconomic Stability: An Exploration," Working Paper 2856, Washington, DC: World Bank.

—— and —— 1999. "Restoring Banking Stability: Beyond Supervised Capital Requirements," *Journal of Economic Perspectives* 13 (Fall), 43–64.

Caprio, Gerard and Daniela Klingebiel 1996. "Bank Insolvencies: Cross-Country Experience," Policy Research Working Paper 1620, Washington, DC: World Bank.

Carkovic, Maria and Ross Levine 2002. "Does Foreign Direct Investment Accelerate Economic Growth?," draft, Minneapolis, MN: University of Minnesota (June, available at papers.ssrn.com).

Cashin, Paul, Paolo Mauro, Catherine Pattillo, and Ratna Sahay 2001. "Macroeconomic Policies and Poverty Reduction: Stylized Facts and an Overview of Research," Working Paper WP/01/135, Washington, DC: International Monetary Fund.

Cassel, Gustav 1922. *Money and Foreign Exchange After 1914*, New York: Constable.

—— 1918. "Abnormal Deviations in International Exchanges," *Economic Journal* 28, 413–15.

Chamon, Marcos 2002. "Why Can't Developing Countries Borrow from Abroad in Their Currency?," draft, Washington, DC: International Monetary Fund (December, available at papers.ssrn.com).

Chang, Roberto and Andres Velasco 2000. "Liquidity Crises in Emerging Markets: Theory and Policy," in Ben Bernanke and Julio Rotemberg, eds., *NBER Macroeconomics Annual 1999*, Cambridge, MA: MIT Press, 11–58.

Chen, Shaohua and Martin Ravallion 2001. "How Did the World's Poorest Fare in the 1990s?" *Review of Income and Wealth* 47, 283–300.

Chenery, Hollis and Alan Strout 1966. "Foreign Assistance and Economic Development," *American Economic Review* 56, 679–733.

Chopra, Ajai, Kenneth Kang, Meral Karasulu, Hong Liang, Henry Ma, and Anthony Richards 2002. "From Crisis to Recovery in Korea: Strategy,

Achievements, and Lessons," in David Coe and Se-Jik Kim, eds., *Korean Crisis and Recovery*, Washington, DC: International Monetary Fund.

Christofides, Charalambos, Christian Mulder, and Andrew Tiffin 2003. "The Link Between Adherence to International Standards of Good Practice, Foreign Exchange Spreads, and Ratings," Working Paper WP/03/74, Washington, DC: International Monetary Fund.

Claessens, Stijn, Daniela Klingebiel, and Luc Laeven 147–80 "Financial Restructuring in Banking and Corporate Sector Crises: What Policies to Pursue?," in Michael Dooley and Jeffrey Frankel, eds., *Managing Currency Crises in Emerging Markets*, Chicago: University of Chicago Press, 147–80.

Clark, Peter, Natalia Tamirisa, Shang-Jin Wei, Azim Sadikov, and Li Zeng 2004. *Exchange Rate Volatility and Trade Flows—some New Evidence*, Occasional Paper, Washington DC: International Monetary Fund, forthcoming (May 19 draft available at www.imf.org).

Clarke, Stephen V. O. 1967. *Central Bank Cooperation: 1924–31*, New York: Federal Reserve Bank of New York.

Coase, Ronald 1992. "The Institutional Structure of Production," *American Economic Review* 82, 713–19.

——— 1960. "The Problem of Social Cost," *Journal of Law and Economics* 3, 1–44.

Collyns, Charles and Russell Kincaid, eds. 2003. *Managing Financial Crises: Recent Experience and Lessons for Latin America*, Occasional Paper 217, Washington, DC: International Monetary Fund.

Commission for the Study of Economic and Monetary Union 1989. *Report* [Delors Report], Luxembourg: Office for Official Publications of the European Communities.

Committee of the Board of Governors of the Fund on Reform of the International Monetary System and Related Issues [Committee of Twenty] 1974. *International Monetary Reform: Documents of the Committee of Twenty*, Washington, DC: International Monetary Fund.

Cooper, Richard 1999a. "Exchange Rate Choices," in *Rethinking the International Monetary System*, Conference Series No. 43, Boston: Federal Reserve Bank of Boston, 99–123.

——— 1999b. "Should Capital Controls Be Banished?," *Brookings Papers on Economic Activity* 1, 89–125.

——— 1998. "Should Capital-Account Convertibility Be a World Objective?" in Peter Kenen, ed., *Should the IMF Pursue Capital-Account Convertibility?*, Essays in International Finance No. 207, Princeton, NJ: Princeton University, International Finance Section, Department of Economics, 11–19.

——— 1992. "Fettered to Gold? Economic Policy in the Interwar Period," *Journal of Economic Literature* 30, 2120–8.

——— 1990. "Comment," in William Branson, Jacob Frenkel, and Morris Goldstein, eds., *International Policy Coordination and Exchange Rate Fluctuations*, Chicago: University of Chicago Press, 102–5.

Cordella, Tito 2003. "Can Short-Term Capital Controls Promote Capital In-flows?" *Journal of International Money and Finance* 22, 737–45.

Corden, Max 2002. *Too Sensational: On the Choice of Exchange Rate Regimes*, Cambridge, MA: MIT Press.

———— 1999. *The Asian Crisis: Is There a Way Out?*, Singapore: Institute of Southeast Asian Studies.

Corsetti, Giancarlo, Bernardo Guimaraes, and Nouriel Roubini 2003. "International Lending of Last Resort and Moral Hazard: A Model of IMF's Catalytic Finance," Working Paper 10125, Cambridge, MA: National Bureau of Economic Research.

Council of the European Communities 1970. *Interim Report on the Establishing by Stages of Economic and Monetary Union* [Werner Report], Luxembourg: Office for Official Publications of the European Communities.

Council on Foreign Relations 1999. *Safeguarding Prosperity in a Global Financial System: The Future International Financial Architecture*, Washington, DC: Institute for International Economics.

Crafts, Nicholas 2000. "Globalization and Growth in the Twentieth Century," in *World Economic Outlook: Supporting Studies*, Washington, DC: International Monetary Fund, 1–51.

Crow, John, Ricardo Ariazu, Niels Thygesen, and Jonathan Portes 1999. "External Evaluation of Surveillance Report," in *External Evaluation of IMF Surveillance*, Part 3, Washington, DC: International Monetary Fund.

Daban, Teresa, Enrica Detragiache, Gabriel di Bella, Gian Maria Milesi-Ferretti, and Steven Symansky 2003. *Rules-Based Fiscal Policy in France, Germany, Italy, and Spain*, Occasional Paper 225, Washington, DC: International Monetary Fund.

Deaton, Angus 2003. "How to Monitor Poverty for the Millennium Development Goals," *Journal of Human Development* 4, 353–78.

Dell'Ariccia, Giovanni, Isable Schnable, and Jeromin Zettelmeyer 2002. "Moral Hazard and International Crisis Lending: A Test," Working Paper WP/02/181, Washington, DC: International Monetary Fund.

Demirguc-Kunt, Asli and Enrica Detragiache 1998. "Financial Liberalization and Financial Fragility," in *Annual World Bank Conference on Development Economics 1998*, Washington; DC: World Bank, 303–31.

De Soto, Hernando 2001. "The Mystery of Capital," *Finance and Development* 38 (March), 29–33.

———— 2000. *The Mystery of Capital: Why Capitalism Triumphs in the West and Fails Everywhere Else*, New York: Basic Books.

Despres, Emile 1973. *International Economic Reform: Collected Papers of Emile Despres*, Gerald M. Meier, ed., New York: Oxford University Press.

————, Charles P. Kindleberger, and Walter S. Salant 1969. "The Dollar and World Liquidity: A Minority View," *The Economist* (February 1, 1966), 526–9. Reprinted with minor additions in Lawrence H. Officer and Thomas D. Willett, eds., *The International Monetary System: Problems and Proposals*, Englewood Cliffs, NJ: Prentice-Hall, 41–52.

Detragiache, Enrica and Antonio Spilimbergo 2001. "Crises and Liquidity—Evidence and Interpretation," Working Paper WP/01/2, Washington, DC: International Monetary Fund.

De Vries, Margaret 1985. *The International Monetary Fund, 1972–1978: Cooperation on Trial*, Washington, DC: International Monetary Fund.

———— 1976. *The International Monetary Fund, 1966–71: The System Under Stress*, Washington, DC: International Monetary Fund.

Diamond, Douglas and Philip Dybvig 1983. "Bank Runs, Deposit Insurance, and Liquidity," *Journal of Political Economy* 91, 401–19.

Diamond, Douglas and Raghuram Rajan 2001. "Banks, Short Term Debt and Financial Crises: Theory, Policy Implications and Applications," *Carnegie-Rochester Conference on Public Policy* 54, 37–71.

Diaz-Alejandro, Carlos 1985. "Good-Bye Financial Repression, Hello Financial Crash," *Journal of Development Economics* 19, 1–24.

Dobson, Wendy and Gary Hufbauer 2001. *World Capital Markets: Challenge to the G-10*, Washington, DC: Institute for International Economics.

Dollar, David and M. Hallward-Driemeier 2000. "Crisis, Adjustment, and Reform in Thailand Industrial Firms," *World Bank Research Observer* 15 (No. 1), 1–22.

Dollar, David and Aart Kraay 2003. "Institutions, Trade, and Growth: Revisiting the Evidence," Policy Research Working Paper 3004, Washington, DC: World Bank.

Domar, Evsey 1957. *Essays in the Theory of Economic Growth*, Oxford: Oxford University Press.

———— 1946. "Capital Expansion, Rate of Growth, and Employment," *Econometrica* 14, 137–47.

Dooley, Michael 2000a. "A Model of Crises in Emerging Markets," *The Economic Journal* 110 (January), 256–72.

———— 2000b. "International Financial Architecture and Strategic Default: Can Financial Crises Be Less Painful?" *Carnegie-Rochester Conference Series on Public Policy* 53, 361–77.

———— 1996. "A Survey of the Literature on Controls over International Capital Transactions," *IMF Staff Papers* 43, 639–87.

Dooley, Michael, Rudiger Dornbusch, and Yung Chul Park 2002. "A Framework for Exchange Rate Policy in Korea," in David Coe and Se-Jik Kim, eds., *Korean Crisis and Recovery*, Washington, DC: International Monetary Fund, 483–521.

Dooley, Michael and Jeffrey Frankel, eds. 2003. *Managing Currency Crises in Emerging Markets*, Chicago: University of Chicago Press.

Dooley, Michael and Carl Walsh 2003. "Capital Movements: Curse or Blessing?" in L. Aurnheimer, ed., *International Financial Markets: The Challenge of Globalization*, Chicago: University of Chicago Press, 79–102.

Dornbusch, Rudiger 2002a. "A Primer on Emerging-Market Crises," in Sebastian Edwards and Jeffrey Frankel, eds., *Preventing Currency Crises in Emerging Markets*, Chicago: University of Chicago Press, 743–54.

—— 2002b. "Malaysia's Crisis: Was it Different?," in Sebastian Edwards and Jeffrey Frankel, eds., *Preventing Currency Crises in Emerging Markets*, Chicago: University of Chicago Press, 441–54.

—— 2001. "Fewer Monies, Better Monies," *American Economic Review* 91, 238–42.

—— 1999. "Emerging Market Cirses: Origins and Remedies," draft (July, available at www.mit.edu/~rudi/media/PDFs/imf-imf99.PDF).

Dornbusch, Rudiger, Ilan Goldfajn, and Rodrigo Valdes 1995. "Currency Crises and Collapses," *Brookings Papers on Economic Activity* 2, 219–93.

Dornbusch, Rudiger, Yung Chul Park, and Stijn Claessens 2000. "Contagion: How It Spreads and How It Can Be Stopped," *World Bank Research Observer*, 15 (No. 2), 177–97.

Dornbusch, Rudiger and Alejandro Werner 1994. "Mexico: Stabilization, Reform, and No Growth," *Brookings Papers on Economic Activity* 1, 253–98.

Drazen, Allan 2002. "Conditionality and Ownership in IMF Lending: A Political Economy Approach," *IMF Staff Papers* 49 (Special Issue), 36–67.

—— 2000a. "Political Contagion in Currency Crises," in Paul Krugman, ed., *Currency Crises*, Chicago: University of Chicago Press.

—— 2000b. *Political Economy in Macroeconomics*, Princeton, NJ: Princeton University Press.

Dziobek, Claudia and Ceyla Pazarbasioglu 1997. "Lessons from Systemic Bank Restructuring: A Survey of 24 Countries," Working Paper WP/97/161, Washington, DC: International Monetary Fund.

Easterly, William 2002. *The Elusive Quest for Growth*, Cambridge, MA: MIT Press.

Easterly, William and Ross Levine 2002. "Tropics, Germs and Crops: How Endowments Influence Economic Development," Working Paper 9106, Cambridge, MA: National Bureau of Economic Research.

——, ——, and David Roodman 2003. "New Data, New Doubts: A Comment on Burnside and Dollar's 'Aid, Policies, and Growth' (2000)," Working Paper 9846, Cambridge, MA: National Bureau of Economic Research.

Edison, Hali, Ross Levine, Luca Ricci, and Thorsten Slok 2002. "International Financial Integration and Economic Growth," *Journal of International Money and Finance* 21, 749–76.

Edison, Hali and Michael Melvin 1990. "The Determinants and Implications of the Choice of an Exchange Rate System," in William S. Haraf and Thomas D. Willett (eds.), *Monetary Policy for a Volatile Global Economy*, Washington, DC: AEI Press, 1–44.

Edwards, Franklin 1999. "Hedge Funds and the Collapse of Long-Term Capital Management," *Journal of Economic Perspectives* 13, 189–210.

Edwards, Sebastian 1999. "How Effective Are Capital Controls?," *Journal of Economic Perspectives* 13, 65–84.

Edwards, Sebastian and Jeffrey Frankel, eds. 2003. *Preventing Currency Crises in Emerging Markets*, Chicago: University of Chicago Press.

Edwards, Sebastian and Igal Magendzo 2003. "A Currency of One's Own? An Empirical Investigation on Dollarization and Independent Currency Unions," Working Paper 9514, Cambridge, MA: National Bureau of Economic Research.

—— and —— 2001. "Dollarization, Inflation and Growth," Working Paper 8671, Cambridge, MA: National Bureau of Economic Research.

Edwards, Sebastian and Miguel Savastano 2000. "Exchange Rates in Emerging Economies: What Do We Know? What Do We Need to Know?," in Anne Krueger, ed., *Economic Policy Reform: The Second Stage*, Chicago: University of Chicago Press, 453–510.

Eichengreen, Barry 1999a. "Kicking the Habit: Moving from Pegged Rates to Greater Exchange Rate Flexibility," *The Economic Journal* 109, C1–14.

—— 1999b. *Toward a New International Financial Architecture*, Washington, DC: Institute for International Economics.

—— 1996. *Globalizing Capital: A History of the International Monetary System*, Princeton, NJ: Princeton University Press.

—— 1993. "European Monetary Unification," *Journal of Economic Literature* 31, 1321–57.

—— 1992. *Golden Fetters: The Gold Standard and the Great Depression*, Oxford: Oxford University Press.

—— 1989. *Elusive Stability: Essays in the History of International Finance, 1919–1939*, Cambridge, England: Cambridge University Press.

—— and Michael Bordo 2003. "Crises Now and Then: What Lessons from the Last Era of Financial Globalization?," in Paul Mizen, ed., *Monetary History, Exchange Rates and Financial Markets: Essays in Honour of Charles Goodhart*, Vol. 1, Northampton, England: Edward Elgar.

Eichengreen, Barry and Ricardo Hausmann 2002. "How To Eliminate Original Financial Sin," *Financial Times* (November 22), p. 15.

——, ——, and Ugo Panizza 2003. "Currency Mismatches, Debt Intolerance, and Original Sin: Why They Are Not the Same and Why It Matters," Working Paper 10036, Cambridge, MA: National Bureau of Economic Research.

Eichengreen, Barry and Peter B. Kenen 1994. "Managing the International Economy Under the Bretton Woods System: An Overview," in Peter Kenen, ed., *Managing the World Economy: Fifty Years After Bretton Woods*, Washington, DC: Institute For International Economics, 3–57.

Eichengreen, Barry, Kenneth Kletzer, and Ashoka Mody 2004. "Crisis Resolution: Next Steps," in Susan Collins and Dani Rodrik, eds., *Brookings Trade Forum 2003*, Washington DC: Brookings Institution Press, 279–352.

Eichengreen, Barry and Paul Masson, with Hugh Bredenkamp, Barry Johnston, Javier Hamann, Esteban Jadresic, and Inci Otker 1998. *Exit Strategies: Policy*

Options for Countries Seeking Greater Exchange Rate Flexibility, Occasional Paper 168, Washington, DC: International Monetary Fund.

Eichengreen, Barry, Paul Masson, Miguel Savastano, and Sunil Sharma 1999. *Transition Strategies and Nominal Anchors on the Road to Greater Exchange Rate Flexibility*, Essays in International Finance No. 213, Princeton, NJ: Princeton University, International Finance Section, Department of Economics.

Eichengreen, Barry and Ashoka Mody 2000. "Would Collective Action Clauses Raise Borrowing Costs?," Working Paper 7458, Cambridge, MA: National Bureau of Economic Research.

Eichengreen, Barry, Michael Mussa, Giovanni Dell'Ariccia, Enrica Detragiache, Gian Maria Milesi-Ferretti, and Andrew Tweedie 1998. *Capital Account Liberalization: Theoretical and Practical Aspects*, Occasional Paper 172, Washington, DC: International Monetary Fund.

Eichengreen Barry, Andrew Rose, and Charles Wyplosz 1996. "Contagious Currency Crises," *Scandinavian Journal of Economics* 98, 463–84.

——, ——, and —— 1995. "Exchange Market Mayhem: The Antecedents and Aftermath of Speculative Attacks," *Economic Policy* 21, 249–312.

Eichengreen, Barry and Nathan Sussman 2000. "The International Monetary System in the (Very) Long Run," Working Paper WP/00/43, Washington, DC: International Monetary Fund.

Feldstein, Martin, ed. 2002. *Economic and Financial Crises in Emerging Market Economies*, Chicago: University of Chicago Press.

—— 1998. "Refocusing the IMF," *Foreign Affairs* 77 (March/April), 20–33.

Fischer, Stanley 2003. "Globalization and Its Challenges," *American Economic Review* 93 (No. 2), 1–30.

—— 2002. "The Asian Crisis: Lessons for the Future," Fifth Hong Kong Monetary Authority Distinguished Lecture (May 21, available at www.iie.com/fischer/sl.html).

—— 2001a. "Ecuador and the International Monetary Fund," in Alberto Alesina and Robert Barro, eds., *Currency Unions*, Stanford, CA: Hoover Institution Press, 1–10.

—— 2001b. "Exchange Rate Regimes: Is the Bipolar View Correct?," *Journal of Economic Perspectives* 15, 3–24.

—— 2001c. "The International Monetary System: Crises and Reform," the Robbins Lectures (October 29, available at www.iie.com/fischer/sl.html).

—— 1999. "On the Need for an International Lender of Last Resort," *Journal of Economic Perspectives* 13, 85–104.

—— 1998. "Capital-Account Liberalization and the Role of the IMF," in Peter Kenen, ed., *Should the IMF Pursue Capital-Account Convertibility?*, Essays in International Finance No. 207, Princeton, NJ: Princeton University, International Finance Section, Department of Economics, 1–10.

Fishlow, Albert 1985. "Lessons From the Past: Capital Markets During the Nineteenth Century and the Interwar Period," *International Organization* 39, 383–439.

Fleming, J. Marcus 1962. "Domestic Financial Policies Under Fixed and Under Floating Exchange Rates," *IMF Staff Papers* 12, 369–80.

Flood, Robert and Peter Garber 1984. "Collapsing Exchange Regimes: Some Linear Examples," *Journal of International Economics* 17, 1–13.

Flood, Robert and Nancy Marion 1999. "Perspectives on the Recent Currency Crisis Literature," *International Journal of Finance and Economics* 4, 1–26.

Flood, Robert and Andrew Rose 1995. "Fixing the Exchange Rate Regime: A Virtual Quest for Fundamentals," *Journal of Monetary Economics* 36, 3–37.

Flood, Robert and Mark Taylor 1996. "Exchange Rate Economics: What's Wrong with the Conventional Macro Approach?," in Jeffrey Frankel, Giampaolo Galli, and Alberto Giovannini, eds., *The Microstructure of Foreign Exchange Markets*, Chicago: University of Chicago Press, 261–94.

Folkerts-Landau, David and Carl-Johan Lindgren 1998. *Toward a Framework for Financial Stability*, Washington, DC: International Monetary Fund.

Forbes, Kristen 2003. "One Cost of the Chilean Capital Controls: Increased Financial Constraints for Smaller Trade Firms," Working Paper 9777, Cambridge, MA: National Bureau of Economic Research.

Fraga, Arminio, Ilan Goldfajn, and Andre Minella 2004. "Inflation Targeting in Emerging Market Economies," in Mark Gertler and Kenneth Rogoff, eds., *NBER Macroeconomics Annual 2003*, Cambridge, MA: MIT Press, forthcoming (also available as NBER Working Paper 10019, Cambridge, MA: National Bureau of Economic Research).

Frankel, Jeffrey 1999. *No Single Currency is Right for All Countries at All Times*, Essays in International Finance No. 215, Princeton, NJ: Princeton University, International Finance Section, Department of Economics.

Frankel, Jeffrey and David Romer 1999. "Does Trade Cause Growth?," *American Economic Review* 89, 379–99.

Frankel, Jeffrey and Andrew Rose 2002. "An Estimate of the Effect of Common Currencies on Trade and Income," *Quarterly Journal of Economics* 117, 437–66.

—— and —— 1996. "Currency Crashes in Emerging Markets: An Empirical Treatment," *Journal of International Economics* 41, 351–68.

—— and —— 1995. "Empirical Research on Nominal Exchange Rates," in Gene Grossman and Kenneth Rogoff, eds., *Handbook of International Economics*, Vol. 3, Amsterdam: North Holland, 1689–729.

Frankel, Jeffrey and Nouriel Roubini 2003. "The Role of Industrial Country Policies in Emerging Market Crises," in Martin Feldstein, ed., *Economic and Financial Crises in Emerging Market Economies*, Chicago: University of Chicago Press, 155–278.

Frankel, Jeffrey, Sergio Schmukler, and Luis Serven 2000. "Global Transmission of Interest Rates: Monetary Independence and Currency Regime," Working Paper 8828, Cambridge, MA: National Bureau of Economic Research.

Fratianni, Michele and Jürgen von Hagen 1992. *The European Monetary System and European Monetary Union*, Boulder, CO: Westview Press.

Freund, Caroline 2000. "Current Account Adjustment in Industrialized Countries," International Finance Discussion Papers No. 692, Washington, DC: Federal Reserve Board.

Froot, Kenneth and Kenneth Rogoff 1995. "Perspectives on PPP and Long Run Real Exchange Rates," in Gene Grossman and Kenneth Rogoff, eds., *Handbook of International Economics*, Vol. 3, Amsterdam: North Holland, 1647–88.

Furman Jason and Joseph Stiglitz 1998. "Economic Crises: Evidence and Insights from East Asia," *Brookings Papers on Economic Activity* 2, 1–135.

Gagnon, Joseph 1993. "Exchange Rate Variability and the Level of International Trade," *Journal of International Economics* 34, 269–87.

Garber, Peter 1998a. "Buttressing Capital-Account Liberalization With Prudential Regulations and Foreign Entry," in Peter Kenen, ed., *Should the IMF Pursue Capital-Account Convertibility?*, Essays in International Finance No. 207, Princeton, NJ: Princeton University, International Finance Section, Department of Economics, 28–33.

—— 1998b. "Derivatives in International Capital Flow," Working Paper 6623, Cambridge, MA: National Bureau of Economic Research.

Geithner, Timothy 2003. "Structural Conditionality in IMF Programs," in Martin Feldstein, ed., *Economic and Financial Crises in Emerging Market Economies*, Chicago: University of Chicago Press, 437–42.

Gelos, Gaston and Shang-Jin Wei 2002. "Transparency and International Investor Behavior," Working Paper WP/02/174, Washington, DC: International Monetary Fund.

Gennotte, Gerard and Hayne Leland 1990. "Market Liquidity, Hedging, and Crashes," *American Economic Review* 80, 999–1021.

Ghosh, Atish, Anne-Marie Gulde, and Holger Wolf 2000. "Currency Boards: More than a Quick Fix?" *Economic Policy* 15, 271–335.

Ghosh, Atish, Anne-Marie Gulde, Jonathan Ostry, and Holger Wolf 1997. "Does the Nominal Exchange Rate Regime Matter?," Working Paper 5874, Cambridge, MA: National Bureau of Economic Research.

Ghosh, Atish, Timothy Lane, Marianne Schulze-Ghattas, Ales Bulir, Javier Hamann, and Alex Mourmouras 2002. *IMF-Supported Programs in Capital Account Crises*, Occasional Paper 210, Washington, DC: International Monetary Fund.

Giovannini, Alberto 1990a. "European Monetary Reform: Progress and Prospects," *Brookings Papers on Economic Activity* 2, 217–91.

—— 1990b. *The Transition to European Monetary Union*, Essays in International Finance No. 178, Princeton, NJ: Princeton University, International Finance Section, Department of Economics.

Gold, Joseph 1979. *Conditionality*, Pamphlet Series No. 31, Washington, DC: International Monetary Fund.

Goldsmith, Raymond 1969. *Financial Structure and Development*, New Haven, CT: Yale University Press.

Goldstein, Morris 2003a. "An Evaluation of Proposals to Reform the International Financial Architecture," in Michael Dooley and Jeffrey Frankel, eds., *Managing Currency Crises in Emerging Markets*, Chicago: University of Chicago Press, 225–62.

—— 2003b. "Debt Sustainability, Brazil, and the IMF," Working Paper 03-1, Washington, DC: Institute for International Economics.

—— 2003c. "IMF Structural Programs," in Martin Feldstein, ed., *Economic and Financial Crises in Emerging Market Economies*, Chicago: University of Chicago Press, 363–437.

—— 2002. *Managed Floating Plus*, Washington, DC: Institute for International Economics.

—— 2001. "IMF Structural Conditionality: How Much Is too Much?," Working Paper 01-4, Washington, DC: Institute For International Economics.

—— 1998. *The Asian Financial Crisis: Causes, Cures, and Systemic Implications*, Washington, DC: Institute for International Economics.

—— 1997. *The Case for an International Banking Standard*, Washington, DC: Institute for International Economics.

—— 1980. *Have Flexible Exchange Rates Handicapped Macroeconomic Policy?*, Special Papers in International Economics No. 14, Princeton, NJ: Princeton University, International Finance Section, Department of Economics.

Goldstein, Morris and Peter Isard 1992. "Mechanisms for Promoting Global Monetary Stability," in Morris Goldstein, Peter Isard, Paul Masson, and Mark Taylor, eds., *Policy Issues in the Evolving International Monetary System*, Occasional Paper 96, Washington, DC: International Monetary Fund.

Gourinchas, Pierre-Olivier and Olivier Jeanne 2003. "The Elusive Gains from International Financial Integration," Working Paper 9684, Cambridge, DC: National Bureau of Economic Research.

Grossman, Sanford and Joseph Stiglitz 1980. "On the Impossibility of Informationally Efficient Markets," *American Economic Review* 70, 393–408.

Group of Five 1985. "Announcement of the Ministers of Finance and Central Bank Governors of France, Germany, Japan, the United Kingdom, and the United States," September 22.

Group of Ten Deputies 1993. *International Capital Movements and Foreign Exchange Markets*, Rome: Bank of Italy.

Hacche, Graham and John Townend 1981. "Exchange Rates and Monetary Policy: Modeling Sterling's Effective Exchange Rate, 1972–80," *Oxford Economic Papers* 33 (Supplement), 201–47.

Haggard, Stephan 2000. *The Political Economy of the Asian Financial Crisis*, Washington, DC: Institute for International Economics.

Haldane, Andy and Mark Kruger 2001. "The Resolution of International Financial Crises: Private Finance and Public Funds," Bank of England and Bank of Canada (available at www.bankofengland.co.uk).

Hall, Robert and Charles Jones 1999. "Why Do Some Countries Produce So Much More Output Per Worker Than Others?," *Quarterly Journal of Economics* 114, 83–116.

Harrington, Richard 1992. "The Financial System in Transition," in Henry Cavanna, ed., *Financial Innovation*, London: Routledge, 1–13.

Harrod, Roy 1939. "An Essay in Dynamic Theory," *Economic Journal* 49 (March), 14–33.

Hausmann, Ricardo, Michael Gavin, Carmen Pages-Serra, and Ernesto Stein 1999. "Financial Turmoil and the Choice of Exchange Rate Regime," Working Paper 400, Washington, DC: Inter-American Development Bank.

Hausmann, Ricardo, Ugo Panizza, and Ernesto Stein 2000. "Why Do Countries Float the Way They Float?," *Journal of Development Economics* 66, 387–414.

Hayek, Friedrich von 1941. *The Pure Theory of Capital*, Chicago: University of Chicago Press.

Helleiner, Gerald 2000. "Markets, Politics, and Globalization: Can the Global Economy Be Civilized?," the Tenth Raul Prebisch Lecture, Geneva: UNCTAD (December 11).

Heller, Peter and Sanjeev Gupta 2002. "Challenges in Expanding Development Assistance," Policy Discussion Paper PDP/02/5, Washington, DC: International Monetary Fund.

Helliwell, John 1998. *How Much Do National Borders Matter?*, Washington, DC: Brookings Institution Press.

Hoelscher, David, Marc Quintyn, and others 2003. *Managing Systemic Banking Crises*, Occasional Paper 224, Washington, DC: International Monetary Fund.

Horsefield, Keith 1969. *The International Monetary Fund, 1945–1965: Twenty Years of International Monetary Cooperation*, Washington, DC: International Monetary Fund.

Hunt, Benjamin, Peter Isard, and Douglas Laxton 2002. "The Macroeconomic Effects of Higher Oil Prices," *National Institutes Economic Review* 179, 87–103.

Ikenberry, G. John 1993. "The Political Origins of Bretton Woods," in Michael Bordo and Barry Eichengreen, eds., *A Retrospective on the Bretton Woods System: Lessons for International Monetary Reform*, Chicago: University of Chicago Press, 155–98.

Independent Evaluation Office 2003a. *Fiscal Adjustment in IMF-Supported Programs*, Washington, DC: International Monetary Fund (available at www.imf.org).

—— 2003b. *The IMF and Recent Capital Account Crises: Indonesia, Korea, Brazil*, Washington, DC: International Monetary Fund (July 28, available at www.imf.org).

International Monetary and Financial Committee 2003a. "Communiqué," Washington, DC: International Monetary Fund (April 12, available at www.imf.org).

—— 2003b. "Communiqué," Washington, DC: International Monetary Fund (September 21, available at www.imf.org).

International Monetary Fund 2004. "Report of the Managing Director to the International Monetary and Financial Committee on the IMF's Policy

Agenda," Washington, DC: International Monetary Fund (April 19, available at www.imf.org).

——— 2003a. "A Guide to Committees, Groups, and Clubs: A Factsheet," Washington, DC: International Monetary Fund (December 18, available at www.imf.org).

——— 2003b. "Analytical Tools of the FSAP," Washington, DC: International Monetary Fund (February 24, available at www.imf.org).

——— 2003c. *Annual Report*, Washington, DC: International Monetary Fund.

——— 2003d. "Collective Action Clauses: Recent Developments and Issues," Washington, DC: International Monetary Fund (March 25, available at www.imf.org).

——— 2003e. "Enhancing the Effectiveness of Surveillance: Operational Responses, the Agenda Ahead, and Next Steps," Washington, DC: International Monetary Fund (March 14, available at www.imf.org).

——— 2003f. "Fifth Review of the Fund's Data Standards Initiatives," Washington, DC: International Monetary Fund (June 18, available at www.imf.org).

——— 2003g. "Financial Sector Assessment Program—Review, Lessons, and Issues Going Forward," Washington, DC: International Monetary Fund (February 24, available at www.imf.org).

——— 2003h. "IMF Concludes Discussion on Access Policy," Public Information Notice 03/37, Washington, DC: International Monetary Fund (March 21, available at www.imf.org).

——— 2003i. "Initiative for Heavily Indebted Poor Countries—Status of Implementation," Washington, DC: International Monetary Fund (September 12, available at www.imf.org).

——— 2003j. "International Standards—Background Paper on Strengthening Surveillance, Domestic Institutions, and International Markets," Washington, DC: International Monetary Fund (March 5, available at www.imf.org).

——— 2003k. "Poverty Reduction Strategy Papers—Progress in Implementation," Washington, DC: International Monetary Fund (September 12, available at www.imf.org).

——— 2003l. "Report of the Managing Director to the International Monetary and Financial Committee on a Statutory Sovereign Debt Restructuring Mechanism," Washington, DC: International Monetary Fund (April 8, available at www.imf.org).

——— 2003m. "Reviewing the Process for Sovereign Debt Restructuring Within the Existing Legal Framework," Washington, DC: International Monetary Fund (August 1, available at www.imf.org).

——— 2003n. "Review of Contingent Credit Lines," Washington, DC: International Monetary Fund (February 12, available at www.imf.org).

——— 2003a. "The Fund's Transparency Policy—Issues and Next Steps," Washington, DC: International Monetary Fund (September 29, available at www.imf.org).

—— 2003p. *World Economic Outlook*, September issue, Washington, DC: International Monetary Fund.

—— 2002a. "Assessing Sustainability," Washington, DC: International Monetary Fund (May 28, available at www.imf.org).

—— 2002b. "Guidelines on Conditionality," Washington, DC: International Monetary Fund (September 25, available at www.imf.org).

—— 2001a. *Financial Organization and Operations of the IMF*, Pamphlet Series No. 45 (6th ed.), Washington, DC: International Monetary Fund.

—— 2001b. "Structural Conditionality in IMF-Supported Programs," Washington, DC: International Monetary Fund (February 16, available at www.imf.org).

—— 2001c. *What is the International Monetary Fund?*, Washington, DC: International Monetary Fund.

—— 2000. "Key Features of IMF Poverty Reduction and Growth Facility (PRGF) Supported Programs," Washington, DC: International Monetary Fund (August 16, available at www.imf.org).

—— 1998a. *International Capital Markets: Developments, Prospects, and Key Policy Issues*, Washington, DC: International Monetary Fund.

—— 1998b. *World Economic Outlook*, Washington, DC: International Monetary Fund (October).

—— 1998c. *World Economic Outlook and International Capital Markets: Interim Assessment*, Washington, DC: International Monetary Fund (December).

—— 1997. *International Capital Markets: Developments, Prospects, and Key Policy Issues*, Washington, DC: International Monetary Fund.

—— 1995a. *Annual Report*, Washington, DC: International Monetary Fund.

—— 1995b. *International Capital Markets: Developments, Prospects, and Policy Issues*, Washington, DC: International Monetary Fund.

—— 1993. *Articles of Agreement of the International Monetary Fund*, Washington, DC: International Monetary Fund.

Irwin, Douglas 2002. *Free Trade Under Fire*, Princeton, NJ: Princeton University Press.

—— 1998. "From Smoot-Hawley to Reciprocal Trade Agreements: Changing the Course of U.S. Trade Policy in the 1930s," in Michael Bordo, Claudia Goldin, and Eugene White, eds., *The Defining Moment: The Great Depression and the American Economy in the Twentieth Century*, Chicago: University of Chicago Press, 325–52.

Isard, Peter 2000. "The Role of MULTIMOD in the IMF's Policy Analysis," Policy Discussion Paper PDP/00/05, Washington, DC: International Monetary Fund.

—— 1995. *Exchange Rate Economics*, Cambridge: Cambridge University Press.

—— 1994. "Realignment Expectations, Forward Rate Bias, and Sterilized Intervention in an Optimizing Model of Exchange Rate Adjustment," *IMF Staff Papers* 41, 435–59.

Isard, Peter, Hamid Faruqee, G. Russell Kincaid, and Martin Fetherston 2001. *Methodology for Current Account and Exchange Rate Assessments*, Occasional Paper 209, Washington, DC: International Monetary Fund.

Isard, Peter and Hamid Faruqee, eds. 1998. *Exchange Rate Assessments: Extensions of the Macroeconomic Balance Approach*, Occasional Paper 167, Washington, DC: International Monetary Fund.

Isard, Peter and Michael Mussa 1993. "A Note on Macroeconomic Causes of Recent Exchange Market Turbulence," in Group of Ten Deputies, *International Capital Movements and Foreign Exchange Markets*, Rome: Bank of Italy, Appendix V, 139–51.

Ize, Alain and Eduardo Levy-Yeyati 2003. "Financial Dollarization," *Journal of International Economics* 59, 323–47.

Ize, Alain and Eric Parrado 2002. "Dollarization, Monetary Policy, and the Pass-Through," Working Paper WP/02/188, Washington, DC: International Monetary Fund.

James, Harold 1999. "Is Liberalization Reversible?," *Finance and Development* 36 (December), 11–14.

———— 1996. *International Monetary Cooperation Since Bretton Woods*, New York: Oxford University Press.

Jayaratne, Jith and Philip Strahan, "The Finance-Growth Nexus: Evidence from Bank Branch Deregulation," *Quarterly Journal of Economics* 111, 639–70.

Jeanne, Olivier 2003. "Why Do Emerging Economies Borrow in Foreign Currency?," Working Paper WP/03/177, Washington, DC: International Monetary Fund.

———— 2000a. *Currency Crises: A Perspective on Recent Theoretical Developments*, Special Papers in International Economics No. 20, Princeton, NJ: Princeton University, International Finance Section, Department of Economics.

———— 2000b. "Foreign Currency Debt and the Global Financial Architecture," *European Economic Review* 44, 719–27.

———— 1997. "Are Currency Crises Self-Fulfilling? A Test," *Journal of International Economics* 43, 263–86.

Jeanne, Olivier and Charles Wyplosz 2003. "The International Lender of Last Resort: How Large is Large Enough?," in Michael Dooley and Jeffrey Frankel, eds., *Managing Currency Crises in Emerging Markets*, Chicago: University of Chicago Press, 89–118.

Jeanne, Olivier and Jeromin Zettelmeyer 2002. "'Original Sin,' Balance Sheet Crises, and the Roles of International Lending," Working Paper WP/02/234, Washington, DC: International Monetary Fund.

———— and ———— 2001. "International Bailouts, Moral Hazard and Conditionality," *Economic Policy* 16, 409–32.

Jenkins, Roy 1978. "European Monetary Union," *Lloyds Bank Review* 127, 1–14.

Kaminsky, Graciela and Carmen Reinhart 2003. "The Center and the Periphery: The Globalization of Financial Turmoil," Working Paper 9479, Cambridge, MA: National Bureau of Economic Research.

—— and —— 2000. "On Crises, Contagion, and Confusion," *Journal of International Economics* 51, 145–68.

—— and —— 1999. "The Twin Crises: The Causes of Banking and Balance-of-Payments Problems," *American Economic Review* 89, 473–500.

——, ——, and Carlos Vegh 2003. "The Unholy Trinity of Financial Contagion," *Journal of Economic Perspectives* 17, 51–74.

Kaminsky, Graciela and Sergio Schmukler 2003. "Short-Run Pain, Long-Run Gain: The Effects of Financial Liberalization," Working Paper 9787, Cambridge, MA: National Bureau of Economic Research.

Kanbur, Ravi 2001. "Economic Policy, Distribution and Poverty: The Nature of Disagreements," *World Development* 29, 1083–94.

Kane, Edward 1985. *The Gathering Crisis in Deposit Insurance*, Cambridge, MA: MIT Press.

Kaplan, Ethan and Dani Rodrik 2002. "Did the Malaysian Capital Controls Work?," in Sebastian Edwards and Jeffrey Frankel, eds., *Preventing Currency Crises in Emerging Markets*, Chicago: University of Chicago Press, 393–431.

Keehn, Silas 1989. "Banking on the Balance: Powers and the Safety Net, A Proposal," Chicago: Federal Reserve Bank of Chicago.

Kenen, Peter 2003. "Refocusing the Fund: A Review of James M. Boughton's *Silent Revolution: The International Monetary Fund 1979–1989*," *IMF Staff Papers* 50, 291–319.

—— 2002a. "Currencies, Crises, and Crashes," *Eastern Economic Journal* 28, 1–12.

—— 2002b. "The International Financial Architecture: Old Issues and New Initiatives," *International Finance* 5, 23–45.

—— 2001. *The International Financial Architecture: What's New? What's Missing?*, Washington, DC: Institute for International Economics.

——, ed. 1998. *Should the IMF Pursue Capital-Account Convertibility?*, Essays in International Finance No. 207, Princeton, NJ: Princeton University, International Finance Section, Department of Economics.

—— 1992. *EMU After Maastricht*, Washington, DC: Group of Thirty.

—— 1988. *Managing Exchange Rates*, London: Routledge.

Keynes, John Maynard 1925. *The Economic Consequences of Mr. Churchill*, London: Hogarth Press.

Kindleberger, Charles P. 1984. *A Financial History of Western Europe*, London: George Allen & Unwin.

—— 1978. *Manias, Panics and Crashes: A History of Financial Crises*, New York: Basic Books.

—— 1965. *Balance of Payments Deficits and the International Market for Liquidity*, in Essays in International Finance No. 46, Princeton, NJ: Princeton University, International Finance Section, Department of Economics.

King, Robert and Ross Levine 1993. "Finance and Growth: Schumpeter Might be Right," *Quarterly Journal of Economics* 108, 717–37.

Klenow, Peter and Andres Rodriguez-Clare 1997. "The Neoclassical Revival in Growth Economics: Has It Gone Too Far?," in Ben Bernanke and Julio

Rotemberg, eds., *NBER Macroeconomics Annual 1997*, Cambridge, MA: MIT Press, 73–103.

Kletzer, Kenneth 2003. "Sovereign Bond Restructuring: Collective Action Clauses and Official Crisis Intervention," Working Paper WP/03/134, Washington, DC: International Monetary Fund.

——— 1984. "Asymmetries of Information and LDC Borrowing with Sovereign Risk," *Economic Journal* 94, 287–307.

Knight, Malcolm and Julio Santaella 1997. "Economic Determinants of IMF Financial Arrangements," *Journal of Development Economics* 54, 405–36.

Kraay, Aart 2003. "Do High Interest Rates Defend Currencies During Speculative Attacks?," *Journal of International Economics* 59, 297–321.

Krueger, Anne 2003a. "IMF Stabilization Programs," in Martin Feldstein, ed., *Economic and Financial Crises in Emerging Market Economies*, Chicago: University of Chicago Press, 297–346.

——— 2003b. "The Need to Improve the Resolution of Financial Crises: An Emerging Consensus?" speech given at the Harvard University Business School, Cambridge, MA (March 27, available at www.imf.org).

——— 2001. "A New Approach To Sovereign Debt Restructuring," address given at the National Economists' Club, Washington, DC (November 26, available at www.imf.org).

——— 1997. "Trade Policy and Economic Development: How We Learn," *American Economic Review* 87, 1–22.

Krugman, Paul 2003. "Crises: The Next Generation?," in Elhanan Helpman and Efraim Sadka, eds., *Economic Policy in the International Economy: Essays in Honor of Assaf Razin*, Cambridge: Cambridge University Press, 15–32.

——— 2002. "Crying With Argentina," *The New York Times* (January 1), Section A, 21.

——— 2000. "Introduction," in Paul Krugman, ed., *Currency Crises*, Chicago: University of Chicago Press, 1–6.

——— 1999. "Balance Sheets, the Transfer Problem, and Financial Crises," in Peter Isard, Assaf Razin, and Andrew Rose, eds., *International Finance and Financial Crises: Essays in Honor of Robert P. Flood, Jr.*, Boston: Kluwer Academic, 31–44.

——— 1998. "The Confidence Game," *New Republic* 219, 14 (October 5), 23–5.

——— 1992. "Second Thoughts on EMU," *Japan and The World Economy* 4, 187–200.

——— 1979. "A Model of Balance of Payments Crises," *Journal of Money, Credit, and Banking* 11, 311–25.

Lahiri, Amartya and Carlos Vegh 2002. "On the Non-Monotonic Relation Between Interest Rates and the Exchange Rate," draft (June available at www.econ.vela.edu/cvegh).

Lane, Philip and Gian Maria Milesi-Ferretti 2003. "International Financial Integration," *IMF Staff Papers* 50 (Special Issue), 82–113.

—— 2001. "The External Wealth of Nations: Measures of Foreign Assets and Liabilities for Industrial and Developing Countries," *Journal of International Economics* 55, 243–62.

Lane, Timothy, Atish Ghosh, Javier Hamann, Steven Phillips, Marianne Schultze-Ghattas, and Tsidi Tsikata 1999. *IMF-Supported Programs in Indonesia, Korea and Thailand*, Occasional Paper 178, Washington, DC: International Monetary Fund.

Laxton, Douglas, Peter Isard, Hamid Faruqee, Eswar Prasad, and Bart Turtleboom 1998. *MULTIMOD Mark III: The Core Dynamic and Steady-State Models*, Occasional Paper 164, Washington, DC: International Monetary Fund.

Laxton, Douglas and Paolo Pesenti 2003. "Monetary Rules for Small, Open, Emerging Economies," *Journal of Monetary Economics* 50, 1109–46.

Levine, Ross 1997. "Financial Development and Economic Growth: Views and Agenda," *Journal of Economic Literature* 35, 688–726.

Levy-Yeyati, Eduardo and Federico Sturzenegger 2003a. "A de facto Classification of Exchange Rate Regimes: A Methodological Note" (available at www.aeaweb.org/aer/contents/).

—— and —— 2003b. "To Float or to Fix: Evidence on the Impact of Exchange Rate Regimes on Growth," *American Economic Review* 93, 1173–93.

—— and —— 2001. "Exchange Rate Regimes and Economic Performance," *IMF Staff Papers* 47 (Special Issue), 62–98.

Lindgren, Carl, Gillian Garcia, and Matthew Saal 1996. *Bank Soundness and Macroeconomic Policy*, Washington, DC: International Monetary Fund.

Lipworth, Gabrielle and Jens Nysted 2001. "Crisis Resolution and Private Sector Adaptation," *IMF Staff Papers* 47 (Special Issue), 188–214.

Lustig, Nora 2001. "Life Is not Easy: Mexico's Quest for Stability and Growth," *Journal of Economic Perspectives* 15, 85–106.

Madison, Angus 2001. *The World Economy: A Millennium Perspective*, Paris: Organization for Economic Cooperation and Development.

Masson, Paul 2001. "Globalization Facts and Figures," Policy Discussion Paper 01/4, Washington, DC: International Monetary Fund.

—— and Michael Mussa 1995. *The Role of the IMF: Financing and Its Interactions with Adjustment and Surveillance*, Pamphlet Series No. 50, Washington, DC: International Monetary Fund.

Mathieson, Donald and Liliana Rojas-Suarez 1993. *Liberalization of the Capital Account: Experiences and Issues*, Occasional Paper 103, Washington, DC: International Monetary Fund.

Mauro, Paolo 1995. "Corruption and Growth," *Quarterly Journal of Economics* 110, 681–712.

Mauro, Paolo, Nathan Sussman, and Yishay Yafey 2002. "Emerging Market Spreads: Then Versus Now," *Quarterly Journal of Economics* 117, 695–733.

McCallum, John 1995. "National Borders Matter: Canadian–U.S. Regional Trade Patterns," *American Economic Review* 85, 615–23.

McKinnon, Ronald and Huw Pill 1997. "Credible Economic Liberalizations and Overborrowing," *American Economic Review* 87, 189–93.

Meese, Richard and Kenneth Rogoff 1988. "Was It Real? The Exchange Rate–Interest Differential Relationship over the Modern Floating-Rate Period," *Journal of Finance* 43, 933–48.

—— and —— 1983a. "Empirical Exchange Rate Models of the Seventies: Do They Fit Out of Sample?," *Journal of International Economics* 14, 3–24.

—— and —— 1983b. "The Out-of-Sample Failure of Empirical Exchange Rate Models: Sampling Error or Misspecification?," in Jacob Frenkel, ed., *Exchange Rates and International Macroeconomics*, Chicago: University of Chicago Press, 67–112.

Meesook, Kanitta, Il Houng Lee, Olin Liu, Yougesh Khatri, Natalia Tamirisa, Michael Moore, and Mark Krysl 2001. *Malaysia: From Crisis to Recovery*, Occasional Paper 207, Washington, DC: International Monetary Fund.

Meltzer, Allen 1998. "Asian Problems and the IMF," *The Cato Journal* 17, 267–74.

Meltzer Commission 2000. *Report of the International Financial Institutions Advisory Commission* [Allen Meltzer, Chairman], Washington, DC: International Financial Institutions Advisory Commission.

Mendoza, Enrique 2002a. "Credit, Prices, and Crashes: Business Cycles with a Sudden Stop," in Sebastian Edwards and Jeffrey Frankel, eds., *Preventing Currency Crises in Emerging Markets*, Chicago: University of Chicago Press, 335–83.

—— 2002b. "Why Should Emerging Economies Give up National Currencies: A Case for 'Institutions Substitution,'" Working Paper 8950, Cambridge, MA: National Bureau of Economic Research.

Mercer-Blackman, Valerie and Anna Unigovskaya 2000. "Compliance with IMF Program Indicators and Growth in Transition Economies," Working Paper WP/00/47, Washington, DC: International Monetary Fund.

Miller, Marcus and Lei Zhang 2000. "Sovereign Liquidity Crises: The Strategic Case for a Payments Standstill," *The Economic Journal* 110, 335–62.

Mody, Ashoka and Antu Panini Murshid 2002. "Growing Up With Capital Flows," Working Paper WP/02/75, Washington, DC: International Monetary Fund.

Montiel, Peter and Carmen Reinhart 1999. "Do Capital Controls and Macroeconomic Policies Influence the Volume and Composition of Capital Flows? Evidence fro the 1990s," *Journal of International Money and Finance* 18, 619–35.

Mundell, Robert 1963. "Capital Mobility and Stabilization Policy Under Fixed and Flexible Exchange Rates," *Canadian Journal of Economics and Political Science* 29, 475–85.

—— 1962. "The Appropriate Use of Monetary and Fiscal Policy for Internal and External Stability," *IMF Staff Papers* 12, 70–79.

—— 1961a. "Flexible Exchange Rates and Employment Policy," *Canadian Journal of Economics and Political Science* 27, 509–17.

————— 1961b. "The International Disequilibrium System," *Kyklos* 14, Fasc. 2, 153–72.

————— 1960. "The Monetary Dynamics of International Adjustment Under Fixed and Flexible Exchange Rates," *Quarterly Journal of Economics* 74, 227–57.

Mussa, Michael 2002. *Argentina and the Fund: From Triumph to Tragedy*, Washington, DC: Institute for International Economics.

————— 2000. "Factors Driving Global Economic Integration," in *Global Economic Integration: Opportunities and Challenges*, Kansas City: Federal Reserve Bank of Kansas City, 9–55.

————— 1999. "Moral Hazard," in William Hunter, George Kaufman, and Thomas Krueger, eds., *The Asian Financial Crisis: Origins, Implications, and Solutions*, Boston: Kluwer Academic, 385–88.

————— 1997. "IMF Surveillance," *American Economic Review Papers and Proceedings* 87, 28–31.

Mussa, Michael, James Boughton, and Peter Isard, eds. 1996. *The Future of the SDR in Light of Changes in the International Financial System*, Washington, DC: International Monetary Fund.

Mussa, Michael, Paul Masson, Alexander Swoboda, Esteban Jadresic, Paolo Mauro, and Andrew Berg 2000. *Exchange Rate Regimes in an Increasingly Integrated World Economy*, Occasional Paper 193, Washington, DC: International Monetary Fund.

Mussa, Michael and Miguel Savastano 2000. "The IMF Approach to Economic Stabilization," *NBER Macroeconomics Annual 1999*, Cambridge, MA: MIT Press, 79–122.

Mussa, Michael, Alexander Swoboda, Jeromin Zettelmeyer, and Olivier Jeanne 2000. "Moderating Fluctuations in Capital Flows to Emerging Market Economies," in Peter Kenen and Alexander Swoboda, eds., *Reforming the International Monetary and Financial System*, Washington, DC: International Monetary Fund, 75–142.

Neely, Christopher 1999. "An Introduction to Capital Controls," *Federal Reserve Bank of St. Louis Review* 81 (November/December), 13–30.

North, Douglass 1994. "Economic Performance Through Time," *American Economic Review* 84, 359–68.

Nurkse, Ragnar 1944. *International Currency Experience: Lessons of the Interwar Period*, Geneva: League of Nations.

Obstfeld, Maurice 1998. "The Global Capital Market: Benefactor or Menace?" *Journal of Economic Perspectives* 12 (Fall), 9–30.

————— 1996. "Models of Currency Crises with Self-Fulfilling Features," *European Economic Review* 40, 1037–47.

Obstfeld, Maurice and Kenneth Rogoff 2001. "The Six Major Puzzles in International Macroeconomics: Is There a Common Cause?" *NBER Macroeconomics Annual 2000*, Cambridge, MA: MIT Press, 339–90.

————— and ————— 1995. "The Mirage of Fixed Exchange Rates," *Journal of Economic Perspectives* 9 (Fall), 73–96.

Obstfeld, Maurice, Jay Shambaugh, and Alan Taylor 2004. "The Trilemma in History: Tradeoffs among Exchange Rates, Monetary Policy, and Capital Mobility," Working Paper 2004, Cambridge MA: National Bureau of Economic Research.

Obstfeld, Maurice and Alan Taylor 2003. "Globalization and Capital Markets," in Michael Bordo, Alan Taylor, and Jeffrey Williamson, eds., *Globalization in Historical Perspective*, Chicago: University of Chicago Press, 121–83.

OECD Development Assistance Committee 1996. *Shaping the 21ˢᵗ Century: The Contribution of Development Co-Operation*, Paris: Organization for Economic Cooperation and Development.

Ozkan, Gulcin and Alan Sutherland 2008. "A Currency Crisis Model with an Optimizing Policymaker," *Journal of International Economics* 44, 339–64.

Panagariya, Arvind 2003. "Miracles and Debacles: Do Free-Trade Skeptics have a Case?," draft (October), College Park: University of Maryland.

—— 2002. "Potentially Disabling Aid," *Economic Times* (July 31 available at www.bsos.umd.edu/econ/faculty/panagari.htm).

Pauls, Dianne 1990. "U.S. Exchange Rate Policy: Bretton Woods to Present," *Federal Reserve Bulletin*, 891–908.

Pericola, Marcello and Massimo Sbracia 2001. "A Primer on Financial Contagion," Discussion Paper No. 407, Rome: Bank of Italy.

Pesenti, Paolo 2004. "The Global Economy Model (GEM): Theoretical Framework," IMF Working Paper, Washington, DC: International Monetary Fund, forthcoming.

Polak, Jacques 1998. "The Articles of Agreement of the IMF and the Liberalization of Capital Movements," in Peter Kenen, ed., *Should the IMF Pursue Capital-Account Convertibility?*, Essays in International Finance No. 207, Princeton, NJ: Princeton University, International Finance Section, Department of Economics, 47–54.

—— 1991. *The Changing Nature of IMF Conditionality*, Princeton Essays in International Finance No. 184, Princeton, NJ: Princeton University, International Finance Section, Department of Economics.

Polyani, Karl 1944. *The Great Transformation*, New York: Rinehart.

Poterba, James and Jurgen von Hagen, eds. 1999. *Fiscal Institutions and Fiscal Performance*, Chicago: University of Chicago Press.

Prasad, Eswar, Kenneth Rogoff, Shang-Jin Wei, and Ayhan Kose 2003. *The Effects of Financial Globalization on Developing Countries: Some Empirical Evidence*, Occasional Paper 220, Washington, DC: International Monetary Fund (March).

Prebisch, Raul 1950. *The Economic Development of Latin America and Its Principal Problems*, Lake Success, NY: United Nations, Department of Economic Affairs.

Pritchett, Lant 1997. "Divergence, Big Time," *Journal of Economic Perspectives* 11, 3–17.

Quirk, Peter and Owen Evans 1995. *Capital Account Convertibility: Review of Experience and Implications for IMF Policies*, Occasional Paper 131, Washington, DC: International Monetary Fund.

Radelet, Steven and Jeffrey Sachs 1998. "The East Asian Financial Crisis: Diagnosis, Remedies, Prospects," *Brookings Papers on Economic Activity* 1, 1–74.

Rajan, Raghuram and Luigi Zingales 2003. *Saving Capitalism from the Capitalists: Unleashing the Power of Financial Markets to Create Wealth and Spread Opportunity*, New York: Crown Business.

———— and ———— 2001. "Financial Systems, Industrial Structure, and Growth," *Oxford Review of Economic Policy* 17, 467–82.

———— and ———— 1998. "Financial Dependence and Growth," *American Economic Review* 88, 559–86.

Ravallion, Martin 2003. "The Debate on Globalization, Poverty and Inequality: Why Measurement Matters," Policy Research Working Paper 3083, Washington, DC: World Bank.

Reinhart, Carmen 2000. "The Mirage of Floating Exchange Rates," *American Economic Review* 90, 65–70.

Reinhart, Carmen and Vincent Reinhart 2003a. "Twin Fallacies About Exchange Rate Policy in Emerging Markets," Working Paper 9670, Cambridge, MA: National Bureau of Economic Research.

———— and ———— 2003b. "What Hurts Most? G-3 Exchange Rate or Interest Rate Volatility?," in Sebastian Edwards and Jeffrey Frankel, eds., *Preventing Currency Crises in Emerging Markets*, Chicago: University of Chicago Press, 133–66.

Reinhart, Carmen and Kenneth Rogoff 2004. "The Modern History of Exchange Rate Arrangements: A Reinterpretation," *Quarterly Journal of Economics*, 119, 1–48.

Reinhart, Carmen, Kenneth Rogoff, and Miguel Savastano 2003a. "Addicted to Dollars," Working Paper 10015, Cambridge, MA: National Bureau of Economic Research.

————, ————, and ———— 2003b. "Debt Intolerance," *Brookings Papers on Economic Activity* 1, 1–62.

Rigobon, Roberto 2002. "Contagion: How to Measure It?," in Sebastian Edwards and Jeffrey Frankel, eds., *Preventing Currency Crises in Emerging Markets*, Chicago: University of Chicago Press, 269–329.

Robinson, Joan 1952. *The Rate of Interest and Other Essays*, London: Macmillan.

Rodriguez, Francisco and Dani Rodrik 2001. "Trade Policy and Economic Growth: A Skeptic's Guide to the Cross-National Evidence," in Ben Bernanke and Kenneth Rogoff, eds., *NBER Macroeconomics Annual 2000*, Cambridge, MA: MIT Press, 261–325.

Rodrik, Dani 2003a. "Growth Strategies," Working Paper 10050, Cambridge: National Bureau of Economic Research.

—— 2003b. "What Do We Learn from Country Narratives?," in Dani Rodrik, ed., *In Search of Prosperity: Analytic Narratives on Economic Growth*, Princeton, NJ: Princeton University Press, 1–19.

—— 2001a. "The Global Governance of Trade as if It Really Mattered," New York: United Nations Development Project.

—— 2001b. "Trading in Illusions," *Foreign Policy* 123 (March/April), 55–62.

—— 1998. "Who Needs Capital-Account Convertibility?," in Peter Kenen, ed., *Should the IMF Pursue Capital-Account Convertibility?*, Essays in International Finance No. 207, Princeton, NJ: Princeton University, International Finance Section, Department of Economics, 55–65.

Rodrik, Dani, Arvind Subramanian, and Francesco Trebbi 2002. "Institutions Rule: The Primacy of Institutions over Geography and Integration in Economic Development," Working Paper 9305, Cambridge, MA: National Bureau of Economic Research.

Rogoff, Kenneth 2002a. "Moral Hazard in IMF Loans: How Big a Concern?," *Finance & Development* 39 (September), 56–7.

—— 2002b. "Rethinking Capital Controls: When Should We Keep an Open Mind?," *Finance & Development* 39 (December), 56–7.

—— 2001. "Why Not a Global Currency?," *American Economic Review Papers and Proceedings* 91, 243–7.

—— 1999a. "International Institutions for Reducing Global Financial Instability," *Journal of Economic Perspectives* 13, 21–42.

—— 1999b. "Monetary Models of Dollar/Yen/Euro Nominal Exchange Rates: Dead or Undead?," *Economic Journal* 109, F655–59.

—— 1996. "The Purchasing Power Parity Puzzle," *Journal of Economic Literature* 34, 647–68.

Rogoff, Kenneth, Aasim Husain, Ashoka Mody, Robin Brooks and Nienke Oomes 2004. *Evolution and Performance of Exchange Rate Regimes*, Occasional Paper 229, Washington, DC: International Monetary Fund.

Rogoff, Kenneth and Jeromin Zettelmeyer 2002. "Bankruptcy Procedures for Sovereigns: A History of Ideas," *IMF Staff Papers* 49, 470–507.

Romer, Paul 1987. "Crazy Explanations for the Productivity Slowdown," in Stanley Fischer, ed., *NBER Macroeconomics Annual* 1987, Cambridge, MA: MIT Press, 163–202.

Rose, Andrew 2002. "The Effect of Currency Unions on International Trade: Where Do We Stand?" draft (August 7, available at http://faculty.haas.berkeley.edu/arose).

—— 2000. "One Money One Market: Estimating the Effect of Common Currencies on Trade," *Economic Policy* 15, 7–46.

Rosenberg, Tina 2002. "The Free-Trade Fix," *The New York Times Magazine* (August 18).

Roubini, Nouriel 2002. "Do We Need a New Bankruptcy Regime?" *Brookings Papers on Economic Activity*, 1, 321–33.

Rubin, Robert 1998. "Strengthening the Architecture of the International Financial System: Remarks at the Brookings Institution," Washington, DC: U.S. Treasury Department (April 21, available at www.ustreas.gov).

Sachs, Jeffrey 2003a. "Comments," in Martin Feldstein, ed., *Economic and Financial Crises in Emerging Market Economies*, Chicago: University of Chicago Press, 353–56.

——— 2003b. "Institutions Don't Rule: Direct Effects of Geography on Per Capita Income," Working Paper 9490, Cambridge, MA: National Bureau of Economic Research.

——— 1985. "External Debt and Macroeconomic Performance in Latin America and East Asia," *Brookings Papers on Economic Activity* 2, 523–64.

——— and Andrew Warner 1995. "Economic Reform and the Process of Global Integration," *Brookings Papers on Economic Activity* 1, 1–95.

Sala-i-Martin, Xavier 2002. "The World Distribution of Income (Estimated from Individual Country Distributions)," Working Paper 8933, Cambridge, MA: National Bureau of Economic Research.

Salant, Stephen and Dale Henderson 1978. "Market Anticipations of Government Policies and the Price of Gold," *Journal of Political Economy* 86, 627–48.

Santaella, Julio 1996. "Stylized Facts Before IMF-Supported Macroeconomic Adjustment," *IMF Staff Papers*, 43 (September), 502–44.

Sarno, Lucio and Mark Taylor 2003. *The Economics of Exchange Rates*, Cambridge, England: Cambridge University Press.

Savastano, Miguel, Jorge Roldos, and Julio Santaella 1995. "Factors Behind the Financial Crisis in Mexico," *World Economic Outlook* Washington, DC: International Monetary Fund, (May) 90–7.

Scammell, W. M. 1965. "The Working of the Gold Standard," *Yorkshire Bulletin of Economic and Social Research*. Reprinted in Barry Eichengreen, ed., *The Gold Standard in Theory and History*, New York: Methven, 1985, 103–19.

Schneider, Martin and Aaron Tornell 2004. "Balance Sheet Effects, Bailout Guarantees and Financial Crises," *Review of Economic Studies*, forthcoming.

Schumpeter, Joseph 1911. *The Theory of Economic Development: An Inquiry into Profits, Capital, Credit, Interest, and the Business Cycle.* Translated and republished, Cambridge, MA: Harvard University Press, 1934.

Shiller, Robert 1993. *Macro Markets: Creating Institutions for Managing Society's Largest Economic Risks*, New York: Clarendon Press.

Singh, Manmohan 2003. "Recovery Rates from Distressed Debt—Empirical Evidence from Chapter 11 Filings, International Litigation, and Recent Sovereign Debt Restructurings," Working Paper WP/03/161, Washington, DC: International Monetary Fund.

Smith, Adam 1776. *Inquiry into the Nature and Causes of The Wealth of Nations*. Reprinted by Clarendon Press, Oxford, 1976.

Solomon, Robert 1999. *Money on the Move: The Revolution in International Finance Since 1980*, Princeton, NJ: Princeton University Press.

———— 1982. *The International Monetary System 1945–1981*, New York: Harper & Row.

Solow, Robert 1957. "Technical Change and the Aggregate Production Function," *Review of Economics and Statistics* 39, 312–20.

Stiglitz, Joseph 2004. "Capital-Market Liberalization, Globalization, and the IMF, *Oxford Review of Economic Policy* 20, 57–71.

———— 2002a. "Development Policies in a World of Globalization," paper presented at the New International Trends for Economic Development seminar organized by the Brazilian Economic and Social Development Bank, Rio de Janiero (September).

———— 2002b. *Globalization and Its Discontents*, New York: Norton.

———— 1996. "Some Lessons From the East Asian Miracle," *The World Bank Research Observer* 11, 151–77.

Stone, Mark 2002. "Corporate Sector Restructuring: The Role of Government in Times of Crisis," *Economic Issues* 31. x–x. Washington: International Monetary Fund.

Subramanian, Arvind and Devesh Roy 2003. "Who Can Explain The Mauritian Miracle: Meade, Romer, Sachs, or Rodrik?," in Dani Rodrik, ed., *Searching for Prosperity*, Princeton, NJ: Princeton University Press.

Summers, Lawrence 2000. "International Financial Crises: Causes, Prevention, and Cures," Richard T. Ely Lecture, *American Economic Review Papers and Proceedings* 90 (May), 1–19.

———— 1999. "The Right Kind of IMF For a Stable Global Financial System," speech to the London School of Business (December 14, available at http://www.ustreas.gov/press/releases/ls294.htm).

Tavlas, George 2003. "The Economics of Exchange Rate Regimes: A Review Essay," *The World Economy* 28, 1215–46.

Taylor, John 2003. "Testimony Before the Senate Committee on Foreign Relations," Washington, DC: U.S. Treasury Department (March 4, available at www.ustreas.gov).

Tirole, Jean 2002. *Financial Crises, Liquidity, and the International Monetary System*, Princeton, NJ: Princeton University Press.

Tobin, James 1991. "The International Monetary System: Pluralism and Interdependence," in Alfred Steinherr and Daniel Weiserbs, eds., *Evolution of the International and Regional Monetary Systems: Essays in Honor of Robert Triffin*, New York: St. Martins Press, 3–9.

———— 1987. "Agenda for International Coordination of Macroeconomic Policies," in Paul A. Volcker and others, eds., *International Monetary Cooperation: Essays in Honor of Henry C Wallich*, Essays in International Finance No. 169, Princeton, NJ: Princeton University, International Finance Section, Department of Economics, 61–9.

———— 1978. "A Proposal for International Monetary Reform," *Eastern Economic Journal* 4, 153–9.

———— and Gustav Ranis 1998. "The IMF's Misplaced Priorities. Flawed Fund," *The New Republic* 218, 10 (March 9), 16–17.

Triffin, Robert 1960. *Gold and the Dollar Crisis: The Future of Convertibility*, New Haven, CT: Yale University Press.

Tsiang, S. C. 1959. "Fluctuating Exchange Rates in Countries with Relatively Stable Economies: Some European Experiences After World War I," *IMF Staff Papers* 7, 243–73.

Tsikata, Tsidi 1998. "Aid Effectiveness: A Survey of the Recent Empirical Literature," Paper on Policy Analysis and Assessment PPAA/98/1, Washington, DC: International Monetary Fund.

Ungerer, Horst, Jouko J. Hauvonen, Augusto López-Claros, and Thomas Mayer 1990. *The European Monetary System: Developments and Perspectives*, Occasional Paper 73, Washington, DC: International Monetary Fund.

United States Department of the Treasury 2002. "Implementation of Legislative Provisions Relating to the International Monetary Fund: A Report to Congress" (October, available at www.ustreas.gov).

United States General Accounting Office 2003. "International Financial Crises: Challenges Remain in IMF's Ability to Anticipate, Prevent, and Resolve Financial Crises" (June, available at www.gao.gov).

Van Rijckeghem, Caroline and Beatrice Weder 1999. "Sources of Contagion: Finance or Trade?," Working Paper WP/99/146, Washington, DC: International Monetary Fund.

Volcker, Paul 1999. "A Perspective on Financial Crises," in *Rethinking the International Monetary System*, Conference Series No. 43, Boston: Federal Reserve Bank of Boston, 264–8.

Volcker, Paul and Toyoo Gyohten 1992. *Changing Fortunes*, New York: Times Books.

Wall, Larry 1989. "A Plan for Reducing Future Deposit Insurance Losses: Puttable Subordinated Debt," *Federal Reserve Bank of Atlanta Review* 74 (September), 58–69.

Wallis, John and Douglas North 1986. "Measuring the Transaction Sector in the American Economy," in Stanley Engerman and Robert Gallman, eds., *Long-Term Factors in American Economic Growth*, Chicago: University of Chicago Press, 95–148.

Warner, Andrew 2003. "Once More into the Breach: Economic Growth and Global Integration," Working Paper 34, Washington, DC: Center for Global Development.

Wei Shang-Jin 2000a. "How Taxing Is Corruption on International Investors?," *Review of Economics and Statistics* 82, 1–11.

———— 2000b. "Local Corruption and Global Capital Flows," *Brookings Papers on Economic Activity* 2, 303–54.

———— 2000c. "Natural Openness and Good Government," Working Paper 7765, Cambridge, MA: National Bureau of Economic Research.

Wei Shang-Jin and Sara Sievers 2000. "The Cost of Crony Capitalism," in Wing Woo, Jeffrey Sacgs, and Klaus Schwab, eds., *The Asian Financial Crisis: Lessons for a Resilient Asia*, Cambridge, MA: MIT Press, 91–102.

Willett, Thomas 2000. "Managing Financial Crises: The Experience in East Asia, A Comment," *Carnegie-Rochester Series on Public Policy* 53, 69–79.

Williams, John H. 1947. "Economic Lessons of Two World Wars," in Williams, *Postwar Monetary Plans and Other Essays*, New York: Alfred A. Knoff, cviii–cxxxvi.

Williamson, Jeffrey 2002. "Winners and Losers over Two Centuries of Globalization," Working Paper 9161, Cambridge, MA: National Bureau of Economic Research.

Williamson, John 2001. "The Role of the IMF: A Guide to the Reports," Washington, DC: Institute for International Economics (available at www.iie.com).

——— 2000. *Exchange Rate Regimes for Emerging Markets: Reviving the Intermediate Option*, Washington, DC: Institute for International Economics.

——— and Molly Mahar 1998. *A Survey of Financial Liberalization*, Essays in International Finance No. 211, Princeton, NJ: Princeton University, International Finance Section, Department of Economics.

World Bank 2001. *World Development Report 2002: Building Institutions for Markets*, Washington, DC: World Bank.

——— 1998. *Assessing Aid: What Works, What Doesn't, and Why*, New York: Oxford University Press.

Yeager, Leland B. 1976. *International Monetary Relations: Theory, History and Policy*, New York: Harper & Row, second edition.

Young, Alwyn 1995. "The Tyranny of Numbers: Confronting the Statistical Realities of the East Asian Growth Experience," *Quarterly Journal of Economics* 110, 641–80.

——— 1992. "A Tale of Two Cities: Factor Accumulation and Technical Change in Hong Kong and Singapore," in Olivier Blanchard and Stanley Fischer, eds., *NBER Macroeconomics Annual* 1992, Cambridge, MA: MIT Press, 13–54.

Zettelmeyer, Jeromin 2004. "The Case for an Explicit Seniority Structure in Sovereign Debt," forthcoming Working Paper, Washington, DC: International Monetary Fund.

——— 2003. "Bhalla Versus the World Bank: An Outsider's Perspective," *Finance and Development* 40 (June), 50–53.

Author Index

Note: The letter "n" following a number indicates a footnote.

Subject Index

Note: The letter "n" following a number indicates a footnote.